GW00499420

THE TUC OVERSEAS

THE
TUC OVERSEAS
The Roots of Policy

Marjorie Nicholson

London
ALLEN & UNWIN
Boston   Sydney

Allen & Unwin (Publishers) Ltd,
40 Museum Street, London WC1A 1LU, UK

Allen & Unwin (Publishers) Ltd,
Park Lane, Hemel Hempstead, Herts HP2 4TE, UK

Allen & Unwin, Inc.,
8 Winchester Place, Winchester, Mass. 01890, USA

Allen & Unwin (Australia) Ltd,
8 Napier Street, North Sydney, NSW 2060, Australia

First published in 1986

British Library Cataloguing in Publication Data

Nicholson, Marjorie
    The TUC overseas: the roots of policy.
1. Trades Union Congress – History
2. Trade-unions – Commonwealth of Nations
– History
I. Title
331.88′09171′241   HD6664
ISBN 0-04-331103-2

Library of Congress Cataloging-in-Publication Data

Nicholson, Marjorie, 1914–
    The TUC overseas.
Bibliography: p.
Includes index.
1. Trade Union Congress – History – 20th century.
2. Trade-unions – Great Britain – Colonies – History –
20th century. 3. Labour Party (Great Britain) – History –
20th century. 4. International labor activities –
History – 20th century. I. Title.
HD8383.N52 1986   331.88′0941   85–28607
ISBN 0-04-31103-2 (alk. paper)

Set in 10 on 11 point Goudy by V & M Graphics Ltd, Aylesbury
and printed in Great Britain by Biddles Ltd, Guildford, Surrey

To the memory of
WALTER CITRINE

Contents

Foreword

At times, as at present not only in Britain but in some of the other Commonwealth countries which are the subject of this book, governments regard the activities, or even the existence, of trade unions as running counter to their conception of the public interest. In doing this, however, they lose sight of something that Marjorie Nicholson brings out in relief as an essential element of that same public interest. They lose sight of the essential nature of trade unions as democratic associations answerable to their members, but at the same time as great social forces which, whatever governments might think, have a significant and constructive role to play in helping shape the decisions of the societies of which they are a part.

This book is concerned with, and throws light on, much more than the TUC's view of, and contribution to, the development of trade unionism internationally and notably in the colonies of the British Empire – though its publication will establish it as the definitive work in that field. It is indeed more than a carefully documented and discerning record of how, in helping to establish and strengthen trade unions in the colonies, the TUC helped to define and create the stable organizational and even constitutional structure which was critical to their transition to independence. Marjorie Nicholson identifies and describes, in a way which has not been bettered since the Webbs, the essential qualities and characteristics of British trade unionism on which the TUC could draw and to which the trade union leaders in the colonies could respond out of a sense of the special needs of their own unions in their own circumstances.

The narrative and analysis repeatedly revert to the central importance of the fundamental right of working men to share in the decisions which affect them. That is inherent in the representative role of trade unions which governments themselves have no authority to try to weaken or take away. Attempts to do so have been by no means uncommon in the countries which emerged from colonialism to face the problems of establishing their independence while at the same time meeting the aspirations which the struggle for independence had aroused.

In the process of transition to independence, the TUC in Britain saw it as its duty to do what was in its power to ensure that the constitutional frameworks which were established permitted the operation of voluntary and independent trade union organizations in both the public and the private sectors of employment. It was perhaps always open to question whether constitutional guarantees in newly independent countries would maintain their authority and effectiveness in times of political turbulence and economic stress. In some Commonwealth countries, trade union organizations and their leaderships have come under attack from their governments precisely because of the form they took and the objectives they set themselves – because they came to represent a point of influence independent of the government and therefore, mistakenly, regarded as politically hostile to it. Nor has the passage of time since independence led to a diminution of the attacks on trade unions and their freedom of action.

This was among the factors which led to the annual meetings of the Commonwealth worker delegates to the ILO, to which Marjorie Nicholson refers, developing into a Commonwealth Trade Union Council with its own – albeit small – permanent staff, providing the continuity of administration and action on which she properly lays such emphasis. The Commonwealth TUC is indeed living proof that the roots of policy, traced in this book with such skill and perception, were firmly and strongly planted.

Lionel Murray
Loughton, *August* 1985

Acknowledgements

This study had its origins in hours of discussion with my friend and colleague, the late Walter Hood, and the late Sir Vincent Tewson, then General Secretary of the TUC, about the purposes and methods of our work in co-operating with trade unions in what were then British colonies. We had a policy to guide us – laid down in volumes of the TUC's annual Congress Reports and decisions of the General Council – but being faced daily with the evidence that, as Tewson constantly told us, no two colonies were alike and that our British spectacles were best discarded, we found it difficult to interpret, adapt and improve that policy. In 1966 Professor W. H. Morris Jones, then Director of the University of London Institute of Commonwealth Studies, asked me to present a seminar paper which would describe and explain the advice we gave to trade unions in the dependencies, how it had been given, and the kinds of industrial and political situations into which it had been injected. In the ensuing discussion it became clear that, while the academic participants had a wealth of knowledge which in many respects exceeded our own, they started from different premises and in making their judgements frequently arrived at very different conclusions. It ought to be possible, we thought, to explain TUC policies and actions from the standpoint of trade unionists who had actually to take the decisions. For this it would be necessary to go back to the beginning, a task which must be postponed until after retirement.

I had no idea how far back my investigation would lead. Over fifteen years in the TUC had been spent on the upper floors, and as I plodded through the records in the nether regions of Congress House I began to understand that I would need help. It was forthcoming. I wish to thank all those whose generosity, interest and encouragement have enabled me to complete this book.

I must thank the Trustees of the Nuffield Foundation, the Trustees of the Noel Buxton Trust, the Commonwealth Trade Union Council, the Transport and General Workers' Union and the TUC for financial help given at crucial stages of the work, without which it could not have been completed. Professor Morris Jones and his successor, Professor Shula Marks, made available the resources of the Institute of Commonwealth Studies, which has been a constant source of enlightenment and stimulus. Many friends and colleagues read and advised on preliminary seminar papers or on portions of the early drafts of the text which covered subjects of which they had special knowledge: Mr Harry Hurst, Professor J. P. Mayer, Mr Cliff Tucker, and three former general secretaries of the TUC, the late Lord Citrine, the late Sir Vincent Tewson and the late George Woodcock. A fourth, Lord Murray of Epping Forest, has contributed the Foreword. I am deeply indebted to Professor Morris Jones who read a considerable part of the first draft, and to Mr David Morgan who read right through the final draft with the exception of Chapter 8. All gave good advice, which I have taken. Any surviving errors of fact or judgement are, of course, my own. I wish to thank the librarians of the Barbados Archives, the Institute for Social Studies, Amsterdam, the International Labour Office, Geneva, the Labour Party, the Nehru Memorial Library, New Delhi, and Rhodes House, Oxford, for the use of their collections, and I thank the staff of the filing department and the library of the TUC for their forbearance and assistance.

Those who gave me interviews are mentioned in the list of principal sources at the end of the book. Such a list cannot convey the value of their comments, the hospitable atmosphere in which discussions took place, or the warmth of the welcome given to me not only by former trade union and political colleagues but by those whom I had not previously met. I wish also to thank Richard Hart, in London, for his generosity in sharing the fruits of his own researches and experience in the labour movement of the West Indies, and my friends McDonald Moses in Trinidad and Peter and Daphne Abrahams in Jamaica for showing me other aspects of life in the Caribbean.

To the late Lord Citrine there are no thanks that I can offer which will match the great privilege he conferred on me. Not only did he give permission to use the papers he collected and the diary he kept while serving on the West India Royal Commission, but he also read my seminar papers and the early drafts of Chapter 1, most of Chapters 2–4, Chapter 6 and the first part of Chapter 7, and in our discussions commented freely on all aspects of the TUC's overseas work during the period in which he was General Secretary. I was able to discuss his West Indian diary with him while I was reading it, but he did not see the draft of the second half of Chapter 7 in which it was used. This was read by his son Norman, the present Lord Citrine, who kindly gave me permission to publish. It was a great disappointment that Walter Hood died shortly after his retirement. Those who knew him will be able to estimate the debt I owe to him and will, I hope, catch an occasional echo of his voice in these pages.

St Albans, *August* 1985

List of abbreviations used in text

AEU	Amalgamated Engineering Union
AFL	American Federation of Labour
AITUC	All-India Trade Union Congress
ARCCTU	All-Russian Central Council of Trade Unions
ARCOS	All-Russian Co-operative Society
ASLEF	Associated Society of Locomotive Engineers and Firemen
ATSEFWTU	All-Trinidad Sugar Estates and Factories Workers' Trade Union
BGLU	British Guiana Labour Union
BGWILC	British Guiana and West Indies Labour Congress
BITU	Bustamante Industrial Trade Union
BSP	British Socialist Party
BWU	Barbados Workers' Union
CGT	Confédération Générale du Travail
CIO	(Trinidad) Committee of Industrial Organizations (USA) Congress of Industrial Organizations
Comintern	Communist International
Congress Report	Report and Proceedings of annual Trades Union Congress
CPGB	Communist Party of Great Britain
CPI	Communist Party of India
DGB	German Federation of Trade Unions
ECCI	Executive Committee of Communist International
GFTU	General Federation of Trade Unions
GIPRU	Great Indian Peninsular Railwaymen's Union
GKU	Girni Kamgar Union
ICU	Industrial and Commercial Workers' Union (South Africa)
IFTU	International Federation of Trade Unions
ILO	International Labour Organization
ILP	Independent Labour Party
IMF	International Metal Trades Federation
ISB	International Socialist Bureau
ITF	International Transport Federation
ITS	International Trade Secretariats

ITUF	Indian Trade Union Federation
IWMA	International Workingmen's Association
IWW	Industrial Workers of the World
KMT	Kuomintang
LAI	League Against Imperialism
L.P.Imp.A.C.	Labour Party Imperial Advisory Committee
Labour Party Conference Report	Report of Proceedings of Labour Party Annual Conference.
LRC	Labour Representation Committee
LRD	Labour Research Department
LSI	Labour and Socialist International
MIF	Miners' International Federation
MPCA	Man-Power Citizens' Association
NAFTA	National Amalgamated Furnishing Trades Association
NMM	National Minority Movement
NRMU	Northern Rhodesia Mineworkers' Union
NTUF	National Trade Union Federation (India)
NUR	National Union of Railwaymen
OUCRP	Oxford University Colonial Records Project
OWTU	Oilfields Workers' Trade Union
PKI	Communist Party of Indonesia (Dutch East Indies)
PNP	People's National Party
PPTUS	Pan-Pacific Trade Union Secretariat
RILU	Red International of Labour Unions
SATUC	South African Trade Union Congress
SDF	Social Democratic Federation (Great Britain)
SWWTU	Seamen and Waterfront Workers' Trade Union
TGWU	Transport and General Workers' Union
TLP	Trinidad Labour Party
TUAC	Trades Union Advisory Council
TUC	Trades Union Congress (G.C.: General Council, I.C.: International Committee; C.A.C.: Colonial Advisory Committee)
TWMA	Trinidad Workingmen's Association
WFTU	World Federation of Trade Unions
WIR	Workers' International Relief
WWLI	Workers' Welfare League of India

1 Introduction

For over forty years after 1921, when the British Trades Union Congress (TUC) sent its first deputation to the Secretary of State for India, the TUC made a sustained effort to assist the development of trade unionism in the British dependent empire. Its policies and methods were substantially charted before the end of the Second World War and came into full operation after 1945. How should this work be regarded? As a traditional expression of trade union fraternity? Or, in the words of a Trinidadian trade union leader, as 'an instance of colonial paternalism at its best'?[1] Or as a contribution to nation-building, as it was perceived by the General Secretary, Sir Vincent Tewson, who did most to carry out the policy after the Second World War and who constantly asked 'How will they be able to run a country if they can't run a trade union branch?'[2] From a hostile standpoint it could be regarded as a manifestation of cultural imperialism, or even as a form of class struggle in which the 'labour aristocrats' of the British movement allied themselves with the bourgeoisie in order to retain control of colonial markets and raw materials. The former view might be taken in territories conscious of the weight of colonial rule; the latter derives from one strand in European socialist thought rather than from actual trade union experience in the colonies.

What was the TUC, as an organization, trying to do? It was never a body in which committees sat down to construct or analyse theories on which policies might be based. Decisions were taken in specific situations – when an international or overseas trade union body asked for action, when a visitor arrived to make contact with the TUC, when a subject came up for discussion in the International Labour Organization (ILO), or when the British government did (or omitted to do) something which affected trade union interests. This study attempts to trace the decisions, taken within a web of interlocking relationships and events, which followed one another in time and ultimately coalesced into a coherent policy. Since these decisions cannot be understood without a consideration of the development of the TUC itself, the starting point lies five years earlier than the first major venture into the empire.

The most important factor in the history of colonial trade unionism, as distinct from efforts at workers' organization which produced no permanent result, was the pre-eminence of the British movement as the earliest model of what trade unionism could be and could do, as a source of inspiration and tradition and, above all, of experience. British trade unionism was built on the first simple assertion of the right of working men in combination to have a say in determining their wages and conditions of employment. This assertion raised concurrent problems of relations between workers and employers, between workers and workers, and between workers and the community at large; it necessitated definitions in law and the determination of government responsibilities for labour conditions and for intervention, or nonintervention, in industrial relations; it raised expectations in social and political fields extending far beyond the immediate workplace, and formed new channels for expression and for the exertion of influence and pressure through which these expectations might be fulfilled. The growth of this British trade union movement was therefore inseparable from the development of political ideas and institutions, and its example had peculiar weight in the dependencies as one element in the impact of the metropolitan power on the populations it controlled. However, no movement can act beyond the limits of its experience and imagination. British trade union experience was manifestly relevant to the problems of colonial workers where British firms, British laws and British-controlled governments were dominant. It was less obviously applicable where the influence of the imperial government itself was limited either by its own policy of nonintervention in local customs and institutions, by the accelerating transfer of responsibility to elected legislatures and ministers, or by passive or active resistance to British influence.

The assertion of working men's rights was not peculiar to Britain and would have occurred, as it frequently did, amongst Indian and colonial workers who had no contact with the TUC. Nor was the British movement the only source of ideas and experience amongst the industrially advanced countries. In practice, however, other sources were largely ruled out in the colonial period. Had British trade unionism been revolutionary in its aims and methods, colonial unions that followed its example would certainly have been suppressed by colonial governments; had it relied on state machinery rather than on its own efforts, imitation in the colonies would have produced little result from rudimentary administrations. Over time, the British movement had become constitutional, voluntary, independent, representative, empirical and flexible. Its experience was not confined to industry. Unions were formed before working men had political rights, and in the struggle for the vote and for seats in Parliament they were obliged to shape their attitudes towards the political use of union strength, to political parties, and to the various ideas and groupings in the new socialist movement. In fact, during its growth the British movement had encountered most of the problems that confronted colonial unions as they sought to face employers and to establish national centres which could face governments. In most cases, British trade union experience *was* relevant to the varying circumstances and aspirations of workers in the dependencies. Where this was not so, it left no mark.

In India and the colonies the TUC could offer its own industrial knowledge and its influence on the metropolitan government; in the political field it was less sure-footed. The TUC and its affiliated unions had participated in the expansion of workers' political rights within an existing parliamentary system, but the overseas movements operated where that system itself was still under construction, where frequently racial, tribal, communal and linguistic differences cut across class divisions, where even national identities were imperfectly defined. Moreover the TUC worked from the metropolitan seat of power, and its experience did not embrace the sense of exclusion and frustration engendered by colonial status. This deficiency could be remedied only by co-operation with the colonial movements. In 1916, when the first pertinent decisions were taken, these movements did not exist. Scattered attempts at workers' organization had not resulted in the establishment of permanent unions. Only in India was industry developed on a sufficient scale to demand their operation, and it was there that the TUC was to make its first effort in a society which differed profoundly from the domestic conditions in which British unions had grown. It was there that a strong nationalist movement was first encountered, and there that the first major challenge to the TUC's concept of trade unionism was launched from a rival European base. A decade later, when the TUC became fully engaged in the colonies, its experience was by no means limited to Great Britain.

The men who led the TUC out into the wider world had much in common with colonial workers. Ben Tillett,[3] who helped to form the International Transport Federation (ITF), had only a few days' schooling before going to work at the age of 8, and had worked in mining, in fishing and in the Navy – even in a circus – before he became a merchant seaman and founded the Sea Operatives' and General Labourers' Union in 1887. At 13 Ernest Bevin,[4] who was primarily responsible for the establishment of the TUC's Colonial Advisory Committee in 1937, left his job as a farmer's boy to seek work in Bristol, where he became a kitchen boy and ultimately a van-driver. Walter Citrine,[5] architect of the TUC's administration and of its colonial policy, valued his elementary education but beyond that taught himself, and as an electrician wiring houses in Wallasey told himself, 'Some day I and other workers will have electricity just like these people'.[6] Born under Victoria, supposedly heirs to an empire at the height of its power, they had little to learn about deprivation at home.

Yet all the reports made by TUC emissaries to India and the colonies reveal that they did not fully grasp the reality of workers' conditions until they saw them with their own eyes. In India in 1938 Bevin watched men building a house and saw

> stone, mortar, all the building material passed hand to hand up human chains strung from the bottoms and tops of long ladders. The sight sickened me ... I made up my mind that some day I would do whatever I can to raise the standard of living in India.[7]

At about the same time, in the West Indian island of Nevis, Citrine was meeting a woman of 62 who walked five and a half miles each way to work on the roads for 6d. a day. He wrote in his diary:

> I will never again hear talk of our 'trusteeship' of the coloured peoples of the Empire without a feeling of shame at the callous way in which we have neglected them ... I feel so burning with indignation at the neglect I see everywhere, and the stories of poverty I hear, and the wretched houses I can't miss seeing, that it makes me depressed and sick at times.[8]

If their knowledge of the dependent empire was incomplete, the TUC leaders had connections overseas. In America and in the Dominions British immigrants had started new movements, in some cases retaining links with the parent bodies: the Amalgamated Society of Engineers, for example, was formed in Britain in 1851, and by 1854 had set up branches in Montreal and Hamilton in Canada, and in Malta; by 1892 it had eighty-two overseas branches, half of them in Australia and New Zealand. There were also links with the Continent as the common interests of trade unionists were perceived. The Miners' International Federation (MIF) was founded in 1890 and the ITF in 1896. In 1900 there were twelve of these international trade secretariats,[9] in which the constituent unions represented members with the same trade interests and exchanged information relevant to their trades. The leaders of the British unions participated in them, but the TUC itself, although it began to exchange fraternal delegates with the American Federation of Labour (AFL) in 1894, was not affiliated to any international body until it joined the International Federation of Trade Unions (IFTU) in 1919. In the same year the establishment of the intergovernmental International Labour Organization provided an external institution through which national and international trade union bodies might work.

Thus, by the time the TUC turned to the dependencies, its relations with their unions were intertwined with a network of imperial and international connections with the Labour Party, which in turn was in contact with Indian and colonial nationalist organizations, and with the British government which was responsible for colonial administration. But first the TUC had to establish itself as a body willing and competent to represent the British trade union movement in all aspects of its work.

2   The Framework of Activity

In 1916 the TUC was not a trade union national centre in the modern sense of the term. In some ways it was comparable to most of the colonial centres that emerged a generation later: its domestic organization was minimal, it was loosely connected with a political party in an ill-defined relationship, it was uncertain of the purposes of international trade union relations, and it had neither the money nor the staff to fulfil in a responsible manner any external obligations that it might assume. Nor had it established its right to speak for British trade unionism abroad. In fact, it was not mandated to do so.

The strength of the movement lay in the affiliated unions, which organized directly and negotiated with employers. The TUC owed its existence to the emergence of national problems with which individual unions could not deal, such as the need for technical education, arbitration and courts of conciliation, and especially the state of the law as it affected the conduct of trade unions – these, and the government's appointment of a Royal Commission of Inquiry into Trade Unions, were amongst the subjects proposed for discussion in 1868 when the Manchester Trades Council called the meeting which ultimately led to the establishment of a national body. Such subjects fell within the scope of the government and Parliament, and the essential elements of this body were a Parliamentary Committee to represent the views of the movement to them, and a congress to elect and to bring the views of the unions to the Committee. These were domestic functions arising from industrial needs. Unions which required overseas links – notably the seamen – formed them through the international trade secretariats. The idea that the TUC itself should establish international connections was derived primarily from the political Labour movement and lacked appeal until all organizations became immersed in a world war.

The Trades Union Congress in 1916

Organization

When the TUC assembled in 1916, there were 673 delegates representing 2,850,547 members of 227 societies, which now included many large nationally organized unions. The supporting apparatus, however, was rudimentary. The Parliamentary Committee of nineteen members was served by a permanent staff of two – a Secretary, Charles

Bowerman M.P.[1] and a clerk, W. J. Bolton.[2] The Committee's stated aims were to watch all legislation affecting labour, initiate such legislation as Congress might direct, to call the Congress and arrange its programme from resolutions sent in by the trades, and to transact business between congresses. For these purposes in 1916 the total income for the year was £5,381,[3] the contribution (which had not been raised for 14 years) being only 1d. per year for each three members affiliated. But contributions were paid regularly and strictly accounted for, and the amount paid by a union determined its representation. The Parliamentary Committee and the Congress were genuinely representative, and the Committee submitted annually a report on an output of work which in size and quality bore no relation to the paucity of its staff. There was an obvious disparity between the TUC's responsibilities and its organization, which the President of that year, Harry Gosling,[4] pointed out.

As a result, during the following year the Parliamentary Committee prepared a scheme of expansion which was endorsed by the 1917 Congress. It provided for an increase in contributions and staff and for improved information and services to unions, and included a proposal 'to arrange for the exchange of correspondence and journals with the Trade Union movement throughout the world, and to codify and classify them for the use of the Trade Union movement in this country'.[5] For the first time, attention to external relations was envisaged as part of the regular work of the office. It was not clear, however, with whom these relations were to be established.

The Imperial Connection

The most obvious potential link was with the Dominions. The TUC already had relations with the Canadian Labour Congress, with an annual exchange of fraternal delegates initiated in 1913. After the outbreak of war, the existing feeling of kinship was strongly reinforced as thousands of British families were visited by relatives or friends of relatives who might not have seen Britain since their childhood, if at all, but now came to defend it, wearing the uniforms of the Dominions. In 1916, Congress called for the strengthening of kindred ties and for negotiations with representative trade union bodies to secure co-ordination of effort and organization throughout the Empire.

The concept of 'empire' was vague, and the term was habitually used to cover the Dominions, which were already substantially self-governing. Did it include the non-self-governing dependencies? Equally imprecise in matters of race and colour, in 1917 anti-German opponents of a resolution to begin preparation for international co-operation argued that this meant that 'we shall eventually be called upon to meet the people who justify the murdering of our women and children', whereas Australia, Canada, New Zealand, India and the rest of the empire were involved in the war and the economic problems that would arise from it. 'Now is the time,' it was said, 'to get into touch with our comrades who are nearest to us in race and language.' However, a motion calling for an annual British Empire Labour Congress failed on practical grounds and because it cut across the decision on international co-operation which had already been taken.

Although the colonies were included in the 1917 motion, they scarcely impinged on the TUC's consciousness. The same Congress paid no attention at all to one small item in the Parliamentary Committee's Report concerning a deputation to the Secretary of State for the Colonies, Walter Long, to protest against an Ordinance prohibiting for the duration of the war the formation of organizations amongst the labouring classes of St Kitts. The deputation followed a Question tabled in Parliament by Bowerman, to which an evasive reply had been given, suggesting the possibility of disturbances under pro-German influence. Long assured the Committee that the Ordinance had not been brought into force and would be revoked at the end of the war, but the account of the discussion with him shows that the deputation had only the scantiest information at their disposal. They made the best of it, seizing on a recent government initiative to secure a general wage increase as proof that discontent on the island had been justified and stressing the need for workers' representation in negotiations. The matter had been brought to their attention in the first place not by any trade union in St Kitts, for there were none, but by Samuel Gompers, President of the AFL, to whom the Secretary of State's assurance was conveyed.[6] The truth was that until trade unions or political movements existed in the dependencies, there were no bodies with which the TUC could establish fraternal relations, and no call for the Parliamentary Committee to exercise a political responsibility for territories under the authority of a British minister unless information was received, as in this case, through some other channel.

International Connections

Gompers was also responsible for a proposal to which the 1916 Congress did pay attention. The United States was still neutral in the war, but in November 1914 the AFL adopted a resolution calling for an international Labour Congress to be held at the same time and place as the conference which would in the end settle the terms of peace. In March 1916 it issued a formal invitation to 'the Organized Labor Movement of All Countries'. It expressed concern that out of the horrors of war there should come greater opportunity, freedom and protection for those who did the world's work, who bore the brunt of the fighting, and who had always hitherto been excluded from the deliberations of those whose blunders and ambitions caused wars. No agenda for the Congress was suggested, but on representation the proposal was definite: delegates must be either officials or duly accredited representatives of economic organizations of wage earners, two from each affiliate of the IFTU and one each from the labour movement of any country, even if not affiliated. This applied to the TUC, which was not a member of the IFTU.

But the German Federation of Trade Unions (DGB) was affiliated. The Parliamentary Committee urged acceptance of the invitation, but the debate was swayed by emotion directed against the Germans and against the pacifist elements in the British Independent Labour Party (ILP). It was in vain that the Committee's spokesman stressed that only trade unions had been invited. Congress not only refused to participate, but insisted on deleting the offending paragraph from the Parliamentary Committee's Report.

The reasons for the TUC's isolation must be sought in the history of procedural and ideological disputes which bedevilled international labour conferences from their inception. The First International, the International Workingmen's Association, was founded before the TUC, in 1864. It had sections on the Continent connected with its General Council in London through corresponding secretaries[7] and did much to exchange useful information. Some of the British union leaders were associated with it, but not as representatives of the TUC, with its modest aims and organization – there was no Parliamentary Committee until 1871, and even then it was still uncertain whether the committee or the annual congresses would become permanent.[8] The IWMA had its weaknesses, notably the characteristic broad sweep of aims with no clear distinction between political and industrial functions, and in 1876 it foundered on the continuous and bitter dissensions between the supporters of Marx and the anarchist adherents of Bakunin. The idea of international links had taken root, however, and the Parliamentary Committee itself convened a conference in 1888 to discuss industrial problems. There was little meeting of minds: some of the Continental leaders seemed to be more concerned with state action than with union organization, and some turned out to be anarchists advocating universal strikes. As a result, the Parliamentary Committee declined invitations to be represented at further conferences in which bodies other than trade unions were to be allowed to participate.[9]

These included the International Labour Congress held in Paris in 1889 – generally regarded as the first conference of the Second International – and conferences held in Brussels in 1891 and in Zurich in 1893. They were attended by political and trade union organizations and reflected the spread of socialist ideas. This occurred also in Britain, where the Fabian Society and the Social Democratic Federation (SDF) were founded in 1884 and the ILP in 1893. Working men now had the vote, and the unions were quick to realize that they had become important to politicians as a platform and as electoral supporters. In 1895, the TUC Congress decided to confine delegations to Congress to full-time officials of unions and trade unionists working at their trade, a decision clearly aimed at political 'outsiders'. Nevertheless, there was sufficient socialism in the atmosphere to achieve a positive response from the Parliamentary Committee to a deputation from an international committee set up by the Zurich Congress which proposed that a socialist and trade union conference should be held in London. A joint committee was set up and the conference met in 1896.

The TUC Congress which followed recognized that the international conference had been a disaster, not least because it had cost the Parliamentary Committee £300. It was said that the conference had violated every principle of democratic representation, many of the delegates being unknown in this country and probably in their own, and some had disgraced the labour movement by coming to blows. They had been discussing socialism and anarchism, and the conference decided that in future anarchists should be excluded, since they were in any case opposed to normal political action.[10] But Congress had already had enough: it decided that in future international conferences should be constituted by properly chosen representatives of bona fide labour organizations,[11] and in the following year rejected a suggestion from Gompers that such a conference should be held.

Some of the TUC's affiliates were already active in the international trade secretariats and were also members of a mutual assistance body, the General Federation of Trade Unions (GFTU) set up in Britain in 1899 with the Parliamentary Committee's blessing. In 1900, the President of the Danish trade union centre, visiting the GFTU's annual conference, again raised the question of international trade union meetings, and with the co-operation of the DGB the first international conference of trade union national centres was held in Copenhagen in 1901. As further conferences were held, the British representation was provided by the GFTU. Again, in 1904, Tillett tried to persuade the TUC to participate, but Congress voted 246,000 to 83,000 against.[12]

Yet this was a genuine effort to establish co-operation on industrial lines. At Dublin in 1903 the international conference established rules for a skeleton organization to call meetings of secretaries, with a secretary (Karl Legien, secretary of the DGB) to collect and exchange information on legislation, labour statistics, and other relevant material.[13] The meetings continued, and it was decided to admit fraternal delegates from the trade secretariats. They attended for the first time in 1913 and held a meeting of their own – their first.[14] The conference of 1913 reconstituted itself as the IFTU and marked the beginning of a change of attitude on the part of the TUC. Bowerman attended, and French and German fraternal delegates were invited to the TUC Congress in that year.

The relative success of these trade union conferences in excluding divisive political controversies was partly due to changes in the socialist camp. The Second International had no standing organization until its Paris Congress established an International Socialist Bureau (ISB) in 1900. Its conferences – the TUC declined an invitation in 1903 – became regular and provided a forum for the protagonists of varying socialist creeds to thrash out their differences. This enabled the international trade union conference, in 1907, to exclude from discussion a motion submitted by the French Confederation of Labour (CGT) on international trade union action against war and to remit it to the Socialist International as a political question.

The trade union Secretariat could not entirely avoid semipolitical questions, as some of these arose within the trade union movements themselves. The Amiens Charter adopted by the CGT at its own congress in 1906 held that unions must not be made the instruments of political parties, nor must their members introduce differing political views into the unions. This was not a statement of nonpolitical trade unionism – on the contrary, the union itself was seen as the vehicle of political change, pursuing immediate industrial demands, but with the ultimate aim of securing the abolition of the wage system and expropriation of the capitalist class by means of a general strike, after which the unions would play a key role in social organization. This was the syndicalist view, propagated in Britain by the Industrial Syndicalist Education League founded by the engineers' leader, Tom Mann[15] and in America and Australia by the Industrial Workers of the World (IWW), founded in America in 1905. The IWW, initially organizing workers who could find no place in the craft unions of the AFL, became a threat to the established unions when it tried to bring skilled and unskilled workers into single industrial unions. Thus the syndicalist movement raised both theoretical and organizational problems affecting representation. In 1909 the international trade union conference restated the objects of conferences called by the International Secretariat as:

to consider the closer union of the trade unions of all countries, uniform trade union statistics, mutual help in economic struggles, and all questions in direct connection with the trade union organization of workers. *All theoretical questions, and those which affect the tendency or tactics of the trade union movement in the separate nations will not be discussed.*[16]

Two years later the IWW sent a representative to the seventh conference at Budapest, but only the CGT supported his admission against the opposition of the AFL.[17]

Bowerman's attendance at the 1913 conference suggested a recognition by the TUC that the International Secretariat had disposed of the confusions which had caused trouble in the past. However, the outbreak of war dealt a shattering blow at the new IFTU. Except for the AFL and an affiliate in the Transvaal, all its affiliates were in divided Europe and its headquarters, together with those of 27 of the 32 international trade secretariats, were in Germany.[18] Only the neutrals could hope to maintain some links across the battlefronts, and a subsecretariat was hastily set up in Amsterdam under J. Oudegeest, secretary of the Dutch trade union centre. But with the German invasion of Belgium and France the desire for links began to evaporate and leaders in the Allied countries set up a Central Office of Correspondence in Paris under Léon Jouhaux, secretary of the CGT. This kept Allied affiliates in touch, and representatives of France, Italy and Belgium attended the GFTU's annual meeting at Leeds in July 1916. So when Gompers' proposal came before the TUC Congress in that year, it encountered not only the strong anti-German feeling engendered by the war, but also a latent rivalry between the TUC and the GFTU.

The Political Dimension

There were also historic political tensions reflected in the TUC. The unions were conscious that the numerical and financial strength in the political labour movement lay with them, and that they had been the first in the field. When even returning officers' expenses had to be paid by election candidates, they had borne them, and before Members of Parliament were paid, they had maintained theirs. The first two, the miners Alexander Macdonald and Thomas Burt, were elected in 1874 before the Labour Party, the ILP, the SDF or the Fabian Society existed, and the first to become a minister, the stonemason Henry Broadhurst,[19] who served for 12 years as Secretary to the Parliamentary Committee, was appointed under-secretary of state at the Home Office in 1886. Broadhurst was privileged to have his fire poked by the Prince of Wales when he was invited to stay at the Palace, and it was generally appreciated that a man who had worked with his hands in building the Houses of Parliament had been enabled to sit there.[20] These early members generally worked with, or sat as, Liberals, and even after the formation of the ILP James Mawdsley, Secretary of the Operative Spinners' Association and with 11 years' service on the Parliamentary Committee, unsuccessfully contested the double-member constituency of Oldham in 1899 in harness with a Conservative, Winston

Churchill.[21] It was as a result of a Congress decision in 1899 that a Labour Representation Committee was set up to coordinate union efforts in elections with those of the sympathetic political societies, and in 1904 Ramsay MacDonald, speaking as fraternal delegate from the committee to Congress, acknowledged that it was 'neither sister nor brother to Congress, but its child'. 'We come,' he said, 'to offer our filial respects'.[22]

The Labour Representation Committee prospered and, after the 1906 general election, changed its name to the Labour Party. In that election, 23 of the 29 successful candidates it sponsored were union candidates, and 22 others secured election who had been put forward by Liberal associations or by their unions alone. These formed a separate trade union group in Parliament until 1910, when the Miners' Federation affiliated to the Labour Party.[23]

In Parliament the two groups co-operated, especially during the passage of the Trade Disputes Act 1906, and outside, from 1905 onwards, a Joint Board constituted by the TUC, the GFTU and the LRC/Labour Party discussed both policy and organizational matters.[24] Despite its coherence in Parliament, with Arthur Henderson[25] as Chief Whip, the Labour Party remained a federation of groups – the affiliated unions, the ILP, the Fabian Society, and the SDF which subsequently split. The internal strains nearly reached breaking point in 1914 when the ILP declared its opposition to the war and, after conscription was introduced in January 1917, some of its leaders were gaoled for refusing the call-up, in contrast with the Parliamentary Committee, which was convinced by the German invasion of Belgium, and with Henderson himself, who joined the government in May 1916.

Such strains were magnified in the ISB, with which the Labour Party became formally associated in 1908. While the IFTU confined itself to limited industrial functions, the Socialist International had set out to change the whole system of society, and attracted not only the parliamentary socialist parties but also those of countries with no political freedoms. The nature of its theoretical controversies ranged from the curious debate on whether or not the Labour Party was eligible for admission – it was finally accepted on the grounds that although it did not avowedly recognize the class struggle, it actually carried it on[26] – to the bitter disputes between the Bolsheviks and Mensheviks of the Russian Social Democratic Workers' Party, split after 1903, with the exiled Menshevik headquarters in Paris and Lenin's Bolshevik group in Switzerland. When the war came, such divisions cut right across national boundaries.

At the outset, the Secretary of the ISB, Camille Huysmans, transferred his office from Belgium to Holland and summoned a conference of neutrals, which called on socialists in the belligerent

countries to stop the war. When this failed, the antiwar elements called
conferences at Zimmerwald in Switzerland in 1915 and at Kienthal in
April 1916 which were attended by delegates from neutral countries
and from belligerents on both sides. The importance of these
conferences lay less in their calls for peace than in the process of
subdivision of the International that they began. The antiwar groups
were now distinct from the main socialist parties of the Allies and of the
Central Powers, and Lenin had failed to gain majority support for the
Bolshevik view that it was the duty of socialists to transform the
imperialist war into civil war within their own countries. On 15 March
1917 the Tsar abdicated,[27] and in April the Bolshevik Party decided to
take the initiative in creating a third international.[28]

A Change of Course

In January 1917 the ISB executive decided to call a full meeting of the
Social International. Germany began unrestricted submarine warfare
and the USA declared war in April. The Russian war effort was
disintegrating, opening up the eastern flank of the Allied blockade of
Germany. The war was taking an appalling toll and seemed to have
taken a new lease of life, but the neutrals persisted. A joint Dutch-
Scandinavian committee was set up under Hjalmar Branting of Sweden
to prepare the conference, and a series of intricate moves began which
ultimately brought the TUC into the International.

In Britain the antiwar groups in the labour movement came to the
fore. The ILP and the British Socialist Party (BSP), the successor to the
SDF, had nominated delegates to the Zimmerwald Conference in 1915,
but they were refused passports. In 1916 the BSP split, and its antiwar
wing set up a United Socialist Council with the ILP. This Council called
a Convention at Leeds in June 1917 which became almost as notorious
as the International Conference in 1896. In Russia, state institutions
were being undermined by the formation of workers' and soldiers'
councils, one of which, the Petrograd Soviet, also issued a general
invitation to an international conference, to be held at Stockholm to
formulate a working-class peace policy. Inspired by the revolutionary
dawn, the Leeds Convention pledged itself to work for a peace
without annexations or indemnities, and called on the organizations
represented to establish soviets to co-ordinate this effort. Ramsay
MacDonald – then treasurer of the Labour Party, but speaking for the
ILP – exhorted the delegates: 'Let us lay down our terms, make our own
proclamations, establish our own diplomacy; see to it that we have our
own international meetings. Let us say to the Russian democracy
"Maintain your Revolution ... put yourselves at the head of the
peoples of Europe"'.[29]

The Convention responded to the Petrograd invitation, and amid a blaze of hostile press publicity its delegates prepared to leave from Aberdeen on 10 June. They were frustrated by the refusal of members of the Seamen's and Firemen's Union to carry MacDonald on any ship. In the event, the Stockholm conference was postponed and no soviets were set up, but the Labour Party and the Parliamentary Committee were almost equally embarrassed by the behaviour of MacDonald and the seamen and the attendance of many trade unionists at Leeds.

The TUC and the Russian Revolution

The Parliamentary Committee were already aware that the situation in Russia was more complicated than they had realized in March when they had hailed 'the triumph of representative and democratic government by the Duma' and expressed the hope that the labour forces in Russia would unite in support of the new government. This message was sent through Will Thorne,[30] a member of the Committee, who was appointed with James O'Grady by the Labour Party to join representatives of the French Socialist Party who were going to Petrograd. Thorne was also asked to invite the official representatives of the organized Russian workers to send a fraternal delegate to the TUC's Congress in September.

Whether there were any workers' organizations capable of responding to this invitation was not known. Unions were allowed to operate in Russia after 1912, but became fully legal organizations only after the February revolution in 1917. Their relationship – if any – with the soviets that were spreading throughout Russia was unclear. The situation of the political parties was also uncertain. The Russian parties opposed to the Tsar had disturbed international conferences for decades and exhibited the usual characteristics of suppressed organizations. The Mensheviks of the Social Democratic Workers' Party were the nearest in outlook to the parliamentary parties of western Europe, but the Social Revolutionaries, with a following amongst the peasantry, condoned and practised terrorism. When the first Duma (Parliament) was established in 1906, there were disagreements on the desirability of fighting the elections, and when the war came, some of the leaders were in the Duma and some still in exile. By the time the Parliamentary Committee heard the delegates' report in May, Menshevik and Social Revolutionary leaders had joined the Provisional Government, but the Bolshevik leaders were still outside, though with contacts inside, Russia.

Thorne and O'Grady reported that ordinary trade unions were in existence – there were twenty in Moscow, including a strong compositors' union. In the factories British foremen had been dismissed, workers were securing wage increases, and new unions were being formed. However, there was no central trade union body with which to make contact, and the workers' and soldiers' councils, including the 3,000-strong soviet in Petrograd, consisted mainly of middle class men – lawyers, journalists, bank clerks and the like – not workmen themselves. Although it had not been possible to obtain a true impression of the feeling of the industrial workers and the peasants, the delegates had no doubt that the revolution was popular, and they thought it might be helpful if the Parliamentary Committee would send one or two representatives to Russia, even though in the existing chaos they might be able to do little more than watch events and advise the unions. The Petrograd Soviet and the Provisional Government were in opposition to one another, and the delegates had advised a coalition. The Soviet had asked their opinion of a manifesto in favour of peace without annexations, on the basis of the right of every people to control their own destinies, but in the discussion there had been no agreement on what these terms meant.[31]

The manifesto arose from the ISB's decision to call an international conference. Representatives of the Dutch–Scandinavian commitee had met the German Social Democrat leaders and had gone on to an enthusiastic welcome from the Menshevik and Social Revolutionary majority in the Petrograd Soviet, which began to take an active part in securing support for the conference. At this stage the Parliamentary Committee wished to stand aside. In accordance with the advice given by Thorne and O'Grady, they provisionally chose two representatives to go to Russia and cabled the Soviet in June expressing willingness to send them if it would be thought useful, and also referring to a visit paid to the TUC office by two emissaries of the Provisional Government who had inquired about British methods of trade union organization. At the same time they asked Henderson, who was going to Russia for the British Government, to make it clear to the Soviet that no action would be taken until an invitation had been received and that their mission, if sent, would go on a purely trade union visit 'in no way involved in the Stockholm or any other conference'.[32]

On 11 July an invitation to an international socialist conference, to be held in Stockholm on 15 August, was published by the Dutch-Scandinavian Committee and a Russian committee, thus carrying the authority of the ISB, the Scandinavian and Dutch parties, and of all the Russian socialist parties except the Bolsheviks. In accordance with the practice of the prewar International, both majorities and minorities of parties, and rival parties, were invited. On 17 July, on his way home from Russia, Henderson declared publicly in Stockholm that he was now convinced that the conference should be held, and in his turn was attacked by the press as pro-German.[33]

The Parliamentary Committee had had no reply from the Petrograd

Soviet when they received an invitation to an international trade union
conference to be held in Berne in October. This proposal stemmed
from the Allied conference of IFTU affiliates held at the time of the
GFTU's meeting in Leeds in July 1916, which had drawn up a
programme of social demands which later had a direct bearing on the
establishment of the International Labour Organization. The IFTU
followed it with a trade union conference in Stockholm on 6 June
1917, to which all IFTU affiliates were invited, but at which only the
CGT, the neutral countries and the Central Powers were represented.
The Swiss then tried again with their invitation to Berne, where they
hoped to discuss both the Leeds programme and the future of the
international trade union movement. The Parliamentary Committee
would probably have responded positively but for the rejection of the
Gompers proposal at the 1916 Congress, and if the whole idea of
sitting down to discuss anything with Germans had not been called into
question by the extraordinary conduct of the Leeds Convention and by
the much-publicized humiliation of Ramsay MacDonald at the hands
of a TUC affiliate. In this heady atmosphere they decided not to reply
immediately to the Swiss, but first to discuss the international situation
with the Labour Party Executive.[34] Before they could do so, four
delegates from the Petrograd Soviet arrived in London, and the Labour
Party Executive invited the Committee to meet them on 25 July.

The joint meeting with the Russians was unsatisfactory: when asked,
they gave no reason for the Petrograd Soviet's failure to reply to the
TUC's offer to help the trade unions. When the Parliamentary
Committee met afterwards, however, it emerged that the Labour Party
Executive had previously met the Russian delegation separately and
had decided to appoint delegates to go with them to meet the French
Socialist Party. In an extraordinary *volte face*, which could only have
been due to the prevailing controversies, the Committee took objection
to the Labour Party acting alone, appointed three of their own number
to go to Paris, and informed the party executive that they wished 'to be
consulted with and made part of any joint body responsible for the
convening of any International Labour Conference arising out of the
war', and that in their view 'such a Conference should be called, so far
as the British Labour representation is concerned, only on the
responsibility of the Labour Party Executive and the Parliamentary
Committee'. It was explained in reply that the Labour Party had been
invited to Paris to discuss the conditions under which the ISB's
Stockholm conference would be held; however, there was to be a
preliminary conference of Allied representatives, and although the
TUC was not affiliated to the ISB, the Executive invited the
Parliamentary Committee to appoint 8 of the 44 delegates that would
be allocated to the British Section of the ISB at the Allied conference.[35]

Swallowing their pride, the Parliamentary Committee withdrew their nominations for the Paris meeting.

Thus the visit from the Petrograd Soviet did not lead to co-operation between the TUC and the Russian trade unions, but in this bizarre manner it started the Parliamentary Committee on the road that led the TUC into joint working with the Labour Party in international affairs.

'Stockholm' and the 1917 Congress

Although the Parliamentary Committee now saw themselves and the Labour Party Executive as the only international representatives of the British Labour movement, the British Section of the ISB consisted of the Parliamentary Labour Party, the ILP, the BSP and the Fabian Society – a composition which would give half the votes to the socialist societies, and none to any other groups. The Petrograd delegates on the other hand had wanted the Stockholm conference – which was again postponed – to be all-embracing, and to have the task of framing a peace programme which would be binding on both majorities and minorities. At a difficult conference called by the Labour Party in August it was decided to send a delegation, but the miners' union succeeded in restricting its composition to members to be appointed by the party executive and the Parliamentary Committee. Immediately 'Stockholm' again became a national bone of contention when Henderson spoke at the conference in favour of participation, and was forced to resign from the Cabinet. It also became known that the Government would withhold passports, as the Italian and American Governments intended to do.[36]

Immediately before Congress the Parliamentary Committee's eight representatives attended the Inter-Allied Socialist Conference. Support for the Stockholm Conference was not unanimous, and on two essentials the delegates went counter to the Parliamentary Committee's views: they supported the representation of minorities, and they failed to agree on the general war aims of the Allies. The Parliamentary Committee accordingly reported to Congress their opinion that agreement on aims amongst the Allied representatives was essential to the success of an international conference, but that an international socialist conference was a necessary preliminary to the conclusion of a lasting peace. While ruling out Stockholm, they asked for powers to arrange and take part in such a conference, with representation by national delegations in which minorities within them would be governed by the majority or, alternatively, that each section should be given voting powers according to the number of persons it actually represented.[37]

Their report was introduced to Congress by the miners' leader Robert Smillie.[38] There was great opposition to the inclusion of minority groups in a British delegation, though Smillie pointed out that they had kept alive a British link with the International while Congress had ignored it. The seamen's leader, J. Havelock Wilson[39] then made it clear that if a further attempt were made 'to parley with the enemy', his members would again refuse to carry a British delegation, and he countered Smillie's argument by citing the activity of British unions in the international trade secretariats. He was opposed to mixing trade union and socialist conferences – as he had been since 1896 – and he set the TUC's 3 million membership against the Labour Party's 4,000, urging the delegates – as trade unionists – to act for themselves. Wilson's political reputation was not above criticism, however, and the Parliamentary Committee's proposal that minorities should have votes only in accordance with their strength was reasonable. Congress accepted it.[40]

This controversy over the Socialist International had left the Parliamentary Committee uncertain how to reply to the Swiss trade unions' invitation. The Allied affiliates of the IFTU had arranged to meet after Congress to discuss the invitation, and in August the Parliamentary Committee had agreed to join the meeting. But on 4 September they rescinded this decision. They did not record their reasons, but some of the statements at Congress suggested that they were now concerned that the GFTU would be attending as an IFTU affiliate, and also that they had committed themselves to co-operate with the Labour Party, which would not be represented.

On 6 September, at Congress, the Parliamentary Committee and the Labour Party Executive together decided that no further steps should be taken towards calling an international conference without either body consulting the other.[41] The committee were left to explain their reversal to the fraternal delegates at their own Congress, and the Inter-Allied Trade Union Conference again took place without the TUC. Thus the year ended with the Parliamentary Committee still outside the IFTU in a position of acute embarrassment. The trade union conference at Berne was held on 1 October, but with representation only from the neutrals and the Central Powers. The political conference at Stockholm never took place.

The neutrals had failed to bring the belligerents together, but their efforts and the 1917 Congress led the TUC into the international arena. The Parliamentary Committee's proposals for improved organization, including exchange of information with trade unions elsewhere and the provision of extra staff, were adopted, and consultation on international matters with the Labour Party Executive was agreed. On 27 September 1917 a joint meeting of the Parliamentary Committee and the Executive set up an International Joint Committee, and in February 1918 Fred Bramley[42] took up the post of assistant.

War Aims

The first task of the International Joint Committee was to consider a memorandum on war aims adopted by the Labour Party's Special Conference in August. Three important members of the committee – MacDonald, Henderson and Sidney Webb[43] – had contributed to it, expressing ideas that had been developing in the Labour movement since the early days of the war. In three meetings from October to December the new committee re-drafted it. The final version, adopted by a special conference representing societies affiliated to the TUC and to the Labour Party on 28 December, was taken by deputation to the Prime Minister.

There can be little doubt that this work had some effect. On 5 January 1918 Lloyd George chose a conference of trade union representatives originally called to discuss manpower, to make public a statement of war aims agreed between the British and Dominions governments. Lloyd George believed that without his declaration it would have been impossible to maintain the co-operation of the unions in the most critical phase of the war. The British government was now committed to independence for Poland and to self-determination – or government with the consent of the governed – in Austria–Hungary, the Turkish Empire and the German colonies, and to the creation of an international organization to settle disputes and to reduce the burden of armaments. Three days later, President Wilson, who had been sent the Labour Party's first statement, published his Fourteen Points of Peace.[44]

In February 1918 the memorandum was amplified by an Inter-Allied Labour and Socialist Conference in London. By this time the October revolution had taken place in Russia, and the Bolshevik Government refused passports for the Menshevik and Social Revolutionary delegates, but the socialist parties of Britain, Belgium, France and Italy were represented, and the TUC for the first time. In its final form the memorandum was a detailed statement on self-determination, the establishment of a League of Nations, and the need for international labour legislation. Hoping for a negotiated peace, the conference sent their statement to the socialists of the Central Powers. The Bulgarian, Austrian and Hungarian parties expressed willingness to meet on this basis, but by the time Congress met in September there was still no response from the majority Social Democrats in Germany.[45]

The 1918 Congress was notable for the attendance of Gompers. The AFL had sent a delegation to meet the Parliamentary Committee and the Labour Party Executive in April, and subsequently the CGT and the French Socialist Party. It was also represented at a further Inter-Allied Labour and Socialist Conference which met in London after

Congress. This reaffirmed the demand that workers should be represented at the peace conference and decided that a world labour conference should be held at the same time and place. So Gompers had obtained support for his original proposal, and the conference also took special note of various propositions that the AFL wanted to have incorporated in the peace treaty, such as a statement that the rights of free association, free speech and free assembly should not be abridged, and that it should be recognized in law and in practice that 'the labour of a human being is not a commodity or an article of commerce'.[46]

In October rebellions began in Austria–Hungary; on 9 November a German Republic was proclaimed. On 11 November the armistice between the Allies and Germany was signed. The terrible war was over.

'Representative Internationalism'

The Parliamentary Committee and Congress had thrown their weight behind the plans for the postwar world, but the main work of preparing them had been done by the Labour Party and the affiliates of the IFTU.

The part played by the GFTU in this was by no means negligible. Its secretary, W. A. Appleton, had been primarily responsible for organizing the Allied trade union conference at Leeds in July 1916. It was sparsely attended and held in private, but Appleton sent a report of the proceedings to Gompers, and the agreed resolutions to the British government. Oudegeest sent the resolutions to all IFTU affiliates. Proposed by Jouhaux, they demanded that the peace treaty should include provisions for international labour standards on such subjects as hygiene, safety, hours of work and social insurance, with an international commission to give effect to them. Nor was the work of the neutral affiliates fruitless. The Leeds resolutions were considered together with proposals from Legien in Berlin at the conference of IFTU affiliates from the neutral and Central Powers held in Stockholm in June 1917. Finally, the conference called by the Swiss, and held in Berne on 1 October 1917, brought both sets of recommendations together in a common programme which covered specific labour questions and demanded that the International Labour Office at Basle should call intergovernmental conferences on labour standards and should grant representation to the IFTU.[47]

The office at Basle had been set up in 1901 as a result of the work of the International Labour Association founded in Paris in 1900. Its method was to examine specific subjects and to devise proposals for legislation which could be set out in international conventions, and then try to persuade governments to sign and implement them. Though it attracted some subsidies from governments, it was essentially a voluntary body without the capacity to drive governments into action. However, sufficient progress was made before the war to influence the thinking of some of them, including the British Government, and of some leading figures in the labour movement, including Arthur Henderson, who was treasurer of the association's British section.[48] The international trade union proposal for intergovernmental conferences was a modest one, but it was the first step towards the establishment of an intergovernmental body.

Having embarked on this work, the GFTU naturally reacted unfavourably to the 1917 Congress decision on organization which empowered the Parliamentary Committee to start work in the international field, and at the Inter-Allied Trade Union Conference which followed that Congress its representatives left the foreign delegates in no doubt that they disputed the Parliamentary Committee's right to assume the lead in British representation. There were also domestic causes of friction – some political and some even personal[49] – and an underlying tension due to the character of the GFTU as an organization largely composed of small skilled unions practising the same kind of 'business trade unionism' as the AFL.[50] While the Parliamentary Committee was drawing up plans for its international work, the GFTU produced and publicized a scheme of expansion which would have made it, not the TUC, the central British body in international affairs.

One of Bramley's first tasks was to analyse the TUC and GFTU memberships to find the extent of overlapping. He established that the GFTU represented fewer than 900,000 members, of whom 800,000 were affiliated to the TUC. After consultation with the AFL delegation in April 1918, the Parliamentary Committee called a conference of TUC unions with international affiliations, which met on 9 July and 8 August. Fifteen unions with nearly 2½ million members sent delegates. At present, the Parliamentary Committee's paper prepared for the conference said, the British trade unionist is in practically complete ignorance of the work done by his colleagues abroad. International trade union conferences in the past had not been fully representative, and some of the alleged international Socialist and Labour conferences had been entirely dominated by people who neither represented nor had any substantial influence with the great mass of organized labour. 'Internationalism has not yet failed. Fully representative internationalism has not yet been tried.'

The conference adopted the Parliamentary Committee's suggestions, and it was decided to recommend to the forthcoming Congress in September that the Committee should establish an international department to be responsible for developing a close relationship with the trade union movements of the Allied and neutral countries, the colonies[51] and the United States. It would establish an information bureau which would co-operate with the British sections of the international trade secretariats and would produce immediately an

International Review to give TUC affiliates information on foreign trade unionism. The proposals meant, as the conference had agreed in principle, that the Parliamentary Committee would become the central international trade union bureau for Great Britain.[52]

However, they had attached too little weight to the GFTU. At Congress, Tillett urged delegates not to disregard a body which had dealt with international questions from the purely economic and trade union standpoints and Tom Shaw,[53] secretary of the International Textile Association, claimed that the GFTU had started to prepare its scheme three years before, and the Parliamentary Committee should meet them, though the GFTU should realize that they could no longer claim to do the work in the international movement. The Committee met the GFTU immediately and, with a working arrangement in sight, Congress endorsed its action in preparing to establish an international department.[54]

At a joint meeting in October Appleton offered to co-operate in arranging joint affiliation to the IFTU, but with the bureau under the auspices of the Parliamentary Committee.[55] Discussions had not been completed at the end of the year, when the peace conference supervened. Provided that the IFTU would sanction joint representation, the TUC's participation in both the trade union and socialist international movements was assured, but on what terms remained to be decided.

Restoring the Internationals

The Berne Conference

Since the French government took the view that it would not be in their own interests for German delegates to go to Paris, where the Peace Conference opened on 18 January 1919, the Labour Conference was held in Berne on 3–9 February. The geographical separation may have had some effect on trade union attitudes towards the structure of the ILO which emerged from the work of the Commission on Labour Legislation of the Peace Conference. Gompers was included in the American delegation and became president of this Commission, and Jouhaux played some part after the Berne Conference. However, Gompers did not go to Berne, and the British Labour representatives who were called to Paris for consultation with the British government's delegation went there before they went to Berne. It is possible, though unlikely, that they would have taken a different line in the consultations if they had first heard the debates at Berne. As it was, there were few outside the Labour Commission who were fully aware of its work.[56] In other respects, the separation of the two conferences was probably immaterial.

The status of the Berne Conference was uncertain. In December 1918 Henderson had set out some of the procedural problems for the Labour Party and the Parliamentary Committee. First, who should call the conference – the ISB? the IFTU? If either of these bodies called only its own affiliates, the most representative British labour organization, the TUC, would be left out. Should it be the AFL, which was now proposing to call a conference itself to establish a new trade union international? Their delegation which had visited Britain in the preceding April had been adamant that the American Socialist Party had no representative character at all, and in September Gompers had confirmed that if that party were invited the AFL would not attend. However, if means were found to include the TUC, Henderson asked, how could an actual affiliate of the ISB be excluded? These questions were never satisfactorily resolved, but the very lack of clarity enabled two conferences – one trade union, one socialist – to assemble in Berne and join together to agree an International Labour Charter.

The Parliamentary Committee appointed their delegates to the 'Labour and Socialist International Conference'[57] and adhered to their decision despite an impassioned plea from Gompers, who arrived in January 1919 with an AFL delegation. They would not go to Berne, he said, they were not yet ready to meet representatives from the ex-enemy countries (the Belgians took the same view), and they refused to be subject to the domination of any political party or combination of parties in Europe. They were anxious to meet the real workers of the organized labour movement of the world, to help organize the unorganized, to work out problems of an international character, and to help in having clauses on conditions of labour incorporated in the peace treaty. Gompers continued with a prophetic passage: 'he was so overwhelmed with the importance of this hour that he found difficulty in translating these thoughts into words, for now was the opportunity that had come to the workers of the civilized countries of the world ... they did not know when such another time would come and such another opportunity be afforded them, and if frittered away on political parties and issues, and the real interests of Labour were lost sight of for political party advantages, the world of Labour would hold them responsible for decades, if not for centuries to come'.[58]

Even if they had wished to do so – and there is nothing to suggest that they did – the Parliamentary Committee could not at this stage retreat from a policy adopted at their own instigation in 1917 and twice endorsed by Congress. Nevertheless, it was evident that though the divisions between the former belligerents might be overcome, there was now another within the socialist world that was so fundamental that it was no longer possible to hold an all-embracing international socialist congress of the old type. Throughout 1918, as the outlying provinces of the former Tsarist Empire fell to the Germans, and Allied forces moved to meet them in Europe, Russia was engulfed in civil war. The Bolsheviks had established their secret security policy (Cheka) in December 1917. In January 1918 Lenin disbanded the elected constituent assembly, in which the Social Revolutionaries were the largest party; in July a small Social Revolutionary and anarchist rising was suppressed in Moscow; and after the attempted assassination of Lenin on 30 August the real Terror began. The situation was obscure and still fluid, but it was clear that for the time being at least no system of government that the western labour movements could recognize as democratic would be found in Russia. If the Bolsheviks had regarded their dictatorship as a necessary but temporary deviation from socialist ideals there need have been no split but, on the contrary, they denounced the very concept of parliamentary democracy as a bourgeois sham and the socialists who believed in it as traitors to the working class.

This difference was not to remain an internal matter. The encircled Bolsheviks looked outside Russia for allies. The rebellions they had expected in the belligerent countries came in the German and Austrian empires, but not to the benefit of the small communist groups. Yet there was everywhere sufficient disorder to keep alive their hope that the working class would rally internationally to the Bolshevik cause, and this resulted in an irredeemable split in the international labour movement. In December 1918, faced with the prospect of a potentially hostile socialist conference at Berne, the Bolshevik Party Central Committee denounced it in advance, and implemented their decision of April 1917. In January 1919 an invitation was issued from Moscow in the names of the Communist Parties of Russia, Poland, Finland, Latvia, Germany, Hungary and Austria, the Balkan Revolutionary Social Democratic Federation and the Socialist Workers' Party of America, to a conference which would be 'the first congress of the Communist International'. The new international would be based on the propositions that the proletariat must immediately seize state power, destroy the apparatus of the bourgeois state by mass action up to open armed conflict, and substitute the dictatorship of the working class in the form of soviets, expropriating capital and transferring private property in the means of production and commerce to the nation. This invitation was sent to existing communist parties, to elements in the Second International which were considered to be actually or potentially revolutionary, and to some industrial groups such as the IWW in America and Australia and the shop stewards' movement in Britain.[59]

The International Labour and Socialist Conference was held in Berne under Henderson's chairmanship. Except for Canada, it was a

European conference: the AFL did not attend, and a delegation from Australia arrived too late to participate. It did bridge the gulf between the former belligerents: most of the Allies except for Italy and Belgium attended, with the Central Powers, Poland and Finland and the neutrals except for Switzerland. From Russia itself, and from the arc of former dependencies on its western and southern borders over which the Bolshevik Government had not yet established control, Menshevik and Right Social Revolutionary delegates came, from Latvia, Estonia, Georgia and Armenia, and a delegation from the Ukraine that was too late to join the conference. What was their status? Nobody knew. In June 1918, before the Armistice, when the dispossessed Russian Prime Minister Kerensky had urged the British Government to support constitutional forces in Russia, it had seemed to Lloyd George that he was overestimating the strength of the 'chattering conventicles' that he represented.[60] Now in Berne Jean Longuet for France and Friedrich Adler for part of the Austrian delegation did not question their good faith, but argued that these delegates represented only a minority of the Russian working class. The Conference decided to send a commission of inquiry to Russia which would report back to the International, but it was killed at birth by the refusal of passports.

The conference also passed a resolution proposed by Branting which declared that socialism and democracy were inseparable, and which defined the institutions of democracy as governments responsible to parliaments, with universal suffrage and the rights of association, assembly, free speech and freedom of the press. These institutions, the resolution asserted, also provided the working classes with the means of carrying on the class struggle.[61] Not only did this resolution run counter to the entire Bolshevik thesis, but it was supported by the various groups from Russia. Its adoption made it certain that the Bolsheviks would not join the reconstituted Second International, and within the conference there were non-Bolshevik revolutionary elements which opposed it.

The conference elected a committee to draft a new constitution for the International. On 4 March the rival conference in Moscow transformed itself into the first congress of the Communist International (Comintern). Although at Berne the whole British delegation had taken the view that every effort must be made to co-ordinate and keep in touch with the various currents of opinion that were bound to appear in the revolutionary period following the war,[62] the Parliamentary Committee decided in June to endorse the draft rules for the revived Second International and to recommend affiliation to the ISB. In September, Congress agreed,[63] but few of the parties represented at Berne took the same step.

On 5 February 1919, at Berne, a trade union conference was held.

Like the British, most of the delegates also attended the socialist conference, but at the trade union conference the Swiss and Italian trade unions were represented and the controversial Russian delegations were absent. The other delegations came from France, Britain, Germany, Austria, Bohemia, Hungary, Bulgaria, Greece, Norway, Sweden, Denmark, Holland, Spain and Canada. The conference advocated the speedy reconstruction of the IFTU and instructed Jouhaux and Oudegeest to arrange a further meeting. It specified demands on working conditions to be included in the Peace Treaty and demanded the creation of an International Labour Bureau as a component part of the League of Nations. This Bureau was to be based on an international labourers' parliament attended by delegates of all countries and all trades, which would be an international legislature making laws which 'from the moment of their acceptance must have the same validity as national laws'. These demands were included in a proclamation to the workers of all countries, which began with the declaration originally proposed by the AFL at the Inter-Allied Conference in September 1918, that human labour is not an object of barter. There was a breath of the old syndicalism in the statement that workers were aiming at the abolition of wage labour, that the management and distribution of production should be in the hands of the producing masses, and that the effort to realize social reforms did not betoken that an ultimate ideal must be relinquished. The proclamation was adopted without discussion: the Parliamentary Committee's delegates refrained from objections to the details, which differed from the proposals agreed by them with the British government's delegation in Paris, presumably because they wished to reach a broad agreement in Berne.

The combined trade union and socialist conferences finally affirmed the principle of self-determination, demanded the establishment of a permanent League of Nations and the adoption of the agreed International Labour Charter, and appointed a deputation which presented the resolutions to the French Prime Minister, Clémenceau, on 17 February for submission to the Peace Conference.[64] Although the Peace Treaty that was signed on 28 June contained many features that the labour movements opposed, there can be little doubt that the Berne Conference had fortified those who secured the inclusion of some of its more liberal provisions.

The IFTU: Resumption of Activities

The ad-hoc trade union conference at Berne was useful, but improvised. The American, Belgian and British (GFTU) affiliates of the IFTU did not attend, and in some of the delegations – appointed as they had been to the socialist conference – the most important trade union leaders of their countries were not included.[65] In other moves to reconstitute the trade union international, there were consultations between the Parliamentary Committee and the AFL and with representatives of the International Metal Trades Federation, with which the Committee had co-operated in calling their conference of internationally affiliated British unions in July 1918. Gompers was working closely with the CGT, and in February a meeting of AFL, CGT, and TUC representatives was held in Paris to discuss his proposal that an international trade union conference should be held in Washington to coincide with the founding conference of the ILO. Oudegeest was preparing to call an IFTU conference, and in March expressed the hope that the TUC would attend and offered his help to bring about an understanding between the GFTU and the Parliamentary Committee. Eventually these moves and further discussions with the GFTU brought a combined TUC/GFTU delegation to Amsterdam for a conference to reconstitute the IFTU held from 28 July to 2 August 1919.[66]

The aims agreed for the reconstituted IFTU were the traditional ones: exchange of information, mutual support, and the promotion of social legislation. The rules provided that only one national centre in each country might be represented, and that representatives must be resident and organized in the countries represented by them. The size of delegations to the biennial conference and on the management committees raised some difficulties, the American and British delegations arguing that it should be in proportion to paid-up affiliated membership. A compromise was accepted providing for one vote for every 250,000 members or fraction of that. These rules ensured that affiliates would be organizations of substance, and a provision that national centres would retain their autonomy permitted affiliation by those which were not prepared to submerge their authority in that of the international. Characteristically, these included the TUC and the AFL. The rule was tested immediately, when an attempt was made to bind national centres to refuse to attend the ILO Washington Conference unless, contrary to the arrangements made by the Peace Conference, the ex-enemy countries were invited. Both British and American delegations protested against the attempted violation of a constitution adopted only on the previous day and refused to be bound by any such decision.[67] Gompers was also displeased by references to the Berne trade union conference and by the semipolitical character of some of the Amsterdam resolutions. He believed that some socialist trade union leaders wished to use the IFTU to rebuild the Socialist International, but he agreed to advise his AFL executive to re-affiliate. Although he had been so active internationally, the AFL had not paid any affiliation fees since 1914, and the mood of America was now turning back to isolation. When a Special Congress of the IFTU was held in London in November 1920, the AFL did not attend. In March 1921 its executive finally decided against affiliation, on the grounds that the fee was too high and the organization too socialist, and that the pledge of autonomy for national centres had not been kept. The AFL did not rejoin the IFTU until 1937.[68] It was similarly excluded from the ILO by the national decision to reject membership of the League of Nations.

All the Amsterdam delegates except the Americans came from Europe, but the new rules included a provision for the promotion of trade union objects in countries where there were no affiliates. Within two years, organizations in Canada, Peru, Argentina and South Africa had joined, and others followed, but until the AFL rejoined no affiliate outside Europe won a seat on the IFTU executive.[69]

At Amsterdam Appleton was elected President of the IFTU, and the GFTU and TUC delegates worked well together. However, the GFTU's persistent attempts to maintain its international position, and continuing hostility to its domestic policies amongst powerful elements in Congress, alienated a sufficient body of opinion to ensure support at the 1920 Congress for a resolution which excluded it from the international field in which it had performed so well. The resolution declared that the British trade union movement should be affiliated to the IFTU only through the TUC, and that the Parliamentary Committee should not co-operate with any other body.[70] The decision was hard on the GFTU, but in terms of practical working it was realistic.

The International Labour Organization

When the Parliamentary Committee sent their delegates to Berne they had given little thought to the possible structure of the International Labour Bureau that the conference ultimately proposed, and it was not discussed at their meeting with Gompers and the IMF representatives on 20 January 1919. Nor did the Berne decisions make clear what its structure and powers were to be, or how governmental responsibilities could be reconciled with the conference's proposal for an 'international Labourers' Parliament'.

The effective proposals on structure were made by government officials in Paris. Immediately after the first armistice was signed with Bulgaria on 29 September 1918, officials of the British Ministry of Labour began work on possible schemes for submission to the Peace Conference. They had available the various trade union proposals that had been made, but apparently at this stage they did not have

consultations with the TUC. In Paris they had conversations with their
counterparts in other Allied delegations, all of whom were preparing
drafts of their own, but none in such detail. By the end of January 1919
the British delegation had a scheme ready and the Minister
Plenipotentiary, G. H. Barnes,[71] a former General Secretary of the
Amalgamated Society of Engineers, consulted Henderson and J. H.
Thomas,[72] who were already in Paris, and invited the Parliamentary
Committee to send representatives for discussion before the plan was
presented to the special Labour Commission of the Peace Conference.
At two days' notice, the Committee's chairman, J. Stuart-Bunning[73] of
the Postmen's Federation, Bowerman, and Robert Shirkie[74] of the
Scottish Colliery Engine and Boilermakers' Association, who happened to be passing through London on his way to Berne, went to Paris
without adequate preparation. There they met the minister and
representatives of the governments of Canada, Australia, New-
foundland, New Zealand and India, and secured some important
changes in the draft. The officials also had correspondence, but no
meeting, with the British employers. It is clear that the meetings with
the labour representatives on 27 and 28 January were decisive.

The provisions of the Labour Charter produced at Berne and the
attempt at Amsterdam to make decisions binding on national centres
were manifestations of what might loosely be termed a 'Continental'
approach to the construction of institutions. The tendency was to lay
down requirements in detail and to secure their enforcement by law. It
had the merit of providing maximum application of standards after
unions had secured their inclusion in legislation, but it did not allow
much scope for subsequent union action. The British attitude –
displayed by the Parliamentary Committee when it first convened an
international conference in 1888 – was fundamentally different.
Although state intervention was used, the primary responsibility was
held to lie with the parties to industrial relations, the unions and
employers. So the Fair Wages Clause in government contracts and the
Trade Boards Act of 1919 provided statutory protection for workers
who could not protect themselves, but used for comparison wages and
conditions negotiated for organized workers by unions and employers.
Similarly, the Conciliation Act of 1896 provided for the intervention
of government officials only after existing procedures for the avoidance
and settlement of disputes had been exhausted, and there were many
industries in which unions and employers had built up their own
voluntary machinery for this purpose. When union practices were
sacrificed to the war effort and strikes were forbidden, the concept of
standing but voluntary machinery for the avoidance of disputes lay
behind the recommendations of the Committee set up in 1916 under
the chairmanship of J. H. Whitley MP to consider the relations

between employers and workmen. Such conventions were ultimately carried into industrial relations in India and in the colonies, and since in their cases the practice of the ILO was of considerable importance, the initial structure of the ILO was particularly significant. When officials of the British Ministry of Labour began their consideration of international labour standards and their application, they naturally looked for standing machinery which would allow scope for negotiation and be capable of flexibility and further development, rather than for particular measures to deal with specific needs.

The Ministry's scheme discussed with the TUC's representatives[75] proposed a permanent office with a permanent director and an international staff, and an advisory council composed of government representatives with permanent seats for the Great Powers. There would also be an annual conference, with national delegations consisting of representatives of governments and representatives chosen from organizations of workers and of employers, to prepare conventions for implementation by governments, and a procedure for complaints to be made and heard if undertakings were not kept. Henderson at once noticed the weakness of the advisory council, and proposed instead an administrative board including representatives of employers and workers. Stuart-Bunning proposed that it should consist of tripartite national delegations, and that in each separate state a tripartite committee should be set up to be in permanent liaison with the office. The amended draft, with the purely governmental advisory council replaced by a tripartite 'Governing Body', was approved by the whole British Empire delegation, and on 1 February the Labour Commission of the conference began its work with the amended British draft as the basis for discussion. Thomas, Stuart-Bunning and Shirkie went on to join the rest of the TUC delegation at Berne. Bowerman returned and reported to the Parliamentary Committee, emphasizing that throughout the negotiations they had insisted that the participating governments should agree the labour representatives in their delegations with national associations. The Committee, and later Congress, approved the report.[76]

The Labour Commission considered the Labour Charter drawn up at Berne, and nineteen points from it were included in the preamble to Part XIII of the Treaty of Versailles which established the International Labour Organization. The Commission's final proposals on structure differed in three respects from the Charter. Berne had proposed a permanent commission consisting of equal numbers of representatives of the states members of the League of Nations and of the IFTU, and the inclusion of labour clauses in the Treaty in a form which would make them immediately binding on the signatories. The Berne proposal for an international labourers' parliament also fell by the wayside, and with it the old concept of the international working-class movement dominating over national governments by its unity and strength. The full Versailles conference adopted the Commission's proposals.

Jouhaux remained dissatisfied, but can surely not have expected governments to agree to equal representation between themselves and the IFTU, or that they would have implemented the mandatory decisions of the proposed 'parliament'. The alternative procedure – to make the labour standards themselves binding on the governments in the Treaty – would have reduced agreement on them to those which could be forced on the least willing government. Instead, the major governments – those represented on the Governing Body – were committed by their very membership, and even more by the tripartite character of the Governing Body and the Conference. The final method adopted for the selection of workers' and employers' representatives on the Governing Body – that they should be elected at the conference by workers' and employers' delegates respectively – gave the unions for the first time an opportunity to develop a functional unity in an international forum in which governments could be directly influenced.

Before the Treaty was signed on 28 June 1919, an organizing committee to prepare for the first conference, to be held in Washington in October, met in London in May. It began by preparing reports on hours of work, unemployment, and the employment of women, young persons and children, all of which had been included in the Labour Charter. Since the Treaty had to be ratified, and the League of Nations established, it was not certain whether Germany would be allowed to send a delegation to Washington. The IFTU's Amsterdam conference decided to co-operate only if all countries without exception were invited and further insisted that only representatives of IFTU affiliates should represent workers – a condition that was in direct contravention of the Treaty provision that workers' representatives should be nominated in agreement with the most representative workers' organization in each country. On 25 August an IFTU delegation led by Appleton informed Barnes that without the necessary changes their affiliates would be unable to nominate any delegates to Washington.[77]

Workers' Representation

The Parliamentary Committee took no part in the IFTU delegation, their representatives at Amsterdam having already refused to be bound by the conference resolution. But they were anxious not to fall foul of the international that they wished to join, and urged Barnes to secure the inclusion of Germany. They did not finally decide to nominate delegates themselves until he informed them that the United States government had agreed to invite the ex-enemy countries to send delegations to Washington, leaving it to the Conference to decide whether they should be admitted.

Selection of the British workers' representatives also presented problems. In August Barnes attended a meeting of the Parliamentary Committee with a list of names he had prepared, but it was agreed that the Committee themselves should propose names, from which the government could choose. They chose four of their own members for selection of the delegate, and for the advisers chose four from the Committee and four from outside – a clear claim that the entire workers' delegation should be chosen from Committee nominees, including any from unions or elsewhere.

The Committee was uncertain about the type of advisers it wanted. At one point in the discussion the names of Henderson and G. D. H. Cole, then Secretary to the Labour Party's Advisory Committees, were suggested, but not agreed upon. On the minister's suggestion that a woman should be included (presumably because women's employment was on the agenda), the Committee proposed Mary Macarthur, Secretary of the Women's Trade Union League. After a deputation from the Labour Party Executive, Henderson was included. In the event, Margaret Bondfield[78] went instead of Mary Macarthur, and Henderson did not go, but the issue of Labour Party representation was dropped. By 1921 the Parliamentary Committee's claim to submit names for the full delegation for the annual conference and for specialist meetings had been established, and it was accepted that if information was required from unions for inquiries by the ILO, it should be transmitted through the Parliamentary Committee.[79]

One advantage of the flexible structure of the ILO was that it facilitated the application of conventions to the dependencies of member states. At first the British government proposed that when these states ratified conventions, they should 'consider' applying them to their colonies, but that a definite decision by the governing power should be necessary before they became applicable. Under pressure from the French government and from Jouhaux, the saving formula was agreed and embodied in Article 421 of the Treaty: that they would apply ratified conventions, but subject to local conditions, and that they would notify to the ILO the action they had taken in respect of each territory.[80] So the colonies would be affected, but as non-self-governing territories they would have no right to send representatives of their own to ILO meetings, where the metropolitan powers would speak on their behalf. At this stage, the Parliamentary Committee did not grasp that this would place a special obligation on the shoulders of their nominees. When they grasped the implications of this obligation, some years later, they took it seriously.

However, one dependency – India – was represented at the Peace Conference, signed the Treaty, and became a member of the ILO. At Washington, India put forward a claim, later upheld by the Council of the League of Nations, to be included in the group of states of chief industrial importance which were to have permanent representation on the ILO Governing Body. This representation had an important effect on the development of the Indian trade union movement, whose leaders made effective use of it. Initially, the problem was to choose the Indian workers' delegate to the conference. There were few unions, and no union national centre, in India in 1919. The Government of India unilaterally selected as delegate a former teacher, N. M. Joshi,[81] who held no trade union position at the time, and as adviser chose the militant Hindu nationalist leader, Bal Gangadhar Tilak, who was then in England. When Tilak declined, B. P. Wadia, President of the Madras Labour Union, was appointed.

There was no doubt of Joshi's dedication, or of his competence. Since 1909 he had worked for the Servants of India Society, which required its members to pay in all outside earnings and accept such provision as the Society could make for their maintenance. He was one of the founders of the Bombay Social Service League, which provided night schools and libraries and pioneered the formation of co-operative societies. More immediately relevant was his association with the Kamgar Hitawardhak Sabha (Association for Watching the Interests of Indian Workingmen), which had supported the Government of India against the millowners' opposition to the 1912 Factories Act and had shown a firm grasp of industrial needs in a petition submitted to E. S. Montagu during his visit to India as Secretary of State in 1917.[82]

Protests against the appointment of a middle-class man, and a Brahmin at that, were raised in Parliament and in India. Both appointments were opposed by the London-based Workers' Welfare League of India (WWLI),[83] and on his return to Bombay Tilak carried his protest to a welcome meeting of 10,000 workers. In 1920 Joshi's appointment to the ILO Maritime Conference brought the radical political leaders' activity to a head in a mass meeting of Bombay workers which claimed the right to appoint their own representatives and resolved to set up an Indian TUC.[84] The inaugural session of the All-India Trade Union Congress (AITUC) met on 31 October 1920, and thereafter the Government of India accepted its nominations for the ILO.

For the TUC, the consequences were that they had no responsibility for India at the ILO, but instead had a new opportunity for co-operation. This began at Washington, in discussions on hours of work for children and young persons in India.[85] But first the TUC's horizons were widened by the spectacular appearance of Wadia at the 1919 Congress.

The Congress of 1919

Since the Washington Conference did not meet until 29 October and British workers' participation was not yet confirmed when Congress met on 6 September,[86] the full significance of the Parliamentary Committee's report on the ILO was not apparent to delegates, who endorsed their actions without comment. Nor did they discuss the IFTU, except in regard to the contribution that would have to be paid.

First Link With India

This did not mean that the delegates were wholly inward-looking. The star of the Congress turned out to be Wadia, appearing as representative of the Madras Labour Union, the first Indian union to contact the TUC.[87] It was also the first modern trade union in India, though attempts at organization can be traced back to N. M. Lokhande's formation of the Bombay Millhands' Association in 1890 and to railway associations that were primarily benefit societies. As in Britain, the wartime need for army supplies brought expansion in factory employment, and the dislocations that followed the cessation of hostilities caused much suffering and discontent. In 1918 two strands in British labour history became interwoven in Madras, where Mrs Annie Besant, champion of the London match-girls in their strike in 1888, had established her Theosophical Society centre and a newspaper of which Wadia was assistant editor.

Wadia had given little thought to labourers' problems until two members of a religious association – which, unknown to the educated classes of the city, was doing social work amongst them – went to the newspaper office to seek help. These two, G. Shelvapathi Chetty and C. R. Naidu, had observed the half-hour lunch break in a neighbouring mill which gave its workers inadequate time to get cooked food, and had helped to write anonymous letters to management to point out this and other grievances such as physical assaults by supervisors. Wadia returned with them, and addressed a meeting. The establishment of the Madras Labour Union had begun. The workers themselves, in his view, were unable to express their grievances,[88] and in the following period ill-defined aims became clarified in strikes and lock-outs amongst textile workers, tramwaymen and rickshaw-pullers. Labour problems were publicized in the newspaper, and Mrs Besant herself addressed meetings which – with her great prestige as religious leader and scholar

and as a former President of the Indian National Congress – gave the
workers confidence and brought the union into the mainstream of
public life.[89] Both Chetty and Naidu became long-serving union
secretaries, and the union undertook such practical tasks as starting a
cheap food store and instituting prosecutions for assaults.[90] Most
important, it was properly conducted with regular subscriptions and,
when it asked to send a delegate to Congress, sent in credentials.

Mrs Besant and Wadia both attended the Congress and Wadia
addressed the delegates. Helped no doubt by his handsome appearance
and considerable height, he thoroughly roused his audience. Speaking
of the unions forming in Madras and Bombay, of outdated factory
legislation and appalling wages and housing conditions, and of the
threat to British workers' standards while British capitalists exploited
the people of India, he appealed to the delegates to join hands with
Indian workers. A special resolution welcoming the formation of trade
unions in India, and instructing the Parliamentary Committee to raise
funds from affiliated unions to help them, was enthusiastically carried.
It was a reflection of spontaneous generosity rather than mature
consideration, and its weakness was perceived by a young delegate
from the Dock and Riverside Workers, Ernest Bevin. He wanted
permanent results. The Parliamentary Committee, he argued, should
try immediately to get in touch with workers' representatives and build
up information on the various movements in eastern countries, so that
Congress could be properly informed. 'This is a case where even from
selfish motives we ought to support these people,' he said; 'there is,
however, a better plan, and that is to work along the lines we have
always done in support of downtrodden people, for their own sake and
without the least selfish consideration.'

This double theme was well illustrated by other resolutions before
Congress. The Sailors' and Firemen's Union, which supported the
appeal for help to India, where it was trying to organize seamen, moved
a resolution demanding immediate steps to abolish underpaid Asiatic
labour in the British mercantile marine in which, it was claimed,
15,000 Chinese were employed, to the detriment of British white and
coloured seamen, and it was argued that wages should be the same for
all seamen. Another called on affiliated unions and the Parliamentary
Committee to work for an approximation of wages and conditions
within the Empire, asserting that labour in Britain, Australia and
Canada was adversely affected by conditions in India and South Africa
which degraded the lives of workers for whom the British movement
had some responsibility. Both were carried. A third, referred to the
Parliamentary Committee without discussion, asked for visits to
eastern countries to investigate conditions and recommend the best
methods of helping to raise the standard of living.

Organization

In addition to the domestic problems pressing on them, the Parliamentary Committee were now committed in the ILO, the IFTU and the Empire to tasks which the TUC had neither the resources nor the expertise to perform. Since 1916 affiliated membership had increased, and 851 delegates represented 5,283,676 members in 266 affiliated societies. Income for the year was nearly £9,000, with £8,000 of it derived from affiliation fees at £1 10s per thousand members. It was not nearly enough – the IFTU alone required £1 per thousand, which would have to be paid by a levy on unions. Despite improvements in staffing, the Committee had too few for the work demanded. With its terms of reference still unchanged, it was lacking in authority, and was obliged in the following year to call four ad hoc Special Congresses.

Once again, Congress passed resolutions on reorganization, and in the next two years the Committee put forward proposals for reconstruction. This time, they were all-embracing, and the new General Council elected for the first time in 1921 was a very different body from the Parliamentary Committee. Internationally, in the dependencies, and at home, a new era was about to begin.

3 Co-operation with the Labour Party: Organization and Policy

The Parliamentary Committee's plunge into international politics in 1917 had left it with a decision to affiliate to the ISB and a combined TUC/Labour Party International Joint Committee. The 1919 Congress confirmed affiliation to the IFTU, but there was no specialized committee to deal with the TUC's responsibilities in the IFTU or with international trade union affairs generally. This deficiency was paralleled on the domestic front by the inadequate definition of the Parliamentary Committee's duties, which gave it no power to co-ordinate the activities of the movement. The Labour Party had earlier seen the need to reorganize and had adopted a new constitution at a Special Congress in February 1918.

Reorganization

The TUC

The TUC's reorganization began with the appointment of a Co-ordination Committee whose report pointed out that the functions of the Parliamentary Committee, as defined in Standing Orders, were a survival from the period when there was no separate Labour Party. It proposed that a scheme should be drawn up for a reorganized structure with adequate staff to support it, and that there should be consultations with the Labour Party on the development of departments under joint control which could serve both bodies and avoid overlapping. A Special Congress endorsed the report on 9 December 1919.

Proposals for the reorganized structure adopted by the Portsmouth Congress in September 1920 provided for the replacement of the Parliamentary Committee by a larger General Council to be elected by the whole Congress from nominees put forward by groups of unions classified according to occupations. Its duties under the new rules were to promote common action on any matters of general concern that might arise between unions, between unions and employers and between the movement and the government, and to enter into relations with the trade union and labour movements in other countries with a view to promoting common action and solidarity. To pay for the development of administrative departments sufficiently staffed and equipped to provide an adequate trade union centre the affiliation fee was raised to 1d a member, and the annual contribution to the IFTU was written into the rules.[1]

Another survival was Bowerman's position as a Member of Parliament. In 1921 Congress decided that the General Secretary should devote his whole time to the work, albeit with a rider that this did not preclude his being a candidate for or a Member of Parliament, provided that in this event he was prepared to sign the constitution of the Labour Party. When Bowerman submitted his resignation in 1922, the General Council still intended to allow their officers to run as candidates, with their position to be reviewed if elected, but when Bramley was appointed General Secretary he acknowledged a strong contrary opinion by resigning his prospective candidature.[2] Yet the political tradition died hard: when the General Council finally decided to propose the amendment of Standing Orders to state simply that the General Secretary should devote his whole time to the work of the Council, the proposal was carried by only one vote. The change was endorsed by the 1923 Congress, at which Bowerman retired. It was no longer necessary for the TUC to have its own secretary on the floor of the House of Commons, where there were now 140 Labour members.[3]

Thus Bramley became the full-time General Secretary of an organization whose responsibilities were no longer primarily parliamentary in character. The process of differentiation of function might be regarded as completed when he was followed in 1926 by Walter Citrine, who was very conscious of the need to build the TUC into a competent organization in its own right. Already as assistant general secretary he had pointed out to a Parliamentary Labour Party gathering that while the Party was composed of people who believed in socialist principles, the trade unions catered for all workers irrespective of their politics, and had explained to the puzzled Chairman of the All-Russian Central Council of Trade Unions (ARCCTU) that despite their close relationship with the Labour Party the unions had found during the first Labour Government's term of office in 1924 that it was necessary to preserve their own independence.[4]

The success of the Labour Party in the 1923 general election brought about another change. Members of the General Council who sat in the House of Commons were full-time officers of their unions – only as such were they eligible to be delegates to Congress – and it was for their unions to decide whether they regarded service in Parliament as union business. However, when the Labour government was formed and three members of the General Council – Margaret Bondfield, Thomas

and Gosling – became ministers, it was decided that Members of
Parliament might retain their seats on the Council, but the three who
had accepted office were forthwith replaced.[5]

The position of members of the Labour Party Executive was settled
as far as the TUC was concerned when the first General Council was
elected in 1921. The leadership had been kept distinct by a clause in the
Labour Party's constitution, originally adopted in 1908, which
excluded members of the Parliamentary Committee from election to
the Party Executive. This was retained in the Labour Party's new
constitution, but the Parliamentary Committee would no longer exist.
When nominations for the new General Council were made, they
included John Bromley of the Associated Society of Locomotive
Engineers and Firemen (ASLEF),[6] who was then a serving member of
the Executive. The outgoing Parliamentary Committee decided that the
nomination could not stand, Bromley withdrew from the Party
Executive and was elected to the General Council.[7] Dual membership
was in any case precluded by the practice of holding Executive and
General Council meetings at the same time on the same day.

The Labour Party

The Labour Party's new constitution provided for the first time for
individual as well as affiliated membership in local Labour parties. The
executive was to consist of representatives of affiliated trade unions,
local Labour parties, women's sections and socialist societies. Thus the
party remained a conglomeration of groups, but all brought together by
the provision that the conference voted as a whole in the election. The
change weakened the ILP. At local level its branches were outbid by
divisional Labour parties and on the executive it lost its separate
representation. It continued for a time to pursue its own international
policies and its Members of Parliament remained a distinct group, until
in 1932 it disaffiliated from the Labour Party altogether. In
composition the Labour Party remained predominantly trade union: in
1923, after five years of individual membership, 106 affiliated trade
unions accounted for 3,120,149 out of a total membership of
3,155,911. Some of the unions were still uncommitted: in the same
year the TUC had 195 affiliates with 4,369,268 members,[8] and it was
open to individual trade union members to contract out of
subscription to union political funds. However, the returns showed
clearly that the strength of the main unions was behind the Labour
Party.

Although the TUC itself was never affiliated to the party, the Co-
ordination Committee's proposal for closer co-operation was a
development of previous practice. The Joint Board was wound up in
1917, but the Parliamentary Committee and the Labour Party

Executive then began to hold regular meetings and put out a joint appeal to all unions to affiliate to the party. The party's new constitution specifically provided for co-operation with the Parliamentary Committee in joint political or other action, and after the TUC's Special Congress in December 1919 a joint committee was set up to prepare the proposed scheme, which was adopted in 1921 by Congress and by the Labour Party Conference. The Joint Executives remained, and there was a National Joint Council which brought them together with the Parliamentary Labour Party. In addition, there was to be continuous co-operation below executive level.

Joint Committees and Departments

The scheme envisaged departments jointly financed and controlled by the General Council and the Labour Party Executive which would undertake work for them and for the National Joint Council. Each was to be in the charge of a responsible officer and to be supervised by a joint subcommittee representing both bodies. They would deal with research and information, publicity, legal matters and international affairs. The administrative requirements were considered at the first meeting of the National Joint Council on 18 November 1921 and determined by the Joint Executives on 4 January 1922. In the same month the Joint Research Department became the first to serve both bodies. There was also a joint publicity department which produced a new monthly *Labour Magazine* from May 1922 onwards. The last issue of the TUC's *International Trades Union Review* appeared in January 1922. Thereafter, one of its main features – a collection of news and information on trade union developments in other countries – appeared regularly in the new publication.

The Joint International Department and its committee presented some difficulty. The joint committee set up in September 1917 was still in existence[9] and the Labour Party assumed that all the international work of both bodies would be handled by the new joint department.[10] However, at their first regular meeting in 1921 the General Council had set up a Trade Union International Committee[11] to handle their work in the IFTU, and they were determined to keep this under their own control. They insisted on amendments to the scheme which stated that the new joint department was to be at the service of the General Council and its General Secretary on industrial questions, and of the Labour Party and its secretary on political questions. Correspondence between the General Council and the IFTU was to be dealt with by a TUC official attached to the department for this purpose.[12] The joint department was put under the direction of the Labour Party's international officer, William Gillies, who became secretary to the Joint International Committee, but the TUC kept its International

Committee separate while all the Labour Party's international work was handled through the new joint committee.

The new regime considerably improved the background information available to the TUC. The former International Joint Committee had in practice been serviced by the Labour Party's advisory committees, which had prepared briefs for the Berne Conference under the direction of G. D. H. Cole. These had a direct bearing on the discussions preceding the establishment of the ILO and were subsequently published by the Labour Party, not the TUC.[13] The new Joint Research Committee, with Sidney Webb as chairman, now reconstituted the Labour Party's advisory committees by adding trade union members, and it was agreed that the joint research and international departments would co-operate in briefing delegates to ILO Conferences.[14] At first the Joint Research Department had the key role, with the Joint International Advisory Committee reporting to it. In 1924 this advisory committee was transferred to the Joint International Department, and formed an Imperial Affairs Sub-Committee. It was there that the major contribution to colonial policy was made. Leonard Woolf had been secretary of the Labour Party's International Advisory Committee, and continued as secretary of the Joint International Advisory Committee with Tom Shaw as chairman. He was also secretary of the Imperial Sub-Committee, with Charles Roden Buxton as chairman.

The Imperial Sub-Committee was nothing if not expert. Woolf had already made his mark on overseas policy with his publications *International Government* and *Empire and Commerce in Africa*, and he and Buxton were highly respected. Woolf had started his career in the district administration of Ceylon and was one of the very few people in British public life who foresaw that the justified revolt of subject peoples would continue and would become a central problem of the modern world. Buxton regarded work for the protection of backward peoples as a moral crusade to be fought through all available channels. Like Woolf, he worked unflaggingly for the Labour Party without financial reward, but he was closer to the centre of affairs than Woolf. Elected to Parliament in 1922, he became Parliamentary Adviser to the Labour Party in 1926 and in that capacity provided interested Members with information and suggestions for Questions and for colonial debates until September 1939. He co-operated with the Anti-Slavery Society and kept track of the work of the League of Nations' Permanent Mandates Commission, on which he spoke in the League Assembly as delegate for the second Labour Government. With W. G. H. Ormsby-Gore, who subsequently became Secretary of State, he was joint secretary of the Joint Select Committee of both Houses of Parliament which considered the closer union of the three East African

territories in 1930–31, and after his defeat in the 1931 election he
visited East Africa and the Gold Coast and Nigeria. His papers reveal
his contacts with sympathetic officers in the colonial service, with
organizations like the Kikuyu Central Association, and with men like
Arthur Shearly Cripps in Southern Rhodesia and Tshekedi Khama,
Winifred Holtby and W. G. Ballinger in South Africa.[15] He was thus
familiar with all the 'causes' – especially in areas of white settlement –
which were the bones of contention in land and labour policy in the
colonies throughout the 1920s and 1930s.

Another important link with Parliament was Harold Snell,[16]
secretary of the Labour Party's Labour Commonwealth Committee
which met weekly from 1922 onwards. Others recorded as attending
the Joint International Advisory Committee and its Imperial Sub-
Committee at different times[17] included some with a special interest in
India, such as the theosophist Major Graham Pole and Shapurji
Saklatvala.[18] The lawyer H. S. L. Polak, who had worked with M. K.
Gandhi in South Africa and was the moving spirit of the Indian
Overseas Association in London, was well informed on the Indian
immigrant communities scattered throughout the Empire from British
Guiana to Fiji. E. D. Morel, former Elder Dempster shipping clerk who
became a journalist and exposed the scandals of the Belgian Congo in
his book *Red Rubber*, had made an important contribution to Labour
Party policy in the previous decade through the Union of Democratic
Control which he – together with Buxton, Ramsay MacDonald and
Charles Trevelyan – had founded in 1914. His ideas persisted, but he
died in November 1924.

Yet Woolf found the Advisory Committees 'difficult teams of
intellectuals and trade unionists'[19] and the work of the Imperial Sub-
Committee did not at first appear to arouse any particular interest in
the General Council. Nevertheless, their documents were available to
the staff and were still being used after the committee itself was
disbanded. When this happened, it was not long before the TUC was
obliged to turn to the outside experts again.

The End of the Joint Departments

The problems of the Second International were a preoccupation which
had sparked off the process which had led to joint working. Their
resolution marked the beginning of the end of the joint departments.
The General Council suddenly questioned their own role in June 1923,
when the new rules of the re-established Labour and Socialist
International (LSI) came before them for approval. Instead of passing
them, the General Council asked its own International Committee to
consider whether in future all international political work should be
confined to the Labour Party, while the TUC dealt with industrial

matters in the IFTU. The committee approved this separation, and its recommendation against affiliation to the LSI was endorsed by Congress in September.[20] The General Council then decided that it would be inappropriate to appoint their members to the Joint International Committee, and also asked the Joint Executives to investigate the staffing and general administration of the joint departments. Despite the evident consternation of the Labour Party, the Joint Executives had no alternative but to agree, and in return the General Council appointed their members, giving the Joint International Committee 2 more years of life.[21]

By this time, the General Council had a competent Finance Committee, which demanded detailed statements of expenditure and noted that the joint departments had exceeded their estimated costs.[22] The General Council then set up a Functions Committee to inquire into the functions, personnel and work of their own committees and of committees on which they were represented. It concluded in July 1925 that it was impossible for the work of Congress to be carried on adequately by the joint departments. 'The identity of the trade union and political Labour movements is kept entirely distinct both nationally and internationally,' they reported, 'and while the closest collaboration between the two Movements is necessary, the work of each necessitates its own machinery. ...'

This view that there were two movements, not one, was put to representatives of the Labour Party, who urged that nothing should be done to create the impression of separation between the General Council and the party executive. However, by December 1925 the General Council had decided to set up their own research and international departments. In January 1926 they decided to discontinue the Joint International Department with its joint committee and its two advisory committees: that is, if the TUC had any political business to do in international and imperial affairs, it would do it through its own International Department and committee. The Joint Research and Joint Publicity Committees were also disbanded.[23] 'Joint Working' was over, and only the common library, Labour Magazine and the links at executive level remained.

In the TUC's attitude the administrative difficulties had been decisive, for the advent of Citrine as assistant general secretary in January 1924 had initiated a new era of improved management. He found the joint departments loosely manned and under very little control, and for this reason alone would have advocated separation.[24] Even before he arrived the General Council had insisted that trade union business was a matter for them, and this included not only the IFTU and the ILO, but all the industrial matters arising from their new Indian trade union contacts. When a joint TUC/Labour Party deputation met the secretary of state for India in July 1924, it was decided beforehand to keep industrial and political issues separate, and when a question on the trial of four Communists at Cawnpore – a matter that had been raised by the deputation – was put at Congress, A. A. Purcell[25] replied on behalf of the General Council that that was a question for the Labour Party.[26] When the same Congress instructed them to examine and report on labour conditions in eastern countries, especially India, the General Council made no use of the still-existing Joint International Department and its committees, but set up a special Far Eastern subcommittee of their own International Committee in March 1925[27] and brought in the former leader of the SDF, H. W. Lee, to service it.[28]

It was not suggested that the joint committees and the Joint International Department had not done good work, but it was mainly on political issues. In the long run the greatest benefit came from the Advisory Committee on Imperial Questions, where the long-term issues underlying colonial policy could be thrashed out. The principal result was the publication of a memorandum on Africa but, since industry in Africa was in its infancy, the General Council did not grasp the importance of what had been written, though its representatives in the ILO did so later when the subject of forced labour was placed on the agenda. In the decision-making committee, the Joint International Committee, the most important work was the preparation of the British Commonwealth Labour Conference of 1925. Political matters considered included political developments in India, the Palestine mandate and the report of the Ormsby-Gore Commission on East Africa in 1925.[29] These were clearly of more interest to the Labour Party than to the TUC.

With the separation came an improvement in the General Council's own staffing. An assistant was appointed to allow Bolton to devote more time to international work, and in Lee they had for the first time an able man who could specialize in Indian and colonial work. Originally appointed for six months – presumably, in the opinion of the General Council, the time required to produce material for the Far Eastern Labour Committee – Lee arrived on 26 June 1925[30] and remained to make his last recorded attendance at the International Committee on 18 June 1931. He had turned out to be 'pure gold'.[31] In the General Council, Citrine emerged into full light as General Secretary at the 1926 Congress, and Bevin had been elected a member in 1925. The principal architects of the TUC's colonial policy were now in position.

It had taken the TUC many years to define the organizational limits of co-operation with a political party. The problems it encountered in the process arose in the colonial trade union movements when, influenced by nationalist rather than by labour parties, they built up their own trade union centres. The TUC had also learnt that it could not act effectively through a Member of Parliament and one clerk,

whether in domestic, imperial or international affairs, and that to do so
it must have funds, staff and expertise. Nor could it claim to represent
British workers until it had the will and the authority to secure
agreement amongst its affiliates. On all these points, the TUC's
experience in this formative period conditioned the advice given to
colonial movements when they came to ask for it – but before 1924
they had not asked for advice. With the single exception of the
Parliamentary Committee's intervention on behalf of St Kitts in 1917,
the TUC had no knowledge of colonial labour problems. It began to
learn during the period of joint working.

Joint Working and the Colonies

After the demise of the joint committees, the Labour Party set up its
own Imperial Advisory Committee and Woolf remained secretary
until 1946. It is significant that in his autobiography Woolf made no
distinction between this and the Joint Advisory Committee, and no
reference to any TUC contribution to the policies formulated. All the
indications are that he was broadly right, and that the real work of the
Joint Advisory Committee was done by the outside members.[32] In
colonial policy, the General Council followed the lead of the political
movement.

Colonial Policy

In its keynote policy statement of 1918, *Labour and the New Social
Order*, drafted by Sidney Webb,[33] the Labour Party envisaged an order
founded 'not on an enforced dominion over subject nations, subject
races, subject colonies, subject classes, or a subject sex, but ... on that
equal freedom, that general consciousness of consent, and that widest
possible participation in power, both economic and political, which is
characteristic of Democracy'. This did not entail the abandonment of
the Empire but, specifically, its maintenance and its development into a
Britannic Alliance based on the absolute autonomy of the Dominions
and a constant progress in democratic government in every part,
especially in India.

For territories which had not yet reached the stage of demanding
democratic government, Webb stressed the special obligations to
fellow-citizens overseas and the moral claims on Britain of 'the non-
adult' races. In the context, it was evident that no complete solution
was expected while capitalism prevailed. The consequent dilemma of
the socialist was scarcely discussed in Britain, and in their nine months'
office in 1924 the members of the first Labour government did not
begin to resolve it. Concentrating as they did on the League of Nations
and on relations with the Dominions, they made little impression on

the colonies, though J. H. Thomas as Secretary of State took particular pleasure in returning King Prempeh from exile to Ashanti.[34]

The question had been faced, however, in the briefs prepared by the former Labour Party Advisory Committees for the Berne Conference. Considering the problems of 'Native Labour' – with ideas pioneered by the Anti-Slavery Society and by the Union of Democratic Control – they looked for the agents of change. Ruling out reliance on the middle-class nationalist movements already active in Egypt and India, and in the absence of local stimulus from trade unions, they identified the bureaucracy. Though subject to opposition by British capitalists, it was also open to stimulus from Britain, where pressure must come from organized labour. The machinery of the League of Nations must be used to establish minimum labour standards, especially the abolition of forced labour. In examining the dependent territories, they distinguished between India with its developing industries, where the right of combination should be recognized, and three groups of colonies: areas of white settlement, territories such as Fiji with immigrant labour, and West Africa, where maintenance of native land tenure might yet prevent the peasantry sinking into mere wage slavery. The Berne Labour Charter included little of all this, but these briefs provided the starting-point of the Joint Advisory Committee's statement on Africa, published jointly by the TUC and the Labour Party in 1926 as *Labour and the Empire: Africa*.

This began as a memorandum drafted by Buxton, in which land rights were seen as central to freedom, enabling Africans to sell their labour only if they wished, unforced by pressure from the tax system, from their own chiefs, and from the exercise of government influence on behalf of settler farmers or of the mining companies. Buxton demanded that the 'European' policy pursued in East Africa should not be extended, and if necessary governments should re-enter upon alienated lands; if concessions were granted to Europeans, it should be on short leases only, over restricted areas, and with the consent of the native community affected, while native land rights must be legally recognized. In employment, there should be no forced labour, no criminal sanctions for the enforcement of labour contracts, and no colour bar. In government, native systems of local self-government should be encouraged and there should be progressive admission to Legislative Councils and to representative and responsible government. In addition, there should be a complete educational system for all sections of the populations. It was a programme conceived in the tradition of humanitarian paternalism for preindustrial societies; trade unions were not mentioned.[35] Re-drafted by the Joint Advisory Committee on Imperial Questions in a shorter and more popular form, with a preface by J. H. Thomas, this became the official policy of the

Labour Party and the TUC. It was the point of reference for all the
Labour Party's work on colonies for the next 10 years, and was used
particularly by Buxton and his parliamentary colleagues to bring
pressure to bear on Sidney Webb (Lord Passfield) as Secretary of State
in the second Labour government. For the TUC – since it did not deal
with trade unions – the pamphlet's immediate value lay in its relevance
to work in the ILO.

At Scarborough in 1925 Congress expressed other ideas in a
resolution declaring opposition to imperialism as a form of capitalist
exploitation, support for workers' efforts to organize trade unions and
political parties, and for the right of all peoples in the British Empire to
self-determination, including the right to complete separation.[36] How
these objectives were to be achieved was not explained.

This dichotomy exemplified the dilemma inherent in colonial
policy: whether to use available government machinery to bring about
improvement, or to hand over, to what? As the TUC and the Labour
Party emerged from their period of joint working, there was still a great
gap in their policy. Governments, Parliaments, colonial administrations, Legislative Councils, the League of Nations, the ILO, were all
in the picture, laying down standards, exercising trusteeship, protecting
the native, leading the backward on to democracy, perhaps even to
socialism; the missing element was still the organized native worker.
Given the right of combination, no doubt he would appear in time, but
so far he had not arrived. Meanwhile the Labour Party were conscious
of their lack of contact with the colonial peoples – as distinct from India
– and of their frequent ignorance of the results of official action and of
the growth of new sentiments and new hopes.[37]

The Commonwealth Labour Conference

An opportunity to improve contacts came from the British Empire
Exhibition held at Wembley in 1924. The General Council saw its
potential for employment and was represented on the planning
committee, and there was similar interest in the Dominions. In 1923
the New Zealand Labour Party proposed that some method of co-
operation should be established between Labour parties in the
Commonwealth, and the South African Labour Party suggested that a
meeting might be held in London during the exhibition. As they could
not find a date on which a full conference could be held, the Joint
Executives proposed an informal meeting as a first step. It was held on
17 September 1924 and consisted of Labour Party and TUC
representatives and accredited delegates of colonial Labour parties and
trade unions then in London.[38]

E. L. Poulton,[39] the General Council's ILO delegate, took the chair,
and the overseas representatives came from the Australian Labour

Party, the Victoria Trades Hall Council, the Federated Labour Party of British Columbia, the Rhodesian Labour Party (Jack Keller), the Northern Ireland Labour Party and Hubert Critchlow from the British Guiana Labour Union (BGLU). Meeting amongst themselves between sessions, the Dominions representatives agreed a proposal which they moved in the full conference, and which was adopted, that in future regular Commonwealth conferences should be held. It was the 1917 Congress motion in another form, but this time the practical difficulties could be overcome. The Joint Executives agreed to hold biennial conferences and timed the first for July 1925, when delegates would be in Europe for the ILO and LSI conferences. The Joint International Committee was entrusted with the arrangements.[40] It was realized that such conferences could not take binding decisions: noting the problems before the third conference in 1930, after this issue had been raised, Citrine recorded that Australian letters took six weeks, three months with replies, and that if delegates were to be mandated there must be further time for conferences and executive meetings of the constituting bodies.[41]

The first formal British Commonwealth Labour Conference was a major event lasting six days.[42] This time Southern Rhodesia and British Columbia were not represented, but the Canadian Labour Party and Independent Labour Parties of Ontario and Manitoba sent delegates, and new associates were the Irish Labour Party and TUC, the All-India TUC, the Jewish Labour Federation of Palestine, the South African Association of Employees' Organizations, the Parliamentary Labour Party, and fraternal delegates from the IFTU and the LSI. New Zealand was again unrepresented, but submitted documents on migration and on inter-Dominion trade relations. The TUC and the Labour Party submitted a joint memorandum on state trading within the Commonwealth, and the Labour Party initiated discussions on the Geneva Protocol for the Pacific Settlement of International Disputes and on the constitutional position of the Dominions in the event of a declaration of war by the Crown.

The AITUC delegates, Joshi and Diwan Chaman Lall, confronted the Conference with some of the root problems that had not been completely faced in the Labour Party's declarations and in the TUC/Labour Party pamphlet on Africa. They began with the ILO, which the TUC had placed on the agenda for discussion. They pointed out that on the existing basis of representation, workers in colonies, mandated territories and in protectorates, including the Indian princely states, had no direct voice at Geneva, and urged that advisers representing them should be appointed in the appropriate metro-politan delegations. Chaman Lall also suggested that all Common-wealth representatives of workers at the ILO should meet among

themselves to discuss matters of common interest. Both proposals
were ultimately adopted by the TUC.

Their move made it clear that the Indian delegates regarded the status
of the dependencies as a matter of concern to the whole
Commonwealth and to the international organizations, and not merely
as an issue between them and the metropolitan powers. Traditionally
the Indian National Congress, like the Government of India, took a
keen interest in the conditions of Indians settled outside India, and in
so far as these stemmed from the former system of indentured labour
Critchlow, from British Guiana, recognized that they were an
appropriate subject for discussion in an industrial context. However,
the South African delegate, H. W. Sampson, while agreeing that the
South African delegation to the ILO would be strengthened by the
inclusion of 'an intelligent Native', refused to agree – in the case of the
Indians – to Joshi's request for a straight declaration of principle
opposing racial discrimination in employment, residence, and the
franchise. Considering that such a resolution would have no impact in
South Africa, and that they were not mandated to vote on it, the other
delegates suggested that instead the Labour Party and trade unions in
South Africa and the AITUC should try to reach agreement on these
matters amongst themselves. It was evident, however, from the bitter
little duel that took place that neither the Indian nor the South African
organizations would take constructive action to deal with them, and
nothing resulted.

Chaman Lall also tabled a motion in favour of self-determination for
subject peoples, which the conference referred to a commission
composed of George Lansbury,[43] Joshi, Ben-Gurion (Palestine),
Sampson, T. Johnson (Ireland) and J. MacDonald (Canada). In the
absence of specific mandates, the delegates agreed without discussion
to recommend their constituent bodies to support immediate self-
government for India. But the commission's other suggestions aroused
opposition. Lansbury put forward their proposal that the views of the
constituent organizations should be obtained on whether Labour
policy should be to develop subject peoples so that they might
ultimately be fitted to elect and control their own governments.
Ramsay MacDonald objected to wording which cast doubt on the
fitness of any people to govern themselves, and proposed instead that
the commission, which Critchlow joined, should draw up a
questionnaire to pinpoint specific problems.

The questionnaire on subject peoples (excluding India) was
endorsed by the conference for circulation, with several others, in
advance of the next meeting. It posed such questions as 'whether these
peoples should be granted self-government immediately? If not, how to
apply our principle of self-determination? How to prevent their

economic exploitation?' The conference ended with the most difficult questions of all still to be answered. The Joint Advisory Committee on Imperial Questions made some progress in drafting replies before the joint committees were disbanded.[44]

The Entry of the West Indies

One man much influenced by the Commonwealth Labour Conference was Hubert Critchlow. He told the conference that he knew nothing about the trade union movement until he read in the *Daily Herald* 'what a union was like' and wrote to Henderson, who gave him advice on what was needed.[45] He was a natural organizer, however, and as early as 1905 resentment at working 10½ hours a day on the docks, which left him no time for sport, had caused him to lead a strike in Georgetown. He was arrested then, and again in a strike in 1906, though without penalty and without success on both occasions. In 1917, to avoid a wartime strike, he acted by petition and won a wage increase with the support of the Governor, but when he organized another petition, for an eight-hour day, he was sacked. By contrast with the strikes of 1905 and 1906, this effort led to permanent organization. He was again supported by the Governor, Sir Wilfred Collet, and started a union. A Trade Union Ordinance followed in 1921, and in July 1922 his British Guiana Labour Union was registered.[46] By the time he came to address the Commonwealth Labour Conference in 1925 he had manifestly become a confident and well-informed trade union leader.

Impressed by the conference, on his return to Georgetown Critchlow organized a conference of West Indian labour leaders and invited his Commonwealth colleagues to attend. The TUC and the Labour Party decided to send a joint representative.[47] On New Year's Day 1926, the Rt Hon. F. O. Roberts MP landed in Port of Spain *en route* to British Guiana. He was the first TUC representative to arrive in the West Indies.

Roberts was a good representative of the British movement: a compositor who had worked hard in his spare time to improve his education, a district secretary and national executive member of the Typographical Association, and a Member of Parliament who had been Minister of Pensions in the first Labour government. For the Caribbean, where political, trade union and social activities were commonly conducted under one umbrella, his broad experience of co-operative and friendly societies was particularly appropriate. So was his personality. At home he had the habit of playing his violin at Labour meetings, and evidently his early training as a choirboy stood him in good stead in the West Indies, where he earned the title 'Sweet singer of the stage'.

He was to meet equally colourful characters on arrival, the first being

Captain Arthur Andrew Cipriani, horse trainer, auctioneer, former soldier, Member of Legislative Council and President of the Trinidad Workingmen's Association (TWMA). The TWMA had a long-standing link with the Labour Party, and actually applied for affiliation in 1906. It was refused on the grounds that the Party had no provision for overseas affiliation, but help was promised and J. Pointer MP, who came to be known as 'Member for Trinidad', began to raise parliamentary Questions and went to Trinidad in 1912 on a visit jointly financed by the Labour Party and the TWMA.[48] In 1921, when the Trinidad government refused it recognition as the representative of Trinidad workers,[49] the TWMA sent its organizer, W. Howard-Bishop to London. Bishop met Labour Party officials, but there is no indication in his report that he might have called next door to see the TUC.[50]

In one sense this lack of contact with the TUC was understandable: while the Parliamentary Committee had been inactive in colonial matters, most colonies were accustomed to receiving emissaries from Westminster, often as members of Empire Parliamentary Association delegations or of commissions of inquiry, and colonial politicians were quick to identify sympathetic Members who might help them in Parliament, where much might be gained from a Question or a debate. However, Bishop was not new to industrial action. He had been fined in the aftermath of a dock strike in 1919 which culminated in the arrival of two British warships,[51] and when he was received by the under-secretary of state in 1921 he asked for trade union legislation to be introduced in Trinidad. When Cipriani won election to the Legislative Council, it was on a platform which included demands for trade union legislation, an eight-hour day, and workmen's compensation. For an industrial – as distinct from a political – link, much depended on Roberts.

On arrival, still feeling decidedly ill from a rough crossing, Roberts was conducted in a demonstration through Port of Spain to Woodford Square, where he addressed a great crowd as well as his physical condition would allow. At other public meetings in the city and outside he had the same enthusiastic reception. He was shocked by the housing conditions and the widespread employment of children in the rural areas, and left for Georgetown strongly impressed by demands for compulsory education, universal suffrage, more elected seats in the Legislative Council and payment of Members.

He had a similar experience in British Guiana, where he chaired the opening day of the First West Indian Labour Conference. It was attended by delegates from the BGLU and the TWMA, the British Guiana East Indian Association and three other Guianese associations, and by two delegates from the Surinam Porters' Union who could not speak English but were pleased to be there. The demands Roberts had already heard in Trinidad were made again, together with a resolution for the repeal of all penal sanctions in the British Guiana Master and Servant Ordinance. The conference also called for a Federation of the West Indies with a form of self-government which would enable them to conduct their own affairs in a Colonial Parliament, with Dominion status. It decided to set up a Guianese and West Indian Federation of Trade Unions and Labour Parties and appointed a committee led by Cipriani to draft the rules.

As the attendance at the conference showed, this last was an expression of hope rather than reality at that time. Jamaica was still a world away, and Roberts did not go there; but he did go on to Barbados, where he found no labour party or any recognized union, but met the executive of the Democratic League, which had two Members in the Colonial Parliament. In the smaller islands, although some employers and estate managers told him that the people were happy and did not need agitation, he found sympathy amongst the clergy and some supporters of the labour cause. Despite the gap between hope and reality, he concluded that 'though only very slightly, Democracy has been recognized', and urged that any help from Britain should be aimed at widening and strengthening its basis, so that it could be used in achieving immediate reforms and making them operative, and in bringing an understanding of what must be done in the future and of how to do it.[52]

It was a small but important beginning. The path to self-government had been charted, and the elementary industrial demands formulated. The movements were no longer isolated, but had a nucleus to which other organizations in the West Indies could turn as they were formed. The West Indian labour movement had reached out to the wider world, and the two-way flow of information – the bedrock of all assistance and co-operation – had begun. At the 1928 Commonwealth Labour Conference Trinidad was represented, and Grenada in 1930. Since the third was also the last of the TUC/Labour Party Commonwealth Conferences, and the West Indies sent no representatives to the ILO, the links were still tenuous, and were to remain so until the explosions of the next decade brought the second TUC representative to the West Indies – Citrine, in the guise of a Royal Commissioner, in 1938.

Joint Working and the Internationals

By January 1926 the Labour Party and the TUC had arrived at some conclusions about colonial policy which remained unchanged throughout the colonial period. For themselves, they intended to work through parliamentary institutions which provided, as the Branting resolution at Berne had asserted, not merely the channels of political expression, but also the means of pursuing changes required by workers as such. 'Democracy' was indeed a sort of goddess, written with a capital letter, presiding over the New Social Order, and, more practically in the Roberts report, enabling labour movements to define their aims and to achieve an understanding of what needed to be done and how to do it. Democracy was not to be confined to Britain, but extended to the empire, itself to be transmuted into Webb's Britannic Alliance, in which self-government was seen as the end-product of the development of democratic institutions, as it had been in the Dominions.

But these were European concepts, and the existence of problems involved in applying them to territories with different cultural backgrounds had been recognized at the first Commonwealth Labour Conference. The unlikely possibility that such territories might not wish them to be applied at all was not considered. In Palestine and in the West Indies the claim was for parliamentary government, and the Labour Party and the TUC were seen as allies. However, the Indians at the Commonwealth Labour Conference asked for nothing but independence, and it was remarkable that the Indian nationalist parties were not represented. Nor did they attend the second and third conferences: but for the TUC's link with the AITUC, there would have been no Indian representation at all. Moreover, the Indians at the 1925 conference had placed the question of colonial status in an international context, and the Labour Party was bound to recognize that this was inherent in the Covenant of the League of Nations.

The TUC leaders showed little interest in such theoretical considerations, but these questions had implications for them. In India, and to a lesser extent in the West Indies, the pace of change was too slow to satisfy either political or purely industrial demands. There was every prospect that the nascent trade unions would be swept up into nationalist movements which would subordinate labour interests to national aims; at worst, if the unions were too weak to gain industrial objectives by their own strength, and alternative political means were denied, the organization of workers en masse under revolutionary political leadership would be virtually inevitable. There was very little revolutionary leadership in British territory, but it was encountered as soon as entry was made into the international scene. This entry had now been made, and although the ideological disagreements that divided the socialist and trade union internationals had originated in Europe, they were not irrelevant to the dependencies outside, which proved highly susceptible to alternative political leadership throughout their advance to independence. Gompers had believed that it was possible to build a trade union international which would not be entangled in political battles. It proved to be impossible in Europe. The danger in the international dimension was that European conflicts would be defined in universal terms and carried down into the new labour movements elsewhere by the very bodies which in their different ways claimed to aim at world unity and peace.

The Labour and Socialist International

The opposition of some delegates to the Branting resolution at Berne and the formation of the Comintern set off a series of international and domestic rifts. In an attempt to devise a set of rules which all its former affiliates could accept, the ISB sent out an invitation in April 1920 to a full conference at Geneva, in which it stressed the need for unity but acknowledged that the International must trust its affiliates to use methods of action which were in their view best calculated to lead to the socialist transformation at which all aimed.[53] The Labour Party and the Parliamentary Committee decided to participate. However, in May three influential leaders of the IFTU – Appleton, Edo Fimmen of Holland and Corneille Mertens of Belgium – expressed their personal opinion to the Parliamentary Committee that to avoid a trade union split along the lines of the international political divisions, trade union national centres should not be represented.[54] Nevertheless, the Parliamentary Committee persisted.

At Geneva in July the British delegation was by far the largest, and the majority socialists of Germany and Austria, but not of France, were represented. The delegates decided to move the headquarters from Brussels to London and asked the Labour Party to negotiate with the sections that had not attended. Reluctantly, the Labour Party and the Parliamentary Committee accepted this responsibility provided that the transfer was temporary and that MacDonald and Gosling acted as secretaries.[55]

The Labour Party was already embarrassed in the British section. In April the national conference of the ILP had decided not to affiliate to the ISB and in May sent a mission to Moscow to discover the exact terms of affiliation to the Comintern. The British Socialist Party had decided to affiliate at the end of 1919,[56] and on 31 July 1920 – the day after the Geneva Conference opened – formed the largest contingent at a national convention of socialist societies which decided to form the Communist Party of Great Britain (CPGB) as an affiliate of the Comintern. The key resolution was moved by Purcell, already a member of the Parliamentary Committee. The ILP was not satisfied with the report of its delegation to Moscow, but instead of returning to the ISB, joined in December with the Swiss and German independent socialists in a preliminary Reconstruction Conference of parties that would not join either international but were prepared to mediate between them.

In a joint appeal for unity,[57] the TUC and the Labour Party challenged both the theoretical manifesto adopted by the Reconstruction Conference and the Bolshevik method of seizing and holding political power by armed force and changing the economic structure of society by decree and suppression. But in February 1921 representatives of 14 parties, mostly from the 1915 Zimmerwald group, met at Vienna and formed the International Working Union of Socialist Parties with Freidrich Adler as secretary. This became known as the 'Vienna Union' or the 'Two-and-a-Half International', and aimed at the conquest of power by revolutionary class struggle.

Despite the failure of their initiative, neither the TUC nor the Labour Party was in a position to abandon it. At the Second Congress of the Comintern in 1920 an International Council of Trade and Industrial Unions had been set up, and by January 1921 it had a British Bureau in existence with Tom Mann as president. For the Labour Party, the adherence of the ILP to the Vienna Union mocked at its own affiliation to the ISB. The effort to secure unity continued throughout 1921 and 1922 in a series of meetings, of which the most important was held at Berlin on 2 April 1922. There representatives of all three political Internationals considered the terms on which they could co-operate, and set up a Committee of Nine which met in May, but failed to reach agreement. In June the ISB decided that no understanding could be achieved with the Comintern, but that Vienna should again be approached. Finally, in May 1923 at Hamburg a joint conference of the ISB and the Vienna Union set up the LSI.

The LSI was considered to be the successor to the Second International. Affiliation was open to socialist organizations which accepted the economic emancipation of workers from capitalist domination as their object and the independent political and industrial action of workers' organizations as the means of attaining it. The LSI was to maintain a close connection with the IFTU and the International Cooperative Alliance and to be ready to call joint meetings with them to discuss common problems. The rules[58] made decisions binding on affiliates.

The TUC General Council made no pronouncement on the resolutions or the rules, but noted that the TUC was the only trade union body directly represented at Hamburg. The question of duplicate representation of unions through the TUC and the Labour Party was raised, and it was argued that the conference had judged matters from a purely political standpoint. It was at this point that they instructed their International Committee to consider the separation of functions. The committee's report recalled that in 1917, in war conditions which no longer existed, the TUC had adopted joint action with the Labour Party to restore the International. This had been achieved, but in the LSI it would always be difficult to gain adequate expression for a strictly trade union point of view. The TUC did not affiliate and the process of winding up the joint departments was begun.

Considering that the first congress of the Comintern had approved Lenin's theses rejecting bourgeois democracy and parliamentarism, this persistent effort to achieve a united International requires some explanation. Why did the socialist parties and the TUC discuss unity at all? One reason may be that the situation in Russia was still fluid. It could not be assumed that the Bolsheviks would prevail, and even if they did, there were differences amongst them. It was not until the Tenth Congress of their party in March 1921, after the defeat of the Workers' Opposition which claimed the right of independent trade unions to elect their own officials, that party members were forbidden to enter 'fractions' advocating policies different from those of the established leadership. In 1922 some members of the Workers' Opposition actually appealed – unsuccessfully – to the Comintern, and the Eleventh Party Congress rejected a disciplinary committee's recommendation that its leaders should be expelled from the party.[59] On the other hand, a delegation sent in May 1920 by the Parliamentary Committee and the Labour Party saw enough to indicate that the terror was real. They had to hope that it was temporary.

The European socialist parties judged the revolution by comparison with the former Tsarist oppression and in the context of their own governments' armed intervention in the continuing civil war. The report of the TUC/Labour Party delegation called for the unconditional recognition of the Soviet government,[60] London dockers refused to load the ship *Jolly George* with munitions for Poland, and in August a National Conference of Executive Committees and members of TUC and Labour Party affiliates warned the British government that if necessary industrial power would be used to frustrate British assistance for an attack on Russia through the Polish intervention. Similar action was taken by other parties in the ISB and the IFTU, and much effort went into organizing famine relief. There was no corresponding goodwill in the Bolshevik camp. In November 1920 the London Conference of the IFTU protested against the 'calumnies and insults' directed against their organization, couched in language which 'could not possibly be considered as proper methods of discussion between free and civilized men'.[61] However, in time such language had to be accepted as characteristic of Russian propaganda.

The meeting of the executives of the three Internationals in Berlin in April 1922 exposed three fundamental differences. The Comintern

representatives proposed that a general conference should be held
which would initiate union. The ISB representatives agreed, but on
three conditions: that the Comintern practice of cell-building
everywhere within all parties would be abandoned, that a group of
Social Revolutionary prisoners who had been held for three years in
Russia would be given a fair trial, and that Russia should acknowledge
the right of self-determination of all peoples, notably those of
Georgia.[62]

It was almost impossible for the Comintern to concede the first. The
Statutes adopted at its Second Congress in August 1920 required every
communist party to organize cells inside trade unions, workers'
councils and factory committees, co-operatives and other mass
workers' organizations. To the TUC and the Labour Party this meant a
conspiracy inside every trade union branch and every local Labour
party, but the cell was the bedrock of communist organization.

The second was also difficult. There was no question that the
Mensheviks and Social Revolutionaries were hostile to the Bolshevik
regime, and the Social Revolutionaries were particularly dangerous to
it since they had been the largest party in the Constituent Assembly
which the Bolsheviks disbanded and, moreover, had always condoned
or practised terrorism. For the Comintern, Karl Radek agreed to
recommend to the Soviet government that representatives of the
socialist Internationals should be allowed to attend the trial and that no
death penalty should be inflicted. Lenin considered that these
concessions went too far,[63] but a trial was held. The representatives of
the ISB and the Vienna Union were housed outside Moscow and
accompanied everywhere by government officials. In court they were
insulted, independent shorthand notes of the evidence were not
permitted, and in their view the judges threw aside all pretence of a
judicial trial.[64] Death sentences were imposed, but not carried out.

The demand for recognition of the right of self-determination was a
test case for Russia's handling of the former Tsarist dependencies. It
was not conceded. In the socialist view, the subject peoples should
have a right to expect that the revolution would bring them freedom,
but the Bolsheviks regarded nationalism as a manifestation of
bourgeois philosophy. The Baltic countries and Poland gained their
independence, but as an outcome of the war, not of the revolution. As
the Bolsheviks lost control of outlying provinces in face of German,
White and then Allied attacks, Georgia remained under Menshevik
administration and European socialists hoped that the young republic
would demonstrate that social change could be carried out democratically.[65] With other leaders of the Second International, Ramsay
MacDonald visited Georgia in 1920 and was impressed by their
enthusiastic reception, by the land reform, the nationalization

measures, the free elections and the free speech.[66] But the work of the local Bolshevik parties was directed by a Caucasian Bureau in Moscow,[67] and first Azerbaijan, then Armenia, became Soviet republics. In February 1921 attacks were mounted on the Menshevik regime in Georgia internally and by the Red Army, and also by Turkey. A new Soviet Republic of Georgia was proclaimed, which was federated with Armenia and Azerbaijan in a Trans-Caucasian Federation. The Menshevik version of these events was known to the ISB since the leaders, including I. Tseretelli, who had been a minister in the governments of Prince Lvov and Kerensky, had joined their fellow exiles in Paris, and delegates from Azerbaijan and Georgia had attended the ISB's Geneva Conference in July 1920.

In Berlin MacDonald asked for the military occupation to be withdrawn so that the people of Georgia might decide on their own government. Radek replied that there was evidence that the so-called independent Georgia had rested on the support of German and British imperialism.[68] It was agreed that all three executives would collect and submit their evidence, but at the Committee of Nine on 23 May 1922 MacDonald accused the Comintern representatives of going back on their undertakings, and demanded a commission of inquiry into the situation in Georgia. Radek insisted instead that a date should first be fixed for a general conference of the three Internationals. Recognizing the obvious, Adler stated on behalf of the Vienna Union that the minimum agreement required for a general conference did not exist, and the Committee of Nine came to an end.[69]

According to the Comintern, the Second International had frustrated the attempt to build a united workers' front 'from above', and it must now be built 'from below': workers in parties affiliated to the Second and Two-and-a-Half Internationals must organize to compel their leaders to join a world congress. 'Fight the leaders of the Second International who are splitting the working class'[70] was the message from Moscow. At the LSI's Hamburg Conference in May 1923, delegates from the Russian Mensheviks and the Georgian Social Democratic Party attended, and the conference demanded the complete abandonment of party dictatorship in Russia, the release of persons convicted or condemned for their political opinions, and the evacuation of Soviet troops from Georgia, expressed sympathy with the socialist victims of Bolshevik terror in Russia and Georgia, and declared it to be the duty of all affiliated organizations to give moral and material support to all Russian socialists who worked in the spirit of the resolution. The entire British delegation – Labour Party and TUC, ILP, SDF and Fabian Society – regarded this as intervention in the domestic affairs of the Soviet Union and abstained, but they were alone. Yet this conference did put the colonial issue in the forefront of

socialist concern: not only was Bolshevik imperialism condemned but
also, in a separate resolution, all imperialism, and the exploitation of
native peoples and the violent destruction of their economic systems.[71]
Later developments were to show that the TUC, which supported this
resolution, paid too little attention to the view that the Bolsheviks also
might be guilty of imperialism.

The Communist International

While the three Internationals were arguing about self-determination
in 1922, the Bolsheviks were implementing their policy for the former
Tsarist empire. They had begun in 1917 by proclaiming the equality of
the peoples of Russia and the right to sovereignty to the point of
separation and the formation of independent states. This right was
recognized in the case of Finland. It was quickly modified when the
provisional government of the Ukraine called for Ukrainians in the
army to return home and refused to allow Soviet Government troops
to cross its territory to reach the south, where civil war had begun.
While negotiations for a peace with Germany had not been completed
and there were Japanese intervention forces in Siberia, the Russian
republic could not, for its own safety, concede the Ukrainian or any
similar claim on its borders.

The change of policy that ensued was not caused entirely by the
dangers of outside intervention. The Ukrainian government had also
dispersed local soviets by force. In January 1918 the third All-Russian
Congress of Soviets, against Menshevik opposition, adopted a
proposal by Stalin[72] that the principle of self-determination for small
nations

> ought to be understood as the right of self-determination not of the
> bourgeoisie but of the toiling masses of a given nation ... [and] used
> as a means in the struggle for socialism, and it ought to be
> subordinated to the principles of socialism.

This re-formulation could conceivably have been acceptable to the
other parties that claimed to be socialist if they had been allowed to
function, but by the time the Berlin international conference discussed
Menshevik Georgia in 1922, it was clear that the right of the toiling
masses meant the right to decide within the limits of communist policy
and organization. In the Russian Soviet Socialist Republic, which
stretched down to the borders of Persia, Afghanistan and China,
Russian control, such as it was, rested on those elements in the former
Tsarist administration and its forces that chose to cast in their lot with
the new regime proclaimed in Moscow and on the Russian workers and
others in the towns, who were not all Bolsheviks. They were

surrounded by non-Russian Muslims in what had been, and in effect still were, colonial dependencies. At the end of 1922, when the Red Army had brought Georgia into line and advanced beyond the Caspian Sea, new republics were proclaimed in the south-east, and were brought together with the Transcaucasian Federation and the rest of Russia in the Union of Soviet Socialist Republics (USSR). Their right to self-determination was contained by the extensive powers reserved to the central government and by the steel frame of Communist Party direction, reinforced as this was over the years by massive Russian settlement.[73]

In the Asian republics the Russians were facing problems similar in some ways to those experienced by the British, French, Dutch and Belgian empires. Since none of the Internationals had a monopoly of wisdom, it was regrettable that there was no useful discussion between them. Nor was there any useful discussion in the Comintern. It was a curious feature of that International that such issues as the degrees of self-government appropriate in different areas that were unable to sustain immediate independence, or land tenure, or the recruitment of labour for economic developments, were not argued out, except obliquely – while the future of Georgia was still in doubt and resistance amongst the Turkic peoples of Central Asia was still being suppressed, the Second Comintern Congress held a theoretical debate on the worldwide need to rally peasants to the side of the proletariat.[74] No constructive ideas emerged, just as no contribution was made to the work of labour administration in the ILO, which the Soviet Government refused to attend. By contrast with the LSI and the Commonwealth Labour Conferences, the colonial revolution was seen in the Comintern as an essential element in the destruction of capitalism – that is to say, as something which would occur in other empires.

In this setting, the revolutionary potential of the colonial question was taken seriously. The Second Comintern Congress in August 1920 appointed a special commission to draft a report on it, with Hendrik Sneevliet (Maring),[75] representing the Dutch East Indies Communist Party (PKI), as secretary. Then and at successive congresses a basic policy was formulated. Bourgeois nationalism was ultimately a sham, but it could be utilized. Nationalist parties should be supported, provided the alliance was only temporary and that the independence of the proletarian parties was maintained. It was the duty of communist parties in countries with colonies to support colonial liberation movements by all means, including agitation amongst the armed forces of their own countries. Thus the vision of an existing free union of soviet republics was uncritically accepted as an aim, with the subjects of other empires joining it when their revolutions succeeded.

Already at the first Congress consultative delegates attended from Georgia, Azerbaijan, Turkestan, Persia, China and Korea, to be joined at the second by spokesmen from India and the Dutch East Indies. In September 1920 the President of the Comintern, Gregorii Zinoviev, presided over the first Congress of Peoples of the East at Baku, with the stirring call, 'Brothers! We call you to the holy war, to the holy war above all against English imperialism'. It was followed in January 1922 with a Congress of Toilers of the Far East, with delegations from China, Japan, Korea, India, Java, Mongolia and the Soviet Union. A Communist University of the Toilers of the East was set up in Moscow. This was a great attraction. 'To be modern, to understand the revolution,' the future Chinese Red Army leader Chu Teh was told by his Communist mentors in France and Germany, 'you must go to Russia. *There you can see the future*.'[76] The University soon claimed a student body of 700.[77]

This issue of self-determination could not be dissociated from the basic disagreement between the Internationals on the meaning of democracy. In the British dependencies, parliamentary government was in its infancy, but the history of its development in Britain and the Dominions predisposed a man like Roberts to assume that it would be a natural growth in the West Indies. The Bolshevik leaders had not had his experience. They were not working men who had seen great reforms in their own lifetime, but highly educated intellectuals who had starved for years in foreign libraries and concluded that parliaments had no inherent value but were merely trappings of the bourgeois state; they had never been allowed to build a movement openly by persuasion: their business was not to represent, but to lead. They had seized and held power by force, and in Lenin's view, 'generally speaking, it is not voting, but civil war, that decides *all* serious questions of politics when history has placed the dictatorship of the proletariat on the order of the day'. The bourgeois state apparatus must be smashed from top to bottom, and all attempts to return to capitalism must be suppressed. Only the dictatorship of the proletariat, which was 'soviet government, or proletarian democracy', would give real liberty and equality to the workers, who must be undeviatingly trained for revolution in a class struggle in which parliamentarism and bourgeois 'liberties' should be utilized, but in which it would be necessary to resort to mass actions beyond the bounds of bourgeois legality.[78]

In 1920 Lenin spelt out the organizational implications of this doctrine in *'Left Wing' Communism: An Infantile Disorder*, in which he answered the view that the British Communist Party, then being formed, should have no truck with Parliament or the Labour Party. On the contrary, he advised, the new party should participate in Parliament and offer an electoral pact to the Labour Party. However, these moves would be purely tactical:[79]

> If I address the masses as a Communist, and invite them to vote for
> Henderson against Lloyd George, I most certainly will be listened to.
> And ... I shall be able to popularize the idea, not only that Soviets are
> better than Parliaments, and that the dictatorship of the proletariat is
> better than the dictatorship of Churchill (disguised under the name
> of bourgeois 'democracy'), but also that I am prepared to support
> Henderson by my vote in just the same way as a rope supports the
> man who has hanged himself.

In the same way, affiliation to the Labour Party – as long as it continued
to be the representative party of the trade unions – would give the
Communist Party access to a 'platform that is higher and more visible
to the masses than their own'.[80] The first requirement was contact with
the masses. The second was contact with the Comintern. Every
Communist Party must act in accordance with its policy. There was no
doubt about this. The Statutes adopted by the Second Comintern
Congress in August 1920 empowered the Executive Committee
(ECCI) to issue instructions binding on member parties, which would
be sections of the International. All were required to give
unconditional support to any Soviet republic contending with counter-
revolutionary forces, and to work through their trade union cells for a
break with the 'yellow' Amsterdam International and support for the
new 'red' trade union international then being formed. All must fulfil
the Twenty One Conditions of Affiliation which the ILP was unable to
accept: applicant parties which still retained their old social democratic
programmes must revise them, parliamentary fractions must be purged
of unreliable elements and made subordinate to the party presidium,
and the whole party press must be run by reliable communists and
must publish all important official documents of the ECCI. All parties
must be organized on the principle of democratic centralism, with 'iron
discipline' and periodic 'cleansing' of any petty bourgeois elements
which might have crept in.

Although these Statutes were subsequently revised, the essential
features did not change. At the third Congress in July 1921, it was laid
down that each party must make a quarterly report to the Comintern,
every organization within the party must report to its immediately
superior committee, and the directives and decisions of the leading
party bodies were to be binding on subordinate organizations and on
individual members. These disciplined parties must win the masses by
leadership and persuasion, but since the leaders of the social
democratic parties and trade unions could not be persuaded, they must
be fought 'by detaching their adherents from them, by convincing the

workers that the social-traitor leaders are just the errand boys of capitalism'.[81]

As the Committee of Nine concluded, such regulations made the union of the three internationals impossible. They also cut across the Labour Party's organization at every level, with the natural consequence that the Communist Party's application for affiliation to the Labour Party was refused. That party itself failed to live up to expectations, and in 1923 the Comintern set up a special committee to study 'the British question'. The party was reorganized – abandoning its initial federal structure – and the leadership was changed. Many of the early members, including Purcell, left it. The Labour Party consistently refused to play the role Lenin had assigned to it. Rejecting a new application for affiliation in 1924, it also decided that no member of the Communist Party might be a member or be eligible, whether proposed by a local Labour party or by a trade union body, to stand as a Labour candidate in parliamentary or local government elections.[82]

However, exclusion did not end the Communist Party's attempt to influence the Labour Party from within. Still seeking the platform higher and more visible to the masses than its own, it made special efforts to influence the trade unions. This occurred over the whole range of policy, but could be specially effective in imperial affairs, about which most rank-and-file members were relatively ignorant and which constantly provided occasions for heartfelt protest. In addition, all communist parties in the metropolitan countries were obliged to support colonial movements and were required to pay special attention to trade unions in the dependencies in order to emancipate them from nationalist ideology and from the trade union bureaucracies of the fatherlands.[83] Thus, in their work in India and in the colonies, the TUC and the Labour Party had to contend with a permanent opposition within their own ranks and, where this could be achieved, in the dependencies themselves. This opposition arose from a consistent programme born of a political doctrine that was legitimately concerned with fundamental issues and had merits of its own, but which was essentially destructive and fundamentally incompatible with what the Labour Party and the TUC were trying to do. Not only were the Labour Party's beliefs challenged, but the type of trade unionism advocated by the Comintern and its associated trade union international could not be reconciled with the advice offered to overseas unions by the TUC. Nor did it spring from the needs and ideas of the workers themselves, but was handed down through structures which deprived their organizations of any genuine representative capacity. In the succeeding years the TUC suffered much trouble but was able to deal with it, but by 1929 the young Indian TUC was irremediably split.

The Red International of Labour Unions

The Red International of Labour Unions (RILU) was established after
a year's preparatory work by the International Council of Trade and
Industrial Unions set up in July 1920 to act as a militant international
committee for the reorganization of the trade union movement,
working in conjunction with the ECCI.[84] The founding congress was
held in July 1921 at the same time as the Comintern's Third Congress,
and both bodies endorsed a Programme of Action which affirmed that
the general class struggle could be adequately organized only when
revolutionary trade unions acted in perfect unity with the communist
parties of their respective countries. It was agreed that at top level a
representative of the RILU should sit on the ECCI and vice versa, and
that joint sessions of the two executives should be held at intervals.
These decisions were not lightly made. There was a strong syndicalist
element at the congress which based its plea for trade union action
independent of political schools of thought on the CGT's Amiens
Charter of 1906, but ultimately those who had spoken against co-
operation with the Comintern withdrew their opposition in the
interests of unity of the revolutionary trade unions. Four years later the
RILU's secretary, S. A. Lozovsky, was able to write that the work of the
Comintern and the RILU was frequently performed 'by one and the
same organization, sometimes even by one and the same person'.[85]

The leaders of the two organizations habitually spoke as if they were
of equal status, but this could not be so. The founding congress rejected
a proposal by delegates from the IWW and by German and Italian
syndicalists that it should aim at replacing the established unions by
new unions. Thus many of the RILU's adherents were minorities
within the broader existing unions, and unlike the communist parties
affiliated to the Comintern, they could have no independent status of
their own. Moreover, the communist elements within them were
subject to the discipline of their local parties, which were in turn under
the direction of the ECCI. The RILU itself reinforced this position, as
was made clear in a searing report on the conduct of the British Bureau
made by the RILU Executive to its Third Congress in 1924. It was said
that after reiterated instructions to the Bureau to remedy its loose
connections with the industrial department of the British Communist
Party, the Executive had appointed new members in August 1923, but
still their showing at the TUC Congress in September had been
unsatisfactory. There had also been a dock strike in which the two
leaders 'appointed by the Communist Party to direct the strike' had
fallen far below the mark, and altogether the British Bureau had failed
to combat effectively the tendencies of the non-party revolutionary
workers to keep their organizations independent of communist
influence.[86] At the highest level Lozovsky recorded 'that before the

opening of this Third Congress the basic line of action had already been marked out by the Fifth Congress of the Comintern.[87]

In practice, the RILU was ultimately subordinate to the Comintern, and its aim was that of the Comintern – the destruction of capitalism, if necessary by violence. On this point Lozovsky was surprisingly frank. Fascism, then in its first stages in Italy, had adopted much from Bolshevism, he explained, in its violent methods, its repudiation of democratic forms, its rapidity of action, and its recognition of the necessity to raze to their foundations the organizational centres of the class to which it was opposed. The difference was that Fascism used these methods to destroy not the bourgeoisie, but the working class: 'it is not the external traits that define this or that movement, but its social basis'.[88] The external traits of the RILU presaged continuous disruption. Always with the aim of revolution in mind, unions must make general 'every local uprising, every local strike, and every small conflict'[89] in order to win concessions from the ruling classes. These guided activities were to be pursued through factory committees and at every level up to national unions – which in the view of the RILU should be industrial unions – and national centres.

In the colonies and semi-colonies, the first task was to establish industrial unions standing on the principle of the class struggle and fighting for trade union rights. The second was to make a systematic effort to place native labour on the same footing, with regard to wages, hours and conditions of work, as workers emigrating from the mother countries – an effort that was much needed throughout the British Empire, though it was not specifically named. At the same time the RILU gave general advice in line with that of the Comintern: colonial workers must take into their own hands the leadership of the peasant masses and of the agrarian revolution which was essential to the emancipation of the colonies; they must participate in the national movements, but not be misled by them; they must not fall prey to racial hatred, which must be replaced by class hatred; and they must recognize the growth of a capitalist class at home which they would have to fight, exposing always the hypocrisies and half-hearted efforts of such movements as Gandhism in India, Kemalism in Turkey, and the Homidan [sic] in China. The revolutionary unions and minority movements in the metropolitan countries, like the communist parties, must help the colonial unions.[90]

In this last task also the British Bureau was failing. In 1924 its connections with the dependencies were reported to be extremely weak and limited to accidental correspondence. In part this was due to the Bureau's general weakness. Though it claimed a circulation of 10,000 for its journal *The Worker*, it was still working only through local branches and trades councils, unrecognized by the headquarters of any national union.[91] However, the failure in the empire was also due to the RILU's allocation of responsibility for all British dependencies to the British Bureau. Whatever effort was made from that quarter, it was undertaken at first remove, and it is difficult to see how, in the absence of representative affiliates in the dependencies themselves, the actual conditions, needs and desires of colonial workers could have been the determining factors in the formation of RILU policies concerning them – but these were not intended to be the determining factors. The foundation of all trade union and communist work in the colonies and in Britain itself was the theoretical analysis made in the Comintern and the RILU. The effect of the theories, methods and structures of both communist internationals was that their propaganda was in a sense an unnatural intrusion into the British labour movement, and even more unnatural in the dependencies.

This did not mean that it could not be attractive to some elements, and its appeal was increased by the provision of funds in quantities that could only be guessed, since its adherents in Britain and elsewhere were able to produce publications and sustain organization at levels which appeared to be beyond the capacity of their membership and circulation returns. In addition, their Russian affiliates were the largest in both bodies and could not be regarded as independent of the Russian state apparatus. Hostile critics of the Comintern and the RILU could reasonably regard them as being subject to government influence, and possibly using government funds. In the occasional exposures of the deployment of 'Moscow gold' in Britain, the channels of distribution varied, but the source could generally only be suspected. In the first scandal concerning the £75,000 in jewellery provided for, and refused by, the *Daily Herald* in 1920, the source was apparently the Soviet Government,[92] and in 1921 the subsidy of £6,000 a year to the Labour Research Department[93] went through the Russian trade delegation.[94] In that year the British Government insisted that the first Anglo-Soviet trade agreement should include a Russian undertaking not to engage in hostile propaganda against the British Empire – especially with regard to activities against the Government of India organized from Tashkent. After allegations that this had not been kept, the trade treaty negotiated by the Labour Government in 1924 again included a promise on both sides to refrain from hostile propaganda and interference in internal affairs. Such provisions assumed an intimate link between the Soviet government and the Comintern, and in handling the affair of the Zinoviev Letter the Foreign Office had no doubt that such a link existed.[95] Whatever its origin, it was known that money came in – for example, the British Government's seizure of documents in 1925 purported to reveal that only about one-seventeenth of the British Communist Party's expenditure came from its members. On the other

hand, the 250,000 roubles sent by the ARCCTU to the TUC for the
general strike in 1926, which the General Council declined, was
collected voluntarily and enthusiastically by Russian workers.[96]

The continuous uproar in the British press about 'Moscow gold' was
so hysterical that a large section of the Labour movement habitually
discounted it. Nevertheless, it was evident that the Communist Party
and the British Bureau of the RILU were systematically trying to build
an opposition to TUC policy amongst its affiliates. In August 1924 it
was co-ordinated in the formal launching of the National Minority
Movement (NMM). Purporting to be an organization of British trade
unionists, this body developed a newspaper, a full-time secretariat, and
an administrative structure with industrial sections and branch
committees, again apparently financed from outside.[97] For a long time
the General Council tolerated it, but its factions were observed at
work at the Bournemouth Congress in 1926, in trades councils, and in
union elections. In 1927 the General Council decided to refuse
recognition to any trades council affiliated to or associated with the
NMM, and such trades councils were to be excluded from participating
in any work carried out under the General Council's auspices.[98]

The memory of these methods persisted long after the NMM and the
RILU had disappeared, and coloured the attitude of the TUC wherever
it met communist influence in the trade unions. Other representative
trade union organizations elsewhere had similar experiences, and it was
partly for this reason that the Comintern and the RILU, although able
to supply financial help and some highly competent and dedicated
advisers, failed to achieve a revolution or to build up or win over a
united trade union movement in any British dependency.

The Widening Breach

When the TUC/Labour Party Joint International Department came to
an end in March 1926, the Labour Party had disbarred the Communist
Party from its electoral platforms. The TUC could not exclude
Communists from its ranks, and had still one more international effort
to make in pursuit of unity. Its industrial work, both domestic and
international, had been kept separate, but in both spheres an
organizational differentiation was taking place between political
tendencies within the wider labour movement, and this could not be
halted as long as the Comintern insisted that all trade union activity
must be politically directed, that it had the right and duty to intervene
in any country, and that the Comintern and the RILU must work in
unison.

The IFTU and the RILU

The IFTU had resumed activities when the Second International was still floundering, and it had a more stable base. Its affiliates had been built from the bottom, where the members were, and were established bodies which were required to pay their dues to the international and to send forward delegates who were resident and organized in the countries that they claimed to represent. Its first objection to the RILU was that its affiliates did not truly represent workers, and that internationally it did not represent trade unions.

This charge was levelled at the heart of the RILU, the Bolshevik-led unions in Russia. At the outbreak of war such unions as did maintain a precarious existence had been driven underground, and it was now said that after the February revolution in 1917 they had had no time to organize themselves fully before they faced the Bolshevik attack.[99] The TUC/Labour Party delegation in 1920 saw the work of destruction nearly completed when they attended, on 23 May, a meeting of some thousands in Moscow led by the Printers' Union, which claimed to have set up the first soviets during their Moscow strike in the 1905 revolution, and whose existence in 1917 Thorne and O'Grady had reported. The 1920 delegation heard allegations that printers' leaders in the principal towns had been arrested, their elected committees dissolved and their union journals suppressed both directly and indirectly by withholding paper supplies, and that their members had been deprived of rations. It was said that the claim of the Communist-controlled unions to represent working men was false, and the Menshevik leader, A. Kefali, told the delegates that all international socialism would have to decide whether the movement would go forward by way of the democracy of working men or by way of transforming the working masses into a scattered human herd subject to benevolent dictators. Three weeks later all the members of the union's administrative council were arrested and its office was occupied by force. This was the end of independent unions.

Delegates also met the executive of the Communist-led ARCCTU, set up in 1918. They were told that the new unions met the workers' desire for organization on an industrial rather than a craft basis, and that membership of these unions was not 'compulsory', but 'obligatory'. The unions joined with the state in social operations, and with the Communist Party, which had at its Ninth Congress (March–April 1920) approved a scheme for compulsory labour service which was considered justified in war conditions. These conditions could not be ignored; nor could the fact that the protests from the independent unions were being voiced by Social Revolutionary and Menshevik leaders, and some of the delegation were sufficiently inspired by the aims of the revolution to minimize the significance of the means. When the report[100] was presented to Congress,[101] Purcell declared

> of all the opportunities that were ever presented to the working classes ... of all occasions on which these opportunities were seized upon and a united effort made to make the most of them, we have the best example in Russia at the present time. ... In eliminating the employers they have done what many trade unionists in this country regard as essential for the future of trade unionism and of the working classes (loud cheers).

Although the TUC's records give no indication that they had any authority from the Parliamentary Committee to do so, or that their actions were reported to the Committee or to Congress, two of the British delegates, Purcell and Robert Williams,[102] joined in the discussions associated with the Second Congress of the Comintern which resulted in the establishment of the International Council of Trade and Industrial Unions. Despite the TUC's affiliation to the IFTU, they expressed themselves in favour of the creation of a new trade union international, though they were not there when the final decision was taken.[103] The manifesto subsequently issued by the International Council to the trade unions of all countries, published in the communist press, included England in the list of countries whose unions had founded the Council.[104] In 1921, when the founding congress of the RILU took place, a British delegation – Tom Mann, N. Watkins and J. T. Murphy[105] – attended, though how these three had been chosen and mandated was not explained, even in the report that Murphy wrote on the Congress. According to the London secretary of the International Council's British Bureau, Harry Pollitt, he personally asked Tom Mann, on his retirement from the Amalgamated Engineering Union (AEU), to attend, and to become the first chairman of the British Section.[106] These were not representative procedures.

Not only were minority groups urged to challenge national centres affiliated to the IFTU, but the international trade secretariats were subject to the activities of international propaganda committees set up for each industry by the RILU's first congress to secure the establishment of single united industrial internationals. With their affiliations from national unions as distinct from national centres, it might have been possible for the secretariats to pursue common industrial issues, or even to allow double affiliation. At their conferences, the metal workers welcomed the Russian revolution but agreed it was impossible to work with communists; the transport workers refused to hear Murphy, who had asked to be allowed to speak to them on behalf of the RILU; the textile workers invited the Russian textile union to be represented, but on receiving no response rejected the credentials of a French delegate who claimed to hold its mandate; the printers refused an actual application for affiliation from the Pan-Russian Typographical Association. The IFTU took a definite decision against double affiliation in May 1921,[107] and its Rome Congress in April 1922 agreed an amendment to rules providing that each national trade union should be affiliated both to its national centre and to the relevant international trade secretariat.[108] Eventually, it was decided at the Vienna Congress in 1924 that the secretariats should have three voting representatives on the IFTU Management Committee.[109] Thus they became more closely tied to the IFTU, but they remained autonomous bodies and retained their freedom of action, unlike the international propaganda committees of the RILU.

The RILU in turn charged the IFTU with being unrepresentative of workers, not because of its structure, but because it did not sufficiently oppose capitalism and imperialism. Besides claiming a representative status for itself, the International Council's manifesto in 1920 referred to the split between trade unions of the belligerent countries during the war, and particularly to the IFTU's collaboration with the 'infamous' ILO – both organizations together serving the interests of the capitalist class. Despite these strictures, the IFTU leaders were astonished at the open letter that the International Council and the ECCI addressed to its 1920 London Congress as 'the World Congress of the Yellow Leaders of the Trade Unions in London'. The signatories included Zinoviev, Lenin and Radek for the ECCI and Lozovsky and Mikhail Tomsky, leader of the ARCCTU, for the International Council. 'You are the watchdogs of capital, barking furiously at all those who approach your master's lair,' the message told them,[110] and

> Pygmies! Just as a tattered handkerchief cannot hide the sun, so your manifestoes, patched together with lies and hypocrisy, cannot vanquish the Communist International ... the sun of the working class ... shining more and more ardently over the entire earth, over all the oppressed and exploited, over all the working masses you have deceived and betrayed ...

In their reply the IFTU Congress declared that they did not believe that the Russian proletariat were responsible for such attacks. They had invited the ARCCTU to send delegates to their founding congress in 1919, but had been rebuffed. In April 1920 they had hoped to send representatives to Russia at the same time as, but independently of, an ILO mission,[111] but the ILO mission was refused entry, and by the time the IFTU London Congress met in November, the independent unions had been suppressed. During 1921 the Kronstadt rising was crushed, in the Russian Communist Party the views of the Workers' Opposition were condemned as an anarcho-syndicalist deviation, and the RILU was set up. Trade unionism on the Bolshevik pattern was now fully established in Russia and as a model for RILU affiliates – actual and potential – elsewhere.

When the expected revolution did not happen and the Comintern sought a new entry to western Europe through a unity conference with the Second International, the RILU made a parallel approach to the IFTU. Its efforts never culminated in an actual meeting, but the IFTU still had some hope of agreement with the ARCCTU, and again invited it to be represented at the Rome Congress in 1922. In January 1923, when the IFTU eventually informed the RILU that there would be no further reply to its appeals, communications or invitations, the letter made it plain that it would consider the affiliation of the ARCCTU if the Russian organization was willing to adhere to the IFTU's constitution.[112]

The TUC General Council were not happy with this decision, or with their own position in the international trade union movement. Since the AFL had not joined the IFTU, and its German affiliate was weakened by the collapse of the German currency under inflation, the TUC was the main contributor to the IFTU's funds. The cost was considerable – in 1921 and 1922 the affiliation fee was the largest single item of expenditure in the accounts submitted to Congress, and this did not include the expenses of delegations and contributions to relief funds. All through 1923 the General Council were discussing the IFTU's finances: they questioned the need for four secretaries, and there was some tart correspondence on the cost of new premises, before they decided to send two of their own members to inquire into the whole administration.[113] It was argued that some way must be found to strengthen British representation in the IFTU and its Management Committee, and as late as 1931 Citrine pointed out that except for the textile workers' international, none of the international trade secretariats had a British secretary or any British official in an important administrative post.[114] Members of the General Council found the approach of their Continental colleagues doctrinaire,[115] and the position was not improved in this respect when Purcell succeeded Margaret Bondfield as chairman of the General Council when she became a minister in 1924, and he followed J. H. Thomas as President of the IFTU. Although he had left the Communist Party, Purcell made no attempt to conceal his distaste for what he regarded as the narrow-minded rigidity of the IFTU or his enthusiasm for the Russian experiment.

When the first Labour Government took office in January 1924, MacDonald intended to work for peace and reconciliation on all fronts. In February, Britain accorded full diplomatic recognition to the Soviet Union, and in April opened negotiations for a trade treaty. The General Council sent the Council of People's Commissars an expression of their 'profound regret' at the death of Lenin in January,[116] and gave wholehearted support to the trade negotiations. Before these were completed, the IFTU's Vienna Congress met in June and considered the Bureau's report on its correspondence with the ARCCTU. There had been little progress towards affiliation, but the British delegation secured the adoption of a congress decision that the consultations should be continued in so far as this was possible without prejudicing the dignity of the IFTU. In reply to further inquiries from Amsterdam, the ARCCTU returned to the proposal for a world labour congress originally put by the RILU, but in this case to be preceded by an exploratory conference, without prior conditions, between the IFTU and the ARCCTU. Bramley supported this proposal in the IFTU General Council at Amsterdam in February 1925, arguing that differences of tradition and the circumstances of each country must be taken into account. He was heavily defeated.[117] At that point a major cause of the British isolation in the IFTU was a new venture that had been set in train at the TUC's Hull Congress in the previous September.

The TUC's Russian Venture

The treaty negotiations had brought four Russian trade union leaders, including Tomsky, to London, and they were in contact with the TUC and well pleased with the British initiative at Vienna. Although the NMM was launched in August, the Russians were invited to Congress and a special meeting with them was arranged at which it was agreed to recommend the incoming General Council to accept a reciprocal invitation to send a delegation to Russia.[118] Congress responded enthusiastically to Tomsky's fraternal speech and empowered the General Council to take steps through the IFTU to bring the different elements in the international movement together.

At Congress Oudegeest, speaking as IFTU fraternal delegate, set out in general terms the conditions that must be fulfilled for affiliation. Every affiliate had its autonomy and freedom of action guaranteed by the IFTU's rules, but none might interfere in the domestic affairs of any other. The international trade union movement could exist only on the basis of democracy, and its policy must be determined by its members. The British movement had the right to criticize the Labour Government, and all IFTU affiliates should have the right to criticize theirs. The British movement was independent of any political party: the IFTU had exactly the same liberty of action, and any national centre that was truly independent could endorse its platform and become affiliated.[119]

There was no evidence that the ARCCTU even wished to meet such conditions. The best course would have been to send an IFTU mission to find out on the spot how far they could be fulfilled, but the Russian invitation was extended to the TUC, not the IFTU. A TUC delegation, led by Purcell and including Bramley and Russian-speaking advisers,[120] arrived in Russia on 11 November 1924 and spent a month there, travelling as far south as Georgia. Much of the responsibility for the worsening in relations with the IFTU that resulted must be attributed to Purcell. He had seen Russia at its low ebb in 1920, and responded to his warm welcome with speeches of such enthusiasm that they drew protests, when reported throughout Europe, from the other affiliates of the IFTU, of which he was, after all, the president. There was also resentment at the news that the delegates had committed themselves to seeking an unconditional conference between the IFTU and the ARCCTU – an agreement which on their part was merely to make such a recommendation to the General Council, but which was trumpeted throughout the international press and presented to the ARCCTU congress with a proposal for the establishment of an Anglo–Russian committee.[121]

The delegation's task was to report on conditions in Russia. They were not asked to find out whether the ARCCTU could meet the IFTU's requirements for affiliation, but these requirements were of interest to the TUC itself. Were the Soviet unions free to differ from the RILU? Did they interfere in the domestic affairs of other movements? Were they in a position to determine their own policy? Had they the right to criticize their own government? If not, could they fully represent their members' views? Were they allowed to elect their own officers? If not, did they truly represent Soviet workers? If not, were these workers free to form other unions of their choice? If so, would such unions be allowed to function? In sum, was the ARCCTU a bona fide trade union organization? If not, could and should the TUC work with it? If so, why? In the atmosphere that developed round the delegation, if such questions were posed, they were insufficiently answered.

Looking broadly at the position of trade unions in Russian society, the mission concluded that the system was a form of state socialism, or state capitalism, in which there was no exploiting ruling class. The unions had retrieved their moral status as workers' organizations when Lenin's new economic policy relieved them of responsibility for managing industry, and employment was now based on free contract and collective bargaining. Unions had representation on all the councils of the Soviet government. Questioned further by Citrine a year later, Tomsky replied, 'It is all one movement; there is no difference ... how can we use the instrument [the state] against ourselves? We are the state', with unions performing functions that in other countries were carried on by state departments, such as looking after all questions of social insurance, unemployment and health.[122] The mission referred to the unions' work in training and education, but they were not specific on such matters as the negotiation of wages and conditions and the representation of workers' grievances. The report[123] expressed the general view that workers now enjoyed 'a new life and a new liberty'. This did not include rights of opposition which were regarded elsewhere as essential to political liberty, but it was suggested that the majority of workers and peasants were reconciled to renouncing them, partly because they had been replaced by other rights of greater value, partly because recent movement had been towards their restoration.

This argument was of special interest to the LSI, which had been set up in the previous year on the basis that its affiliates accepted the independent political and industrial action of workers' organizations as the means of attaining the economic emancipation of workers. It infuriated Adler: in his view the authors of the report still saw the Russian worker or peasant as a slave under the Tsars – 'for them he is still the "native" who can be quite rightly clapped in jail if he is fool enough to dare to yearn for the liberty and the rights of the British citizen', and the same argument for his subjection could be used by imperialist capitalism and by Mussolini, Horthy, and the whole Fascist reaction.[124] Equally distasteful was the report's conclusion on the Social Revolutionary prisoners – not executed despite the 1922 death sentence – whom the delegates had visited in jail. They found them now without a programme or a following, but rejecting release on any condition restricting their freedom of action. The mission advised clemency, but thought that for the 'irreconcilables' exile might be preferable to further confinement.

Although the mission asked for a general amnesty, it was clear that the one-party state was regarded as inevitable, if not acceptable. The exact relationship between the unions and the Communist Party was not analysed – this was scarcely necessary in view of the public pronouncements of the Comintern and the Bolshevik leaders. All the members of the delegation endorsed a section of the report written by one of the advisers, Young, who saw the Party, with its cell in every factory, as a nucleus vitalizing a mass of nonpartisans who apparently contentedly accepted the status of a line regiment from which the best men were continually being drafted into the communist guard.

Acceptance evidently did not extend to Georgia, where there had been a revolt three months before the visit. Both advisers drafted this section of the report. They found that the rebellion had had a genuine appeal to nationalist sentiment and had probably been supported by the majority of Georgians. They rejected the Bolshevik claim that the opposition consisted merely of mountain banditti, Tsarist officers and nobles anxious to regain their land, but they noted that the Georgians were allowed their own language and enjoyed improvements in prosperity, education and land distribution. The rebels were alleged to have expected foreign military support, which had not materialized, and some Mensheviks who had participated urged that the Paris exiles should refrain from further disruptive agitation. The delegates were told that there had been no elections in the Menshevik party since 1918, and no affiliation fees paid to the Socialist International since 1920. Leaders living comfortably in Paris, they concluded, had for the time being killed the Menshevik cause by sacrificing brave followers who had fought with swords and pistols against machine guns. The report did not mention that some of the Georgian Communists had also been in dispute with Moscow.[125]

The delegates recommended that the security apparatus in Georgia should be dissolved and the Red Army withdrawn. They were assured by the authorities that this was largely a question of time, as the area was still an object of foreign intrigue. Since previous history suggested that this was likely to be true, the report concluded that it was in the interests of the workers and peasants of Georgia that the Trans-Caucasian Federation should remain in the USSR. There was no imperialist argument, Adler wrote, which could not be found in this chapter, which was of inestimable value for the imperialist policy of Great Britain itself.

The mission's conclusions were not as foolish or unprincipled as their critics maintained. The population of Transcaucasia was an agglomeration of different communities, often mutually antagonistic; it could not be in their interest to be exposed by their own weakness to outside attack, or to sink into anarchy. The delegates believed that more liberty would come as more peaceful conditions developed, and if in the meantime restrictions were necessary to protect the people from external and internal threats, then, as Adler rightly pointed out, they were accustomed to that in the British dependencies. They did not, it appears, stop to reflect that the Bolsheviks did not pretend to approve of nationalism, and supported nationalist movements even in capitalist empires only as a tactic. In this respect, their whole inquiry in Georgia was irrelevant to the Soviet purpose – but it should not have been irrelevant to their own support for self-determination as a principle. The problems to be solved in British territories would not be less difficult than those in Georgia, and they should at least have tried to draw some lessons from the Russian experience, if indeed there were any to be drawn. And they should have gone to Tashkent. But it is obvious that in 1924 the colonial problem was not uppermost in their minds.

The most important question was the practice of trade unionism in Russia. The delegates had seen improvement since 1920, had found no competent opposition to the Bolsheviks, legal or illegal, and had been assured that relaxation of restrictions was contemplated for the future. The whole apparatus of Bolshevism was new to them – and to everybody else – and they had evidently not understood its continuing force, or the one phenomenon that was totally outside their experience, and of which Bertrand Russell had given warning after his visit in 1920. Bolshevism, he wrote, was not merely a political doctrine, but a religion equipped with dogmas and inspired scriptures; a great part of the Bolshevik despotism was inherent in its social philosophy, and would have to be reproduced in some form wherever that philosophy became dominant.[126] Citrine sensed the same danger in 1925 when he produced a stunned silence amongst his hosts by remarking, in response to constant appeals to Lenin's authority, that Lenin was not Jesus Christ.[127]

Citrine had travelled back to Russia with Tomsky after Tomsky's second visit to Congress in September 1925. Perhaps his most valuable experience lay in their discussions on the long train journey, for his tour was cut short by Bramley's death. Much more level-headed than Purcell, he was still optimistic. On his second visit in 1935, when he found Tomsky in a minor job, he recorded only 'doubts' about whether the dictatorship would prove to be temporary.[128] Yet within two years the leaders of the Comintern were led to their deaths and Tomsky was driven to suicide. In 1924, no-one could possibly have foreseen this.

At that time the TUC was seeking some accommodation with the ARCCTU. This could not be achieved by a frontal attack on the whole Soviet system. If there was any potential common ground, it was the delegates' business to find it in the trade union movement. That differed from their own, but trade unions existed, they had important functions and responsibilities, and their members were workers. Not only they, but the General Council, expected a genuine dialogue with the Russians, to the point that in May 1925 an editorial in *Labour Magazine* argued that their participation in the international movement might modify the principles and practice of Bolshevism, and that the TUC should not be distracted by the imbecilities of Zinoviev and Lozovsky. In March 1926, in an article on the Russian unions and their relationship with the Communist Party, it was noted that Tomsky himself was not satisfied with their existing situation.[129]

On the mission's return, Purcell defended himself at the IFTU's General Council meeting in February 1925, and he and Bramley argued that the possibility of bringing in new members should induce a less rigorous and exclusive attitude on the part of the IFTU. Their proposal

that at least an informal conference with the ARCCTU should be held
was voted down. In December the TUC tried again, but the IFTU
General Council decided finally that before any further steps were
taken the ARCCTU must make a formal application for affiliation.[130]
The ARCCTU did not do so, and the trade union internationals
continued on their separate ways.

The TUC's relations with the IFTU did not improve until after its
Paris Congress in 1927, at which Purcell was not re-elected president,
Oudegeest resigned, and John Sassenbach became the sole secretary.
After a short interval Citrine was elected in Purcell's place, and
remained to face the same problem of relations with the Russians in
1936 and 1939. It was not resolved before the outbreak of the Second
World War.

The Anglo–Russian Joint Advisory Council

Meanwhile the Anglo–Russian Joint Advisory Council was set up to
exchange information and develop contacts for the purpose of
promoting international unity. It held its first meeting when Tomsky
attended Congress in 1925, and it was decided that the General
Council and the ARCCTU should be recognized as the sole medium of
expression on international trade union unity in Great Britain and in
the USSR, respectively. Thus the Russians went over the heads of the
NMM and the British Communist Party. The committee met again on
8–9 December 1925, immediately after the IFTU General Council had
refused to hold any talks until the ARCCTU had applied for affiliation.
After this, since the ARCCTU did not apply, the main purpose of the
committee was already unattainable.

However, it would still have been possible to promote understanding and to identify points of common interest. The committee
met again on 30 July 1926, after the British general strike, on 25 August
1926, and on 30 March 1927. At this March meeting both sides agreed
on an additional provision which excluded intervention in domestic
affairs and acknowledged that the fraternal alliance must not impair the
internal authority of the TUC and the ARCCTU. The Russians did not
keep this agreement. On 18–19 June 1927 the chairmen and secretaries
of the two organizations met for the last time before the TUC's
Edinburgh Congress in September decided that no useful purpose
would be served by continuing negotiations with the ARCCTU as long
as their existing attitude and policy were sustained.[131]

The actions to which the TUC objected were essentially attempts to
intervene between the General Council and its affiliates and between
the General Council and Congress, particularly by the publication in
Russia and in the British Communist press, and directly to Congress, of
continuous criticisms of the General Council as a whole and of

individual members. These began in June 1926 with a bitter public attack on the general strike as conducted by the General Council – in the Russian view, it should have become a revolution, and the General Council's rejection of their offer of financial support was resented. In September there were no Russian fraternal delegates at Congress, since the Conservative government refused them entry to the country. Instead the ARCCTU sent a telegram to Congress in the guise of a fraternal messge. This reiterated the previous attacks. These persisted in 1927 after the March agreement, with the (false) allegation that the TUC had done nothing to protest when the British authorities raided and closed the offices of the Soviet Trade Delegation and the All-Russian Co-operative Society (ARCOS). They continued till the eve of Congress.[132] All were couched in language which the TUC, like the IFTU, found intolerable, and they were supported by the activities of the NMM.

The ARCCTU had applied the tactics of the RILU and the Comintern, and had indeed consulted both bodies before issuing their statement on the general strike, as Stalin explained when the British Communist Party complained tht it had not been informed.[133] In the end, except for the question of trade, and its possible effect on employment,[134] no one had identified a specific trade union issue on which the TUC and the ARCCTU might usefully have co-operated after the battle for international trade union unity had been lost.

The TUC had found their movement distracted and confused, yet Citrine was glad that the attempt had been made.[135] There was some disappointment also in the Comintern, where some had hoped that the Advisory Council would pave the way to co-operation with the millions of workers who were outside the Comintern and the RILU. There is evidence, however, that if Tomsky intended this, some of his superiors did not.[136] From their stand-point the TUC was an unreliable channel for the export of their own views, and no two-way traffic in ideas was contemplated. Despite Tomsky's friendliness and his frequent tributes to the TUC's long experience, it really counted for nothing with the Bolsheviks.

The end of the road was reached when the 1927 Congress brought the Anglo–Russian Joint Advisory Council to an end and endorsed the General Council's decision to exclude trades councils which associated with the NMM from the work of the TUC. Both internationally and at home, the breach was complete.

The Political Background

In their decisions on internal reorganization and on their international relationships, the TUC and the Labour Party had finally determined

the character of their own movements. They had faced the greatest
revolution of the century, had tried to come to terms with it, and had
then fallen back on the basic principles of democracy in the form of
parliamentary government and civil liberty with independent trade
unionism as the channel through which workers' needs might be met.
The experience had left them divided from the quasi-revolutionary
elements which had previously been associated with the British Labour
endeavour, and which now had to stand on their own. The same
clarification had taken place in the political and trade union
internationals.

In the joint Commonwealth Labour Conference and their mission to
the West Indies, the TUC and the Labour Party had also seen the
expression of the second great change in the world pattern – the
movement towards independence in the empires of Britain and its
former Allies. With this they were in sympathy, but had to take
decisions within a different relationship. In this case they were not
dealing with organizations of equal status, as the TUC and the
ARCCTU had been. The Labour Party was required to make decisions
in Parliament and in government which could be imposed, and the
TUC, though less obviously, was also part of the social structure of the
imperial power. The Commonwealth Labour Conference had chosen
the right title for its questionnaire on 'the Subject Peoples' – these
peoples *were* subject, and in regard to their future the TUC and the
Labour Party had hardly progressed beyond the formulation of general
principles. The Indian challenge at the Commonwealth Labour
Conference had exposed the need for a ruthless analysis of purpose and
possibilities.

But there was no *tabula rasa* on which the conclusions could be
written, nor could the TUC and the Labour Party write them alone.
Russia claimed international leadership and offered a model of
revolutionary practice in every country into which the Comintern and
the RILU could penetrate, as they did with some success in Asia. Of
greater importance, in India, was the powerful indigenous nationalist
movement, and the growth within it of a new challenge to British
authority which, while totally different in character from the Russian,
was equally revolutionary. India was the key to the whole British
dependent empire, the first country in which theories concerning
constitutional progress towards democracy and independence would
have to be put into practice – that is to say, proved in day-to-day
decisions which would have immediate consequences and which would
determine the relationships of the participants.

During the period of joint working the TUC and the Labour Party
were involved in such decisions, and after 1926 they continued to
co-operate.

The TUC's concern was with trade unionism rather than nationalism, but it was committed to democracy if only because, as Russia had shown, the political climate in which trade unions had to grow could be decisive for them. Thus the political decisions taken on domestic, international and imperial matters could not be separated from decisions directly affecting the unions as industrial organizations. Together they represented a common effort to build new institutions and new relationships in a changing empire in which workers would have their legitimate place.

4 Co-operation with the Labour Party: Application of Policy

The Subject Peoples

In settling their domestic and international relationships in the period from 1918 to the end of 1927, the TUC and the Labour Party were acting within the broader Labour movement which they had known for a generation. When they took decisions about the dependencies they were concerned with territories in which they had no natural allies, for there were no labour parties and such unions as existed were in their infancy. They had given their support to the principle of self-determination and were now taking part in its implementation in practice. This process had followed a familiar path in the 'white' Dominions, but elsewhere the way was yet to be charted. A start had been made in India, but there nationalism was the strongest developing political force. The problems of coming to terms with that in Ireland had been encountered in Britain for over a century and were at the time being experienced in one of the most bitter of the conflicts that continually beset that unhappy country. This was an experience that no one wanted to repeat.

In the intellectual climate of the day nationalism was not accepted as wholly beneficial – it was thought that one cause of the war had been its excesses in Europe, and support for the new League of Nations was seen as a move towards curbing them. Moreover, nationalism was not socialism. The briefs prepared for Berne had specifically ruled out reliance on the middle class nationalist movements of India and Egypt. For a working-class party, an Indian mill-owner in Bombay or Ahmedabad was not inherently better than a British company in Madras or in Lancashire, and Purcell was expressing a widely-shared view when he told Congress in 1924 that he was not prepared merely to accept the demands of educated Indians who aired their political grievances in Britain, because they came mainly from the employing, merchant and professional classes which could not be trusted to give their own workers a square deal, and therefore India must not be handed over to 'mere politicians'.[1] Self-determination could not be interpreted as a simple acceptance of demands: there were two sides to the political relationship, and when TUC representatives examined a colonial situation in which they had no self-interest, in Georgia, they almost instinctively placed the nationalist claims in the context of the whole Soviet Union, just as Webb had envisaged a future Britannic Alliance in which all progressive forces would work together. Finally, self-determination required the consideration of methods, for it was seen as the end of a process of developing parliamentary democracy in each territory, in which social reform would give reality to freedom and equality in the new nation whose status was to be determined. This was the future that Roberts glimpsed for the West Indies – the British Labour approach proved to be consistent wherever the colonial problem arose.

However, this approach was not compatible with, for example, Chaman Lall's insistence at the 1925 Commonwealth Labour Conference that India must be excluded from the discussion on subject peoples, with the implication that all that was required was a declaration in support of immediate independence. Nor did it do justice to the positive element in his demand. There had always been forces of social regeneration within the Indian national movement, evidenced in the remarkable tradition of social service which extended beyond the political leaders, and this was true in some degree of nearly all the nationalist movements which emerged in British territories. It could also be argued that although the British government and the various colonial and Indian authorities under their direction saw their administration – sometimes justifiably – as protective and progressive, it was often an actual obstruction to social reform, engendering inertia by the mere fact of dependence, or by acting in support of reaction as exemplified by the Indian Princes, or through sheer neglect, as in the West Indies.

Yet the administration was, for the Labour Party, the instrument of change most ready to hand, though a weak one. It could be influenced even if Labour was in opposition, with the limitation that every statement was regarded as a pledge to be implemented when the party was next in power. When the first Labour Government took office on 22 January 1924, it commanded 191 seats in the House of Commons, and could face the opposition of 259 Conservatives only with the support of 159 Liberals. Few of its members, from the Prime Minister downwards, had ever held office before, and the whole country was familiar with the gibe that Labour was not fit to govern. It survived for only nine months, and although MacDonald was able to form a second government in 1929, real power was not achieved until 1945.

Thus experience during these twilight years brought home to the Labour Party and to the TUC the complex nature of the processes by which self-government might be attained in the dependencies, but it did not allow them to act in a manner which would gain recognition of their ultimate aims. Though these were broadly in harmony with the principal nationalist objective – the removal of alien rule – and though they might hope to work in co-operation with nationalist politicians, it remained to be seen whether the leaders would be prepared to work with them. The crucial test was in India. Here they did begin to define their attitude towards nationalist movements, but they failed to evoke a comparable response.

India: Non-Co-operation

The institutional foundations of responsible government were laid by the Government of India Act 1919, based on the recommendations of the Montagu-Chelmsford Report. It established a system of 'dyarchy' in the British Indian Provinces by which 'transferred' subjects were to be handled by ministers responsible to legislatures with elected majorities, while other subjects, including finance and law and order, were reserved to the Governors. At the centre, there were no ministers, but only an Executive Council firmly under official control. Both houses of the central legislature had elected majorities, but these were balanced by the Governor-General's reserve powers for the enactment of essential legislation. The princely states, scattered throughout India, remained without any elections at all, and with power to restrain their rulers vested entirely in the Governor-General in his capacity as Crown Representative.

The provisions posed many problems for the nationalists. If they won seats on the narrow franchise available, would they be able to achieve anything useful in the legislatures? There were nominated seats for labour in some of the provinces and at the centre, but would the nominees be merely placemen for the Governors and the Governor-General? If elected members became provincial ministers, would they incur public odium for the Governors' administration of finance and law and order, and would those who entered the central Executive Council be merely puppets? If these limitations were accepted, for how long would they continue? The Preamble to the Act repeated the Montagu Declaration of 1917 that the policy of Parliament was

> to provide for the increasing association of Indians in every branch of Indian administration and for the gradual development of self-governing institutions, with a view to the progressive realization of responsible government in British India as an integral part of the Empire.

After ten years a Statutory Commission was to be appointed to inquire into the working of the system and to report on

> whether and to what extent it is desirable to establish the principle of responsible government, or to extend, modify or restrict the degree of responsible government then existing therein ...

The Preamble also declared that the time and manner of each successive stage of further progress would be determined by Parliament, on whom lay the responsibility for the welfare and advancement of the Indian peoples. If Indian politicians could stomach this last humiliating assertion, it was manifest that what Parliament gave it could also take away, and that it might give no more.

According to their reactions to the Montagu-Chelmsford Report, some of the different groups which had previously worked under the umbrella of the Indian National Congress began to hive off from it, beginning with the Liberals. In 1918 the National Congress itself demanded a statutory guarantee that full responsible government would be established within 15 years. The eminent lawyers in all the groups involved must have known that Parliament could not be bound in advance, but this obstacle might have been overcome if the Act had been less restrictive and if it had got off to a quick start. However, it was passed in December 1919 in all the turmoil of the aftermath of the war, and after the events of that year had destroyed confidence.

Non-Co-operation

The first came in March with the enactment, against the opposition of all the unofficial Indian members of the unreformed central legislature, of public safety legislation to be operated in emergency in areas to be designated. The agitation against it brought M. K. Gandhi into the political arena, using methods of non-co-operation which he had begun to develop in South Africa, and which proved to be unique.

Gandhi's *satyagraha*, embodying 'firmness' and 'truth', aimed at substituting self-respect for the regime's psychological dominance of the people by non-violent but determined opposition to injustice, demonstrated by some simple public act of law-breaking. His campaign was launched in Bombay in April, with the sale of two innocuous but proscribed books, and with protest meetings. Since the police turned a blind eye to the books and Gandhi himself led the demonstration, there was no disturbance, but in this as in all the other civil disobedience campaigns which followed, a traditional form of protest was also used – the *hartal* or complete suspension of business, to be observed with fasting and prayer. A *hartal* could become, or include, a strike, and its use had an effect on the Government of India's attitude to trade union activity. It could also become violent, and on this occasion the mill-workers in Ahmedabad went on strike, an attempt was made to take up railway lines, and a government officer was murdered. Gandhi admitted to a 'Himalayan miscalculation' in calling upon people to disobey unjust laws before they had fitted themselves to do so by first obeying the just laws of society and disciplining themselves to nonviolence.[2]

The second decisive event occurred on 13 April in Amritsar, when after a ban on public meetings following a *hartal* and riots in which five Europeans were murdered, a gathering in an enclosed area, the Jallianwala Bagh, was dispersed by troops firing without warning. Martial law was declared and continued into June; no public inquiry was appointed until October. Even then the December session of the Indian National Congress decided to work the machinery provided by the new Act, unsatisfactory though it was, in order to secure responsible government.

However, the National Congress had appointed its own inquiry, which began to uncover evidence which was by any normal standards incredible. Its report was published in March 1920, and though the government claimed that it was exaggerated, naturally it influenced opinion. The report of the official Hunter Commission, which followed in May, had to be accepted. It established, *inter alia*, that 379 people had been killed in the Jallianwala Bagh and that 1200 wounded had been left without assistance where they fell.[3]

At the same time it became known that the peace treaty offered to Turkey dismembered the Turkish empire. This fuelled the Khilafat movement amongst Muslims who had anticipated the disruption of their religious hierarchy by the Sultan's defeat. In the belief that the Muslims had been betrayed, Gandhi launched a new non-co-operation movement in alliance with the Khilafat leaders. At a special session of the National Congress in September 1920 the Congress leaders threw their weight behind his campaign, with the aims extended to include the attainment of *Swaraj* – self-rule – and the methods extended to include the surrender of titles and honorary offices and the boycott of foreign cloth, government schools and colleges, law courts, and the impending elections to the reformed legislatures. In December the regular session of the Congress endorsed the decision and adopted new rules, drawn up by Gandhi, which greatly improved the organization and declared the aim of Congress to be *Swaraj*, to be obtained by 'peaceful and legitimate' means, not – as formerly – by 'constitutional' means.

The full Congress-backed campaign came to fruition on 17 November 1921, the day the Prince of Wales landed in Bombay for a tour of India. A riot greeted his arrival, which was followed as he went round the country with *hartals*, the burning of imported cloth, and silent streets. The various boycotts took place, and in some rural areas no-tax campaigns were conducted. On 8 February 1922, at the village of Chauri Chaura, 21 policemen were hacked to death and thrown into their burning police station. Gandhi forthwith called off the disobedience movement and instructed his followers to concentrate on constructive work.[4] On 18 March, the day on which the Prince left India, Gandhi went to gaol with a six-year sentence for sedition.

The Labour Response

After Chauri Chaura the National Joint Council representing the TUC General Council, the Labour Party Executive and the Parliamentary Labour Party issued a policy statement,[5] emphasizing that the antagonisms growing in India could be disastrous for the future relations of the Indian and British peoples.

They had first to form an opinion on non-co-operation. One powerful factor, which was always present in the many upheavals that occurred in India and in the colonies, was the British Government's continuous defence and explanations of its policies and actions in Parliament. Governments always had information which was inaccessible to others, and their views could be challenged, but could never be wholly counteracted or wholly rejected. A non-co-operation movement against elections ran counter to all the British Labour leaders' instincts, and threatened all future plans for the development of responsible government in India, including those which a Labour government would have to make. Non-co-operation might be condoned only if it clearly represented the overwhelming will of the Indian people. This campaign did not do so. The National Congress boycott of the elections held in November 1920 had not deterred non-Congress candidates from standing, about one third of the electorate voted, and Indians accepted office in the provinces and at the centre. In the new legislatures which met in January 1921 the National Congress was unrepresented, but there had been no constitutional breakdown.

It was true that the total electorate was only 6 million, but it was the educated political classes which had demanded responsible government in the first place. Did the National Congress now represent them? The Liberals and Moderates did not attend its session in December 1919; at the special session in September 1920 the Punjab Arya Samajist leader, Lala Lajpat Rai, who was the first president of the AITUC, advised against non-co-operation, as did C. R. Das and the Muslim leader, M. A. Jinnah, who left the National Congress. The Servants of India Society, in which Joshi was prominent, was opposed. So was Mrs Besant: she did not go to the Nagpur session in December 1920, denounced Gandhi's methods as mad and dangerous, and ceased to call him 'Mahatma'.[6] C. R. Das accepted the decision to back the non-co-operation movement, but Lajpat Rai remained privately unconvinced.[7] Moreover, this session adopted the new rules, which axed the overseas branches, including the British Committee of the Indian National Congress, of which the ILP leader, Fenner Brockway, had become joint secretary.[8] This direct link between the Congress and the Labour Party disappeared.

Mrs Besant's link continued. During the war she had been in touch with George Lansbury, who was president of the British Division of her Home Rule League, then associated with the National Congress, and Philip Snowden contributed to her Madras newspaper, *New India*. She rejoined the Labour Party with acclaim at the Southport Conference during her visit in 1919, and in the Parliamentary Labour Party the views of her Theosophist colleagues, John Scurr, Colonel Josiah Wedgwood,[9] Major Graham Pole, and later Dr Haden Guest, carried considerable weight, and Wedgwood and Pole served on the TUC/Labour Party joint committees. Thus the extent to which Mrs Besant's attitude was losing her support in India was unlikely to be fully understood in London.

The National Joint Council's statement of 21 February 1922 recognized that law and order must be maintained in India, but deplored the political arrests and 'no less the action of the Non-Cooperators in boycotting those Parliamentary institutions recently conferred upon India, by means of which grievances should be ventilated and wrongs redressed'. It urged Indian democrats and the Government of India to join in a conference, reflecting all shades of political thought, to consider the possibilities of peace based on an amnesty, the dropping of non-co-operation, a time-limit on the transition stages of partial self-government, and fresh elections, at least to the Legislative Assembly.

These constructive suggestions were ignored. No elections were held until December 1923, after the assemblies had completed their allotted term. With Gandhi in gaol, the Swarajist group in the National Congress, led by C. R. Das and Motilal Nehru, contested with considerable success both at the centre and in the provinces. But they did so with the intention of exposing the limitations of the constitution, and succeeded in doing this at the centre by voting down the budget, which was duly certified as essential legislation and enacted by the Viceroy. The idea of a conference bringing different groups together was echoed in a different form by a Central Legislative Assembly resolution demanding a round table conference to settle the terms of Indian freedom, but the Government of India did not respond until the next Viceroy, Lord Irwin, announced the British Government's decision to call a round table conference in his statement of 31 October 1929, when the second Labour government was in office.

The National Joint Council statement also asserted that it was the settled policy of Great Britain, under the Government of India Act 1919, to place India as soon as may be in the position of a self-governing Dominion. This particular interpretation of the Montagu Declaration was not universally shared, but the Labour Party never wavered from it. Was 'the progressive realization of responsible government' a pledge of Dominion status? The 1919 Act did not say so. In 1929 the Irwin Declaration stated that it was implicit in the Montagu Declaration that Dominion status was 'the natural issue of India's constitutional progress'. This was vigorously attacked in Parliament although it was formally expressed in the Viceroy's Instrument of Instructions from the King.[10] The Labour Party's commitment on this point was important, but it was not certain what exactly Dominion status implied until the Imperial Conference of 1926 described Great Britain and the Dominions as united in their common allegiance to the Crown, and as equal in status and in no way subordinate one to the other in any aspect of their domestic or external affairs. It was acknowledged that some legal, administrative and conventional adaptations would be necessary to secure this position in the various countries, and these remained to be determined in succeeding committees and conferences in 1929 and 1930 and finally enacted in the Statute of Westminster 1931.[11] So there was still plenty of scope for nationalist doubts in 1922.

These doubts also attached to the Labour Party. Even if its interpretation of the Montagu Declaration was correct, what was meant by 'as soon as may be'? What was clear was that the National Joint Council had condemned non-co-operation, and had thus distanced itself from what proved to be the mainstream of Indian nationalism.

The First Labour Government

By setting their sights on parliamentary democratic institutions, the Labour Party and the TUC in effect required the solution of the problems involved in creating them before power was transferred. The nationalist leaders also thought in terms of parliamentary democracy, but within a time-scale that did not allow for the difficulties inherent in devising a constitution on the scale of India, far less for the development of the social and economic conditions required to support it. The Swarajist method of using the legislatures as tactical instruments rather than as embryo parliaments was a negative, and ultimately sterile, form of protest.

Gandhi's approach was quite different. His demand for the removal of the imperial power was essentially a claim that its existence prevented Indians from learning to solve their problems for themselves. Before going to prison he had expressly stressed the need for constructive work – by which he meant work against untouchability and for Hindu–Muslim unity, and particularly work in his campaign amongst the peasants for domestic spinning and weaving, to build self-confidence by increasing income and reducing indebtedness. To him the towns were of secondary importance, but he also engaged in trade union activity, aimed at the evolution of labour leadership from self-reliant workers' organizations. Such activities were not intended to have an immediate political aspect: as he expressed it, a nonpolitical cause was helped by being kept within its nonpolitical limits.[12] But there would be political effects. As he said of his trade union work, 'Its direct aim is not in the least degree political. Its direct aim is internal reform and evolution of internal strength. The indirect result of this evolution when, if ever, it becomes complete, will naturally be tremendously political'.[13] There could scarcely have been an expression of view more consonant with the long-term aims of the British Labour movement.

The first Labour government took office at what was perhaps the last point at which it might have been possible to marry this attempt to make the Indian people fit for *Swaraj* with political advance in a joint effort. On 5 February 1924 Gandhi was released, four years before the expiry of his sentence. Though there were those in the National Congress who resented his preoccupation with what they saw as minor nonpolitical issues,[14] they did not prevail at the Belgaum session in December. Gandhi presided, and all the emphasis was on the constructive programme. There were some outbreaks of communal tension and of terrorism in Bengal, and the Government of India discerned the hand of the Comintern in an alleged revolutionary conspiracy for which four communists, and the Comintern representative M. N. Roy in his absence in Europe, were tried at Cawnpore in March. However, there was no prospect of civil disobedience, and overall India was quiet enough to justify a major political initiative to secure co-operation in the legislatures. It did not come.

In May the Government of India appointed a Reforms Inquiry Committee under Sir Alexander Muddiman, but this was primarily concerned with administrative imperfections revealed in the working of the 1919 Act. Its terms of reference did not satisfy the Swarajists. Nor did they satisfy the Labour Party Executive and the General Council. The newly formed Imperial Questions Sub-Committee of the Joint International Committee took up the Indian question with a will, and a joint deputation from the Labour Party and the TUC was sent to put their proposals to the Labour Secretary of State, Lord Olivier. They had their first meeting on 25 July, when Mr (later Sir) Atul Chatterji, Member of the Viceroy's Council responsible for Industries and Labour, was present. The TUC representatives asked for trade union legislation and raised a series of industrial issues, of which the most important was a request for a full-scale government inquiry into the economic conditions of labour and industry. At the second, on 31 July, the Labour Party spokesmen asked Olivier to make a definite statement that the British Government itself intended to send a commission to India to examine the breakdown of the political reforms.[15] Neither proposal had been implemented before Parliament was dissolved on 9 October, and on 6 November Lord Birkenhead became Secretary of State for India in the new Conservative government.

The Muddiman Reports

When the Muddiman Committee reported in 1925, the Imperial Questions Joint Advisory Committee was in the middle of mapping out a new policy and had reached four main decisions. The most important was that the aim of Labour policy must be full Dominion status as soon as possible. Meanwhile, the Indian members of the Viceroy's Executive Council should be chosen from the elected members of the Central Legislative Assembly, further powers should be transferred from the centre to the provinces, and in the provinces the franchise should be extended to town workers and the peasants and the governments should be made fully responsible to the legislatures.[16]

This policy was changed when two reports came from the Muddiman Committee. The majority (including two Indian members) considered that their terms of reference precluded suggestions for any fundamental change, but the minority of four Indians, including the Liberal leader, Sir Tej Bahadur Sapru, concluded that dyarchy had proved to be intrinsically unworkable. The Joint Advisory Committee recommended that the Labour Party should support the minority report and call for the immediate appointment of the statutory review commission due, under the 1919 Act, in 1929. The Joint Executives accepted their proposal.[17]

Birkenhead had from the first profoundly mistrusted the Montagu–Chelmsford policy, and upheld the rejection of dyarchy in July. But instead of announcing the statutory commission, he challenged the nationalists to produce a constitution which would carry a fair measure of general agreement in India and which could be considered by the Government of India, by himself, and by the statutory commission 'whenever that body may be assembled'.[18]

At the Labour Party Conference in October 1925, the Executive seized on Birkenhead's statement. The National Congress leaders had not produced a constitution, but were organizing a 'national demand' for a round table conference which would draw one up on the basis of full Dominion status. Mrs Besant, who rejoined the National Congress at its Belgaum session in December 1924, had prepared a draft Commonwealth of India Bill for Dominion Home Rule. This Bill in its final form had been drafted by Henderson's son and it had been taken into account when the Joint Advisory Committee prepared its recommendations for the Joint Executives. Gandhi did not approve it because it recognized the King-Emperor as Sovereign, and the National Congress leaders did not attend a conference which Mrs Besant called in April. The conference mandated her to take the Bill to the Labour Party, and she had been lobbying in its support before the party conference began.[19] With no other constitutional proposals to hand, the party executive presented a resolution, moved by Lansbury and embodying amendments proposed by the ILP, which asked the Secretary of State to examine the Commonwealth of India Bill and any other proposals that might be submitted, and to call a conference of representatives of the various Indian parties with a view to the immediate application of a constitution in accordance with the wishes of the Indian people. Since this resolution did not mention the statutory commission, it was compatible with the 'national demand', and it also expressed the view that the British government should co-operate with the Indian people to achieve full self-government and self-determination.[20] There had been no move forward by December, when Lansbury introduced the Commonwealth of India Bill in the Commons as a private Member's Bill, backed by Scurr, Wedgwood and Haden Guest. It had its first reading, and died.

The Labour Party's attempt to please everybody overlooked one issue which should have received more attention. Since the franchise instituted by the Montagu–Chelmsford Reforms was so limited, the need for labour representation had been recognized by the provision of five special seats in the provincial legislatures and one at the centre, which Joshi held from 1920 to 1947. Since Parliament had not followed the recommendation of the Joint Select Committee which had previously examined the subject – that some form of election to these seats should be devised – the six labour representatives were nominated. On Wadia's motion, the first inaugural session of the AITUC called for election,[21] on the same principle as had been adopted for the greater number of special representatives of industry and commerce, who were effectively chosen by trade associations and chambers of commerce. There was an inherent difficulty in establishing union constituencies, since until 1926 there was no legislation providing for unions to register their membership and rules, and in 1920 it was feasible to argue that the unions did not represent the majority of Indian workers. However, they were the only bodies in existence that had any claim to do so, and the choice of representatives could have offered scope for educating union members, offering them a voice in a new field of activity, and extending organization. Representation of special interests in the legislatures – whether accompanied by separate electorates as in the case of the Muslims, or whether filled by nomination – was a barrier to the attainment of majorities by political parties trying to organize across the board, and the National Congress was opposed to it. A different remedy for under-representation was a general extension of the franchise, and the central Legislative Assembly asked for a wider franchise but rejected the introduction of election to the special seats. At the Labour Party Conference in 1925, when Brockway gave the terms of the Assembly's resolution, nobody pointed out that if the widest possible franchise were not conceded, the unions would be left with nominees.

In the central Legislative Assembly debate on the Muddiman Report, Joshi demanded the vote for every adult, man or woman.[22] There was no likelihood that this would be granted, and a wider franchise would not necessarily meet the same need as special seats. One certainty was that Indian labour needed a stronger voice, especially at the centre where labour legislation was enacted. Joshi was alone there until the Swarajists fought the 1923 elections and the trade union leaders Chaman Lall and V. V. Giri[23] were elected. Even then many of the upper-class nationalists were still ignorant of workers' needs, and Joshi attributed the failure of his Maternity Benefit Bill, which was defeated by four votes in 1925, to the indifference of Motilal Nehru. A very wide extension of the franchise would have given the politicians an incentive to seek workers' votes, but they were more than likely to place nationalist demands first. Alternatively, a Labour party could have been formed, but the unions and the AITUC had no funds for such a venture. Nor, in Joshi's view, was it desirable for them to try, since politicians who were united in their ultimate aim were still divided in their attitude to the legislatures, and would carry their divisions with them into a Labour party.[24] In other words, the politicians could, if they tried, utilize such industrial strength as the unions could contribute, but it was insufficient to bring much electoral weight to bear on them.

In such circumstances, the Muddiman Report's proposal for an increase in the number of labour seats had merit, as was recognized by the AITUC, which asked for the nomination of its own chairman, Chandrika Prasad, to the central Council of State, where there was no labour representation at all; it also asked for twelve representatives in the central Assembly to be chosen by the AITUC, and for seventy-six members in the provincial councils to be chosen by the AITUC's provincial committees.[25] But the Report proposed that nomination should be continued.

The Labour Party and the TUC had missed an opportunity here.

There was at the time no regular exchange of information with the AITUC, and although the Joint Advisory Committee knew of the AITUC's 1920 decision,[26] it was apparently given insufficient weight when they prepared their recommendations to the Joint Executives, stressing the need for an extension of the franchise, and the Labour Party Conference preferred the nationalist demand. Eventually the Government of India provided four more nominated labour seats in the provinces, but still left only one at the centre. The franchise became a matter for the future statutory review of the constitution and the issue of labour seats was left over, to be dealt with eventually by the Royal Commission on Labour in 1929, by the Round Table Conferences and by the Government of India Act 1935.

The Simon Commission

As early as December 1925 Birkenhead decided to bring forward the statutory review, fearing that if Labour won the next general election, its appointment would be transferred into their hands.[27] He agreed with Lord Irwin, who arrived as Viceroy in April 1926, that since it would be impossible to appoint representatives of all opinions, no Indians should be included. It was envisaged that when the commission of inquiry had reported, a draft Bill based on its recommendations should be discussed between a Select Committee of both Houses of the Indian central legislature and a Joint Select Committee of both Houses of Parliament.[28]

While their private correspondence continued, patience was wearing thin in India. The Swarajists formally withdrew from the legislatures in March 1926, precipitating the formation of a new non-Congress alliance to work for *Swaraj* by all constitutional means and to reject civil disobedience. Mrs Besant and Joshi, who was a Liberal, joined its executive committee.[29] This group was doing what the Labour Party and the TUC had suggested in 1922, but in 1926 it could not survive without a clear signal from the government that constitutional means would yield results. There was still a gap between the Labour leadership and the Indian National Congress. Jawaharlal visited Britain in 1926 and Motilal Nehru in 1927, but though Motilal sent a friendly message to the TUC's Congress in 1926[30] and Jawaharlal, on a visit to Derbyshire, was moved by the plight of the striking miners,[31] apparently neither of them considered actually visiting the TUC. In 1927 the Labour Party Conference declared that the statutory commission should be so constituted, and its method of work so arranged, that it would enjoy the confidence and co-operation of the Indian people.[32]

In November the Commission, under Sir John Simon, was announced. As a parliamentary inquiry, it had no Indian members, but provision was made for the central and provincial legislatures to elect representative committees to co-operate with it. Two members were appointed from each of the three British parties, the Labour members being Major C. R. Attlee and Vernon Hartshorn, a South Wales Member of Parliament with miners' backing.

Though it seemed obvious in Britain that the Labour Party must perform its duties in Parliament, where the final decisions would be made, it did not seem obvious to Indians. This was not a round table conference at which all could equally express their views: it was an inspection of Indians' fitness to receive a further instalment of self-government. The central Assembly refused to co-operate, and the National Congress, including Mrs Besant, called for a boycott. During the Commission's first visit, in February and March 1928, it was met by huge black flag demonstrations. At one of these, Lala Lajpat Rai – who had taken a stand against the Congress in 1926 – was beaten by an English police officer. Expect nothing from the British Labour Party, he subsequently told the All-India Congress Committee,[33] and died shortly afterwards. An all-parties conference was called to draw up a constitution, and when it met in August 1928, Jawaharlal Nehru spoke against Dominion status and against any idea of co-operating with the British, especially with 'the sanctimonious and canting humbugs who lead the Labour Party'.[34]

Yet during the Commission's first visit, two representatives of the TUC were having a very different welcome in India. They were completing a tour begun in November 1927, after the Commission had been announced. They travelled to all the main industrial centres, and everywhere they held meetings, mostly outdoors, with audiences varying from a few hundred to thousands.[35]

The Revolutionary Alternative

The TUC representatives went to India in response to an invitation from the AITUC to send a delegation to its Cawnpore Congress in November 1927. 'We want you to send out your men, your money, your advice, your cooperation,' the AITUC fraternal delegate, G. Sethi, had told the TUC Congress in September,[36] stressing one strand in the relationship between the two organizations. It was not the only strand: as Wadia had emphasized in 1919, the standards of British workers in certain trades were undercut by the poor wages and conditions prevalent in industry in Asia. The seamen came regularly to Congress with their complaints, and at Hull in 1924 the delegate from the Amalgamated Weavers pointed out that his union's protests went back to Lord Morley's time,[37] while the shameful conditions in the textile factories of Bombay should make every Britisher blush. In 1921 the Textile Workers' International Congress stressed the importance of bringing the textile workers of India, China and South America into their international and appealed to the IFTU for help.[38] The British unions raised the question at Congress in 1922, 1923 and 1924, sweeping aside the General Council's initial view that the IFTU should deal with it. By 1924 the TUC's preoccupation with its own reorganization was over, and the Congress decision in that year that the General Council must make its own investigation[39] resulted in the establishment of the Far Eastern Labour Committee in 1925 and Lee's appointment.

It met first on 25 June 1925 with E. L. Poulton, member of the ILO Governing Body, in the chair, and was reconstituted after the 1925 Congress with the new Chairman of the General Council, Arthur Pugh,[40] Poulton, Purcell, Thomas and Tillett as members. A preliminary report was made to the 1925 Congress and the committee continued until August 1926.[41] Appeals for assistance in Indian trade disputes were considered in this committee, but its basic work was a well-researched inquiry – Lee had prepared 19 memoranda by April 1926 – on India, China and Japan, which for the first time provided the General Council with a sound basis for its decisions.

The General Council also set up a Committee on International Trade and Conditions, again served by Lee, and the Labour Party established a committee with Philip Snowden as chairman to examine the problem of sweated goods. This committee suggested[42] that if a country persistently refused to adopt and give effect to any particular ILO Convention, and produced goods under conditions less favourable than those laid down in it, all the states that had adopted the Convention should exclude those goods. This was the only step likely to be effective, the committee noted, since a discriminatory tariff might intensify sweating, and even if it kept sweated goods off the home market in one country, they would still compete in other markets unless countries acted together. But it was a gospel of perfection.

The General Council's Far Eastern Labour Committee quickly reached the conclusion that a documentary inquiry could touch only the fringe of the problem. In 1925 the Dundee Jute Workers sent Tom Johnstone MP and J. F. Sime to India, followed in November 1926 by a delegation from the Textile International led by its secretary, Tom Shaw MP, with two representatives of the British cotton workers and two from Germany. The TUC's Scarborough Congress in 1925 instructed the General Council to consider sending delegations to India, China and Egypt to recommend how best the TUC could help their workers in trade union organization. Since the Far Eastern Labour Committee's interim report had been accepted, the resolution was formally moved and attracted only one speech. Bevin wanted action this time, and insisted that it be passed as a definite instruction to be carried out.[43]

The General Council were not yet ready to undertake work that had previously been regarded as outside the TUC's scope. They considered that at least three months' work would be necessary in each of three countries – India, China and Japan – and questioned whether responsible trade unionists could be spared for this period. Nor could funds be spared, after the general strike in 1926. At that year's Congress, when the full report of the Far Eastern Committee was complete, even Bevin, who was now on the General Council and had examined the balance sheet, was obliged to agree. He proposed instead that the Textile International should be asked to broaden their inquiry and make their information available to the TUC. This was done.[44]

Before further action was taken in India, there was an eruption in China that brought its troubles within the purview of the British government, the TUC and the Labour Party, the IFTU, the Comintern and the RILU.

China

British interest in China centred on the treaty ports from which foreigners enjoying extraterritorial rights were allowed to trade. In the concessions attached to Chinese towns, foreign police and volunteer forces maintained order and municipal authorities composed of foreigners ran their own services, but thousands of Chinese also lived there, many employed in these services, in trading establishments, and in foreign and Chinese-owned factories and workshops. Britain also had a leased territory, Kowloon, the island colony of Hong Kong from which warships could descend on mainland ports at will, and a naval force based on Hankow which operated right up the Yangtse River. China had two governments, one in Peking which claimed authority throughout the country but could not control the nominally subordinate war-lords in the provinces, and one in Canton under the control of the nationalist party, the Kuomintang (KMT). In March 1925 the nationalist leader Sun Yat Sen died while visiting Peking in an attempt to reach agreement between the two governments.

Given the proximity of Hong Kong to Canton, it was natural that the unions developing there should look to China. The Mechanics' Union was associated from 1918 with the Kwangtung Mechanics' Association, and in 1920 the Hong Kong Seamen's Union was founded as a branch of the Chinese Seamen's Union. During a seamen's strike in 1922 the Governor declared their union illegal and closed the Seamen's Hall. Seamen went to Canton, and printers, electricians, transport and shipyard workers and others joined in a general strike, after which the union president was deported. The TUC reported these events,[45] but was not invited to play any part.

Hong Kong had no trade union legislation, but the government began to tackle the worst abuses in the factories. An Ordinance which came into force on 1 January 1923 regulated hours of work and prohibited the employment of children under 10, or under 12 years of age in dangerous trades. The Municipal Council of the important International Settlement in Shanghai, under pressure from the local YWCA, appointed a commission of inquiry in June 1923. Its most expert member, Dame Adelaide Anderson, had been a senior factory inspector in Britain. Its report presented a terrible picture of children working 12-hour shifts in cotton mills, of boy apprentices in workshops and home industries working for five years with little or no pay, and of adult wages so low that the wives and children of unskilled workers were forced on to the labour market unprotected by any legislation or regulations. Since the Municipal Council had no powers to inspect or prosecute, a new bye-law was drafted and the Foreign Secretary instructed the British consul in Shanghai to support it, but by the time the Far Eastern Committee's report was put before Congress in September 1926, the majority on the Municipal Council had still not agreed to enact it. In the rest of China, the Peking government promulgated factory regulations without effect.[46] With the backing of the IFTU, Poulton raised the question of child labour at the ILO, and the Governing Body instructed the Director-General to obtain information.[47] The ILO succeeded in establishing a correspondent in China, who became convinced that it was useless to wait for a stable administration there before setting up a branch office, but was compelled by events to revise his opinion.[48] China was on the verge of civil war.

At the beginning of 1925 there were strikes in foreign-owned factories throughout China, but it was one in a Japanese-owned cotton mill in Shanghai that sparked the blaze. One of the strikers was killed, arrests were made amongst demonstrators, and 30 May British-led police fired on a crowd of several thousands outside the prison. Twelve men were killed.[49] In the International Settlement martial law was proclaimed and a general strike followed, spreading to concessions in other towns and to Hong Kong. The strikes had merged into a general nationalist movement against the foreign concessions. There was a shooting in Hankow on 12 June when a stone-throwing crowd trying to enter the concession refused to disperse.[50] On 23 June British, French and Portuguese police fired in Canton, killing fifty-two, and while the Scarborough Congress was meeting in September a telegram from the Chinese Information Bureau in Peking reported a further firing in the Shanghai International Settlement.[51]

After the first shooting in Shanghai the General Council asked the Prime Minister to prevent the use of British armed forces against Chinese workers in an industrial struggle, but Baldwin was reluctant to intervene. The Joint Executives then demanded that industrial grievances should be redressed, and that Britain should call an international conference to negotiate the ending of extraterritorial rights. The AFL Convention in October urged the US government to concede customs autonomy to China.[52] By December Kuomintang (KMT) forces, advancing northwards from Canton, had occupied Hankow and set up a new Nationalist government, and the British government indicated willingness to negotiate. British troops were withdrawn to their ships in Hankow and Fukien, but the National Joint Council sent a deputation to the Foreign Secretary in January 1927 when the government announced its intention to bring reinforcements from Britain and India to the Shanghai International Settlement. The National Joint Council also issued a statement calling for peaceful negotiations and cabled it to Eugene Chen, the Trinidadian Chinese journalist and lawyer who was Foreign Minister in the new government at Hankow, receiving from him an assurance of willingness to negotiate and the information that their message had made the resumption of negotiations possible.[53] This was the only success the TUC and the Labour Party had throughout the Chinese controversy. The agreement by which the British concessions in Hankow and Fukien, and subsequently in two other ports, were relinquished was reached in February 1927. It was the first treaty signed by the Nationalist government with any foreign power. None of the other countries concerned gave up any of their treaty rights.[54]

News of the General Council's first representations to the British Government in June 1925 brought requests from the Chinese Information Bureau in London, from Shanghai and from the Chinese Railway Workers' Union in Peking, for a TUC delegation to be sent to investigate conditions in China. Considering that the question of the treaty ports was international, the TUC approached the IFTU, but the IFTU Executive took the view that China's condition of civil war did not permit an objective inquiry, and began by trying to obtain information from the unions that had made the request. Despite all efforts, they failed to obtain it.[55]

The TUC faced the same difficulty. Gathering information for the Far Eastern Labour Committee, the international department secured from the Foreign Office reports on the trade unions made by British consuls, which had originally been requested by MacDonald during his term of office in 1924, and which began to reach the Foreign Office in November 1924. They showed how powerless the Peking government was. When a general labour union formed in Changsha in 1921 started a strike, the secretary and the editor of the union newspaper were executed, and in 1923 the military governor in Hupeh had a strike leader beheaded and forty workers shot. Where unions did function, it was not clear whether they were workers' organizations or guilds, whether they were still active in 1925, or whether they were under political leadership. Seven genuine trade unions in Canton were named, and there were no doubts about the industrial bona fides of the union formed in the workshops of the Peking-Hankow Railway in 1921, or of the Chinese Seamen's Union and the Chinese Electrical Workers' Union. The nucleus of a movement appeared to be there if the unions could stand the strain. In the Shanghai International Settlement a Shanghai Labour Union was formed after the May shooting, but its partner in organizing the general strike that followed was the Amalgamated Union of Commerce, Labour and Education, which included shopkeepers' street organizations and students. One of the telegrams sent to the TUC came from the All-China Labour Federation, but carried no address. It was known that a conference had been called in Canton in May 1922 to form a national centre, but that the meeting was too small and unrepresentative for action to be taken.[56] Was there a national centre in 1925 with which the TUC could deal? In response to inquiries, only the railwaymen's union sent definite particulars, and information promised from Shanghai and Canton never materialized.[57]

In June 1925 Canton and Hong Kong followed Shanghai with a general strike, said to have been organized by the All-China Labour Federation. Once again many Hong Kong workers moved to Canton, where a Canton–Hong Kong Delegates' Conference instituted a successful boycott of Hong Kong shipping, ran schools and hospitals, maintained municipal services with the help of funds from the Chinese chambers of commerce, and set up tribunals to punish transgressors.[58] The Hong Kong strikers put forward genuine industrial claims, but the Governor refused to negotiate with them and attributed the movement to Bolshevik intrigue. His fear of Communist influence was shared by the KMT army leader, Chiang Kai Shek, who took control of Canton in March 1926, surrounded the strikers' headquarters with troops, arrested the leaders and disarmed the volunteer corps. After a British naval action in September, the KMT negotiated with the Hong Kong Government and ultimately ended the boycott. The strikers gained nothing.[59]

All this was accompanied by press reports of appalling atrocities. Though all may not have been true, atrocities by the strikers did occur,[60] and there seemed to be little to choose between the different combatants. As Shanghai awaited the arrival of the KMT armies in March 1927, the General Labour Union called a strike in the Chinese city. It was put down with executions and a public display of heads. A second strike became an insurrection in which a workers' militia took over all the city except the International Settlement, and as the northern troops withdrew, handed it over to Chiang Kai Shek's army. On 12 April organized gangs from the secret societies together with KMT troops – allegedly supported with money and arms from commercial interests in the French Concession and the International Settlement – raided the workers' headquarters and forcibly suppressed a retaliatory strike. Canton followed three days later, and in June the garrison commander in Hankow disarmed the local unions' volunteer brigades.[61]

Appalled by the news in March, the General Council called on all the authorities in China to recognize freedom of association.[62] They were whistling in the wind: there was no element in control in China – the warlords, the military governors, the KMT, the British administration in Hong Kong, the strike volunteers themselves – that was prepared to allow this.

In 1927 the chief fear of the TUC and the Labour Party was that the British government would be drawn into large-scale hostilities. During the Canton shipping boycott in 1925–6 British warships had protected the shipment of supplies to the foreign concession. In March 1927, before Chiang Kai Shek took over Shanghai, the forty-five warships in the river took no action when troops of the northern garrison were repelled from the International Settlement, but two days later British and American ships shelled Nanking to cover the escape of foreigners from the concession, which was overrun. According to naval records, ten Chinese were killed, but on this and all other such occasions claims of thousands of casualties were made and reported throughout the world. The National Joint Council took up the contradictory reports and appealed to the British government not to make any ultimatum to China.[63] In a dispirited note prepared before the 1927 Congress, the only satisfaction that Bolton could find was that no actual war had occurred. The TUC, he wrote, had been bombarded with hundreds of conflicting messages and reports coming in daily from China, Hong Kong, Berlin, Paris and Moscow, and from the Foreign Office, business houses, communist agencies and the Chinese Information Bureau in London. Yet withdrawing warships might save bloodshed in one direction and increase it in another, and although the concessions were under foreign administration, thousands of Chinese chose to live there. The labour conditions in European-owned factories were bad, but worse in those owned by the Chinese.[64]

Since it plainly could not influence the situation, why did the General Council concern itself with China? The decision to examine labour conditions in Asia was taken before the outbreaks in 1925 which destroyed all hope of helping the trade unions, but still the General Council persisted, partly because the full picture had not yet been revealed. It would have done better to concentrate on Hong Kong and the settlements, where the British government had some responsibility, but it had no choice. The Soviet Union, the Comintern and the RILU were interested in China, and they made it a world issue. The subject was regularly raised at Congress, beginning in 1925 with a resolution inspired by the NMM and the circulation of a Chinese Information Bureau leaflet calling for the withdrawal of British forces.[65] A vigorous 'Hands off China' campaign was pursued in Germany and France as well as in Britain, where trades councils and local Labour parties were rallied without reference to the TUC or to Labour Party headquarters.[66] The British government published documents after the ARCOS raid in May 1927 which purported to show that this campaign was supported by Soviet government agencies, and there was evidence that messages from the Shanghai Labour Union and the All-China Labour Federation to the TUC after the Nanking shelling might have been sent at the suggestion of the Russian chargé d'affaires in London. The Nanking shelling also became a point of dispute at the last meeting of the Anglo–Russian Trade Union Council.[67] The 1927 Congress defeated a motion to refer back the Chinese section of the General Council's Report[68] and began the move against NMM penetration, but not before the whole affair had demonstrated the ease with which the best instincts of British trade unionists could be manipulated in a matter outside their normal experience and knowledge.

In China itself the dominant outside influence on the trade unions was initially nationalist. Reporting to the Comintern Executive on the Hong Kong seamen's strike in 1922, Maring recorded that it was run, led and financed by the KMT, which he described as embracing workers, the leading intelligentsia and the Chinese bourgeoisie overseas which contributed to its funds and had recently begun to found firms in China. He himself had been in daily communication with the KMT strike leaders. At that time Maring found no connection with the small Communist group in Canton,[69] but leading members of the Chinese Communist Party, which originated in Peking and Shanghai, helped to set up the railway union in the north and unions of railwaymen, miners and others in central China. In May 1923 its third congress, held in Canton, decided that Communist Party members should join the KMT as individuals and co-operate with it to the extent – on Maring's insistence – of sharing control over the labour movement.[70]

This was achieved in Canton after the arrival in October 1923 of M. M. Gruzenberg, known in the Comintern as Michael Borodin and to the British police as George Brown. Mentor of M. N. Roy in Mexico in 1919, in Britain in 1922 Borodin was influential in the reorganization of the British Communist Party and in the formation of the NMM before he was imprisoned, as an alien without a passport, and deported to Russia in February 1923. A man of outstanding ability, Borodin brought stimulus, training and organization to the trade union movement. Whereas Maring had found no RILU publications in Canton in 1922, in June 1924 a conference of Transportation Workers of the Pacific brought in foreign RILU delegates. It was followed by a further strike in which, by contrast with 1922, the Chinese Communist Party played a leading role. The RILU Executive Board was now able to report that it was in contact with the Chinese National Secretariat of Trade Unions – evidently the body that held its second national conference in Canton on 1 May 1925, at which the All-China Labour Federation was established and declared its affiliation to the RILU.[71]

The Russian government also supported the KMT. Borodin was a government emissary, as was the military adviser, General Galen, and Chiang Kai Shek was trained in Moscow. A steady stream of Chinese students went to Moscow and returned to work in the Communist Party, the KMT and the trade unions. The alliance proved to have been tactical on both sides but, even when it was wearing thin in 1926 and 1927, important Communists visited China – including Tom Mann, Earl Browder of the United States and Jacques Doriot of France in February 1927, during the brief heyday of the Left KMT government in Hankow. M. N. Roy, as Comintern representative, arrived in April, just in time for Chiang Kai Shek's suppression of the Shanghai unions and his establishment of a new 'right' KMT government in Nanking. In July Communists were expelled from the KMT, the army and Hankow, and Borodin, Eugene Chen and M. N. Roy left for Russia, followed by Mme Sun Yat Sen. In December the Chinese Communist Party under the leadership of the Comintern representative Heinz Neumann seized Canton, but failed to hold it against the KMT army. These disasters, in which one of the few redeeming features was the undoubted courage and dedication of its representatives, had a shattering effect on the Comintern, but did not end its activity, or that of the RILU.

The Pan-Pacific Trade Union Secretariat

For the RILU, China was the base for Asia and the whole Pacific area, in which there were great variations in union strength. In the Dutch East Indies the leading political organization, Saraket Islam, was Muslim and nationalist in outlook, but the PKI was able to influence a Revolutionary Trade Union Centre[72] which was later suppressed. In Singapore a Nan-Yang (South Seas) Branch of the Communist Party of China was formed in 1925 and a Nan-Yang Federation of Labour in 1926. The party was quickly suppressed; the union organization held two annual congresses and advocated violent methods in strikes before the British authorities declared it illegal and deported the leaders back to

China.[73] But the RILU hoped to win adherents in India, Australia, the USA and Japan, where there were substantial movements.

A start was made with the establishment of port bureaux which were intended to serve as links between these trade union movements and the RILU, which called its Pacific Ocean Conference of Transport Workers in Canton. However, a meeting called in Sydney in July 1926, intended to be a Congress of Trade Unions of the Pacific Countries, was so badly attended that it was decided to make another attempt to hold a full congress in Canton in May 1927.[74]

Although the NMM was represented at Sydney, the TUC did not become involved until March 1927, when an invitation to Canton arrived by cable from the Preparatory Bureau, Pan-Pacific Labour Congress, in the names of the All-China Labour Federation and the Commonwealth Trade Union Congress, Australia – a body whose existence in anything but name was in doubt.[75] This invitation was typical of the RILU's organizing methods. Though the RILU was not mentioned, it could not have been expected that the TUC would endanger its relationship with the IFTU, not to mention Australia, by attending. But at least the cable listed important industrial subjects for the agenda. It was followed by a Draft Propaganda Thesis which stated that it had been decided at Sydney in 1926 to point out to workers of all Pacific countries the need to join forces against international capitalism and preparations for war, and to take an active part in the struggle for international trade union unity. The TUC declined, referring to the short notice, but the British press began to question the role of Tom Mann, who was to attend for the NMM. The Australian government was reported to have refused passports to a proposed delegation to be led by J. S. Garden, the Communist secretary of the Sydney Trades and Labour Council. The Indian government refused passports for a delegation selected at the instance of M. N. Roy,[76] and fourteen of the Japanese delegation were arrested before they could leave Japan. However, delegates from Korea, Japan, Java, the USSR and the 'revolutionary minorities' in the USA, France and Britain arrived in China.

As Canton was no longer under Communist control, they were obliged to find their own way to Hankow, where the congress was held under the wing of the 'left' government at the end of May. It decided to set up a Pan-Pacific Trade Union Secretariat (PPTUS) in which the All-China Labour Federation and the ARCCTU would each have two representatives and the other countries would have one – in the case of Britain, Tom Mann.[77] The Secretariat was not to be affiliated to the RILU, but since it would pursue the same objects as the revolutionary workers of all countries, all RILU affiliates should support it. Its enemies would be the reformists – Purcell was specifically named – who were helping the imperialists in Europe and the USA to strangle the Chinese revolution, and whose aim in colonial countries was to control and disorganize workers' organizations. This message was carried in four languages in the Secretariat's journal from Hankow. Subsidiary themes were attacks on the IFTU and the ILO, the need to create a single trade union international, support for the NMM and denunciation of the TUC Congress decision to wind up the Anglo–Russian Joint Advisory Council.[78]

The Secretariat could not stay in Hankow, but managed to function from Shanghai, where the International Settlement traditionally provided a refuge for revolutionaries. Its Chinese members must have been working underground, since the remnant of the Hankow government combined with Nanking in a new National Government in September 1927, and both Nanking and Peking were hunting down Communists and suspected communists – the public executions continued into 1928.[79] But conferences were held in Shanghai in February and October 1928, the second being entrusted with the task of drawing up practical measures to implement the decisions of the Fourth RILU Congress, 'with which the PPTUS had declared itself in agreement'. Earl Browder edited the journal, and in 1929 – because the Australian government would not allow it to be held in Australia – the conference was held in Vladivostok.[80]

Such events played their part in the TUC's domestic moves against the NMM, but TUC decisions throughout were based on conclusions reached by observation rather than from exact knowledge of the workings of the RILU and the Comintern. Sometimes it acted from what could only be called instinct, as in 1931 when the General Council was asked to join a deputation to the Chinese legation in London to press for the release or open trial of the secretary of the PPTUS and his wife, Mr and Mrs Ruegg. It was said that when on trade union business they had travelled under an assumed name, and that they appeared to have been accused of conducting communist propaganda. In Shanghai, the International Settlement police had arrested and handed over to the KMT government a teacher, Hilaire Noulens, who had three passports and twelve cover names and was thought to be a Swiss Communist, Paul Ruegg. British intelligence had been led to him by the discovery of a Shanghai address in the papers of a French Comintern agent arrested in Singapore, where a Malayan Communist Party and a Malayan General Labour Union had been formed in 1930 under the direction of the Comintern and the PPTUS. The Noulens papers in Shanghai included documents and accounts of the PPTUS and of the Far Eastern Bureau of the Comintern, and showed that Noulens headed both offices. They received funds from the Western European Bureau of the Comintern in Berlin, and in Hong

Kong there was a Comintern Southern Bureau which maintained contact with the communist parties of Malaya and Indo-China. This was directed by Nguen Ai Quac (Ho Chi Minh), who was in turn arrested.[81] The TUC gave no reply to the invitation to join the London deputation – not because it had any knowledge of the documents unearthed in Shanghai, but because the invitation came from the British Section of the League Against Imperialism,[82] with which the TUC refused to have any dealings.

The League Against Imperialism

Apart from its methods and its questionable credentials as a representative trade union body, the PPTUS had the merit that it tried to fuse the two great liberating ideas of the century, the emancipation of workers and the emancipation of peoples. However, the unions were too weak to provide a firm foundation: such strength as the Secretariat had came from the Comintern/RILU apparatus and the Soviet government behind it. Seeking, as Lenin had advised, a platform higher and more visible to the masses than their own, the Communists turned to the political movements, and concurrently with the moves to call the Pan-Pacific trade union congress, prepared a political conference to be held in Brussels in February 1927.

Again the TUC was invited at the last moment, the invitation being signed by, amongst others, Mme Sun Yat Sen, Jawaharlal Nehru, George Lansbury, Bertrand Russell, Saklatvala, the French Communist Henri Barbusse, and the German Communist Willi Muenzenburg, who ran the office of the Workers' International Relief (WIR) in Berlin. The purpose of the conference was to discuss the creation of a permanent international organization to link up all forces fighting international imperialism. There were no trade union sponsors, but a covering letter from L. Gibarti, General Secretary of the League Against Colonial Oppression, Berlin, included the Ceylon Labour Council and the South African Trade Union Congress amongst organizations which had already nominated delegates.[83]

The TUC declined on the ground that its channel for international representation was the IFTU.[84] The Labour Party refused, and later published an analysis of the procedures adopted: the IFTU and the LSI were not invited, nor any of the LSI's non-British affiliates except (a few days before the opening of the conference in their capital city) the Belgian Labour Party; individuals and small organizations like the Plebs League were invited, and at the conference itself every individual had been given one vote irrespective of his representative capacity.[85]

The Congress was of the type that the TUC abhorred, bringing together trade union and non-union bodies on a haphazard system of representation that cut across trade union affiliations. Even some of the leading participants did not know how it had originated. Jawaharlal Nehru happened to be in Berlin when preparations were being made, and correctly secured permission to attend from the Indian National Congress. He thought that the left KMT might have started the idea.[86] Fenner Brockway, secretary of the ILP, thought that the KMT had financed it, but wrote in 1942 that there was no doubt that the initiative came from the Comintern.[87] However, the Congress was a great success. From all accounts the true organizer, Willi Muenzenburg, was one of those Communists like Harry Pollitt and S. A. Dange who evoked respect and some affection even from their opponents, and he knew how to arouse enthusiasm in a large audience full of hope. As well as Nehru, a whole galaxy of future prime ministers and presidents attended from the British, French and Dutch colonies. There were also delegates, claiming to speak for nearly 8 million trade unionists of all races, who signed a joint resolution of solidarity with oppressed peoples, stressing such estimable objectives as the right to organize and the end of racial discrimination amongst workers, and calling for unity between the RILU and the IFTU. Pollitt signed for the NMM, S. O. Davies for the Miners' Federation of Great Britain, and Edo Fimmen, secretary of the ITF, on behalf of a Mexican organization.[88]

The main achievement of the Congress was to launch a new League Against Imperialism (LAI), with Brockway as its first international chairman and Fimmen amongst the vice-presidents; Nehru, Muenzenburg and Saklatvala were elected to the executive. Reginald Bridgeman, who had been connected with the Chinese Information Bureau and the British Labour Council for Chinese Freedom,[89] became Secretary of the British Section, to which in due course the NMM and NAFTA affiliated. The All-India Congress Committee adhered to the League as an associate member. Evidently, the support of the AITUC was also expected, for the League attributed the failure of its Cawnpore Congress to affiliate to the influence of the British fraternal delegates.[90]

A bizarre feature was the affiliation of the PPTUS and of the WIR.[91] In 1925, after accusations by the secretary of the LSI, the TUC had concluded that the WIR did not devote all the money it received to the specific work of relief.[92] It was regarded as one of the 'communist solar system' of organizations which purported to be independent of the Communist Party. As early as March 1925 Bramley had drawn the General Council's attention to this phenomenon, citing the LRD and other bodies,[93] and since then there had been the proliferation of fringe bodies supporting 'China'. The Labour Party had paid special attention to the *Resolution on the Development of Methods and Forms of Organization of the Masses under the influence of the Communist Parties*, passed by the Enlarged Executive of the Comintern in 1926, which referred to independent sympathizing mass organizations formed for special purposes and cited the WIR as an example. Whether independent or autonomous, such organizations 'must be in reality under Communist leadership'; in form they should be as flexible as possible, providing for both individual and collective membership; in each country agreement should be reached with the Communist Party executive as to which of these organizations should be authorized to solicit the collective affiliation of trade unions. The Resolution also said that organizations against colonial atrocities and oppression of Eastern peoples were new types which would come into consideration in many countries in the immediate future. Was the new LAI one of these? According to the LSI, its forerunner was the League Against Colonial Oppression, which had originated in a meeting held in Berlin in February 1926. This was called by the WIR and the League Against Atrocities in Syria, and there Muenzenburg announced that the first steps had been taken to call an international anti-colonial conference.[94]

Bridgeman, who was a member of the Labour Party and stood unsuccessfully as a Labour candidate in the 1929 general election, denied this attribution. He insisted that the League was started at the Brussels Congress, that by rule membership in the British Section was open to members of all parties, and that none of its officers was or had been a member of the Communist Party.[95] Yet the invitation to the TUC had come from the League Against Colonial Oppression, Berlin. It was also noted that in July 1928 the Sixth Comintern Congress instructed all its sections to affiliate to the LAI – a decision welcomed by the League's Executive, which contrasted it with the attitude of the LSI. At the same time the Executive declared that the League was not a Communist organization or one of the Comintern's sections.[96]

The LSI Executive had condemned the League. Obliged to choose between his membership of the Executive and the chairmanship of the LAI, Brockway withdrew, and the ILP decided that James Maxton should replace him in the League.[97] The LSI's objections were based on theoretical as well as on organizational grounds. While expressing sympathy with the fight against imperialist oppression, it held that the chief task of the International was to rally the working-class elements of the colonial nations under the banner of international socialism, 'and not to create *a new international organization having for its aim the blending of these elements into a pan-national movement*'.[98] They were not alone in seeing a possible discrepancy between nationalism and the international form of organization prescribed for the LAI. In a confidential report to the Indian National Congress Working Committee on the Brussels Congress, Nehru recommended affiliation, but he pointed to the possibility of conflict between Indian nationalist interests and the interests of workers outside. The League, he wrote, had a socialist character, and Saklatvala had criticized the boycott of Lancashire goods in India as harmful to British workers.[99]

This tension between nationalism and international socialism could not be resolved within the LAI. Like Nehru, most of the colonial delegates were first and foremost nationalists, and the appeal of the Brussels Congress lay precisely in this gathering together of representatives of subject peoples. Unfortunately, this was its only appeal. Conditioned by its origin, the LAI never became a forum for the serious discussion of colonial problems. It was another weapon in the communist revolutionary challenge to the European metropolitan powers, as the LSI had perceived.

It was also a challenge to the LSI in its efforts to face the same problems. The Indian boycott did harm British workers, but was not India entitled to build up its own industry for its own market, and were not all the subject peoples entitled to look forward to controlling their own countries? Slogans about international socialism did not answer such questions, and the LSI was trying to probe beneath the generalities. There had been a discussion on colonies at its Second Congress in Marseilles in 1925, and preparations were being made for a full-scale examination at its Third Congress. This was held in Brussels in August 1928, when Olivier chaired the colonial commission. Before this took place, fraternal delegates from the IFTU and the LSI attended the Second British Commonwealth Labour Conference in July, and much of the documentation prepared for that Conference was submitted by the Labour Party to the LSI. Thus the ideas that were being hammered out in the TUC/Labour Party joint committees and in the Commonwealth Labour Conferences became absorbed into the policy statements of the LSI.[100]

The Second British Commonwealth Labour Conference

For the Second British Commonwealth Labour Conference in 1928, delegates came from Australia, Canada, the Irish Free State and Palestine; instead of Sampson, W. H. Andrews attended for the South African TUC and R. Maclean for the South African Labour Party; the Ceylon Labour Union and the TWMA were represented for the first time. The Indian delegation[101] was still confined to the AITUC, but the leader, Chaman Lall, was now a Congress member of the Central Legislative Assembly and the British clergyman, C. F. Andrews, was closely connected with Gandhi. In the bitter atmosphere surrounding the Simon Commission, the Indian delegation had seriously debated whether to attend at all. With the TUC and Labour Party representatives, there were 40 delegates in all from the Commonwealth.[102] As in 1925, some of the subjects discussed, such as inter-Commonwealth political relations and reciprocity in social insurance, were of immediate interest mainly to the Dominions and British representatives. For the dependencies, the most important feature was the documentation on subject peoples drawn up in response to the questionnaire agreed in 1925.

The Subject Peoples

The Joint International Department's Advisory Committee on Imperial Questions had produced a draft reply in February 1926. After it was disbanded, various comments and amendments were made,[103] but as in the case of the jointly published pamphlet on Africa in 1926, the main work was done by the Labour Party advisers. One of these, J. F. N. Green, was in charge of Central African affairs at the Colonial Office. He was not officially a member of the Joint Advisory Committee or of the Labour Party's Imperial Advisory Committee which succeeded it, but he consistently produced material for the Labour Party and had actually vetted the joint pamphlet on Africa.[104] The South Africans had also made detailed replies to the questionnaire, but the other delegates were clearly out of sympathy with their views, especially those of Maclean, and they were not adequately discussed.

Nor were those of the British delegates, for the participants tended to comment on particular points – Cipriani pressing for trade union legislation in Trinidad, F. O. Roberts urging the extension of political rights, and Olivier advocating the inclusion of African workers in South Africa in the system of wage regulation operating for white workers. However, the British memoranda, when taken together, amounted to a coherent long-term policy for a Labour government in power. The real significance of these papers is to be found not in the Conference debates, but in decisions taken over the next 20 years in the ILO and the Colonial Office, and in the sustained attempts of the Labour Party, the TUC and the Fabian Colonial Bureau to give practical meaning to the high-principled generalities which had formerly passed muster as the imperial policy of the British Labour movement.

On the question which had caused controversy in 1925, it was recommended that self-government should be granted immediately to the mandated territories of Iraq and Palestine, but to none of the African dependencies: there, it was argued, self-government would in some cases result in white settlers usurping all political power, so that responsible government should not be granted until it was certain that control would be exercized by the African inhabitants. Political education should be advanced by participation in local government and the encouragement of free association, and nobody should be excluded by race alone from any office, activity or occupation in the fields of politics, administration or industry. This time trade unions were specifically mentioned: they should be encouraged, and should be nonracial.

As before, attention was paid to local cultures. Education should be adapted to the needs and traditions of the population, and for all the tropical dependencies a code of native rights was advocated, to safeguard the land, prohibit compulsory labour except for local tribal purposes, and stop government pressure to increase the supply of wage labour. Looking ahead, it was recommended that there should be technical training of all descriptions and that governments should control capital investment and the development of new industries.

Green's memorandum in particular faced the problems of capitalist development, already established in Ceylon, Hong Kong and the West Indies, and elsewhere becoming a threat to subsistence economies with unused resources. He argued that where outside enterprise came in, it should be on strict conditions: land for mining or forest exploitation should be leased for specific periods at a proper rental which could be used for public and tribal purposes, and governments should require the payment of adequate wages and measures to safeguard the health of workers, who should not be separated from their families. These workers would need a voice: Green suggested that there should be inspectors to act as their spokesmen, assisted by representative bodies of employees which could ultimately develop into trade unions, and the trade union bodies of the metropolitan country should be associated with these posts in an advisory capacity and in the selection of candidates. This was a clear example of forward thinking on labour policy which later bore fruit in a different form.

India

India's claim to self-government had been recognized by the delegates to the 1925 Conference and twice ratified by the Labour Party Conference, in 1925 and 1927. The implication that nothing remained to be done beyond tidying up a few loose ends was confirmed by the reference in MacDonald's opening speech to his hope that 'within a period of months rather than years there would be a new Dominion ... that would find self-respect as an equal within the Commonwealth ... India'. Evidently, he had greater faith in the Simon Commission than the AITUC, which had asked for the withdrawal of the Labour members. Chaman Lall now asked the Conference to commit itself by resolution to the alternative nationalist demand for a round table conference.

The British delegation would have had no difficulty in agreeing to this, but not to the withdrawal of Attlee and Hartshorn from the Commission, which was the prelude to a round table conference, a Bill, and a Joint Select Committee which Indians would attend, and it was argued that it would be tragic if Indians had no case prepared or did not participate. Nor would the Commonwealth Conference as a whole agree to pass a resolution. The peculiar bitterness with which Chaman Lall pursued his point left the impression that he was concerned to use the conference and the publicity it provided for a particular aim without regard to the views of other delegates and the long-term interest of the conference itself. When C. F. Andrews remarked that Indians did not regard laws passed by the British Parliament as sacred, Snell retorted that he had made not one constructive suggestion and that the British could not clear out the whole of the administrative service at one stroke or rid themselves of responsibility 'by taking their orders from one section of Indians, however important they might be'. Chaman Lall replied that the Labour speeches left his delegates cold, and led them out of the conference.

The effect of this type of controversy was that the problems inherent in the transfer of power were not discussed. No attention was paid to the warnings of the representative of the Irish Labour Party and TUC, R. J. P. Mortished, that immediate self-government raised as many problems as gradualness, and that the Indian delegates should be careful as to how far they tied up their labour movement with the nationalist parties, speaking from Irish experience. Except for references by C. F. Andrews to South Africa and Ceylon, the Indian delegates made no effective contributions on other matters in which their trade union experience would have been valuable, and they were not there when the ILO and IFTU were discussed. The Labour Party representatives were left in a very equivocal position on India, while the TUC delegates maintained a cautious silence.

Evidently, the AITUC did not associate the TUC with the Labour Party's political stance. In September Bakhale brought the warmest fraternal greetings to Congress, devoted his speech almost entirely to industrial issues, and made only a short reference to the deplorable differences that had arisen, from misunderstanding and suspicion on both sides, between Indians and the 'political wing' of the British movement.[105] As relations between the Labour Party and the Indian nationalists hung by a thread, the industrial link held firm. But this too was about to be threatened by political tensions.

Breaking Points

India: Non-Co-operation Renewed

In India, the All-Parties Conference met in August under Motilal Nehru's chairmanship and agreed the Nehru Report which proposed full responsible government on the basis that India's status would be no lower than that of the existing self-governing Dominions. Taken together with the National Joint Council's interpretation of the Montagu Declaration in February 1922, the Labour Party Conference resolutions of 1925 and 1927, and MacDonald's statement at the Commonwealth Labour Conference in July, it now seemed that the All-Parties Conference decision meant that the Labour Party and the Indian nationalist leaders were all now committed to Dominion status for India, which, since the Imperial Conference statement in 1926, was known to mean equality with the Dominions and with Britain.

Unlike the AITUC's representatives at the Commonwealth Labour Conference a month earlier, the All-Parties Conference could not shy away from the steps required to adapt India's institutions to this change in status. Jinnah was disappointed with the suggestions for the Muslim minority's representation, and when the National Congress met at Calcutta in December 1928 those who, like Jawaharlal Nehru, disliked Dominion status in any case, secured a provision that if the British government did not, within a year, agree to the constitution proposed in the Nehru Report, the claim to full independence should be revived. This was the official position of the Indian National Congress when the second Labour government took office in June 1929. Its Indian policy rested on Dominion status, a round table conference to settle the constitution, and the full-scale inquiry into labour conditions in India which the TUC had demanded in 1924.

Once more the Labour Government was in a minority in Parliament. Its first major pronouncement, in the Viceroy's Declaration of 31 October 1929 that Dominion status was the natural outcome of the Montagu Declaration, was immediately challenged by Lord Reading, the former Viceroy, Birkenhead, the former Secretary of State, and Baldwin, who dissociated the Conservative Party from it.[106] Irwin also announced that the Government would call a Round Table Conference to consider the Simon Commission's recommendations before they were submitted to Parliament, and the Indian leaders accepted, in a Manifesto issued at Delhi. But they also included a condition that the round table discussions must be on the basis of full Dominion status and that, as far as possible in existing conditions, the Government of India would immediately be conducted on the lines of a Dominion government. Aware that Parliament would not agree to forestall completely the report of its own statutory commission, the Viceroy refused. At a final meeting with him on 23 December, the Indian leaders disagreed amongst themselves. The National Congress was now divided not only from Jinnah, but from the Hindu Mahasabha and the Liberals also.[107]

When the annual National Congress met in Lahore, the year of grace was over, a demand for full independence was made, and preparations started for civil disobedience. On 26 January 1930 gatherings all over India challenged the Labour government with an independence pledge which declared that British rule had ruined India economically, politically, culturally and spiritually, and that it was a crime to submit to it any longer; those who took the pledge to resist it nonviolently would carry out National Congress instructions for civil disobedience as they were issued. The Congress members again withdrew from the legislatures, and on 11 March Gandhi formally inaugurated civil disobedience with his Salt March, and a no-tax peasant campaign began in Bardoli.[108]

In January Irwin had made a further statement to the central Legislative Assembly: Britain wished to help India to attain full equality with the self-governing countries of the British Commonwealth; it was hoped that the Round-Table Conference would meet in the autumn; meanwhile, it was his responsibility to maintain order.

Law and Order

Whether or not the National Congress campaign would remain nonviolent, there was violence elsewhere. In the first 12 months of Irwin's viceroyalty there were forty communal riots,[109] in April 1929 a bomb was thrown into the central Legislative Assembly, and as he went to meet the Indian leaders on 23 December, an attempt was made to bomb his train.

There had always been an undercurrent of terrorism in India, but there was now another that the government feared perhaps even more. On 20 March 1929, before the Labour government took office, thirty men were arrested in various towns across India and taken for trial at Meerut, charged with conspiring to deprive the King-Emperor of his sovereignty over British India. Three were British: Ben Bradley, a member of the AEU, Philip Spratt and Lester Hutchinson. Most of them were, or were said to be, Communists. The allegation that the conspiracy had been instigated and financed by the Comitern was given some substance by a manifesto issued by its Executive Committee on 26 March, using the slogan 'Long live the Indian Soviet Republic!' This charged British imperialism with using India as a base for a long-prepared attack on the Soviet Union, accused the Labour Party, the TUC and the Indian nationalist leaders of betraying the Indian revolution, and called on the revolutionary workers and peasants to organize their vanguard in the Communist Party and to rise and confiscate the land.[110]

From the days of Russian activity amongst Indian Khilafat supporters in Afghanistan and M. N. Roy's Military School in Tashkent, where the first Indian Communist Party was formed in 1920, the Indian government had tried to counter Comintern influence in India. Students returning from the University of the Toilers of the East were liable to be arrested, and letters sent by M. N. Roy from Moscow and Berlin to the young pioneers of the Communist Party in India, and their letters to each other, were systematically opened and copied by the police before they were put back into the post or suppressed altogether.[111] This was not fully known at the time, but evidence arising from the Cawnpore conspiracy case in 1924[112] and from the ARCOS raid in 1927 had been publicized in Britain. Some of those arrested in March 1929 had been active in the trade union movement, and there were initial suggestions that the Government of India feared a general strike as the prelude to an armed uprising,[113] but when the actual case for the Crown was opened on 10 June, it was concentrated on the activities of the Comintern and its agents.

A TUC delegation met the new Labour Secretary of State, Wedgwood Benn, on 9 July, and on the basis of evidence received from the AITUC in June asserted that some of the active trade union officials arrested were not Communists. At that time the main issues were the refusal of bail, trial by jury, and the long delays in procedures during which the accused were kept in custody. These dragged on until the verdict in the final appeal was given on 3 August 1933. The TUC's persistent approaches to both Labour and Conservative secretaries of state produced little result, for the matter was *sub judice*, the alleged offences were nonbailable, and both Benn and his successor in 1931, Sir Samuel Hoare, claimed that they had done everything open to them to expedite the case but, Citrine told Congress, 'the Government of India refused advice, and have power to refuse'.[114] The prosecution emphasized that the case was against a conspiracy conceived, directed and financed from Europe, primarily Moscow, and was not directed against trade unionists and nationalists. At the Labour Party Conference in October 1929 the parliamentary under-secretary of state, Dr Drummond Shiels, made the same claim and stressed the Government's wish to encourage genuine trade unionism in India.[115]

The Labour government was in an appalling dilemma. Trial was useless in cases of terrorism when witnesses could be intimidated, and non-violent civil disobedience was an open defiance of authority which could not be met by prohibitions, since each one led to the commission of the action it was intended to stop. When tried, defendants simply admitted their offences which, when multiplied sufficiently, made ordinary administration impossible. The Government of India brought in ten special Ordinances before the First Round Table Conference met, without National Congress representation, in November 1930.

The dilemma was inescapable short of the surrender of power. The British government considered that it was responsible for the welfare of the people of India; the National Congress asserted that this claim unfitted it to rule. 'They cannot persuade themselves to see that the one thing needful for them is to get off our backs',[116] wrote the National Congress leaders in August 1930. They were replying to a last abortive attempt by the Liberal leaders, Sapru and M. N. Jayakar, to get civil disobedience called off before the Round Table Conference met. The signatories included Gandhi, both Nehrus, and Vallabhbhai Patel. At the time of writing, all were in gaol, and the Congress Working Committee was an illegal body.

The Communist Change of Line

The Comintern's attack on the Indian nationalist leaders in March 1929 was part of a world-wide change in the Communist line. By the end of 1927 it was evident that the attempt to work with nationalists had failed in China; in India the great struggles of 1920–22 had ended with Gandhi calling off non-co-operation. There had been no continuous development of a communist party, but only separate and loosely connected groups, and without leadership from a strong and disciplined party their efforts to stimulate the development of combined workers' and peasants' movements threatened to call into question the dogma that the proletariat must always lead. In Russia itself, internal dissension in the Communist Party had led to Trotsky's expulsion from the party in December, and his exile to Alma Ata followed in January 1928. The attempts to merge the trade union and political internationals had failed, and the Comintern had not called a full congress for four years. In Britain, the general strike had not become a revolution, the Anglo–Russian Joint Advisory Council had been dissolved, the TUC had begun to move against the NMM, and the ARCOS raid had started off a new outcry against the Communist Party which, having failed to secure affiliation to the Labour Party, had less than 8,000 members.[117]

Considering these failures, the Comintern Executive in February 1928 adopted a new 'class against class' tactic, applicable everywhere but spelt out for Britain in a *Resolution on the English Question*[118] which asserted that the Labour Party was losing its federal character and increasingly becoming an ordinary social democratic party. Therefore the Communist Party, which had hitherto refrained from contesting elections except in constituencies in which there was no Labour candidate, must now field its own candidates, even in competition – but this was a last resort. The demand for Communist Party affiliation to the Labour Party was to be maintained, and in the constituencies Communists were to aim at securing new Labour Party selection conferences on the basis of the right of all workers, including Communists, to participate; where new conferences were refused, or organized in a purely bureaucratic manner, unofficial selection conferences should be called; if local Labour parties were then disaffiliated, the fullest support should be given to their candidates, and to any candidates who pledged themselves to vote for Communist Party affiliation. This change of line was confirmed at the Comintern's Sixth World Congress in July–September 1928, and in 1929 Communist candidates duly appeared to fight Labour candidates in the general election.

One of these was an Indian, Shaukat Usmani, originally one of the Khilafat volunteers en route for Turkey who crossed into Soviet territory from Afghanistan in 1920 and was diverted first to the military school in Tashkent and – when that was disbanded to secure the trade treaty in 1921 – to the University of the Toilers of the East. Convicted in the Cawnpore conspiracy case in 1924, he attended the Comintern Congress in 1928, and in the British general election in 1929, having been refused bail, contested Spen Valley from Meerut gaol.[119] Standing as a Communist, he won only 242 votes, but his candidature had an effect in the TUC. He was fighting Sir John Simon, who won the seat, but in doing so he also opposed a Labour candidate, H. H. Elvin,[120] who was a member of the TUC General Council. Usmani had the support of the LAI.[121]

Despite its claim to independence, the LAI followed the Comintern's new line. In an extraordinary public incident at its Second World Congress at Frankfurt in July 1929, Saklatvala turned to Maxton, in the chair, and declared that the ILP, which called itself the left wing of the British working-class movement, was in reality protecting the left flank of the Labour Party against both the revolutionary workers in Britain and the colonial masses of the Empire.[122] The League called for a determined struggle against the second Labour government and for the exposure of the Labour Party's and the TUC's imperialist policy in India. Maxton was soon accused of refusing to carry out the decisions of the executive of the British section and was expelled in May 1930.[123] Fimmen also found it necessary to resign and was formally expelled in 1931.[124]

The TUC had already warned trades councils against the LAI, using not only the statements of the LSI, but also an argument that applied to any outside fringe organization that had no substantial membership of its own and relied for prestige, support and money largely on what it could obtain from local and national trade union and Labour Party bodies. Such an organization, the TUC said, 'must necessarily be parasitic in character, drawing its strength from the official organization, and hampering the latter in its legitimate activities'.[125] At the end of 1927 Citrine began to publish a series of articles analysing the structure and activities of the Comintern/RILU apparatus as operated in Britain,[126] and in 1928 the Swansea Congress instructed the General Council to inquire into the proceedings and methods of disruptive elements within the trade union movement. The report of the inquiry was adopted by the Belfast Congress in 1929. The NAFTA delegation tried to secure the reference back of the section on the LAI, but it did not prevail against Elvin, still smarting from his experience in Spen Valley. Yet the General Council's recommendation, adopted by Congress, was mild enough – merely that unions should act in the light of the information provided.[127]

The Labour Party took a stronger line. In October 1930 the Conference endorsed a report listing seven bodies, including the LAI, as organizations ancillary or subsidiary to the Communist Party and ineligible for affiliation to the Labour Party. The effect was that no member of the League could be eligible for individual membership of the Labour Party or for nomination as a local government or parliamentary candidate. This decision could be enforced against open members of the Communist Party or, like Bridgeman, of any of the ancillary organizations.[128] The General Council had no power or wish to exclude Communists from the trade unions. It was only after the Communist Party had started up a new united front campaign that the General Council decided in 1934 to withdraw TUC recognition from any trades council which admitted delegates associated with Communist or Fascist organizations or their ancillary bodies, and affiliated unions were asked to consider adopting rules which would empower them to reject nominations of members of disruptive bodies for official positions within their own organizations.[129]

The General Council had demonstrated in their relations with the Russians a belief that some accommodation should if possible be found even with trade unions pursuing revolutionary aims; but what they found insupportable was the persistent denigration, the parading of the NMM – as at Sydney, Hankow and Brussels – as the true international representative of British workers, the dubious invitations, the front organizations that pretended to be independent, and the constant propagation of day-to-day policies that conflicted with decisions taken by unions and by Congress. Yet still approaches were made to local bodies, to unions, and even to the TUC itself, until in 1934 Bridgeman was informed that no letters from him would be acknowledged.[130]

Four years earlier Jawaharlal Nehru had given the same instruction to the All-India National Congress secretariat.[131] Bridgeman in London and the LAI international secretary in Berlin, V. Chattopadhyaya, had accused him of betraying the Indian masses when he signed the Delhi Manifesto in November 1929, and had demanded withdrawal. Chattopadhyaya followed up with a circular to workers' and peasants' organizations which criticized Gandhi also for chronic reformism and betrayal of their cause. Like Maxton and Fimmen, Nehru was expelled from the League. He had been favourably impressed by the Brussels Congress in 1927 and by what he saw in Russia[132] when he went on to attend the tenth anniversary of the October Revolution. There can be little doubt that the inspiration of both occasions contributed to his uncompromising mood when he returned to India in December 1927, but neither could have prepared him for the Comintern's change of line in 1928.

The ECCI's decision on the English Question in February was followed in September by the adoption of extensive *Theses on the Revolutionary Movement in Colonial and Semi-Colonial Countries* by the Sixth Comintern Congress. In a general analysis of the relations between communist parties and nationalist movements, special attention was paid to India. There, it was said, the revolutionary effort had been terminated in 1922 by the treachery of the national bourgeoisie, afraid of the growing wave of peasant uprisings and of strikes directed against Indian employers. In general, the national bourgeoisie was ultimately 'not significant as a force in the struggle against imperialism', and although it could accelerate the political awakening of the working masses, it retarded the revolutionary movement by securing a following amongst them. Unlike the KMT, the Swarajists had not yet passed over into the counter-revolutionary camp, but there was no doubt that they would ultimately do so, and if communists did not succeed in shaking the faith of the masses in the bourgeois national leadership, it would endanger the advance of the next revolutionary wave. The need was now for independent communist parties acting as sections of the Comintern, fighting against the colonial policy of social democracy which the LSI's Brussels Congress had revealed as a policy of active support of imperialism, and – as their first immediate task – conducting revolutionary propaganda in reactionary trade unions which had a mass working-class membership and, where circumstances dictated, establishing separate revolutionary unions. Here, the leadership of the RILU must be consulted, the IFTU must be exposed, and the communist parties of the metropolitan countries must send out advice and permanent instructors to help the revolutionary unions. In India, the first task was to unite all the scattered communist groups into a single, illegal, independent and centralized party which would unmask the national reformism of the Indian National Congress and, in opposition to all the talk about passive resistance, 'advance the irreconcilable slogan of armed struggle'.[133]

In this they already had the support of the entire communist solar system of organizations. Spratt had arrived in India at the end of 1926, and Bradley shortly afterwards.[134] The evidence given at Meerut, recounted in the British press as the trial proceeded, traced the alleged conspiracy back to M. N. Roy's work in Berlin in the Eastern Bureau of the Comintern and to the British Communist Party's assumption of responsibility for directing the Indian communists in 1925. The prosecution also listed the RILU, the PPTUS, the LAI, the NMM and the LRD. The LRD was alleged to have paid a regular salary to Spratt, while Bradley was said to have been financed by the WWLI. The English defendants were regarded as Comintern agents, working in the trade unions and in the communist auxiliary workers' and peasants' parties in an extraordinary atmosphere of false names, ciphers and invisible ink, with money and propaganda literature delivered over the Afghan border and by British emissaries. Indian Political Intelligence had also identified Percy Glading, a British Communist who was sacked from Woolwich Arsenal as a security risk in 1928, and was sentenced to six years' imprisonment in 1938 for passing secret naval information to the Soviet Union.[135]

The Theses of 1928 laid down that combined workers' and peasants' parties should not be built, since communist party organization should never be founded on a fusion of two classes, but they were already in existence in India at the time, and the ECCI sent a directive for a joint conference of four of them in December 1928. The way forward, it suggested, lay in co-operation in action between peasant bodies and separate organizations of the proletariat. The Communist Party of India (CPI) (whose existence in 1926, though not as a Comintern section, was recognized by the Comintern) contained individual communists, but was a paper organization which must now be separated from the peasant bodies and become a genuinely revolutionary party. These combined internal and external efforts achieved considerable success. If at the end of 1930, as Palme Dutt asserted, there was still no CPI,[136] this was due to police action rather than to any lack of will amongst the revolutionaries, who concentrated on the unions.

Lee had seen this coming. Writing to Joshi in 1925, he noted that the British Communist Percy Glading had addressed the previous AITUC congress as a member of the AEU and Lee inquired tentatively whether his speech, which read 'a little peculiarly', had been at all helpful to the congress. In January 1926 he wrote again privately suggesting that the communists were trying to Bolshevize the Indian trade unions, but Joshi replied that 'these very few people who call themselves communists are ... nationalists before anything else ... hardly connected with the trade union movement in India'. In 1927 Lee wrote that opposition to the Comintern did not arise out of questions of principle or general policy, but from the fact that Communists were under its orders, which often took the form of smashing up the trade unions, labour parties and socialist bodies which could not be forced into agreement with the policy of Moscow.[137]

Before this happened in India, there were disagreements over methods which developed from internal conditions as much as from outside intervention. Though the Comintern and the British TUC both took the view that Indian workers could not rely on Indian capitalists, whether nationalist or not, to improve their conditions, the trade union leaders could see this for themselves. The difference lay between those who aimed at an early revolution, and those who recognized that it would take time to build the internal strength of the unions and considered that this was best done by solid grass-roots organization and by negotiation. Considering the weakness of the unions when compared with the strength of the expatriate and Indian employers, that was a sane view, but it could also be argued that workers' conditions were intolerable and means must be found to change them quickly. In the Legislative Assembly, Joshi warned the Government of India and the employers that if their conduct did not inspire confidence that workers' problems could be solved by agreement and negotiation, the result would be violence or direct action.[138]

A case in point was the experience of the first union to register under the 1926 Trade Unions Act, the Bombay Textile Labour Union, an amalgamation of nine small mill unions formed on 1 January 1926. Its activities, membership and finance were faithfully recorded, and at the end of the first year it estimated its effective membership as nearly 6,000, though there were 9,000 members 'as actually seen on the roll, which does not contain the name of a single member who has not paid for at least a few months'. During the year it had handled 238 complaints, 89 successfully, concerning grievances such as dismissals, withholding of wages, refusal to re-employ workers who went home without permission of the jobbers, accident compensation, and assaults. As such grievances were common to all mills, evidence on them was submitted to the Tariff Board, and as the Government of India was studying deductions from wages, representations were made on fines and on the need for prompt payment of wages. Although Joshi was president and Bakhale was secretary, efforts were being made to bring workers into controlling positions in the union: 42 of the 50 members of the Management Committee had been elected from mill committees, and two had been sent to attend the AITUC Executive Council in Calcutta. A breath of the wider world came in through a meeting with Tom Shaw's international textile delegation and from a send-off for Lajpat Rai as he left for the eighth session of the International Labour Conference. Income for the year was Rs. 17,411 (£1,305) and the expenditure included a contribution of Rs. 334 (£25) to the British general strike fund.[139] This work was the very stuff of

trade union organization. It did not exclude strikes, but prolonged
strikes, and especially unsuccessful ones, laid a burden of suffering on
very poor workers which leaders of Joshi's type were not prepared to
impose if any other way could be found.

A strike came in 1928 against wage cuts and rationalization in the
Sassoon and Wadia mills. The Textile Labour Union and a smaller
affiliate of the AITUC, the Girni Kamgar Mahamandal, which had
brought together three small unions in 1923, wished to confine it to the
mills concerned; but communist elements – both union and political –
organized demonstrations, some violent, to extend it. When the
employers, who began to close down the mills, refused to recognize a
separate strike committee which they had set up, on the grounds that it
did not represent registered unions, they established and registered a
new Girni Kamgar Union (GKU). S. A. Dange was general secretary,
S. S. Mirajkar was assistant secretary, A. A. Alve was President, and Ben
Bradley was a member of the executive.[140] All of them were
subsequently tried at Meerut. Failing to gain concessions from the mill-
owners, the Textile Labour Union and the GKU formed a joint strike
committee, with Bradley as treasurer, and a six-months' strike was
ended in October 1928 by an agreement with the Mill Owners'
Association to refer the dispute to a government-appointed committee.

The establishment of a new union was undoubtedly undesirable, but
the extension of the strike did bring in workers who equally needed
union protection, and the whole Mill-Owners' Association was
brought to the inquiry. However, the GKU did not try to secure full
benefit from the inquiry. It made little contribution to the work of the
Fawcett Committee, where the workers' case was substantially argued
by Joshi and Bakhale, and it continued attacks on Joshi throughout.
The committee's report in March 1929 gave no immediate
improvement to the workers, but included some sensible proposals for
disputes procedures. The Mill-Owners' Association produced a
scheme for standardized wages in the industry, but it was not accepted
and had not been implemented by the time the Royal Commission on
Labour in India (the Whitley Commission) reported in June 1931.[141]

During the strike the GKU had established mill committees, and it
was able to launch a further strike alone in April 1929, although its
leaders had been locked up.[142] This second strike dragged on, with lathi
charges and police firings, until September, when a new court of
inquiry was appointed. Nothing was gained. The workers were left
discouraged, the unions weakened and divided, and the employers with
no effective organization with whom to negotiate.[143]

There were two concepts of trade unionism here, both of them valid
in their way. By Joshi's methods, it would take years to build a union,

but such a union, founded on continuous paying membership, must by definition show benefit to its members and be ultimately responsible to them. A strike against determined employers, who did not shrink from shutting the mills, was almost certain to be unsuccessful, since unskilled workers could be easily replaced by the jobbers or might – as they did in the previous strike and lockout in 1925 – go back to their villages[144] with no guarantee that they would return, or that if they did, they would regain their jobs. Joshi's methods did not secure immediate results in 1928, but neither did the strike of 1929. What mass strike action did achieve, at the cost of considerable suffering, was the maximum civil disturbance. The Bombay Textile Labour Union could not withstand the campaign waged against it in such conditions, and went out of existence in the thirties, while the GKU was revived. In the end the communist-led unions in India established ordinary trade union organization, negotiating with employers, making agreements and seeing that they were kept. That could not be done successfully in 1928 because the employers did not respond, nor in 1929, when the government arrested the GKU leaders.

Nevertheless, Joshi's judgement in 1926 had been wrong. These leaders were, and remained, dedicated Communists. Although many of their actions in 1928 could be appreciated in trade union terms, ultimately they did not rely on their members for contributions or for control of union policy. The Comintern's change of line did not come to full fruition in India until a Red Trade Union Congress was formed in 1931, but already the attack which Lee had foreseen was being launched against existing unions and against the leadership of the AITUC itself. When its congress met in December 1929, the AITUC could no longer contain the diverse pressures that were being exerted upon it.

The All-India TUC

In British terms, it was a strange feature of the AITUC's Nagpur Congress that Jawaharlal Nehru presided, but it was customary for the AITUC to choose influential outsiders as president for a year, such as C. F. Andrews in 1928. Politicians had inspired its formation, and its inaugural meeting in October 1920 was attended by a galaxy of political leaders, including Colonel Wedgwood, together with a sprinkling of mill-owners, merchants, lawyers, and even 'staid upper middle class women's leaders'.[145] Nehru had been chosen at the 1928 session, when he was secretary of the National Congress, and considered it a sign of weakness in the trade union movement that a newcomer and nonworker should have been chosen, and in his absence. He hoped the labour movement would co-operate with the National Congress despite its bourgeois outlook, but that Labour would keep a distinct ideology and identity of its own.

The Nationalist Pressure

The dilemma inherent in this view was exposed at the congress, which carried a resolution to boycott the Whitley Commission. Joshi and Chaman Lall had been appointed to the Commission, which had already started work, and there was no industrial interest to be served by a boycott. Yet Nehru sympathized with the resolution as corresponding with the National Congress policy. As he recorded, 'It seemed absurd to cooperate with official Commissions when we were carrying on, or going to carry on, a direct action struggle'.[146] Faced with a potential split on a range of issues that divided a moderate centre from two opposing factions, he criticized both factions in his presidential speech for not waiting for the forthcoming session of the National Congress, which might have made the split unnecessary.[147] Later in the month the National Congress decided on civil disobedience. Such movements dislocated organized trade union activity, not least by provoking restrictions on meetings.[148] At Nagpur a sustained attack was made on the AITUC leadership. It was alleged that Moscow had sent a directive calling for the removal of Joshi, Giri and Shiva Rao, and of the nationalist 'extremists' like Nehru and Subhas Chandra Bose,[149] but the nationalist group was strong enough to secure the election of Bose as president for the coming year. This was the first powerful external pressure on the trade union movement.

The Communist Pressure

The second came from the communist attack. At previous sessions in 1927 and 1928 the communists had emerged as a distinct group with their own programme and tactics.[150] Their influence was not entirely negative. Addressing the 1927 congress, Saklatvala emphasized that unions must keep careful accounts, ensure that members received union publications, and conduct research into the conditions of workers and their industries. The thesis adopted at the conference of workers' and peasants' parties in December 1928 made a reasoned case for industrial unions, and stressed the need for members to be organized in branches which would elect representative delegates and discuss and decide policy in regular meetings, for attention to the enforcement of factory legislation, and for industrial action to be planned only when sufficient solidarity and resources were available to ensure success. Given the ability and self-sacrifice of the communist leaders, who constantly paid a heavy penalty for their actions, it seems likely that a naturalized communist movement could have helped Indian workers without destroying their organizations. But they were not left alone. Even this thesis called for affiliation to the RILU, the PPTUS and the LAI,[151] and these demands took precedence in Communist tactics.

Hitherto the AITUC had evaded the international question. In its first year, it did not respond to an invitation to join the IFTU. Although at its second congress a promise of support came from the British Bureau, it did not affiliate to the RILU, and in practice accepted some financial help in strikes from both the internationals.[152] Since they met at the ILO and at the Commonwealth Labour Conferences, the AITUC leaders had closer contact with the IFTU, but when Citrine advised affiliation in 1926, Joshi's concern was to avoid a decision which was likely to cause a split.[153]

In the case of the IFTU, affiliation in any country was secondary to the domestic activities of the trade unions. The IFTU did not control the policy of individual affiliates, nor did it create affiliates for itself. Contributions to strike funds were collected and sent more as tokens of solidarity than as decisive assistance, no full-time organizers were sent from Amsterdam, and affiliates had to pay their way before they could be represented at IFTU conferences. The theory, practice and organization of the Comintern/RILU/ancillary organizations apparatus were the exact opposite. Affiliation to the RILU would mean the loss of the AITUC's independence, not only in internal tactics, but in all outside relationships and activities. In particular, it would end participation in the work of the ILO. It would involve, as Nehru warned the 1929 congress, the adoption in their entirety of methods which had failed in China, and of which he disapproved.[154] At the 1928 session, the communist group secured a decision to affiliate to the LAI. The more important decisions, on affiliation to either of the trade union bodies, the RILU and the PPTUS, were left over, but in February 1929 the AITUC executive decided to affiliate to the IFTU. Since this would have to be endorsed at the full congress, a split at Nagpur was virtually certain unless the international question were set aside by agreement.

The Nagpur Congress 1929

The split occurred in the executive council, where the existing leaders found themselves in disagreement with the adoption of a coherent body of proposals for affiliation to the PPTUS, boycott of the ILO and the Whitley Commission, condemnation of the Nehru Report, and rejection of the Viceroy's proposal for a round table conference. There was a dispute over the representation of the unions which moved most of these resolutions – the GKU and the Great Indian Peninsular Railwaymen's Union, which was also communist-led. The executive conceded the GIPRU's claim to 30,000 members[155] since it was an affiliate of long standing, but the new GKU's claim to 54,000 was challenged by Bakhale and other Bombay delegates, reduced to 42,000, and accepted at that figure by Nehru's casting vote. The resulting delegations, taken together with the militant nationalist element that had voted with them in the executive, produced a majority against the leadership in the congress. Twenty-four unions withdrew, on the grounds that the two unions whose delegations were in question had been mainly responsible for the resolutions, and their adoption meant that 'the policy of the AITUC, under the control and direction of the new majority in the Executive Council, will be fundamentally opposed to the genuine interests of the working class'.[156] There was no proposal to join the RILU, and the resolution to affiliate to the PPTUS was withdrawn, for a year, by its sponsor before the full congress voted. All the other resolutions went through, and one of the leaders of the GKU's 1929 strike, S. V. Deshpande, became general secretary of the AITUC in place of Joshi.

In the TUC's eyes, a union's affiliated membership could be quickly proved by its payment of fees. In the case of the GKU Lee was baffled by figures of 54,000, 6,000, 25,000, 40,000 and 50,000 which were bandied about in the AITUC and in the Bombay press, and even 165,000 in the Communist International Press Correspondence. He noted that the union had been formed in May 1928, registered with 324 members, and reported an increase to 65,000 in January 1929 – a growth, in his view, too phenomenal to be accepted.[157] In 1934 the Bombay Home Department stated that in April 1929 the GKU had over £3,555 in accumulated funds and its claim to 54,000 members was not exaggerated.[158] This did not clear up the question of whether affiliation fees had been paid on this number to the AITUC. The problem appears to have lain in the AITUC's disarray. At its congress in 1931 a further dispute arose over the credentials of the GKU – this time between rival groups claiming to represent it – and the communist element lost the argument. In this and in other cases the decisions of Subhas Bose as president were criticized, and the controversy over representation was cited as one reason for the withdrawal of twelve unions to form the All-India Red Trade Union Congress.[159]

In 1929 the twenty-four seceding unions held a meeting of their own, chaired by Chaman Lall, which decided to establish a new Indian Trade Union Federation (ITUF). A committee with Giri and Bakhale as chairman and secretary was set up to draft a constitution which would exclude unions with communist tendencies from affiliation or representation. The Federation was to unite those unions which wished to work on 'purely trade union lines'. The meeting also put forward nominations for the workers' delegation to the 1930 International Labour Conference and declared that it was essential in the workers' interest to submit evidence to the Whitley Commission. A resolution welcomed the Viceroy's Declaration and the party leaders' Delhi Manifesto responding to it, and demanded representation for labour at the Round-Table Conference. Subsequently, the twenty-four were joined by six other unions and claimed a total of over 96,000 members as against twenty-one unions with 93,000 members remaining with the AITUC. But the Federation had yet to be set up. It had no access to AITUC funds, and could not collect affiliation fees until its constitution was established.

The TUC General Council were predisposed to stand by their friends, trusted colleagues whose concept of trade unionism was in harmony with their own, and who had encountered the same difficulties as the TUC in its battle against disruption. They made a grant of £50 to help with initial expenses and sent the resolution on labour representation at the Round Table Conference to the Secretary of State with a message in support. They did not need to consider any resulting impact on their relationship with the AITUC, since one of the Nagpur resolutions had brought this to an end.[160]

Police Pressures

The third source of pressure on the Indian trade union movement was the police. At its first session in 1920 the AITUC referred to the employment of the military and of armed police in strikes, and a year before civil disobedience was launched in 1930 it was still protesting and warning the government that the use of unwarranted force in the interests of employers was causing grave discontent amongst workers.[161] It was alleged that police influenced shopkeepers to stop supplying food to strikers, that union leaders were followed, and that police reporters habitually attended union meetings. The TUC raised these matters also with the Secretary of State.[162] This type of pressure was continuous. The Meerut case was in a class of its own.

At first the General Council was satisfied that the charges against the Meerut prisoners had not been brought because of their trade union activities. In 1931 Citrine told Congress that the trial had no reference at all to trade union organization, which was still proceeding in India in the ordinary way.[163] As the trial continued, however, it became apparent that some accusations against the accused hung on activities in strikes, that no specific illegal actions were being proved against them, and that mere membership of the Communist Party, which was not illegal, was being treated as incriminating. The long imprisonment seemed indefensible, and when judgement came on 16 January 1933 the sentences were to run from that date, not from the arrests in March 1929. In five cases the judge had overruled all his five assessors, and in another five had overruled four of them. Only three of the accused were acquitted. One, Dundiraj Thengdi, a former president of the AITUC, died before the judgement. For the rest, the sentences were savage, running up to 12 years' hard labour for the leading Communists, Spratt, Dange, S. V. Ghate, K. N. Joglekar, R. S. Nimbkar, all of whom had been active in the trade union movement.[164]

The Labour Opposition in Britain was now thoroughly roused. The National Joint Council called for the immediate release of the prisoners in consideration of the time already spent in gaol and, while the cases went to appeal, published a legal analysis of the trial and sentences, calling on all sections of the Labour movement to publicize its contents and bring pressure to bear on Members of Parliament to secure release. In August the appeal judgement was given: Hutchinson and eight others were acquitted, five were released immediately, and the remaining sentences were substantially reduced. Bradley was released in November and later became secretary of the British Section of the LAI. Spratt remained in India and was arrested again under the Emergency Powers Act in 1934.[165] Lester Hutchinson became a Labour Member of Parliament in 1945.

The case had cast a blinding light on the workings of imperial rule, and of the Comintern. The TUC's concern did not extend to its former emissary, M. N. Roy, who had been formally expelled in December 1929. He had disagreed with the change of line in 1928 and with the ECCI's decision in July 1929 that the Communists should break with the Indian National Congress and organize new 'red' unions. Returning to India in December 1930, he evaded the police until arrested in July 1931 on the outstanding Cawnpore conspiracy charge of 1924. The TUC did not reply to a request for intervention to secure his release.[166]

The Dominance of Politics

Roy inspired a new grouping in the Indian trade union movement which was opposed both to the communists in their acceptance of the disruptive Moscow line, and to the nationalist element which followed the political lead of the Indian National Congress. This political dominance of the movement continued to outweigh industrial considerations throughout the 1930s and during the Second World War. It did not prevent the unions functioning, but it did make the functioning of a national centre impossible, and thus affected the relationships of the TUC. Various attempts were made to rebuild unity, initially concentrated on the group led by Joshi and Shiva Rao and the railway unions that took their lead from Giri and Jamnadas Mehta. In April 1933, these formed the National Trades Union Federation (NTUF), which merged with the AITUC in 1938. The TUC was kept informed of these developments and never lost touch with some constructive grouping.

However, no trade union movement could have resisted the political strains as alignments constantly shifted: the National Congress went from civil disobedience to recuperation and the decision to fight the provincial elections in 1937, from the acceptance of office by provincial governments to their resignation at the outbreak of war; the CPI followed the Comintern's 'class against class' policy with 'red' trade unions, and reversed it when Russia adopted a 'popular front' line as a defence against fascism in Europe. In 1939 both the National Congress and the CPI withheld support for the war effort; the CPI continued to do so for some months after the German invasion of the Soviet Union, and the National Congress resorted to outright civil disobedience in 1942 despite the Japanese advance to the borders of India. The AITUC, strengthened in 1938 by merger with the NTUF, lost the Royist group in November 1941 when a new Indian Federation of Labour, supporting the war as an anti-fascist struggle, was formed with Mehta as president and Roy as general secretary. The AITUC gained the Communists after the CPI had decided that the attack on Russia had changed the imperialist war into a peoples' war, became a legal organization and was encouraged by the Government of India. In 1944 S. A. Dange, former prisoner of Cawnpore and Meerut, representing the AITUC, and A. K. Pillai, representing the Indian Federation of Labour, attended the TUC Congress as fraternal delegates. Miss Maniben Kara and V. B. Karnik of the Indian Federation of Labour, and Dange, visited unions and held discussions with the International Committee,[167] but they remained separate delegations.

The Third British Commonwealth Labour Conference

After the first split in the AITUC in 1929, the new ITUF provided the Indian delegation – Joshi, Chaman Lall, B. Shiva Rao, S. C. Joshi, K. C. Roy Choudhary and Mahomed Umar Rajab – to the Third British Commonwealth Labour Conference in July 1930. This was the last Commonwealth conference held jointly with the Labour Party.[168] Ceylon was unrepresented owing to a general election, New Zealand and Grenada sent delegates for the first time, Critchlow returned for the BGLU and Ben Gurion in the Palestine delegation. The invitation made it clear that the 1928 decision against policy resolutions would be operative, but the Indian delegation gave advance notice that they would wish to discuss the political situation.[169]

India

In June the formal separation of the office and functions of the Secretary of State for Dominions Affairs from those of the Secretary of State for the Colonies had given further clarification to the meaning of

Dominion status, but the Simon Commission's Report had not recommended Dominion status. The immediate question was whether the Labour Party could guarantee that the British Government would accept such a recommendation if made by the Round Table Conference, and if not, what could be gained by Indian participation.

Chaman Lall was convinced that the Labour Government was not in a position to give any guarantee, and that the only way to freedom was by a short cut. Once more he was answered by the Irish Free State Labour Party's delegate, who warned that it was possible to carry on revolutionary agitation for one or two years, but not to live long in a state of constant high tension, and that the revolutionary method was unlikely to put Indians into a position to carry on self-government. The General Council's chairman, John Beard of the TGWU, commented that Ireland had finished up with partition, and there would be many partitions in India if the same line were followed there. Spokesmen from New Zealand, Australia and Palestine urged the Indians to co-operate with the Labour government. The discussion of these immediate issues may have strengthened the hands of those in the ITUF who hoped to use the Round Table Conference to gain the franchise for Indian workers.[170]

The Labour Party's dilemma remained: it was responsible for governing India against the will of the main nationalist movement, and had to negotiate a transfer of power; in the long term, if independence meant the transfer was to Indian capitalism – and there was no doubt that it did – was that the right aim? Joshi insisted that the Party's declarations must be taken to mean what they said, though self-government would not produce any heaven for the Indian worker. He found an ally in Hallsworth,[171] who was not at all sure that the Labour government had done all it might have done. He doubted whether Indian employers, many of whom were more backward than the British firms in India, would do better for their workers than outside exploiters, but that was not an argument against full self-government. Shiva Rao argued that imperial rule necessitated huge expenditure on the army in face of appalling social conditions, while the restricted franchise denied representation to the Indian worker; Gandhi's movement was a genuine mass movement, and the British had asked for it. They were coming close to Nehru's contention, six years later, that independence was the actual prerequisite for social and economic change.[172]

The West Indies

The West Indian spokesmen immediately followed the Indian lead. Speaking to a memorandum put forward for discussion by the TWMA, Cipriani replied to J. H. Thomas that trusteeship would not do for the West Indies. The memorandum claimed self-government on

the grounds of competence. West Indians already preponderated in the
professions and in trade and held important posts in government
departments, but the problems of staffing and promotion in the civil
service were stressed. These were in fact central to the transfer of
power. Cipriani's arguments, however, may not have appealed to the
British working-class delegates. He contended that professionals
trained in Britain should not be forced to put up with the autocracy of
officials transferred from Africa, that they were 'coloured gentlemen'
with the same aspirations as white men; in short, West Indians had the
ability, culture, and civilization to administer their own affairs.[173]
Critchlow, on the other hand, demanded extension of the franchise as
the first requirement.

At the 1928 Conference Cipriani had protested that although West
Indian sugar enjoyed a tariff preference to compete with Cuban sugar,
it was now also in competition with British subsidized beet sugar, and
needed increased preference or some other form of assistance. He
raised this again, and made another exasperated plea for trade union
legislation in Trinidad. Both the TWMA and the BGLU asked for
more comprehensive workmen's compensation legislation, old age
pensions, and minimum wages. Their contributions showed that their
proposals had been carefully prepared, that their organizations gave
close attention to workers' problems, and that they were aware of
legislation in other countries.

They drew a careful reply from Drummond Shiels, now Parliamentary Under-Secretary of State for the Colonies. He pointed to the
Labour Government's establishment of a Colonial Development Fund
as earnest of their intention to break with the conception of colonies as
overseas estates for commercial exploitation, and to the new Ceylon
constitution, which gave universal suffrage, as an important experiment in democracy. But it was indicative of the secretive atmosphere
surrounding Colonial Office business at the time that he did not
enlarge upon any proposals for industrial and trade union legislation
although the Secretary of State, Lord Passfield (Sidney Webb), had
just broached these subjects with colonial governors at the Colonial
Office Conference, and was to issue his despatch on trade union
legislation only two months later.

The Internationals

The Conference also discussed affiliations to the LSI and the IFTU, and
the work of the ILO. The LSI, which like the IFTU was not an
organizing body, provided little more than a forum in which the issues
of the day could be discussed. The IFTU had a more definite role, but
still lacked affiliates. Its Paris Congress in 1927 endorsed a British
resolution calling for an effort to extend organization, and invitations

to consider affiliation were sent to likely bodies outside. The AFL still refused. The Dominions trade unions, partly owing to the size of their countries, had difficulties in achieving a single trade union voice. In Canada there was a division between the purely Canadian unions and the 'international' unions linked with the USA; the Australian flirtation with the PPTUS was over, but it was not followed by formal affiliation to the IFTU; in South Africa the TUC with its 20,000 members was not prepared to be swamped by the ICU with its claim to 100,000. The new Indian Trade Union Federation, while considering affiliation, baulked at the cost; so did the Irish Trades Union Congress, which calculated that the fees would take half its income. In 1930 the only effective Commonwealth affiliates of the IFTU outside Britain were the Trades and Labor Congress of Canada and the Palestine Federation of Labour.

This meant that the most representative forum, for the trade union side only, was still the annual ILO Conference. Even there workers' representation was incomplete. Between 1921 and 1930 New Zealand sent no delegation at all to Geneva; Australia failed to send any workers' delegate in 1922, and South Africa in 1923 and 1927.[174] There was also, except for the British and Indian governments – and their records were patchy – a failure to ratify ILO Conventions, partly because in Canada and Australia the federal structure presented difficulties, and in New Zealand because it was claimed that the Conventions made no improvement on their existing legislation. At the 1930 Commonwealth Labour Conference Poulton called for a greater effort to build up the prestige of the ILO and its capacity to establish international labour standards.

The TUC had hoped for one trade union national centre in each Commonwealth country, all affiliated to the IFTU and working together at ILO Conferences. This could not be achieved, but it was notable that the Indian delegates' determination to ensure continued workers' representation in the ILO was stubbornly maintained throughout the various negotiations towards greater unity that took place in the Indian movement in the next decade.

The Balance Sheet

The TUC and the Labour Party had set out together in 1917 to restore the Second International. They had succeeded, but at the cost of giving formal recognition to the great divide between their own thinking and that of the revolutionaries gathered in the Comintern. The political attempt to overcome this division during the period of joint working had failed; so had the TUC's subsequent effort at inter-union co-operation.

These failures cut at the root of all the British Labour movement's hopes for the postwar world. It was not intended that the revived International should merely repeat the old feuds and theoretical controversies of the previous fifty years, but rather that it should rally the workers of all countries to make a distinctive contribution to the new institutions that were being planned to maintain peace and secure social reform. The Labour Party and the two Labour governments put all their weight behind the LSI and the League of Nations; the TUC made a parallel effort in the IFTU and the ILO. But in each case the USA stood aside, and in the Comintern and the RILU, and in the Soviet government, all the international organizations supported by British Labour were regarded as active agents of imperialism.

Below government level, the Labour Party suffered less from this divide than the TUC. It was able to isolate the Communist Party, and had nothing to fear from it in electoral terms, but this merely concentrated pressure on the trade unions. In its experience of the Anglo–Russian Joint Advisory Council and of the NMM, the TUC demonstrated that an established trade union movement could resist and contain the Comintern/RILU attack. When it looked to the Commonwealth, however, its efforts were seriously undermined by the implementation of the Fifth Comintern Congress theses of 1924 which required all communist organizations to help free the unions in the dependencies from the domination of the metropolitan trade union bureaucracies. This instruction was an astounding inversion of the actual position. The TUC had no organizational means of dominating anybody, nor did it try to create them. Its ventures into the Commonwealth were responses to invitations and appeals; its administrative arrangements were made ad hoc as pressures were exerted from outside. The General Council never tried to build a permanent Commonwealth body with affiliations, contributions, and decision-making machinery. An early precedent was Clements Kadalie's application for the affiliation of the Industrial and Commercial Workers' Union in South Africa. The TUC replied that it was not an international body and advised affiliation to the IFTU. Accordingly, Kadalie attended the IFTU's Paris Congress in 1927.[175] Long after the Second World War the TUC was still refusing applications for affiliation from colonial unions. Even if they had been granted, the TUC did not control its affiliates; nor did the IFTU.

A more pertinent charge would have been that the TUC did not anticipate the extent of the responsibility it would have to assume in the Commonwealth. When the suggestion was made at the 1917 Congress for a Commonwealth organization, it was thought that international co-operation would render it unnecessary, and in the immediately following years such energy as the TUC had to spare from its own task of reorganization was devoted first to the internationals, as was its money, when the responsibilities of affiliation were accepted. Yet the LSI and the IFTU were of little help to the TUC in the colonial field. The empires of the other European powers were more centralized than the British and administered on different lines, and the theoretical analyses current in the Continental labour movements had scant appeal for the TUC leaders and appeared to have little relevance to the immediate problems with which they were confronted. The effective contribution to TUC policy was made by the Labour Party, beginning with the briefs prepared for Berne in 1919 and continued through the period of joint working, and after that, in the Commonwealth Labour Conferences of 1928 and 1930.

Although there were always opportunities for contact with Indian leaders, the three Commonwealth Conferences provided the only forum in which representatives of colonial labour organizations could join their British colleagues in an effort to thrash out a long-term colonial policy. Though not stated in so many words, it was implicit in the discussions on India that nationalism was to be accepted. If so, had Labour any special contribution to make? It was to be found in the painstaking studies prepared for the 1928 Conference, and in the interventions of the West Indian delegates at all three Conferences. Their voice was recognizably the workers' voice, seldom heard at Westminster or, as Albert Marryshow of Grenada pointed out in 1930, in the reports of commissioners and colonial governors. It was heard also in the West Indies, where a 'thrill of pride' ran through the community when Cipriani's speech in 1930 was reported in the local press.[176] The Commonwealth Conferences were landmarks in the history of the West Indian labour movements. The first inspired Critchlow's West Indian Labour Conference, and the second and third brought Trinidad and Grenada into the discussions and into contact with the rest of the Commonwealth and the internationals. In regard to India, however, the Labour Party's problem was not solved. India would have been unrepresented at the Conferences without the trade union delegates, and by 1930 they spoke for only a part of the Indian trade union movement. A policy based on recognition of nationalism presupposed a response from the dominant nationalist party. The Labour Government's invitation to the Round Table Conference was declined by the Indian National Congress, and the British Labour leaders were unable to achieve a meeting of minds with the Congress leaders until after the Second World War.

The development of parliamentary institutions required long and sustained effort, with little result to show at any one time. There had been too many delays and wrong decisions, and there were too many complications, for it to proceed undisturbed in India. Although the nationalist movement aimed at parliamentary government, there were sufficient internal reasons for non-co-operation. But the intervention of outside agencies certainly encouraged distrust on both sides, and presented an alternative to the parliamentary road. At home, the Labour Party and the TUC had made their choice, and the differentiation of political trends in the British movement was completed in 1932 when the ILP disaffiliated from the Labour Party and then split within itself. The Labour Party's domestic base was narrowed, and although different elements continued to be represented in the trade unions, the steps taken to combat disruption tended to restrict channels of representation and to produce a politically homogeneous leadership in the TUC which had little sympathy with revolutionary sentiments or methods.

It was here that the LAI left its legacy. It could not resolve the tension between socialism and nationalism, for no one could work in it – as Maxton, Nehru and Fimmen bore witness – who happened to have noncommunist views of their own. Nevertheless, it could transmit a message, and one that had always appealed to the ILP. Untrammelled by international or domestic discipline, by office or any prospect of office, with no elective responsibility to the main body of the British Labour movement, the ILP leaders like Brockway and Maxton, passionately sincere in their beliefs, carried on what had appeared to be the original impulse of the Brussels Congress. They had little influence in India, but it was to them, not to the Labour Party, that the small group of London-based West Indians led by the disappointed Communist George Padmore turned in the 1930s. This group had some minor influence in the West Indies, and perhaps more amongst many of the emerging generation of educated nationalists in West Africa. Like the LAI, the Padmore group aimed to link nationalism with revolutionary socialism, and to see the colonial world as a whole.[177] In the attitude of negation and continuous opposition which virtually postponed constructive effort until after independence, and in the illiberal, nonsocialist, near-racialist pan-Africanism which followed, there was a dark side to Padmore's International African Service Bureau and to the postwar successors to the Brussels Congress, the Congress of Peoples Against Imperialism and the All-African Peoples' Conference of 1958. However, this was not intended or foreseen in the 1930s, and the mere fact that such movements developed and persisted pointed to a continuing trend of thought which did not find expression in the Labour Party or the TUC, or in any of the internationals, whether socialist or communist, trade union or political.

Yet the work of the Labour Party and the TUC in the 1920s had established ideas and relationships without which these negative trends might have prevailed in colonies suffering from appalling economic distress. It had also established the essential outlines of the Labour Party's colonial policy, and subsequent additions were largely developments of ideas expressed then. Passfield's work in the Colonial Office was again cut short by the fall of the Labour Government in 1931, but it was not lost.

This experience of co-operation with the Labour Party was of immense benefit to the TUC. Left to themselves, the General Council would never have sat down to systematic discussion of colonial policy. They were only marginally interested in the political problems, yet these set the background against which the overseas unions had to grow. The TUC's business was to work with them – a slow and inherently unexciting task, but the only one that by its nature the TUC, and only the TUC, was specifically qualified to perform. The General Council had already begun to tackle it, independently of the Labour Party, in India and in the ILO.

5 The Scope for Trade Union Action

When the TUC began to look overseas, it had neither the knowledge nor the organization for effective action. Three initial essentials may be identified. The first, begun with the publication of the *International Trades Union Review* in 1918 and continued in the Far Eastern Labour Committee in 1925, was the collection and dissemination of information; the second, begun in 1917 with the TUC's internal reorganization, was to develop the capacity to use its knowledge; the third, begun with the conference of TUC unions with international affiliations in July 1918, was to identify and where necessary to construct, or help to construct, the organizations with and through which it could work. There were further extensions of functions as new needs arose, so that the TUC which at home did not organize unions, bargain with employers, or participate in the formation of government policy, ultimately came, after the Second World War, to send organizers into the colonies, to help in union negotiations with British firms operating there, and to join with employers' representatives in standing committees advising the Colonial Office. In the first decade, the scope of action was defined by the TUC's standing as the representative body of British trade unionism – in the IFTU, the ILO, with such overseas unions as sought its co-operation, and with the British government. Its specific contribution derived from experience in Britain.

How far was this experience acknowledged to be relevant to the dependencies? The TUC never encountered a Secretary of State for the Colonies who was opposed to trade unionism as such, from the first deputation on St Kitts, when Walter Long declared that he was sympathetic to trade unions in that island or anywhere else, and would be glad, after the war, to discuss organization in the Crown Colonies with the Parliamentary Committee.[1] Secretaries of State for India – even Birkenhead – took the same line. When Montagu was first approached in 1921, he expressed the view that India could not be industrialized without the help of organized labour, and that the new trade unions there should be welcomed and recognized as one of the essentials of Indian development. This did not imply that ministers accepted a mere transference of British law and practice into dependencies at different stages of organization and industrialization and with different traditions. Montagu argued that the proceedings of the AITUC's second congress did not display the recognition of opposite points of view which enabled the Parliamentary Committee's representatives, accustomed as they were to the hard knocks of public life, to counter an objection with vigour and tolerance as expressed in the forcible but jocular repartee of J. H. Thomas. However, it was not necesary for trade unions in every country to go through the same 'war-worn' history as the British movement: it might be possible to telescope history in India by using British experience, and he accepted Thomas's response, 'It is the only thing we can profit by'.[2]

India

The most effective method of helping the unions at that stage was the Parliamentary Committee's traditional approach to ministers. Deputations were sent to Montagu, Olivier, Birkenhead, the Indian High Commissioner in London, and to Wedgwood Benn.[3] They encountered a difficulty that did not arise in Britain – the status of the Government of India and its obligation to consult provincial governments when enacting central legislation that impinged upon them. As ministerial responsibility was progressively devolved, both in India and later in the colonies, even Parliamentary Questions were restricted, and at all times ministers were inclined to argue that 'the man on the spot' must be trusted. As Birkenhead explained, 'it would be not only unconstitutional but highly inconvenient and improper that I should attempt to dictate to the Viceroy ... who is an Executive Officer of the highest authority ... who is informed of and pressed by the local problems, and whose local knowledge must of course be incomparably greater than that of the Secretary of State'. When Tillett asked what the attitude of his Office would be towards a British trade union inquiry into conditions in India, he replied 'Oh no. I would never consider such a thing at all. It is absurd'.[4] He could not sustain this lofty attitude, but the general position always was that representations to British ministers had the best chance of success if they coincided with pressure in India, if information received from India was incontrovertible, and if the TUC's spokesmen were able to muster arguments from their own experience which ministers would accept as applicable to Indian conditions. Two examples may be given in which these requirements were broadly met.

Trade Union Legislation

In February 1921 the Parliamentary Committee received information from the WWLI that Wadia and nine others had incurred a penalty of

£7,000 for organizing work. A deputation which included the secretary of the League, J. Potter-Wilson, met Montagu on 22 March.[5] The case had originated in the refusal of promotion to an employee of Messrs Binny in Madras, allegedly on the grounds that he was a trade unionist. The refusal of colleagues to take his job led to dismissals, a lockout, and disturbances which resulted in the intervention of armed police and fifteen deaths.

There had been a series of strikes and disturbances in 1920, but in this dispute the employers resorted to the charge, current in Britain before 1871, of conspiracy to interfere in their business by inducing workers to breach their contracts of employment. They secured an injunction prohibiting Wadia from engaging in the Madras Labour Union's activities, and subsequently the employers were awarded damages. By the time the deputation took place a settlement had been reached: the firm did not pursue its claim, Wadia withdrew from the union, and the Government of India accepted a central Legislative Assembly resolution moved by Joshi which called for the protection of trade union activity from charges of civil and criminal liability and for the registration of trade unions. Montagu summed up the legal position for the deputation. The Madras High Court had correctly regarded the union as an illegal conspiracy, since none of the relevant British legislation had been enacted in India: there was no protection for peaceful picketing or against actions for tort in trade disputes, and no legal provision for the registration of trade unions or for vesting union property in trustees with power to sue and be sued in respect of it. As Poulton expressed it, the TUC was asking for the help of the India Office, so that officials in India might understand that trade unions had the right to organize and that their rights would be protected by the Secretary of State.

Montagu said that the new Viceroy, Lord Reading (who had appeared for the Amalgamated Society of Railway Servants in the damages case that followed the House of Lords' Taff Vale judgement in 1902, and had spoken in Parliament in favour of the Liberal Trade Disputes Act 1906), wished to help the unions. The Government of India intended to legislate: it had no constitutional obligation to send the proposed Bill to the Secretary of State, but he expected to receive it and would ask the Parliamentary Committee to comment on it. The deputation also pointed out that there was no machinery such as the British conciliation boards to assist the early settlement of disputes.[6] Pressed by Thomas and Bowerman, Montagu agreed to call the Government of India's attention to the British Act of 1906 which reversed the Taff Vale judgement, and to the need for conciliation machinery.

This discussion suggests that the TUC had not received full

information from the WWLI, either because it was not sufficiently expert to handle the material that the AITUC had sent, or because the new AITUC had not immediately grasped the issues involved. Nevertheless, the deputation was satisfied. They were not attuned to the laborious process of legislation in India. The provincial governments had to be consulted, and when the TUC made enquiries before Congress met in September, it was found that a new Factories Bill had been tabled, but no trade union Bill had emerged. In their opinion, the Parliamentary Committee reported to Congress, no measure would be satisfactory which did not give Indian work-people the same rights as those of trade unionists in Britain.[7]

There were already grounds for caution on two points that always arose for the TUC in its contacts with the government concerning both India[8] and the colonies. Montagu hoped for some *quid pro quo*. Supposing, he said, that his Office kept the TUC informed of developments, and that a trade union in India was being badly conducted, was perhaps fomenting trouble by badly conducted negotiations or on some political grounds, it would be useful if the TUC could use its influence and say 'This is all wrong: you ought not to have done this: we should have done it in a different way'. Thomas replied that if the TUC acted only on official information it would be suspect to Indian trade unions, and Swales[9] suggested that the government should use its influence with the employers to prevent them from killing the spirit of organization by persecuting the leaders who would surely take the place of Wadia. Montagu also expressed the view that many of the bodies that had come spontaneously into existence during the postwar strike wave were not genuine trade unions, and having regard to this and to the migratory character of the workforce it might be necessary to find an appropriate form of organization. This was uncharted territory for the TUC.

The non-co-operation movement and the boycott of the Prince of Wales were in full swing at the end of the year when Montagu gave Bowerman two confidential memoranda on trade union law and workmen's compensation which the Government of India had submitted to provincial governments. The proposals for trade union law included provision for the voluntary registration of unions, with the right to provide benefits for members and to use their funds for political purposes on the same conditions as in the English legislation of 1913. The courts would not interfere in their management, and their activities would cover negotiation on wages, hours and conditions of employment. Unregistered unions would not be illegal, but picketing in any form would not be countenanced, and the unions would not be relieved from civil liability for tortious acts.[10]

In a note prepared for the General Council, Tillett and George

Hicks[11] commented that although the proposals on trade unions in general followed English law, they did not meet the General Council's expressed view that Indian law should approximate to it. The Government of India did not see their way to accepting the English provisions on picketing and liability for actions in tort. Taking into account the vast numbers that would be covered by the legislation and the fact that trade unions in Britain were established for many years before the law granted the freedoms which they now possessed, Tillett and Hicks took the view that it was desirable to get the initial legislation on to the statute book, with the prospect of later improvements being conceded in the light of experience. They considered that the proposals for workmen's compensation were also defective. They did not cover the building trade, and in their view the General Council should insist that employers must be compelled to insure against risks and to provide first aid, that workers should be free to have impartial medical attention, and that compensation should be payable from the first day of incapacity at the rate of 100 per cent of the worker's average earnings.[12] A second deputation, again including J. Potter-Wilson, went to Montagu to press these views on 31 January 1922.[13]

The moment was not propitious: Chauri Chaura was only eight days ahead. Montagu was able to cite the Government of India's reference to the 'acts of violence and intimidation' which had characterized a large proportion of the disputes in which Indian unions had been concerned, and there had even been cases in which funeral services were withheld. He expressed the view that the picketing of shops for political purposes could not be compared with anything that had happened in Britain. The deputation argued that this was not picketing in industrial disputes, in which Indian trade unions needed this method of pressing their case even more markedly than British unions which had other means of publicity. Thomas emphasized that the omission of exemption from liability for tortious acts meant that a union could be completely destroyed by loss of its funds. The TUC recognized that trade union machinery could be used for political purposes, but claimed that legislation giving the unions full rights would be the best safeguard against abuse. Montagu acknowledged that every government should go a little ahead of public opinion, and agreed to convey their views to Delhi.

Until the legislation was enacted the unions were in limbo. Registrars refused them registration under other laws. Strikes continued, and although the employers brought no more prosecutions for damages, civil and criminal liability remained. Although picketing that became violent was acknowledged to be illegal, the limits of legal action were not defined.[14] Nor, apparently, were the limits on actions by the police. Records and even furniture had been destroyed in the Madras Labour

Union's office, and after a further strike, in which there was violence, the union held no more open meetings until 1923. But police informers went in to the religious sabha from which the union had sprung and which workers still attended, though after dark and with their faces covered.[15]

As consultations continued in India, the General Council pressed for legislation, and was able to report to the 1925 Congress that a Bill had been introduced and referred to a Select Committee. It included restrictions on the use of union funds which had not been foreshadowed in the innitial memorandum, but Joshi and Chaman Lall had been appointed to the Select Committee, where they would seek amendments.[16] Finally the Trade Unions Act 1926 passed the Legislative Assembly on 8 February 1926 and received the Governor-General's Assent on 25 March.

It stated that the Societies Registration Act 1860, the Cooperative Societies Act 1912 and the Companies Act 1913 would not apply to any registered trade union, and declared void any registration of a trade union which had already taken place under any of these Acts. It defined a trade union as a combination formed primarily for the purpose of regulating relations between workmen and employers, or between workmen and workmen, or between employers and employers, or for imposing restrictive conditions on the conduct of any trade or business. This definition also covered any federation of two or more unions. Seven or more members might apply to register a union, and there was an appeal to a judge against refusal, withdrawal or cancellation of a certificate of registration. To secure registration, a union must have an office and rules which must set out the whole of the objects for which it was established and the lawful purposes to which its funds might be applied. The rules must cover the admission of members, the conditions of entitlement to benefits, the appointment and removal of officers and the members of its executive, and the custody and audit of its funds. The union must send annually to the Registrar an audited general statement of receipts and expenditure and notify changes of officers and rules.

Various provisions stamped a trade union character on these organizations. By rule, the ordinary members must be persons actually engaged in an industry with which the union was connected, and so must not less than half the members of the executive – the latter being an innovation which later reappeared in some colonial legislation. There was a list of lawful objects to which the expenditure of the general funds must be confined. They included the conduct of trade disputes, the provision of educational, social and religious benefits for members or their dependants, the upkeep of periodicals, and contributions 'to any cause intended to benefit workmen in general'.

Provided it was kept separate and no member was compelled to contribute, a fund for the promotion of the civic and political interests of members might be established, and be spent on meetings and propaganda, electoral candidates' expenses, the registration of electors, and the maintenance of members of legislative bodies or local authorities.

Thus there was a price to pay for registration: a union must, as far as rules and legal requirements could ensure it, be a bona-fide union. A union which could not or would not pay this price was not obliged to register. Some did not, but in practice most of the vigorous organizations did so. By the end of 1929, there were 87 registered unions, with 183,000 members.[17]

The potential threat of liability for criminal conspiracy in trade disputes was specifically removed in respect of any agreement amongst members – excluding an agreement to commit an offence – to further any of the specified lawful objects. The Act also conferred immunity from civil liability in respect of acts done in contemplation or furtherance of a trade dispute, thus ruling out prosecutions for inducement to breach a contract of employment or interfere with an employer's business. Nor would the union itself be liable for tortious acts committed by its agents in a trade dispute if it were proved that the agent acted without the knowledge of, or contrary to the express instructions given by, the union executive. These protections were not given to unregistered unions – a departure from British practice which was an exception to the general character of the legislation, which broadly gave the British trade union liberties which the Government of India had not been willing to concede in 1922. In this it had gone ahead of some chambers of commerce, which had wanted picketing to be prohibited, but despite this their spokesmen in the Legislative Assembly undertook that they would accept and work the legislation.[18]

This was in most respects a satisfactory outcome of the efforts of the Indian trade unions – and especially of the Legislative Assembly Members from the AITUC – and of the British TUC. There remained outstanding the problem of conciliation machinery which the TUC had broached with Montagu. The significance of this gap in the law was revealed in a series of trade disputes in which the TUC was asked to take an interest.

The Bombay Textile Dispute 1925

The general arguments that sufficed for a discussion on the first introduction of trade union law would not meet the needs of a deputation on a specific industrial problem. Here the first requirement was detailed, accurate information from the AITUC. Chaman Lall and Joshi co-operated in the Far Eastern Labour Conditions Committee's inquiry, and information gathered from press and official sources supplemented material supplied by Joshi when a TUC deputation, at his request, met Lord Birkenhead on 3 December 1925 to discuss the textile dispute in Bombay. They were able to submit documents on the origin and progress of the strike, on wages and conditions, and on the system of managing agencies in the industry.[19] They had to be well briefed to face Birkenhead, a former Lord Chancellor who had opposed the English Trade Disputes Act in 1906 and just two months before had urged on Lord Reading the need for a complete reconsideration of the exceptional legal status of trade unions.[20] He interrogated Lee on managing agencies as if he were examining a frightened witness in court, but he evoked some spirited rejoinders.

The strike was against a reduction in food allowance which became operative on 1 September. It was equivalent to an $11\frac{1}{2}$ per cent wage cut, justified by the mill-owners on the grounds of Japanese competition and the Indian excise duty on cotton cloth. There were some small mill unions in existence, but the workers generally were unorganized and without funds. The mill-owners had rejected a suggestion from the Bombay trade union leaders, who had consulted the operatives and feared that they would be starved into submission if they went on strike, that short-time working should be instituted instead. The strike began on 15 September as a spontaneous movement of some 13,000 workers, and soon 150,000 were either on strike, locked out, or had left the city. One of the largest mill-owners, Sir Victor Sassoon, was meanwhile building a private racecourse in Poona.[21] Approached by the union leaders, the Governor, Sir Leslie Wilson, proposed a committee of inquiry and the suspension of wage cuts until it had reported. Again the employers refused. They withdrew the cuts only when Reading suspended the excise duty from 1 December. The TUC deputation went to support the AITUC's demand for a full inquiry – now strengthened by the manner of ending the strike, as if the reduction in food allowance had been used to secure the abolition of the duty.

The union case rested on the AITUC's contention that the duty was not the sole cause of the industry's condition, and on the TUC's arguments, already put to Montagu and Olivier, for statutory inquiry and conciliation machinery. Birkenhead replied that the Government of India intended to introduce trade disputes legislation after the Trade Unions Bill had been passed. Meanwhile, the Indian Tariff Board could start a limited inquiry if an industry demanded tariff protection. The deputation was able to argue convincingly that since the level of production had scarcely fallen in face of Japanese competition, other factors needed investigation, especially the system of managing agencies. Birkenhead expressed his conviction that only ad-hoc inquiries undertaken with the co-operation of both employers and employed could have any value, and in this case the employers had not asked for an inquiry and the workers were insufficiently organized to produce representative spokesmen. He totally rejected the idea of a general inquiry into labour conditions in India, but he undertook to convey the TUC's views to Reading with a request for comments on the practicability of setting up inquiry machinery for individual disputes, and to the Viceroy-designate, Edward Wood (later Lord Irwin), who was already gathering information in the India Office.

In the event the Government of India appointed a special Tariff Board Inquiry with terms of reference which enabled it to investigate conditions in the entire industry, overruling the employers, who again asked for the sole issue of Japanese competition to be examined. Meanwhile, the Textile Labour Union had been established, and it presented its evidence, answering 126 definite questions put to it by the Tariff Board. The deputation to Birkenhead, the General Council reported to Congress, produced better results than had been expected at the time.[22]

The fact that this was the first time a union had been invited to tender evidence in an industrial inquiry, and then only by an extension of a Tariff Board investigation, served to emphasize the gap in the Indian legislation, which provided no bridge between willing negotiations and strike action. In 1927 the Bengal-Nagpur Indian Railway Union was excluded altogether from a management inquiry held after union representations had been made and a strike had taken place which involved violence and a shooting. TUC representatives met the Indian High Commissioner, and after a further strike had been followed by the dismissal of a fifth of the 10,000 employees of the Khargpur railway workshops, went again to Birkenhead to ask for an impartial inquiry.[23] Birkenhead again stressed the delicacy of his own position, but undertook to convey their views. In April 1928 the India Office informed the TUC that the Government of India was ready to introduce legislation to establish machinery for the settlement of industrial disputes.[24]

The Trade Disputes Act 1929

The Trade Disputes Act passed the central Legislative Assembly in January 1929. It defined a trade dispute as any dispute or difference between employers and workmen, or between workmen and workmen, which was connected with the employment or nonemployment or the terms of employment, or with the conditions of labour, of any person. Although it was based on the English Industrial Courts Act 1919, it omitted the establishment of a permanent Industrial Court (which could have developed its own prestige and expertise) and provided only for ad-hoc inquiries and for boards of conciliation, appointed by provincial governments or by the Governor-General as appropriate. A court of inquiry or a conciliation board must be set up if both parties to a dispute applied through persons that the authority was satisfied were representative, and in addition the authority might by order refer any existing or apprehended dispute. A court should consist of an independent chairman and one or more independent persons, and it must inquire into the matters referred to it and report to the authority. A conciliation board should have an independent chairman sitting either with independent persons or with persons appointed on the recommendation of the parties to the dispute in equal numbers. Its duty would be to try to bring about a settlement and, if it failed, to report its findings with a full statement of the facts and circumstances and a recommendation for the determination of the dispute which should 'state in plain language what in the opinion of the board ought and ought not to be done by the respective parties concerned'.

The British Industrial Courts Act supplemented the procedural agreements voluntarily agreed between unions and employers in many industries and the conciliation work of the Labour Department of the Board of Trade (later the Ministry of Labour) which had been initiated by the Conciliation Act 1896. Outside Ahmedabad, India had no parallel to voluntary procedural agreements, and there were no permanent conciliation officers. In July 1929, in discussion with Wedgwood Benn on the Golmuri Tin Plate strike,[25] Tillett stressed the need to attempt conciliation at an early stage instead of allowing a dispute to drag on for months, and the Whitley Commission commented that the Indian Act, by placing such reliance on ad-hoc inquiries rather than on early conciliation, had copied the less valuable part of British legislation on industrial relations. It recommended the establishment of permanent conciliation officers,[26] and that step was taken in 1934 by the government of Bombay in separate legislation. Little could be expected in the years of civil disobedience, but when the new Indian ministers came into office in the provinces in 1937 they made more use of the Act's conciliation provisions in the first year than in all the previous eight years.[27] In 1938 the Bombay government set up a permanent industrial court.[28]

The Act would have got off to a better start if it had not been so long delayed. In 1924 the Government of India had prevented the Bombay government from introducing a similar measure as it wanted to prepare all-India legislation,[29] so Bombay had no statutory provisions when the textile strike occurred in 1925. Moreover, the Trade Unions Act was not passed until 1926, and Birkenhead could rightly point to the absence of organization amongst the textile workers. Since none of the procedures provided by the Trade Disputes Act could result in the enforcement of a decision on an unwilling party, it could be used most effectively in an atmosphere which encouraged a willingness to compromise. However, the Fawcett Committee set up by agreement in 1928, which found that most of the unions' demands were reasonable, did not report until 1929, when its recommendations quickly became submerged beneath the Communist-led strike which started in April. The court of inquiry appointed in that strike marked the first use of the new Trade Disputes Act. Its finding that the prolongation of the strike, with riots and widespread disturbances, was due to the uncompromising attitude of extremists[30] can surely have told the Bombay government little that it did not already know, and with the leaders of the GKU in Meerut gaol and the Textile Labour Union weakened, the union side to the dispute was disintegrating.

The timing was doubly unfortunate in that the final Bill was prepared after the British general strike of 1926 and the enactment of the British Trade Disputes Act 1927. Its provisions on illegal strikes were translated into the Indian legislation. A strike was illegal if it had an object other than furtherance of a dispute within the trade or industry in which the strikers were employed, or if designed or calculated to inflict severe, general and prolonged hardship on the community and thereby to compel the government – if such compulsion might reasonably be expected to result – to take or abstain from taking any particular course of action. There was a fine of Rs. 200, or imprisonment for up to three months, or both, for declaring, instigating, inciting others to take part in, or otherwise acting in furtherance of, such an illegal strike, but not for merely stopping work. Legal action in regard to these provisions might be taken only by a provincial government or by the Governor-General in Council but, although a wide field lay open when civil disobedience started, they were scarcely used. In 1934 the Bombay government prosecuted eight leaders of a textile strike on the grounds that it was not in furtherance of a trade dispute and was designed to inflict severe hardship on the community, but the prosecution failed for lack of proof.[31] In essential services – postal, telegraph and telephone services, sanitation, electricity or water supply, and such railways as might be notified by the Governor-General – there was a fine of up to Rs. 50, or imprisonment up to one month, or both, for going on strike in breach of contract without giving at least 14 days' previous notice of intention.

These restrictions alienated the trade union leaders who might have been more enthusiastic about the provisions for inquiry and conciliation if they had not been included. 'The blackest of all Bills ever passed into law' was the description given to Congress by the Indian fraternal delegate, V. R. Kalappa, in 1929.[32] Nor was the inauguration of the Act helped by the imposition, over the heads of the central Legislative Assembly, which refused to pass it, of a Public Safety Act. Nevertheless, the constructive provisions of the Act were needed, and established a foundation on which it was later possible to build.

If insistence that the British model should be followed had in this case proved a boomerang, there were two divergences from it. The rules concerning union political funds were not touched, perhaps because in practice the unions could not afford to contribute to political parties either directly or indirectly – rather the boot was on the other foot. As late as 1944–5 only four unions maintained political funds.[33] Nor was there any prohibition against civil service unions being affiliated to the AITUC. This was, however, attempted in Ceylon.

Ceylon

As the Conservative government went out of office in Britain, the Ceylon government completed the drafts of four Ordinances dealing with the registration of trade unions, trade disputes, the establishment of a conciliation board, and minimum wages. The TUC was alerted by A. E. Goonesinha, President of the All-Ceylon Trade Union Congress, who stated that notices had been sent to the Post and Telegraph and Hospital Workers' Unions that they must not affiliate to the All-Ceylon TUC or elect nonmembers as officials. He asked the General Council to use their influence to prevent the 'noxious' features of the Trade Disputes Act 1927 being enacted in Ceylon. Citrine reminded the Colonial Office of the TUC's opposition to the 1927 Act, of which the prohibition on the affiliation of public service unions to the All-Ceylon TUC was reminiscent, and pointed out that unions with illiterate members would find it difficult to produce officers from their own ranks. No satisfaction was obtained from the Colonial Office, which referred the matter to the Ministry of Labour. There all action was suspended until the new Labour government declared its policy towards the 1927 Act.

The Labour government was unable to muster a majority in Parliament to repeal the Act, which remained in Britain until after the war. However, in the Ministry of Labour the Ceylon papers were in the hands of the Principal Assistant Secretary in the General Department, F. W. Leggett, who considered that the four Ordinances together constituted a reactionary policy towards Labour. With Citrine's knowledge, he held the papers up, but warned the TUC in May 1930 that the Governor of Ceylon, Sir Herbert Stanley, had arrived in London and was extremely angry that his legislation had been delayed. The Colonial Office approved the introduction of the Bills into the Legislative Council on condition that the offensive provisions were deleted.[34] In September, in his confidential despatch on trade union legislation, Passfield notified all the colonies that he would not agree to the adoption of the 1927 Act's provisions in the colonies.[35] He could not, of course, prevent their adoption after the Labour government fell from power, and in some cases the 'noxious' clauses crept back.

Fraternal Co-operation

The General Council had done fairly well in their approaches to Government on legislative matters in which they could use their own experience and knowledge. But legislation does not build trade unions. Here the second traditional method of assistance was required – fraternal aid. Just as accurate knowledge of local conditions was needed before a deputation could discuss a specific trade dispute with Birkenhead, so the TUC had its own questions to ask when an appeal for help was received. Did it come from a bona-fide trade union, representative of workers, and reliable in its competence and purpose? Was any other body involved, such as a national centre, the IFTU or an international trade secretariat? Nothing effective could be done in China, because these questions could not be satisfactorily answered. If the General Council did wish to respond, had it the ability and resources to do so? The capacity to find the right answers to such questions could be developed only over a period of evolving fraternal relationships.

Two examples may be given, of a successful and an unsuccessful attempt to help Indian workers in dispute with their employers. In the 1925 textile strike the appeal came from Joshi, secretary of the AITUC at the time, and personally known to the TUC since 1919. The General Council made a grant of £250 from its own funds and appealed to its affiliates to subscribe through the TUC to a fund set up by the IFTU. Grants were also made by the International Federation of Textile Workers and the All-Russian Textile Workers' Union. The donations from Europe amounted to over £3,500, of which the TUC and its affiliates contributed nearly a third. With this and donations in India, nineteen relief centres for strikers and their families were opened in Bombay.[36] By good fortune, the Dundee Jute Workers' delegates, Tom Johnstone and J. F. Sime, arrived in Bombay during the strike, and in speeches to the workers gave strong support to the move to amalgamate the small mill unions.[37] Thus the strike produced a competent union able to take advantage of the TUC's representations to Birkenhead.

The effort to help the Tin Plate Workers' Union of Golmuri in 1929 failed. A strike began in April, but it was not until June that the TUC received three requests from the union, to all of which the General Council responded. The strike arose from the introduction of a rationalization scheme and the dismissal of some active workers, but was started against the advice of the union president, M. Daud. With Giri's help, he tried to get a settlement on the basis of reinstatement of the dismissed workers, a conciliation board or joint committee of investigation into the dispute, and the examination of other demands on wages and housing. The TUC was asked to give financial help and to approach the India Office and the Burmah Oil Company, the British firm which was the major shareholder in the Tin Plate Company. When a deputation met Wedgwood Benn in July he hoped the new Trade Disputes provisions might be used. But the Act left the initiative to the local government, and despite pressure from the Secretary of State, the Government of India found itself unable to persuade the Bihar Government to use it. In a direct approach to the main shareholder, Citrine and Tillett secured assurances from the Burmah Oil chairman that former employees on strike would be taken back without victimization as vacancies occurred, and that the company would recognize a properly constituted and representative union.[38] The union was only six months old, but there appeared to be a good chance of recognition, and thus of negotiation. Despite the efforts of Bakhale, then assistant secretary to the AITUC, it made no response to the report of the TUC's meeting with the company until December.

The strike had become politicized, with Daud replaced by an acting president. National Congress leaders went to Golmuri, including Subhas Bose, who joined the picket line and later became president himself.[39] The Workers' and Peasants' Party supported the strike.[40] The RILU attacked the union leaders, saying they were waiting for a favourable opportunity for betrayal, while the 'left Nationalists' Nehru and Bose did not betray the strikers openly because a foreign firm was involved: but the Indian bourgeoisie hoped through them to get a hold on the labour movement and use it to paralyse the class struggle.[41] In this atmosphere of negation and distrust, the strike dragged on, but many returned to work.

In December the union expressed willingness to call off the strike and to select an accredited trade unionist as its president if the management would set an early time limit for reinstatement, withdraw all suits of ejectment from company quarters, and continue to recognize the union. Informed of this by the TUC, the company's London office replied that the works were running to full capacity and not more than 400 men were still on strike; the company was willing to open a register for them with preference as vacancies arose. It was willing to continue to recognize the union, and claimed that none of the strikers had been evicted and no rent had been collected from them.

The General Council felt that they could gain no more, but no response came from the union either to them or to the AITUC. At the AITUC's Nagpur Congress, Bose and the delegates from the union were unwillingly to discuss the matter with Bakhale, who could only advise that there was no scope for further action by the General Council and thank them for their efforts in 'one among many thankless tasks' that they had undertaken for the Indian movement.[42] The strike collapsed after nine months.

It was not to be expected that the first thought of a union secretary with a strike on his hands would be to send information to the AITUC for transmission to the TUC, but the Golmuri experience demonstrated that the TUC could not act effectively without full information at the right time. When an appeal came in February 1929 for help for jute workers in dispute at Howrah, the TUC found that the dispute was six months old, but sent £100 nevertheless.[43] Another problem was to ensure that donations fulfilled their purpose: in one doubtful case Giri forced a union secretary to prepare a statement on all foreign money received, and in a strike in the Lillooah workshops of the East Indian Railway, the TUC sent £250 to the AITUC for disbursement by Joshi. In another, a suggestion was made that part of a grant should go to the defence in a criminal prosecution arising from a strike, but the TUC insisted it must be spent on relief, as intended.[44]

Other cases suggested a need for one channel for appeals on either side, but this was unattainable. In the East Indian Railway dispute a request was made to the TUC, and also to TUC affiliates by the ITF appealing to its own affiliates.[45] In the Bengal-Nagpur Railway dispute in 1927, the WWLI, which had worked with the TUC in 1921, went separately to the India Office, with which the TUC was in communication, and approached the Labour Party and a TUC affiliate directly. It did so as agent for the All-India Railwaymen's Association, which was not affiliated to the AITUC. To avoid overlapping, consultations were held with the WWLI, with apparent agreement, but a further appeal to a TUC affiliate in 1928[46] prompted the General Council to assert its view that all appeals should come directly to it through the AITUC.

Such procedural problems, appearing on the surface as the minutiae of trade union organization, were fundamental to successful fraternal co-operation between trade union bodies, or indeed to any other kind of overseas aid. They also affected the internal status of the AITUC and its external relationships.

Representation

Indian political organizations such as the Indian National Congress and the Home Rule League had established branches or committees in London which acted as their agents, and it was in accordance with this tradition that the AITUC appointed the WWLI as its agent in 1921. The League was founded in 1918, but preparations to form a joint body of Indian and British trade unionists had begun as early as 1916. Chaman Lall became associated with it, and its moving spirit, Saklatvala, had an influence on the Labour Party through his early membership of the ILP.[47] In 1920, before it became agent for the AITUC, the League appealed to the Parliamentary Committee for support. Its stated aim, 'independently of all political aims and movements to advocate the institution in India of provision for the welfare of the working population equivalent to, if not identical with, that granted to the workpeople of Great Britain',[48] coincided with TUC policy. The Parliamentary Committee made no donation of their own, but brought the appeal to the notice of affiliates, at the League's request sent a message of support to the inaugural congress of the AITUC and agreed to receive a fraternal delegate from the League at the Portsmouth Congress. But when the WWLI nominated Saklatvala, the Committee decided that his attendance would be inconsistent with the Standing Orders of Congress and that he could not attend as the representative of Indian workpeople.[49]

There was no hostility to the League, whose secretary joined the TUC's deputations to Montagu in March 1921, and in January 1922 after it had become the AITUC's agent. Nor were Saklatvala's political views the cause of his exclusion. He did not become a member of the Communist Party until April 1921, and as late as 1924 he was a member of the Imperial Sub-Committee of the Joint International Committee and prepared material for the joint TUC Labour Party deputation to Olivier.[50] But he did not represent any trade union, and it was evident that in agreeing to receive a delegate from the League the Parliamentary Committee had anticipated the arrival of an Indian who did.

This domestic disagreement became extended to India when the Executive Committee of the new AITUC decided (without an invitation) to send fraternal delegates to the forthcoming Cardiff Congress, and nominated Saklatvala and B. J. Horniman, the Irish editor of the *Bombay Chronicle*, who had been deported from India in 1919.[51] When the Parliamentary Committee had joined in formulating the IFTU constitution, it had been decided that delegates to the IFTU must be resident and organized in the countries they claimed to represent. They now applied this principle to fraternal delegates, deciding that it was inadvisable to accept anyone unless he was a native of, and came from, the country concerned. Their ruling upset the AITUC, but was reiterated in 1924 when preparations were being made for the first Commonwealth Labour Conference.[52] In 1924 Joseph Baptista, the Bombay barrister who presided over the AITUC's second congress in November 1921, and urged it to follow 'the golden mean of Fabian socialism',[53] was nominated and accepted. He attended a meeting of the Joint Imperial Questions Sub-Committee,[54] but was unable to stay for the Congress, and in 1925, Chaman Lall was correctly nominated and accepted, but did not arrive. In 1926 he arrived without nomination and was irregularly invited to address Congress.[55] Thus there was no properly invited and accredited Indian fraternal delegate to Congress until G. Sethi attended in 1927. He became a vice-president of the AITUC in December 1928.

The confusion over fraternal delegates, together with the AITUC's recognition of the WWLI as its agent, meant that the TUC had no proper flow of information direct from the AITUC until Joshi was elected general secretary at its fifth session in February 1925. In the period between January 1922 and the introduction of the Trade Unions Bill in 1925, there were some appalling strikes in India, on the railways, in textiles, and notably in the Tata Iron and Steel works at Jamshedpur. Some went on for months, with all the suffering for the workers that that entailed, and were characterized by victimizations, disturbances and police firings, while the AITUC leaders, and sometimes the National Congress leaders also, did their best to deal with obstinate employers while even the legal status of their unions was in doubt. Meanwhile propaganda was going into India, when it was not intercepted by the police, from M. N. Roy's Berlin office, from the RILU, and from the British Bureau of the RILU which began with a message from Tom Mann to the AITUC's second congress in November 1921 ridiculing the TUC for refusing to receive Horniman and Saklatvala 'in order to please the India Office'.[56] The existence of these outside pressures was exposed in the Cawnpore conspiracy case in 1924. The Government of India, only recently disturbed by the non-co-operation movement which ended after the Chauri Chaura incident in February 1922, was rightly afraid of disruption and violence in industry if the trade union movement developed on political lines. As Thomas had pointed out, however, the best remedy for this was to accord the unions full rights, thus enabling them to do their job and gain some advantage for their members by negotiation. If orderly and early settlement of industrial disputes was desired in India, the delay in the passage of the Trade Unions Act until 1926, and of the Trade Disputes Act until after the enactment of the British Trade Disputes Act 1927, was a tragedy. As in the political field, these were the crucial years when reform was needed, and they were also the years in which the TUC was least well informed.

The WWLI had no muscle of its own: at the end of 1924 it had 58 individual members, three affiliated Indian unions, and 70 affiliated bodies in Britain, of which some were trades councils.[57] Although the General Council responded politely enough to its requests, its activities at this time were obviously becoming an irritant.[58] It exercised some influence in Congress through Purcell, and secured the adherence of Arthur Pugh. Its main strength lay in Saklatvala, after he was elected to Parliament in 1922. This was a diminishing asset after Communists were excluded from the Labour Party where, H. S. L. Polak warned Joshi in 1926, the WWLI had no influence – rather the contrary.[59] In April 1927 Joshi wrote privately to Lee that he feared the AITUC might again appoint Saklatvala as a fraternal delegate, and asked whether there was any chance of his being well received. Lee replied that if he were nominated, the view might be expressed at Congress that he could not be considered a bona-fide representative of Indian workers.[60]

Apart from the fact that the WWLI began to look more and more like a communist auxiliary, it appeared to be becoming one of those parasitic bodies which the TUC regarded as duplicating or diverting the main efforts of the trade union movement. By invitation, representatives of the League attended the International Committee in November 1927 to explain their position.[61] They admitted that they had only a negligible amount of support from India and that the TUC could deal more effectively with trade union appeals, but claimed to be able to give help in many small matters. The General Council were now determined to work direct through the AITUC, and in 1928 they received a request from its executive to be their agent in Britain. Although it was inconsistent with the TUC's representative status for it to act as a mere 'agent' for a body with which it was not connected by affiliation, the General Council accepted, but only in so far as purely trade union questions were concerned.[62]

Saklatvala himself then took the question of his own position outside the ordinary scope of trade union credentials by sending out circulars denouncing Joshi for leading Indian trade unionists away from their real friends to supporters of British imperialism, and in the highly political atmosphere of the AITUC's Jharia Congress in December 1928 the Executive's decision was rescinded, though the WWLI was not reappointed.[63] When the RILU, commenting on this decision, referred to the League as 'a revolutionary organization connected with the Minority Movement', the General Council was finally provoked into a public response: allegations that the TUC missed no opportunity of joining in the oppression and exploitation of India would have no effect in Britain, they said, but it was another matter to spread them in India amongst people who had no means of verifying the facts; the WWLI had done excellent work in the past, but its present purpose was now made clear; and Saklatvala had no mandate to speak with authority on behalf of or about trade unionism. The WWLI attempted a reply, repudiating any suggestion that it was controlled by any other organization,[64] but the RILU directive for the

Nagpur Congress of the AITUC in November 1929 included the severance of relations with the British TUC. This was done, and the WWLI was reinstated. The RILU recorded the renewal of contact with the League with satisfaction.[65]

The question of representation had proved to be crucial to the TUC's standing, and capacity to help the unions, in India and it played its part in determining the character of the AITUC. It was one factor in the complex of decisions in the Comintern and in the RILU which embraced China, the PPTUS, the LAI and the ultra-left line adopted in India. There the event which had most roused the RILU to make a specific attack on the TUC was the visit of the long-awaited delegation in 1927–8.

The Purcell-Hallsworth Report

The RILU alleged that the TUC had decided on the visit in disappointment at the proceedings of the AITUC congress in March 1927. Saklatvala was invited to address that congress, and S. V. Ghate – later to be imprisoned at Meerut – was elected assistant secretary, but there were no decisions that particularly upset the TUC. The General Council was in fact responding to Sethi's fraternal speech at Congress and to a formal invitation from the AITUC to send a delegation to its Cawnpore congress in November. Its aim, according to the RILU, was to distract Indian workers from the revolutionary struggle, but the creation of workers' and peasants' parties with a revolutionary programme and the occupation of leading posts in the trade union movement by members of those parties, supported by the masses, showed that 'no Purcells or Ben Tilletts' would be able to retard class consciousness.[66]

Tillett and Purcell were appointed, but on account of illness Tillett was replaced by Hallsworth. Except for Tillett, who had long supported the cause of India, Purcell was perhaps the best-fitted of the TUC leaders to make this visit. He had come from a very poor family, beginning work in a woollen factory at the age of 9 before becoming a skilled cabinet-maker and french-polisher. His varied activities and changes in political outlook – from syndicalism, guild socialism and a sort of communism before he finally settled down in the Labour Party – all derived from a hope that it must be possible to build a better society than the one he saw around him. His vision extended beyond Britain, Europe and America, and his inability to work with the IFTU was due largely to frustration at its narrow base, and to his genuine anti-imperialist convictions which lent his utterances on the Empire a revolutionary note which was inconsistent with his industrial reputation as a conciliator. Hallsworth, the shopworkers' general secretary, was an altogether quieter figure, skilled in such subjects as the details of trade boards and, later, of ILO Conventions. They went straight to Cawnpore and then travelled throughout India, arriving back on 31 March 1928 after the most extensive investigation so far undertaken. Piecing together information gathered from unions and individuals with the scanty data available from official sources, they concluded that it was the definite policy of the employing class in India to stabilize poverty on a permanent basis. Indian workers, in their view, should and must be taught that it was wrong to accept their existing state as part of the predestined order of things. At last the full horror of Indian conditions was revealed in their report.[67]

Of fifty-seven unions affiliated to the AITUC, only four had over 10,000 members, of which three were railway unions – which always have the advantage of a ready-made channel for communication with members and collection of dues. They organized some of the best-educated workers in India, in the largest industrial undertaking, for which the government, on the four railways that were state-owned, could not evade responsibility. Yet there were no agreed rates of pay, all rates being imposed without reference to the employees, organized or unorganized, and varying even for similar work. While the old racial discrimination was said to be on its way out in that Indians might now take up railway workshop training, they did not enjoy the grants in aid and reserved junior schools which enabled Europeans and Anglo-Indians to qualify. Similarly, there were no agreed rates of pay in mining or in the cotton mills. The Factory Acts applied only in British India, so that, for example, textile workers in the state of Baroda worked longer hours than in Bombay, Madras or Ahmedabad. Seamen and dockworkers were partially organized, but still seamen were recruited through licensed shipping brokers who were said to take their cut in bribes, and housed with lodging house keepers who were said to take theirs over and above rent. Dockworkers also complained that it was impossible to get a job without bribery.

Conditions were still worse for the unorganized. In mining, family gangs were recruited. For the tea-gardens contractors recruited from outside the district. In 1926 the Workmen's Breach of Contract Act, which had allowed penal sanctions for desertion, had been repealed, but workers displaced from their homes lived secluded on the estates and virtually tied to them. In the Digboi oilfields, in which the Burmah Oil Company had a controlling interest and which the delegates visited, there was no cohesion amongst workers drawn from numerous hill tribes.

In many cases there were no adequate statistics on wages or on hours worked, in jute, silk and woollen mills, in mining, or at Digboi. Thus the elementary substructure for the enforcement of standards from outside was non-existent. Some employers, especially in textiles, provided exceptional welfare facilities but the delegates noted that this was not incompatible with poor pay and unjust conditions: amongst the examples observed in textiles were the deduction of two days' wages for one day's absence and the practice of compelling a worker to buy his own spoilt work at the wholesale price and sell it himself, if he could. Welfare provision might also operate as patronage by associating leading workers with management in its administration. Already, at the request of the Madras Labour Union and of Mrs Besant, who visited the TUC in August 1926, the TUC had raised one such case, where the incentive was to join a rival company-sponsored union, with the Indian High Commissioner in London.[68]

Against this discouraging background, the trade unions had made a good start despite poverty, illiteracy and the multiplicity of languages. They were organized mainly on a local or 'house' basis, but had the potential for development into national unions by amalgamation, especially if employers in the same industry co-operated nationally. The total strength was estimated at 200,000, of which over 150,000 were in unions affiliated to the AITUC. Outside were the Postal Workers' Union, various small unions in municipal and railway employment, and, in private enterprise, the most important of the others was the Ahmedabad Textile Labour Union.

The report was at its weakest in commenting on this union. It consisted of a group of mill unions organized in a federation, it was recognized by the Ahmedabad Millowners' Association, and had a voluntary procedure for the avoidance of disputes which paralleled procedures negotiated by many British unions. It stemmed from Gandhi's intervention in a strike in 1918 when he undertook a fast with the double aim of stiffening the workers' resolve and persuading the employers to accept arbitration,[69] and he continued to represent the union on the standing arbitration board which formed the apex of the grievance procedures. The union, for which the employers operated a check-off, bore the stamp of his determination that workers should be self-reliant. In addition to handling cases and negotiations, the Whitley Commission found it running two dispensaries and a hospital, literacy classes, twenty-five schools, travelling libraries, a savings bank, a cheap grain shop and restaurants, all supported mainly from members' subscriptions.[70] Purcell and Hallsworth acknowledged its record of useful work, but evidently considered that it was doing jobs which should have been done by Government. They noted also that industrial conditions were bad even in the union's chosen field of textiles. But they were unrealistic on both counts. One reason for Gandhi's view that every strike should be ended by arbitration after a maximum of 45 days was that he estimated this to be the limit of workers' endurance,[71] and in this and his other activities he did exactly what Purcell and

Hallsworth considered necessary in teaching workers not to accept an unjust established order. In 1932 an independent British delegation found the union fully engaged in the National Congress anti-drink, boycott and civil disobedience campaigns, but with a good staff and comparing favourably with a well-organized union in Britain.[72] Gandhi saw Ahmedabad as a model, and after the Hindustan Mazdoor Sevak Sangh was set up in 1937 to train leaders, its message was carried elsewhere and remained a permanent strand in the pattern of Indian trade unionism.

The delegates' basic criticism of the union was that they found no convincing reason for its failure to affiliate to the AITUC. They should have read Gandhi's correspondence with Saklatvala, which was published in Britain in 1927.[73] Gandhi argued that there was no concept of national policy or of the general welfare of labour amongst Indian workers, with their communal and caste divisions and lack of social contact and mutual ties across the country. Therefore, an all-India union could exist only on paper. He did not approve the formation of a national centre until 1947. But here Purcell and Hallsworth were on stronger ground. They noted that from the beginning the AITUC had had a national job to do. They saw the AITUC as the engine of organization. It had already undertaken the preparation and distribution of a great mass of pamphlets and leaflets on trade unionism, in many languages, and had raised funds outside the movement to supplement those of the unions, which must remain small as long as wages were so low. A major weakness in the movement, which invited trouble, was the common dependence on lawyers to provide union presidents and secretaries, but they saw this as an inevitable and temporary disability. Moreover, the AITUC outsiders, although quite removed from the actual experience of working-class life, were not out of touch with it, and whatever machinery existed at the time was mainly their handiwork. In fact, there had been a large volume of useful work which must be set down as 'a great record of self-sacrifice and disinterestedness unmatched by any other case in the world of labour'. But the unions needed efficient, practical officers and – given the prevalent illiteracy – it would be some time before they would be forthcoming from the workplaces of India. It was the responsibility of Britain, which had made so much profit from its association with India, to provide help in a practical and lasting form. They envisaged a joint effort of the British and Indian trade union movements to organize to win Indian workers for trade unionism.

In a scheme to implement their recommendation,[74] the delegates suggested that the General Council should appoint four organizers to work with four from the AITUC in sectors selected for their organizing potential. They should have definite instructions to organize industrially, independently of any political body, to avoid the danger that unions would be exploited in support of strictly political and spurious nationalism. They estimated the cost for one year at over £8,000.

The General Council could not easily conjure up £8,000 from current income. After the general strike, affiliated membership dropped over half a million by 1928. As unemployment increased, it went down to just over 3 million in 1934, regaining the 1926 level of 4½ million only in 1938. There was no special fund for India, and the General Council had found the cost of the mission (about £1,500), from the balance of the national strike fund which had been placed at its disposal, while the grants it made for strike relief in India came from ordinary income. The alternative was to go to the unions, but they had taken the brunt of the general strike and already paid to the TUC for the IFTU and to the international trade secretariats to which they were affiliated. Citrine recorded that the Finance Committee had thought it inadvisable to ask Congress for extra money for the *Daily Herald*, and he did not believe the amount proposed for India could be raised from the unions either by grant or by an increased affiliation fee. But it was manifestly unsatisfactory for the General Council to confine its expenditure to ad-hoc grants for strike relief. When compared with the estimates for the cost of the organizers, it can be seen that what appear now to be small grants were not negligible, and they added up to £750 in 1927–8 alone. This was a bottomless pit – in June 1928 three appeals came to one meeting – and grants made after a strike had taken hold were in a sense already too late. The delegates' scheme aimed at a big increase in membership, but would a year's work make it permanent? Citrine proposed an alternative scheme for three to five years at an annual cost that could be borne from current income.[75]

He argued that the organizers could not be withdrawn just when they would have gained some knowledge of the relevant language and become known to the workers and to the principal officials of the firms and government departments with whom they would have to deal. Nor could suitable men be specially recruited for only one year; if they could be borrowed from unions, it would be more difficult to control them. He preferred an adviser who would be directly responsible to the General Council, and would provide impartial information on appeals sent to them, advise the AITUC on legislative, administrative and organizing questions, and if necessary assist in major negotiations. Sir Atul Chatterjee had suggested that an adviser was needed when the TUC representatives at the ILO had met him in June to discuss the Bombay textile dispute of 1928 and the railway dispute at Lillooah,[76] and thus there was a strong presumption that the Government of India would not obstruct and might actually be helpful. Citrine also

proposed a training scheme in Britain, for two years including a period
in appropriate union offices, for Indian trade unionists nominated by
the adviser and the AITUC. He considered that training in India might
be preferable, but not possible. To ensure that trainees would serve the
movement on their return, he proposed that they should be pledged,
but when preparing a similar scheme in 1937 he saw the additional
difficulty that the unions might not be able to pay them when they
returned. In an uncanny way, he had foreseen the difficulties that were
to beset the TUC in its postwar work in the colonies.

The General Council rejected both the Purcell–Hallsworth proposals and Citrine's, giving Congress – which accepted it – the
unconvincing explanation that in the existing state of finances and
organization the unions had felt that money was best spent at home.[77]
It was not until 1937 when – at Joshi's request – Citrine repeated his
proposals, that an office note recorded that one of the principal
reasons why the matter had not been pursued in 1928 was the headway
made by Communists in the Indian unions.[78] If this was the real reason,
the General Council were quickly proved right. At the Jharia Congress
in December 1928 the penetration of the AITUC was exemplified by
the appointment of Bradley and Spratt to vacancies on the Executive
with the status of ex-presidents of the AITUC.[79] For an organizing
scheme to have been successful, it should have been started at the latest
in 1926 after the passage of the Trade Unions Act. There had been a
heavy price to pay for the AITUC's liaison with the WWLI and the
British general strike.

The Whitley Commission

What, then, did the Purcell-Hallsworth mission achieve? It strengthened the morale of the Indian movement at a time when it was still
thought to be dangerous to join a trade union,[80] and its findings were
publicized throughout the British, Indian and international trade union
movements and in the British and Indian press. The long-standing
demand for a full inquiry into labour conditions in India could no
longer be ignored. Birkenhead left office in October, to be succeeded
by Lord Peel for the few months before May 1929 when the second
Labour government took office. On 4 July 1929 the Whitley
Commission was appointed to inquire into and report and make
recommendations on conditions of labour in industrial undertakings
and plantations in British India, on the health, efficiency and standard
of living of the workers, and on relations between employers and
employed. On 11 October the British members arrived in India. Its
appointment as a Royal Commission, from Britain, demonstrated that
even the Government of India could not be a law unto itself. The
members included Sir Victor Sassoon and G. D. Birla, leaders of

British and Indian employers in India, Joshi and Chaman Lall from the trade unions, John Cliff,[81] assistant secretary of the TGWU, and J. H. Whitley as chairman. By appointing assistant commissioners (including women) and taking evidence all over India over a period of a year, the Commission raised the whole level of knowledge and experience amongst the trade unions, the employers, and central and local administrations.

Whitley, when deputy speaker of the House of Commons, had chaired the Committee on the Relations between Employers and Employed set up by the British government in 1916. His committee gave his name to a continuing school of thought in British industrial relations which stressed the need for adequate organization on both sides of industry, for voluntary procedures for the avoidance of disputes which should be fully exhausted before the state intervened, and for statutory provision where these were insufficient. Recommendations for the establishment of joint industrial councils for national negotiations, supplemented by Ministry of Labour inquiries and a permanent court of arbitration, led to the Industrial Courts Act of 1919. Purcell and Hallsworth had envisaged the amalgamation of unions and the organization of employers on a national basis, and the Industrial Disputes Act had been passed before the Commission was appointed. The 'Whitley' philosophy was therefore not entirely new to India, but its practical application required a hitherto unprecedented effort from both sides of industry and from government.

The Commission's recommendations on labour conditions covered matters on which the TUC had earlier made representations, such as the extension of the coverage of the Factories Act and the reduction of hours legally worked under it, the inclusion of building workers, seamen and other excluded categories in the Workmen's Compensation Act, the recruitment of plantation workers, fines imposed on workmen, and the exclusion of jobbers from the engagement and dismissal of workers.[82] Where Purcell and Hallsworth had found labour administration wanting, they recommended the full compilation of labour statistics and the appointment of specialist labour commissioners in the provinces and at the centre. On industrial relations, echoing Montagu, they were moving towards the development of a comprehensive government policy which would recognize the importance of trade unions as an integral part of the industrial structure of the country. Repeating the TUC's earliest criticisms, they pointed to the lack of provision for conciliation, which left government officers with only police reports to provide them with early information on disputes, and they advised the appointment of permanent conciliation officers. In place of the ad-hoc tribunals for which the Trade Disputes Act made provision, they recommended that the merits of standing arbitration machinery be considered. It was evident that national joint industrial councils could not be envisaged until both sides of industry were better organized, but they suggested a standing joint board for the railways, where the All-India Railwaymen's Federation could provide the trade union side. Foreshadowing the National Joint Advisory Council that was established in Britain in 1939 and the labour advisory committees which became a feature of post-war labour policy in the colonies, they suggested that a statutory Industrial Council should be set up, with trade union, employer and government representatives, to discuss policy and examine proposals for legislation.[83]

When considering the unions, the Commission made a classic analysis of the problems of organization with a labour force that was not fully acclimatized to industry. They upheld the principle that legal immunities should be restricted to registered unions, but urged that the conditions of registration should be eased. To give experience and responsibility to ordinary union members, they recommended that two thirds of a union executive – instead of the half required under the trade union legislation – should be engaged in the relevant trade. They did not suggest dispensing altogether with the outsiders, whose voluntary contribution to the movement was appreciated, but the Commission observed that their inevitable lack of complete knowledge of the technical details of the industries with which they dealt placed them at a disadvantage when negotiating with employers. They and the universities and other educational institutions could help in improving the general education of those workers who would become the full-time officials that the trade unions needed, and amongst means of providing industrial training for them, it was suggested that worker delegates and advisers attending the ILO should extend their stay in Europe to study trade union methods.[84]

The Report provided a body of information and of enlightened opinion which paved the way to modern legislation and practice in India. Between 1932 and 1937, nineteen of the twenty-four enactments concerning labour passed by central and provincial legislatures implemented Whitley recommendations.[85] The Commission's work was a trail-blazing achievement, in which the part played by John Cliff was warmly acknowledged in the Indian trade union movement.[86]

The Report dealt with two other questions which became issues at the Round Table Conferences. The TUC had pressed for effective representation there and on the committees which considered the Bill which ultimately became the Government of India Act 1935. In view of the failure of the AITUC and of the Indian National Congress to make constructive suggestions on the constitution, these representatives were the only spokesmen (except for the leader of the untouchables, Dr Ambedkar) that the Indian workers had. They represented substantial trade union strength after May 1933, when the NTUF was formed to bring together the Indian Trade Union Federation and the All-India Railwaymen's Federation, and the NTUF's president, Jamnadas Mehta, was consulted by a committee set up by the National Council of Labour to consider the Bill.[87] However, they were able to secure only minor concessions.

The first issue was the responsibility for labour legislation in the federal constitution that was being devised. There was the administrative problem of the types of legislation which might be best administered from the centre or at the lower level of the provincial governments, but the major concern was that the princely states should be brought into line with British India. By 1933 the Government of India had ratified 13 of the 40 conventions adopted by the ILO up to that date, but for British India only, and the Whitley Commission had referred to the potential danger that some industry might be moved into the states to avoid the restrictions on hours of work and child labour that operated in British India.[88] The Government of India Act 1935 ultimately gave responsibility for labour matters to both central and provincial governments. This enabled the provincial governments elected in 1937 to make some headway but, since the federal part of the Act was not brought into operation, the princes remained unaffected.

The second was the old question of the franchise, stressed again by Joshi in his fraternal speech to Congress in 1931. The qualifications required for the vote again left the mass of workers outside the electoral process, but the peculiar feature of special electorates, which was retained in the new constitution, allowed some scope for the representation of labour. The Whitley Commission pointed out that even after the changes following the Muddiman reports had been implemented in 1926, labour remained underrepresented by comparison with the employers, that the seats were filled by nomination, and that some form of election would be educative and would strengthen the position of labour representatives. Considering various conflicting opinions on methods of election, the Report recommended election by registered trade unions. The 1935 Government of India Act increased the number of special Labour seats, but left the method of selection to be prescribed.[89] In the provincial elections of 1937, this varied from province to province. Thus Bombay had four groups of unions electing to six seats in the Legislative Assembly together with one non-union seat in Sholapur. Bengal had only two union seats, four groups of registered factories, and one each for coalmines and tea-garden labour. Bihar had no union seats at all, the three provided being filled by factory and mining constituencies. Of the thirty-eight for all the provinces, only thirteen were filled by identified union constituencies, and even here the political affiliations of candidates intervened, five of the thirteen seats going to National Congress candidates. Of the remaining twenty-five seats, thirteen went to National Congress candidates, three to other parties and nine to independents.[90] This was a far cry from universal suffrage, and inherently unsatisfactory, but it did give some recognition to the unions, and when representation of special interests was instituted (in different circumstances) in Malaya after the war, trade unions were the medium through which seats allocated to labour were filled.

In Parliament, the Labour opposition voted against the Bill on the grounds that the new constitution did not provide means to realize Dominion status, placed undue restrictions on the exercise of self-government, established an inadequate franchise, and entrenched the forces of wealth, privilege and reaction in the legislatures.[91] On the first point they were technically proved wrong in 1947, but it was left to the constituent assembly which finally drew up the constitution for independent India to give all its citizens a vote and to do away with special representation except in the case of untouchables.

Conclusion

Although the period in which the TUC had a satisfactory working relationship with the AITUC was short, the experience of those years and of subsequent co-operation with the noncommunist sections of the Indian trade union movement effected a marked change in the TUC's outlook. The vague, friendly, wartime feeling of a common British status was replaced by a sustained attempt to utilize British industrial experience in a country with markedly different traditions and circumstances, but in which industry was already developing on lines which proved to be of a world-wide character. The Parliamentary Committee's first intervention arose from the legal challenge to Wadia and the Madras Labour Union, and the Committee was able to act because a British minister responsible to Parliament could be held responsible by a British electorate. In this and in subsequent representations the TUC could claim that the rights of British workers should be enjoyed throughout the Empire, and that it was the responsibility of British workers' organizations to help to achieve this. The self-interest of British workers, which was the driving force in the formation of the Far Eastern Labour Committee four years later, remained a factor in the TUC's activities. The Purcell–Hallsworth mission observed that the industrialization of India at wages one-sixth to one-eighth of the lowest British rates undermined all the advanced industrialized countries – but self-interest was not the only, or the primary factor. British workers' standards were not undermined by failure to negotiate wages on the Indian railways or by the impoverished conditions of workers in the tea-gardens or the Assam oilfields. Self-interest was quickly outpaced by sheer goodwill, as was the case later in regard to the West Indies and Africa, where no element of competition existed. British experience provided a model in trade union law and practice, in industrial relations and labour administration, which was not forced upon India, but used by the Indian trade union leaders themselves as a yardstick in their demands. The Indian trade union movement and the political upsurge of nationalism were of course the main engines of change, but in the process the help of the British movement was specifically requested, and given.

The TUC's experience in India also demonstrated the limitations on its ability to help. Representations to government were only partially successful; the British yardstick was imperfectly applied. The TUC's domestic experience did not equip the General Council to grasp the full force of nationalism, though their underlying distrust of the middle-class nationalist politicians was to some extent vindicated when National Congress governments enacted labour legislation which was more restrictive than the Trade Disputes Act which the TUC and the AITUC had criticized. But the main weakness was organizational: the TUC could not command the resources needed for a full-scale effort to help the Indian movement. Every trade union movement must organize for itself, and the Indian movement was able and willing to do so, but it should not have been confronted and divided at such an early stage of its development by the negative force of the Comintern/RILU attack, which the TUC was unable to counter. Yet the resilience and consistency of the democratic trade union leaders were sufficient to ensure that the movement persisted and expanded throughout the trials of the 1930s and of the war.

This survival was important, for it ensured that at all times a labour voice was heard by the Indian government and by the nationalist politicians. Moreover, India was the forerunner, industrially as well as politically, for the whole dependent empire. If it had been proved there, as it was in China, that industrialization could take place without workers' organization, or that trade unions would be little more than instruments in the hands of nationalist or revolutionary politicians, British governments might have taken a very different line when faced with the problems of Africa or Malaya.

The Indian trade union voice was also heard internationally. Through all their vicissitudes the democratic trade union leaders clung to the right of representation at the ILO, despite allegations of self-interest and subservience to government. It was true that after the AITUC rejected participation in the ILO in 1929 the Government of India appointed delegates from the ITUF and the NTUF, but the

alternative was to deprive Indian workers of any representation at
Geneva. The Indian workers' delegates did not slavishly support the
Government of India. On the contrary, at the ILO's 1934 Conference
they lodged the only complaint against a government made by an
organization during the interwar years. They secured a formal promise
from the Government of India to extend the benefits of the
Washington Hours (Industry) Convention 1919 to all railway workers
without delay.[92] They also spoke up for colonial representation at the
ILO, as they did at the Commonwealth Labour Conference in 1925.
These two questions, the application of conventions and the
representation of the colonies, assumed considerable importance in the
following years.

The International Labour Organization

The provision for workers' representation in tripartite delegations
made the ILO a standing international forum in which trade union
objectives could be pursued. At the first, Washington, Conference in
1919, both the workers' and the employers' representatives combined
into groups to nominate members of committees and of the Governing
Body and to discuss policy. These workers' and employers' groups
became a permanent feature of the ILO, though without any status in its
constitution. The employers' group drew up rules for a new body
which emerged in March 1920 as the International Organization of
Industrial Employers. The workers' group elected Mertens to chair
their meetings, with Oudegeest as secretary, and the IFTU assumed a
co-ordinating role.[93] The initial dissatisfaction in the IFTU with the
ILO's structure and powers was quickly overcome, partly by the
determination of its first Director, Albert Thomas, to build up contacts
with the unions and employers despite misgivings amongst governments and his own staff.[94] Formerly a leading figure in the French and
international socialist movements, Thomas attended the IFTU's Rome
and Vienna congresses and the TUC's 1924 Congress on behalf of the
ILO, and this representation became customary. He also set up a
workers' relations service and provided the type of information on
labour conditions which enabled the unions to make international
comparisons.[95] The ILO's work never aroused enthusiastic interest
amongst rank and file trade unionists, nor was it systematically
discussed at TUC or IFTU congresses, but it provided valuable
experience for the union representatives who attended and the TUC
General Council provided full accounts of its meetings in their own
reports to Congress.

Colonial Representation

In the colonies, which were represented by the metropolitan powers, the ILO was even more remote. The 1927 Conference passed a resolution moved by Giri which drew the attention of member states administering colonial or mandated territories to the desirability of including representatives of workers in these territories in their delegations, especially when questions affecting them were on the agenda. The same proposal in different forms was endorsed in 1928, 1929, 1931 and 1932, at the instance of Joshi, Bakhale and Chaman Lall.[96] The British Government opposed Giri's resolution in 1927, and by 1932 had still not responded, partly because it was thought that if colonial representation were established on the workers' side, a similar demand would come from the employers.[97]

The TUC, however, could not take this line. The General Council refused a request from the General Federation of Jewish Labour, Palestine, in 1926 to include a Palestine representative in their own delegation as an adviser, but reconsidered its position when forced labour, a subject of specific colonial significance, was agreed for discussion, and the IFTU asked its affiliates in the metropolitan countries to make provision.[98]

Conscious that on this subject the General Council's industrial expertise did not meet the standard of exact knowledge that the ILO's procedures would require, Citrine consulted Harold Grimshaw, head of the ILO's Native Labour Section, who came to command the respect and confidence of the TUC's delegates to an unusual degree.[99] He concluded that an expert adviser would be needed for the ILO's Conference in 1929, but it was evident that forced labour concerned mainly the African territories where there were no trade unions from which a representative could be chosen. The discussion with Grimshaw[100] resulted in the appointment of a newcomer to the TUC, William McGregor Ross, a member of the League of Nations Union's Committee on Forced Labour who had been Director of Public Works, Kenya, from 1905 to 1923. Ross attended as adviser in the TUC's delegation in 1929 and 1930, and again in 1938 when contracts of employment were under discussion.[101] The TUC thus secured the help of an expert, but not a trade unionist or a colonial representative. On the other hand, merely to include a colonial as such was not a solution. The Dutch trade union centre nominated an Indonesian, Hadji Agoes Salim, who made a favourable impression at Geneva but came from the political organization, Sarekat Islam. The French delegation in 1930 included the Under-Secretary of State for the Colonies in the French government, the Senegalese, Blaise Diagne. He did not appear as a workers' delegate and his attitude incensed the

TUC's representative, John Bromley. 'What can be the meaning of trade union liberty to peoples without any education?' Diagne had asked the Conference.[102]

When the ILO discussions moved on to the problems of employed workers, the ILO itself suggested that it would be desirable to include colonial representatives. Again the TUC consulted the ILO Office, and nominated for the 1935 and 1936 Conferences, when recruitment was on the agenda, a former member of the AEU, W. G. Ballinger, who was working in South Africa with the ICU under the auspices of the Friends of Africa. At his suggestion in 1935 the General Council also nominated E. N. Nxumalo, who had been representative of the Swazi Nation in Lourenço Marques, and thus in close contact with mine workers recruited under contract for South Africa. Since he was working in South Africa in 1935, the General Council avoided the charge that the TUC was challenging the representative status of the South African TUC by stressing the facts that he was a native of Swaziland and that he and Ballinger would be advising on territories outside the Union. Nxumalo had no trade union status, but he was a member of the Swaziland Progressive Association and of the African National Congress. His appointment was popular, and 'electrified' South Africa.[103]

The TUC did not achieve a wholly satisfactory solution until 1945, when the General Council nominated E. E. Esua, General Secretary of the Nigeria Union of Teachers, for the agenda item Minimum Standards of Social Policy in Dependent Territories. The unions were now able to produce their spokesmen, but since their territories were not yet self-governing they still had to be included in the TUC delegation. In 1954 Frank Walcott, General Secretary of the Barbados Workers' Union, and Matthew Nkoloma, General Secretary of the Northern Rhodesia African Mine Workers' Union, were nominated for items on migrant workers and penal sanctions for breaches of contracts of employment, and for the second discussion of these subjects in 1955, H. K. Choudhury of the National Union of Plantation Workers, Malaya, and Charles Mzingeli, General Secretary of the Reformed ICU in Southern Rhodesia, attended as advisers.[104]

By that time, with the colonies everywhere undergoing constitutional changes that would lead them to self-government, the concept of representation of colonial workers in metropolitan delegations was becoming outdated. In 1954, as a result of proposals initiated by the Workers' Group, the ILO Governing Body agreed, in concert with the metropolitan governments, to invite tripartite observer delegations from appropriate territories. The first, from the Gold Coast, attended the Conference in that year, and in 1955 observer delegations from Barbados, Jamaica, the Gold Coast, Nigeria, Sierra Leone, Malta and

Singapore participated in the work of the committees and of the full Conference.[105]

The Application of Conventions

The agenda items for which colonial advisers were nominated to TUC delegations were of special interest to the colonies, but they were not the only ones that affected them. Member states which ratified conventions adopted by the Conference were obliged to submit reports. on their application to the ILO. The metropolitan powers were obliged also to consider how far they could be applied, in whole or in part, or with modifications appropriate to local conditions, to their dependencies. When they submitted their reports, they were required to notify to the Office the action taken in each case, and where necessary to indicate the reasons why a ratified convention might be regarded as inappropriate to a particular territory.

These rules were of interest to all the workers' delegates because they wished to see as many conventions as possible applied in their countries, particularly the Washington Hours Convention, over which many governments hesitated. Following decisions taken by the Conference in 1926, the governments' reports on ratified conventions were examined first by a technical committee of experts and, secondly, with the experts' report on them, by a committee of the Conference. After 1949, the expert committee considered reports on unratified conventions also. The first experts' report was presented in 1927 and workers' representatives were included in the Conference committee which examined it. To supplement the replies submitted by governments, the IFTU began to collect information from its affiliates and from the AITUC.[106]

This reporting procedure had its effect on governments. As Secretary of State for the Colonies, Passfield found that some colonial governors sent no information, or merely expressed opinions that particular conventions were not applicable to their territories, or that application was undesirable. 'It should be clearly understood,' he warned them, 'that His Majesty's Government are under a moral obligation to apply any conventions which they have ratified to the largest extent and with the smallest possible modifications.' Perhaps they did not realize that ILO committees examined their reports and could readily identify anomalies. Why, for example, was the convention on night work for women, which was applied in Hong Kong, not applied in the Straits Settlements? 'It is difficult to formulate any reason ... which could possibly carry conviction at Geneva.' Night work, workmen's compensation in agriculture, the minimum age for children working in industry – all must be reviewed and a report must be sent on each convention. There followed requests for observations on the applicability of conventions on minimum wage machinery, sickness insurance and seamen's articles of agreement.[107]

The process of inquiry and discussion which preceded the adoption of a convention also had its effect. The ILO collected information on existing practice and sent questionnaires to governments on specific questions which might be embodied in draft conventions to be considered by the Conference. In the case of the Forced Labour Convention 1930, Passfield circulated provisional answers to colonial governments, considered their replies and adopted some of their suggestions, and then circulated the British Government's final answers with the warning that these now constituted a statement of policy that must be implemented.[108] Although the rudimentary administrations that existed in most colonies were scarcely up to these new tasks, in the Colonial Office itself their significance was understood. 'It may be worth reminding the colonies,' an official noted long after Passfield had gone, 'that the terms of labour contracts will shortly come up for consideration ... there is still a good deal to be done and it is important that it should be done quickly so that we may not risk being held up at Geneva as a bad example'.[109]

The final stage was the adoption of a convention by the Conference. When it had been ratified by a sufficient number of states, it came into force as the international standard. Passfield circulated a report on the 1930 conference and told governors that the British Government intended to ask Parliament for ratification of the Forced Labour Convention as soon as possible, adding that although it would not come into force before 1932, any administrative and legislative adjustments that it might require should be made in any case.[110]

Thus the whole slow process was sufficiently exacting to have a cumulative effect on the development of a coherent labour policy in the Colonial Office and in the colonies themselves.

The Native Labour Committee

If the ILO had been solely concerned with the needs of industrial workers its impact on the colonies would have been partial and oblique, but Albert Thomas was responsible[111] for an early decision, which was initially challenged, that agricultural workers came within the scope of Article 396 of the Versailles Treaty. This empowered the Office to make special investigations ordered by the Conference, and to collect and distribute information on all subjects relating to the international adjustment of conditions of industrial life and labour. In addition, the ILO was represented on the Permanent Mandates Commission of the League of Nations from 1921, and on the League's Temporary Commission on Slavery set up in 1924. The powers administering mandated territories were obliged to prohibit forced labour except for essential public works and services, to supervise labour contracts and the recruitment of labour, and to report to the Commission. To make ILO participation effective, Thomas initiated studies into what came to be known as 'Native Labour'.

In 1925 the Temporary Commission on Slavery submitted its first report to the League of Nations Assembly together with a draft protocol presented by the British government's delegate, Lord Robert Cecil. The protocol referred to forced labour as well as slavery, but did not consider detailed regulations on it, and Cecil explained to the House of Lords that no definite request was made to the ILO to do so because the Assembly did not wish to interfere with the autonomy of the Office. Fortified by Cecil's speech and by representations from two British organizations, the Anti-Slavery Society and the League of Nations Union, and pointing out that the metropolitan powers would not accept the ILO's competence unless it was backed by incontrovertible evidence, Thomas asked the Governing Body to sanction consultation with experts. He was supported by the British government and workers' delegates, the latter, A. A. H. Findlay, recalling that the first Commonwealth Labour Conference had already begun discussion on forced labour.[112]

By June 1926 the Governing Body had an outline of work for the Office, and at the annual Conference Lala Lajpat Rai moved a resolution welcoming its proposals. When the League Assembly adopted its Slavery Convention, it asked the League Council to draw the attention of the ILO's Governing Body to the importance of studying the best means of preventing forced or compulsory labour from developing into conditions analagous to slavery. Later the Permanent Mandates Commission also suspended discussion on forced labour, leaving the matter to the ILO.[113] Thus this question passed into the hands of the only body of the League of Nations on which workers had representation.

The experts assembled by the ILO met as a committee for the first time in July 1927 and a special Native Labour Section was set up in the Office under Grimshaw. Material was prepared for the first Conference discussion on forced labour in 1929, and plans were made for further inquiries and conventions on contract labour, covering recruitment and engagement, conditions of labour, renewal of contracts and inspection.[114] This proved to be ten years' work, resulting in the adoption of the Forced Labour Convention 1930, the Recruiting of Indigenous Workers' Convention in 1936, and the Contracts of Employment (Indigenous Workers) and the Penal Sanctions (Indigenous Workers) Conventions in 1939. It was the first, the Forced Labour Convention, which spurred the Colonial Office, the Workers' Group at the ILO, the IFTU and the TUC into action.

The Forced Labour Convention

When the ILO Governing Body decided in 1927 to place the Native Labour Committee's report before the 1929 Conference and to put forced labour on the agenda, the TUC's International Committee was preoccupied with its representations on India and with preparations for the Second Commonwealth Labour Conference to be held in 1928. However, the IFTU circulated information obtained from the ILO which included a list of 24 territories under British control in which forced labour still existed, or at least might be demanded.[115] After consulting Grimshaw and the Labour Party, the General Council decided that they would need not only an expert adviser at the 1929 Conference, but an advisory committee which would help to brief the delegates.[116]

The Labour Party's Imperial Advisory Committee had continued the work started for the TUC/Labour Party pamphlet *Labour and the Empire: Africa*, and had prepared a document for submission to the LSI's conference in 1928. The stalwarts of the former Joint Advisory Committee now came back to help the TUC – Roden Buxton, Norman Leys, H. S. L. Polak, Colonel Wedgwood, Harold Snell, Lord Olivier and Leonard Woolf. With McGregor Ross and Wilfred Paling MP, who had recently visited Tanganyika in an Empire Parliamentary Association delegation, they joined Tillett, Poulton and J. H. Thomas to form the General Council's Advisory Committee on Forced Labour, which held its first meeting on 13 February 1929.[117] At the same time the League of Nations Union publicized the issue,[118] Woolf's Hogarth Press republished Olivier's *White Capital and Coloured Labour*, and the ILP published Buxton's pamphlet, *The Black Man's Rights*.

The TUC had no experience of tribal societies which had little or no surplus labour for public construction such as railways or roads, for public purposes such as transport of officials or essential medical supplies, or for private production in agriculture or in mining, so the advisers were invaluable. The Committee's task was to analyse the ILO's initial questionnaire, and the TUC's final comments on it were sent to the British government and to the IFTU, which circulated them to its other affiliates. Thus their work helped the workers' delegates at the 1929 Conference to strengthen the final questionnaire, for example by inclusion of questions on the use of forced labour underground and on compensation for accident or illness. The same procedure was adopted at the 1930 Conference which considered the draft convention, and John Bromley and Shiva Rao served on the tripartite Conference committee which reported on the draft to the plenary session.[119]

The Convention as finally adopted defined forced or compulsory labour as all work or service exacted from any person under the menace of any penalty and for which he had not voluntarily offered himself. Exemptions included work of a purely military character required under compulsory military service laws, normal civic obligations in a fully self-governing country (such as protection of the dykes in Holland), work exacted in an emergency (such as famine or invasion by insect pests) which endangered the population, and minor communal services for the direct interest of the community which might be exacted only after consultation on the need for the service, and work exacted after conviction in a court of law, provided that it was carried out under the control of a public authority and that the convict was not placed at the disposal of private individuals or companies. Each ratifying member state undertook to suppress the use of forced labour in all its forms within the shortest possible period, subject to the exceptions, for which conditions were laid down. These included requirements that the work must be of immediate necessity, undertaken after it had proved impossible to obtain voluntary labour by offering wages and conditions not less favourable than those prevailing in the area concerned; that, except in the case of communal services, wages must be paid in cash at rates prevailing where the labour was employed, or from where it was recruited, whichever were higher; laws providing for accident or sickness compensation must be applied; all necessary measures must be taken for hygiene and accommodation in the case of transferred workers or workers engaged for considerable periods on construction and maintenance, and definite arrangements must be made for voluntary remittances to families; and finally, the competent authority must have precise rules for receiving and examining complaints from workers and for taking them into consideration. Forced labour for underground work in mines, or for collective punishment was specifically outlawed.[120]

These provisions marked a great advance – so great that for some time only the British and Dutch Governments were willing to ratify the Convention. But they did not satisfy the Workers' Group, which submitted a minority report, signed by Jouhaux, which expressed anxiety that the effect of the Convention might be to legitimize forced labour for public purposes, and doubt as to whether the colonial authorities would fully apply the regulations governing it. These regulations were also regarded as unsatisfactory: the Group failed in the Conference committee and in the plenary session to get hours limited to 8 a day and 48 a week. It also failed to secure a definite time limit for the total suppression of forced labour in any circumstances, but finally agreed to support the Convention because they had a moral obligation to workers who, 'by reason of the lower level of their culture and ... of the prohibitions imposed by the ruling Powers', were unable to defend themselves. The defence they had in mind was, of course, the right to form trade unions. The Convention required that workers' complaints must be 'taken into consideration' – wording drawn from an amendment pressed by the government representatives of France and Portugal against an Office draft which embodied a proposal by the Workers' Group that the rules should bind the authorities to negotiate on the complaints.[121]

This question of the workers' right to bargain had arisen in a different form when the questionnaire for the 1930 Conference was being considered in 1929. The second Labour government had been in office only a few days when its official representatives at Geneva, acting on their previous instructions, helped to defeat a proposal to include the question: 'Do you consider that in order to facilitate the abolition or limitation of forced labour, it would be useful to encourage, or at least not to hinder, the efforts made by the workers to organise themselves freely in the territories which are at present subject to a system of forced labour?' Despite the denials of R. V. Vernon, an assistant secretary at the Colonial Office, Poulton interpreted this opposition as opposition to freedom of association, and informed Citrine.

Citrine's protest to Passfield evoked a reserved response. Passfield wrote (privately, and in his own hand) that he did not see how freedom of association could arise together with the subject of forced labour, and denied that his officials had opposed trade unionism. He found their original instructions satisfactory, and the proposed question ambiguous and possibly irrelevant. He took the view that the constructive course was to draft a questionnaire to which governments could send affirmative replies, adding 'It is the great *variety* of native conditions in the different parts of the world, and the inherent complications of the subject, that prevent the adoption of broad sweeping declarations – the very breadth and generality of which would make them ineffective'. Citrine was not impressed. He blamed official influence on the minister, and told Poulton that the TUC's view should be openly expressed whether or not it embarrassed Labour ministers. Indeed, he added, it might be a good thing if the difference between them was brought to an issue as soon as possible.[122]

The Workers' Group never succeeded in carrying all its recommendations. At the 1939 Conference, when McGregor Ross served on the committee set up to deal with contracts, important gains were made. The Convention that was adopted covered such questions as the minimum age for entering into a contract, the maximum period of service, holidays with pay, safeguards for wages and deferred pay, and the right to repatriation. The Convention on Penal Sanctions for Breaches of Contract by Indigenous Workers was also adopted, but despite the efforts of the Workers' Group and the Government of

India, did not insist on immediate abolition of penal sanctions. However, the Conference did adopt two Recommendations on labour inspection.[123]

Conclusion

Even more than its work on India, this work on colonies in the ILO led the TUC into quite uncharted seas. India, with its political troubles, its army, its princes, and its racehorse owners and cricketers, was always familiar to the British public, though seen through a glass darkly. The colonies aroused scarcely a ripple of interest, except amongst eccentrics in the Anti-Slavery Society, the churches, and the small number of politicians and officials who had personal experience of their problems, and they were interested chiefly in the situation in East Africa, especially the land problems of Kenya. On these the Labour Party put up a continuous fight in Parliament, and since they were related to forced and contract labour its experts were able to help the TUC when the ILO moved into the field of 'Native Labour'. By contrast with India, however, the African colonies had no effective trade union movements able to form their own opinions and influence the TUC. The Advisory Committee on Forced Labour did consult Johnstone [sic] Kenyatta, who was in London in 1930,[124] but in this matter of forced labour the TUC had already been called to act because it provided the British worker representation at Geneva. It thus took on a responsibility that derived not from the interests of its own affiliated unions, or in response to requests from trade unions as in the case of India, but solely from the British government's imperial dominance.

The ILO was the only body that was able in some measure to call the dominant metropolitan governments to account, and it had a Director who was determined to use its powers to the limit. The TUC spokesmen themselves admitted that they had not previously realized, even when forced labour was discussed at the first Commonwealth Labour Conference in 1925, what the ILO could do in this sphere.[125] Having realized it, they had to learn how to use the ILO's machinery, and to equip themselves to do so. In this they were helped by the IFTU and the Workers' Group, and by the ILO's own officials.

Whatever effort the TUC might make in this exacting task on behalf of colonial workers outside its own organization, there could be no satisfactory solution to the problem of representation without constitutional progress and trade union organization in the territories. For the development and implementation of policy in these directions the Colonial Office was responsible. If the TUC was to give practical help to colonial workers, it would have to find a way to influence Downing Street.

6 The TUC And The Colonial Office

In 1929, when the second Labour government took office, the TUC was not yet seeking to exert a continuous influence on the Colonial Office. The issue at Geneva was partially resolved when Drummond Shiels came from the India Office to be parliamentary under-secretary of state. He quickly insisted that the instructions to the British government's representatives must be altered and their efforts positively directed towards the early abolition of forced labour.[1] Though not perfect, the Convention was an achievement. The General Council disbanded their Advisory Committee on Forced Labour, the British government ratified the convention, and by 1932 it was in force in sixteen British dependencies.[2] At the same time the correspondence on labour legislation in Ceylon proceeded by fits and starts, and ultimately the General Council was satisfied that the provisions which it had challenged at the request of the All-Ceylon TUC would not be enacted. However, there were other aspects of Colonial Office policy of which the General Council was unaware.

Labour Policy

Drummond Shiels saw that the impact of ILO conventions on the colonies would go on, and would necessitate changes in law and practice in the territories which only the Colonial Office itself could stimulate. As the despatches on the application of conventions revealed, the days of the noninterventionist Colonial Office were over. Also over, by the time the Labour ministers left office in August 1931, was the almost total grip of the geographical departments on Colonial Office labour policy. Shiels was able to secure the establishment of a Colonial Labour Committee, serviced by the general department, to review, and where necessary to formulate, the general principles on which colonial labour legislation should be based. This committee included officials from the Home Office and the Ministry of Labour as well as the Colonial Office, and held its first meeting on 22 May 1931. Here the subjects that were to come up at the ILO were examined, together with their relevance to territorial legislation such as existing Masters and Servants Ordinances, and the replies from colonial governments to despatches on labour matters were considered.[3] The committee remained in being after the fall of the Labour government. Passfield also circulated to the colonies the papers and proceedings of the conference of governors and senior officials held in 1930,[4] at which considerable attention was devoted to labour problems and the path of further developments was charted. But the TUC knew nothing about the proceedings of the conference or the Colonial Labour Committee.

Citrine had been right in 1929 to distrust the influence of the Colonial Office officials. They deeply resented Shiels's attitude and were determined that the Colonial Labour Committee should be purely official, unlike the Advisory Committee on Education which was set up in 1929. Shiels tried, and failed, to persuade Passfield to appoint Citrine a member.[5] Other considerations besides official opposition may have swayed Passfield, who knew very well that the General Council always wished to appoint its own representatives, whereas all governments were reluctant to acknowledge a representative status and liked to pick and choose. When Bevin was appointed to the Colonial Development Advisory Committee in 1929, the General Council endorsed his acceptance, but asked the Prime Minister to ensure that in future invitations to submit nominations should be sent in the first instance to them.[6] Passfield himself, in the first Labour government, had appointed the Balfour Committee on Industry and Trade without consulting the TUC, and Citrine had protested at this when he spent a weekend with the Webbs in July 1927.[7] In 1930 Passfield did invite nominations for advisers at the Ottawa Imperial Economic Conference, but only three months later the General Council was protesting at the manner of appointments to the Royal Commission on Unemployment Insurance.[8] If this could happen in matters so close to the TUC's domestic interests, it was scarcely likely that the Colonial Office would think it natural for a TUC representative with little, if any, knowledge of the colonies to serve on a standing committee set up specifically to guide and advise its own officials and ministers.

Yet the TUC had performed well on forced labour, and on the other major labour issue that arose under the Labour government – that of trade union legislation – TUC advice was just what was needed, for it is difficult to think of any body of officials less fitted by education, training, experience and outlook to formulate a general policy on trade unions than those in the Colonial Office at that time. On this matter also Drummond Shiels wanted to approach the TUC, and Passfield refused.[9] Perhaps his attitude was due to his acute awareness, emphasized later by Shiels himself, that the pace of improvements would be governed by that of the 'men on the spot' who would have to implement them.[10] Perhaps there was a real divergence of outlook, as

Citrine had anticipated in his letter to Poulton in 1929. Certainly Citrine had found little common ground with the Webbs during his visit in 1927, and had even failed to 'discern any depth of feeling in them, either for trade unionism or for the Labour movement'. Perhaps Passfield was confident that the Labour ministers knew what was needed, and simply wanted to avoid lengthy consultations. He was Dominions Secretary as well as Colonial Secretary until June 1930, and in that year there was an Imperial Conference which adopted decisions later implemented in the Statute of Westminster, introduced in Parliament in November 1931. Passfield was also personally responsible for the reform of the colonial service, and on Shiels's evidence, after the Arab disturbances in Palestine in 1929, the affairs of that territory took up more of the time of ministers and officials than any other subject. Passfield worked mainly by minutes, seldom actually discussing policy either with his parliamentary under-secretary or with his officials.[11] If the despatch had been delayed until full discussion had taken place in the Colonial Labour Committee, full advantage might have been taken of the experience of the Home Office and Ministry of Labour officials; but even the Colonial Office officials were not completely involved, perhaps because they were too hostile. Vernon, whose experience at the ILO left its mark, was the only one to minute before the despatch was drafted, and Passfield accepted his recommendations as providing adequate guidance to governors at the same time as he vetoed the idea of approaching the TUC.[12] The despatch went out on 17 September 1930.[13] It was marked confidential and there is no indication in the TUC's records that its existence was known at the time, nor was there any reference to it in the minutes of the Labour Party's Imperial Advisory Committee. Signed as it was by the leading historian and analyst of the British trade union movement, it acquired in later years, when it was officially mentioned without its text being revealed, a spurious reputation as a sort of Magna Carta of colonial trade unionism.

The Trade Union Despatch

Shiels arrived in the Colonial Office just after a strike in The Gambia. Violence had been used and the police intervened, there were Questions in the Commons from left-wing Members, and it was known that the LAI was receiving information from the colony.[14] On inquiry Shiels became aware of the lack of trade union legislation in The Gambia and most other colonies, and of official opposition to trade unionism. He himself was influenced by his experience in the India Office when the Meerut prosecutions were being prepared, and took the view that the Indian movement had got into bad hands and the TUC had gone into India too late. He hoped that they would be in time to guide the colonial movements on sound constitutional lines. This idea of guidance chimed in well with Passfield's outlook: Woolf referred to the Webbs' axiom that the structure of social institutions was of primary importance in political theory and practice *'and that if you made up your mind what the function of an organization should be, all that was necessary was to create the appropriate structure'*.[15] In those weeks, according to Leggett, Passfield was concerned about what he called 'pseudo trade unions' but which, in Leggett's view, the TUC might regard as genuine.[16] At the Colonial Office Conference Passfield warned the governors that as wage-labour increased, they would begin to be 'troubled' with trade unions, and would have to take steps to regulate their existence and operations. The method of regulation that emerged was compulsory registration.

This represented a new concept. In India, the provisions for registration were protective, requiring a union to have known rules for the appointment of officers and to account for its funds. In return, registration confirmed that the union was a trade union as defined in the law (and not a society subject to the Societies Registration Act), and the law granted it the immunities appropriate to a trade union. In Britain, the principal immunity, that a trade union could not be sued for torts committed by its officials or members, was not conferred until 1906, but by then unions had already been registering voluntarily for 30 years in order to secure the legal status of trade unions and to protect the management of their affairs. In neither case did the trade union law take away the right of a nonregistered union to exist. In most colonies, by 1930, there had been instances of some collective action amongst workers but without permanent organizations emerging. If and when these did emerge, it was reasonable to lay down a definition of what would be regarded as a trade union for the purpose of legislation which recognized them – for the protection of their members – as properly constituted bodies, and enabled them to act in trade disputes without prosecutions for picketing or for inducing a breach of contract. It was in this light that the proposal for compulsory registration was represented when Colonial Office sources began later to refer publicly to the existence and content of the despatch. However, the despatch itself suggested a different reason, pointing out to governors that 'without sympathetic supervision and guidance, organizations of labourers without experience of combination for any social or economic purposes may fall under the domination of disaffected persons, by whom their activities may be diverted to improper and mischievous ends'. This was manifestly true, but it is remarkable that just before the despatch was circulated, Drummond Shiels had condemned an office draft which commented, in the case of the Kikuyu Central Association in Kenya, that such associations would

serve a useful purpose for expressions of opinion provided that they
were 'not allowed to drift into the hands of undesirable extremists' –
words which he persuaded Passfield to delete, as they suggested
supervision and interference and gave an undesirable opening for
oppressive action;[17] but this is exactly what the Passfield despatch
suggested for trade unions.

A trade union does not suddenly appear fully fledged, able to collect
and manage its funds and property, to secure recognition from
employers, and to negotiate wages and conditions on behalf of its
members. In the legislation which followed the Passfield Despatch,
compulsory registration meant that it became an offence to run an
unregistered trade union, which must be dissolved, and this
interpretation was confirmed by the wording used in a model
Ordinance circulated in 1941: 'No trade union or any member thereof
shall perform any act in furtherance of the purposes for which it has
been formed unless such trade union has first been registered. Any
trade union or any officer or member thereof who contravenes the
provisions of this section shall be guilty of an offence punishable with a
fine not exceeding £25'.[18] The requirements for registration, and the
conditions on which it might be refused, suspended or cancelled,
therefore became all important. They varied from territory to
territory[19] and usually were not onerous, but in some colonies after the
Second World War they were extended beyond the conventional
purpose of protecting members' rights into the field of trade union
structure, and after independence many territories adopted restrictive
legislation which covered not only structure but also bargaining rights.
It is difficult to avoid the conclusion that such legislation stands in a
direct line of descent from the concept inherent in compulsory
registration – that a trade union derives its right to exist, as distinct
from what it may do, to the state.

The despatch also departed from current British practice in
Passfield's categorical statement, doubtless elicited by the controversy
in Ceylon, that he would not agree to colonies enacting the provisions
of the British Trade Unions and Trade Disputes Act 1927. Otherwise,
it was an attempt to place colonial trade unionism in a historical setting,
using British experience as a yardstick, and had the great merit of
stressing that the formation of unions would be a natural and legitimate
consequence of social and industrial progress. Recognizing the
divergences of labour conditions between Great Britain and the
colonies, and between one colony and another, Passfield did not lay
down detailed rules for general adoption. He suggested that in
territories where unions or analagous organizations of workers had not
yet been formed, colonial governments should smooth their passage,
when they did emerge, by enacting Sections 2 and 3 of the British Trade

Unions Act 1871[20] which would free them from common law prosecutions on the ground that they were conspiracies in restraint of trade; in dependencies in which trade unions had already made some headway, he asked for review of existing legislation (it did exist in British Guiana, Jamaica and Malta) to determine whether it was still adequate.

The Labour Government resigned on 24 August 1931. So Passfield and Drummond Shiels were not in the Colonial Office to follow up the despatch, and Vernon was the only official to express outright disagreement when the Conservative Secretary of State, Sir Philip Cunliffe-Lister, let it be known that he would not press for colonial governments to implement it.[21] Most of them had reservations, as in Nigeria, where the government and the European employers who were consulted had little difficulty in agreeing that there were too few wage-earners to justify legislation and that local workers were sufficiently protected by the tribal system of mutual assistance,[22] thus defeating the main purpose of the Labour ministers, which was to anticipate the need for trade union law. Tanganyika produced an Ordinance in 1932. In the West Indies, where the wage-earning population was substantial, only the government of Trinidad moved.

The Case of Trinidad

The TUC remained unaware of the issue until 1932, when Cipriani sent a copy of the Trinidad government's draft Bill and expressed concern that it contained no provision for political expenditure by trade unions. The TUC's reply gives some indication of the views that might have been expressed if TUC representatives had been brought into consultation when the despatch was being drafted. First it met Cipriani's anxiety by pointing out that the legislation would allow unions to pursue lawful objects and did not exclude political objects as unlawful. But it went on to draw attention to the vital omission of provisions covering peaceful picketing and protection from liability in tort – the 1906 provisions which the despatch did not mention and which were not included in the 1871 legislation which the colonies had been advised to enact. The reply also noted that the Bill's requirement of compulsory registration was contrary to British law, although in practice the majority of British unions did register. It is not clear what the TUC's comment would have been if it had been known that Passfield had recommended compulsory registration to all colonies, and why,[23] and that it was the one proposal in the despatch which had become permanently embedded in Colonial Office thought on trade unions. The registration provisions in the Bill raised a problem for the TWMA, being, as it was primarily, a political body, but with sections affiliated to it which functioned as trade unions and with some objects in its rules which in the government's view might be regarded as trade union objects.

Citrine sent the texts of the various British Acts and Cipriani in the Legislative Council moved amendments on picketing and immunity which the Trinidad Government refused to accept. In the TUC's eyes, this was the key issue. Asked whether the TWMA should register, Citrine replied that a trade union had no option under the Bill, but insisted that 'it is quite a mockery ... to allow unions to exist but to refuse them the right to take effective action ... and the trade union law of Trinidad must be regarded as utterly unsatisfactory without such safeguards'. As the correspondence went on, it became evident that Cipriani's prime concern was with the political activities of his organization. He was aware that the government did not intend to proceed against the TWMA under the trade union law, but he was prepared to sacrifice the trade union sections if necessary. The TWMA intended to refuse to register and to advise its sections to refuse, and thus throw on the government the onus of prosecuting and proving that they were trade unions within the provisions of the law. In any case the TWMA would not register until the required amendments were incorporated in the law,[24] but nor did the sections register, with the consequence that they 'ceased to exist as trade unions'.[25] The TWMA became the Trinidad Labour Party (TLP) in 1934, and Trinidad was left with unsatisfactory trade union legislation and no trade unions.

This was the position in 1937 when strikes and riots broke out while Cipriani was out of the country, involving groups of workers who were outside the TWMA and were in general hostile to it.[26] Sir Arthur Pugh was appointed to the ensuing Forster Commission of Inquiry, during which he addressed meetings of newly formed unions which Cipriani regarded as 'mushroom' organizations undermining the TWMA.[27] Pugh advised them to register, and in response to a query from the Negro Welfare Association, London, Citrine replied that the earlier advice given to the TWMA should not be construed to mean that trade unions should not be established: 'Whatever the character of the legislation, these should exist in all places where men and women have to sell their labour'.[28]

The disturbances had all the features which Passfield had feared – strikes by workers outside trade union organization, the emergence of the 'agitator' in the person of Uriah Butler, and riots in which a policeman was murdered by the crowd. If the new unions which began immediately to form had not registered, a whole movement would have developed unregulated, and unprotected in any way, by the law. Pugh formed the opinion that Cipriani could no longer be regarded as the mouthpiece of Trinidad's workers, whose only hope lay in the formation of unions on regular lines.[29] He was also impressed by the lack of balanced judgement revealed in some of the demands made after the strikes, and was concerned that legal requirements on the handling of funds should be rigorously enforced.

Against this background, the Commission did not recommend the abolition of compulsory registration. After its report had been published, the TUC was asked whether a union being formed in the distributive trades should register, in view of the Trinidad Labour Party's advice to their clerks' section not to do so. Citrine advised registration, arguing that although the legislation was still unsatisfactory, there seemed to be no prospect of early amendment, so refusal to register would almost certainly mean postponing indefinitely any hope of introducing trade unionism in industries which urgently required organization.[30] In this way the TUC in its turn came to accept, in the case of Trinidad, the compulsory registration of trade unions.

The Forster Commission went further: it recommended that there should be power to withhold registration where the credentials of the applicants were unsatisfactory, or where a new registration would lead to unnecessary duplication of unions in the same trade or calling and so lead to competition and friction.[31] When the TUC's newly formed Colonial Advisory Committee discussed the report with Sir Arthur Pugh, it was already known that the Colonial Office was sending an Industrial Adviser to Trinidad. He was A. G. V. Lindon, a conciliation officer seconded from the Ministry of Labour, who started work in March 1938. The committee recorded no comment on the proposals for registration,[32] but it may be noted that after the war, when the TUC frequently challenged additions to the requirements for registration as they were made in different territories, it did not challenge the provision against duplication (which was not adopted in Trinidad but appeared later in Sierra Leone and Kenya), since it was regarded as a protection against the break-up of the movement by the formation of rival or breakaway unions.

But actually this was the first move towards controlling the structure of a trade union movement. There was a different reaction in the Labour Party's Imperial Advisory Committee, where Green, now retired from the Colonial Office but doubtless still painfully aware of the attitudes of his former colleagues, commented adversely on these proposals. His memorandum was amended after comments from Pugh, but in its final form as approved by the committee it still referred to them as 'doubtful', suggesting that the structure of trade union movements ought not to be determined by the Labour Department but by workers themselves after consultation. Considering the general principle again in 1941, the newly established Fabian Colonial Bureau accepted compulsory registration as a protection for funds and members' rights, and as a means to counter potential hostility to trade unions by conferring on them a measure of public recognition. It followed Green in arguing that registration must not be used to determine the structure of a trade union movement.[33] However these documents do not appear in the files of the TUC, which had no representative on the Labour Party's Imperial Advisory Committee. Arthur Creech Jones, who was a member of the TUC's Colonial Advisory Committee, was the leading figure in the Fabian Colonial Bureau, but in a personal capacity.

Institutional Weakness

Consideration of this experience reveals institutional failure in three places: in Trinidad, where the local government claimed to be acting in accordance with a despatch from Lord Passfield without revealing its contents, and the TWMA was primarily concerned with safeguarding its political role, in the Colonial Office and in the TUC.

The weakness in the Colonial Office was decisive. In its General Division, which handled international conventions and circular despatches, there was no specialist labour section, and there was no adequate co-ordination of the seven geographical departments in regard to labour legislation until Sheils secured the establishment of the Colonial Labour Committee, after the trade union despatch had been sent out. The senior officials were confident that they and the governors knew how to run the colonies without advice from outside – the memory of Shiels's attitude still rankled in 1936, when the head of the East Africa department commented that in Shiels's view the Secretary of State's policy should be to distrust the governor and his staff and be guided by his own inner light and the help of advisers.[34] In the case of Trinidad, the initial refusal to seek outside advice was responsible for the glaring omission of immunities. It was true that the British unions lived for a generation without them, but at the cost of penalties which no trade unions, let alone registered unions, should have been expected to bear. Except for Vernon and Green, there was no echo in the official mind of Montagu's observation in 1921 that it was unnecessary for trade unions in every country to go through the same war-worn history as the British movement.

If the Labour ministers had moved ahead of their officials, there was little danger of this when Cunliffe-Lister took over. There was no drive to stimulate trade union legislation and the Secretary of State himself took an equivocal view on the application of ILO conventions.[35] Although the Colonial Labour Committee continued to examine such matters as minimum wages and workmen's compensation, it held only 11 meetings between 1932 and 1935.[36] An underlying cause was financial stringency following the economic collapse in 1931, affecting administrations in the territories as well as at home. One casualty was the labour department in Tanganyika, and a few labour inspectors in the Kenya Native Affairs Department were the only survivors of early attempts to build up specialist staffs.[37] Cunliffe-Lister began to tackle the economic 'problem by adding economic questions to the responsibilities of the general division and in 1935 a new Economic Department was set up. This had no effect on relationships with the TUC. With the fall of the Labour government, Bevin resigned from the Colonial Development Advisory Committee and no other trade unionist was appointed.[38] Except for the work at the ILO, the TUC's tenuous link with the Colonial Office was broken.

There remained the possibility of ad hoc representations, but where there were no organizations like the TWMA to keep the TUC informed, problems did not come to light. There was also a failure to see colonial labour policy as a whole and to press for a voice in its formulation. In the Trinidad case, as cables crossed letters and consultations took place on the spot in the light of a despatch known only to the government, why was no deputation sent to the Colonial Office to support Cipriani's effort in the Legislative Council? Perhaps the simplest answer is the right one – that Cipriani did not ask for this. Why did no one in the TUC pick up the Trinidad government's reference to a despatch from Lord Passfield and find out what was in it? Probably because Lee had retired in 1931. The advice given to the TWMA was sound, but it was drafted in the research department. In the International Department Bolton was primarily concerned with the ILO, the IFTU and India. There was no advisory committee on imperial questions, there were no joint Commonwealth Labour Conferences after 1930, and there was no replacement for Lee.

In fact, the whole movement was at a low ebb. As the dole queues lengthened, the TUC's affiliated membership touched its lowest point, 3,294,581 in 1934, and did not climb back to the 1926 level, nearly 4½ million, until 1938. In Parliament, after the general election in October 1931, forty-nine Labour Members, with every former Cabinet minister except Lansbury defeated, faced 417 Conservatives. Although in 1935 154 seats were won, these were still fewer than the 192 secured in November 1923. With no strong or general impetus coming from the colonies themselves, it was not to be expected that TUC officials or General Council members would perceive a pressing need to initiate forward policies with the Colonial Office.

The International Committee fulfilled its existing commitments. Green was consulted when Recruitment was put on the ILO Conference agenda for 1935,[39] and right up to 1939 the department was continuously engaged in preparing for the conventions and arranging the representation of colonial workers. As for India, much time was devoted to the Meerut case but the TUC's contact was limited by the disunity that followed the AITUC's 1929 congress. There were helpful initiatives on labour representation and policies at the Round Table Conferences and in the Joint Standing Committee which preceded the enactment of the Government of India Act 1935, and at the ILO.[40]

The main effort in the IFTU was aimed at extending the organization, against increasingly heavy odds. An IFTU visit to the Far East planned in 1931 was postponed because of the British domestic crisis, then indefinitely in 1932 for reasons which signalled the gathering storm: in Asia, because an impartial inquiry was precluded by civil disobedience and the suppression of public assemblies in India and by the military dictatorship in Japan and its invasion of Manchuria, in Europe, because it was inadvisable for the President and the General Secretary of the IFTU – Citrine and Schevenels – to be out of touch with the political situation in Germany.[41] Nevertheless, in 1935 a large section of the Indian movement, the newly constituted National Trade Union Federation, affiliated to the IFTU, and when the IFTU General Council met in Warsaw in June 1937 the sixteen affiliates represented included the Argentine and Mexico, new affiliates – which later materialized – were expected in Australia and New Zealand, and the AFL was accepted into affiliation. The IFTU was breaking out of its European mould, and three years before the ILO had been greatly strengthened by the adhesion of the USA.

However, the international trade union movement was still flawed. The Russian centre sent no reply to the IFTU's invitation to affiliate[42] and when Citrine visited the Soviet Union in 1935 he found Tomsky out in the cold.[43] In 1936, the IFTU and the LSI, shocked by the great trial of the former Comintern leaders, while recognizing that Zinoviev and his associates had always been bitterly hostile to them, appealed to Moscow for a fair trial with independent defending counsel.[44] The next day Tomsky committed suicide and three days later Zinoviev was shot.

Already the Spanish civil war had begun, and in the heart of Europe trade unionists were being driven out. Italy had attacked Abyssinia and the Japanese were moving into central China. In the Congress year 1937–8 alone, the TUC collected nearly £22,000 for the National Council of Labour's International Solidarity Fund, which was expended on German and Austrian refugees, Basque children, and assistance to Spanish and Chinese workers.[45]

In this atmosphere, labour disturbances in many colonies passed unnoticed in the TUC. In the West Indies they occurred in Trinidad (May–July 1934), St Kitts (January 1935), Jamaica (May 1935), British Guiana (September–October 1935) and St Vincent (October 1935).[46] Then in 1937 came the Trinidad eruption, galvanizing into action the Labour Party, the Colonial Office and the TUC.

Labour Party Initiatives

The Labour Party's Imperial Advisory Committee had been concentrating mainly on political questions, on land and education in Kenya, and in labour matters, on the implementation of the Forced Labour Convention. A pamphlet produced in 1933 and adopted as official party policy on the Colonial Empire made little substantial advance on the programme prepared for the LSI in 1928, but it did ask for trade unions to be assisted and not merely permitted and for the establishment of a specialized labour department in every colony.[47] The concept of labour administration as a specialized subject was not new, and was associated with the trend towards positive functions as distinct from mere inspection and protection, just as in Britain the emergence of the Ministry of Labour from the Board of Trade and the development of conciliation and arbitration services marked the acceptance of some state responsibility for industrial relations as well as for conditions of labour. In the ILO conventions and the discussions in the Labour Party's Imperial Advisory Committee the emphasis was still on protection,[48] but in the territories and in the Colonial Office itself even this was inadequately handled.

A change began in 1935, when sporadic outbreaks were already beginning in the colonies. The new intake of Labour Members of Parliament enabled the Imperial Advisory Committee to prepare more effectively for Questions and for the annual debate on the Colonial Office Estimates, and in the Office Malcolm MacDonald, who had followed his father out of the Labour Party but had been brought up within it, had a brief spell from June to November as Secretary of State. He was followed for a few months by J. H. Thomas and then from May 1936 to May 1938 by W. G. A. Ormsby-Gore, who had been parliamentary under-secretary in 1922–3 and chairman of the East Africa Commission which recommended the establishment of labour departments in 1925.[49] In a despatch on labour supervision circulated in November 1935, MacDonald referred to Questions in Parliament and asked governors to review their arrangements and send proposals for improvement. He regarded continuous review as necessary, and stressed that inspection by mines and medical staffs or the ad hoc investigation of complaints about labour conditions by administrative officers did not in themselves provide it. Where there was no need for a separate labour department, there must nevertheless be regular supervision, with adequate and properly co-ordinated arrangements for all the various forms of employment.[50] The fact that two years later some colonies had not yet replied to this despatch was evidence of the rundown state of administration in the colonies and in Downing Street.

In 1936 Drummond Shiels returned to the field with a proposal for a Labour Adviser in the Colonial Office. He had in mind Major Granville Orde Browne, who had ended a long colonial service with five years as Labour Commissioner in Tanganyika and resigned altogether from the service when his labour department was axed in 1931. With his new independence, he pressed his views wherever he could, especially on the Native Labour Division of the ILO, where the comments and information he provided were used when the British government's reports on Tanganyika came before the Permanent Mandates Commission. His direct pressure on the Colonial Office was sufficient to secure his appointment in 1934 as deputy for Lugard on the ILO Committee of Experts on Native Labour – an appointment by the ILO Governing Body which still left him independent of Colonial Office control. He sought to influence the Parliamentary Labour Party to work for specialist labour departments, and in a sustained campaign for the implementation of the Forced Labour Convention in Bechuanaland he worked closely with the British Social Hygiene Council,[51] whose medical secretary was Drummond Shiels.

Drummond Shiels went direct to Ormsby-Gore with his proposal. The official response was mixed, but the parliamentary under-secretary, the Duke of Devonshire, was in favour: 'The policy of Trusteeship is going to be more difficult in labour questions than in any other sphere', he wrote, 'and on grounds of Imperial policy it seems desirable that there should be an Adviser here who would throw his influence on the side of fair wages and better conditions ... There is a special labour point of view in all projects ...' He added that a good Adviser would have detected earlier the 'appalling state of affairs' revealed in a recent report on emigrant labour in Nyasaland. The deputy permanent under-secretary, Sir John Shuckburgh, commented that experience in the Colonial Labour Committee suggested that a whole-time adviser would be valuable, but the cost prohibitive. The project hung fire, and at the end of August 1937 Ormsby-Gore decided that he must first battle with the Treasury on education.[52]

By then the need for change was becoming more evident. In April the Governor of Nigeria, Sir Bernard Bourdillon, decided to introduce trade union legislation. There had been continuous trouble amongst manual workers on the Nigerian Railway since 1931, when a spontaneous strike led by Michael Imoudu led to the formation of a Railway Workers' Association. This became the Railway Workers' Union, which was formally inaugurated in 1932,[53] but it had no legal status. Bourdillon had been approached on behalf of the union by Sir William Geary,[54] whose representations were well known in the Colonial Office.[55] In May the Governor of Kenya asked the Office to approve the introduction of legislation on the lines of the Passfield

Despatch. There had been several strikes in both rural and urban areas since 1934, culminating in a prolonged strike by Indian artisans in Nairobi in 1937,[56] led by the Labour Trade Union of East Africa, first organized in 1934. The governor sent his request during the strike, when some of the employers wanted the union's position to be regularized to enable negotiations to take place.[57] In Parliament, in reply to a Question, the existence of the Colonial Labour Committee was revealed to Arthur Creech Jones. Finding that it was purely official, he wrote to Ormsby-Gore in July asking for an advisory committee like the one on education (to which he had been appointed in 1936), which would review industrial legislation, keep needs under continuous review and advise on new proposals.[58] In the same month the Labour Party's Imperial Advisory Committee decided to take advantage of the situation in Trinidad and Rhodesia to press for a specialist department in the Colonial Office.[59]

Ormsby-Gore had already decided to act. As a result of the Estimates debate on 2 June he discussed with Vernon the reinstatement of labour departments, workmen's compensation, and the recognition of trade unions. In a note prepared after this conversation, Vernon set out his views. It was two weeks before the state of emergency was declared in Trinidad. He suggested that the colonies should be told that the functions of a labour department and its local inspectorate must be to examine the relations between master and servant in agricultural as well as industrial areas and to supervise housing, transport and health services; penal sanctions should be eliminated from Masters and Servants Ordinances, all ILO conventions should be examined to see how far they could be applied; there should be legislation to enable inquiries to be made into the conditions of low-paid workers; trade union law should be reviewed. Here Vernon argued that to prohibit unions or to subject them to the requirements of obsolete features of the English common law was almost bound to encourage the formation of illegal combinations which might easily develop into secret societies and were likely to go outside the industrial and into the political field.[60] This went further than the Labour members had done in the debate, in which trade unions were not discussed. It was as if Vernon, at the end of his career, had gathered together all the positive directions of Passfield, Shiels and MacDonald and made a last effort to have them implemented – but he did not go beyond them.

Ormsby-Gore circulated the official report of the Commons debate to colonial governors, and in a new despatch sent out in August returned to the question of MacDonald's despatch and the replies from the territories. He expressed the view that at least all the larger ones should aim at the establishment of separate labour departments, and accorded prime importance to relations between employers and employees, in agriculture as well as in mines and manufactures. These relations could not be left to the Secretariat or to Native Affairs Departments or the district administration: wherever there was a substantial wage-earning population, colonial governments should 'forthwith' consider establishing an organization of officers whose sole duty would be to examine labour conditions generally and make suggestions for their improvement, in most cases under the control of a chief labour inspector who would act as an adviser to government, whether or not in a separate department. The despatch followed Vernon's references to ILO conventions and included word for word his comments on trade unions, but added that one of the functions of a labour department should be to report on any developments that might have taken place towards the formation of unions, their general conduct and tendencies and their relations with employers. Ormsby-Gore pointed out that the finances of colonies and of colonial enterprises had now improved and that companies operating in mining and agriculture were reaping the benefits of enhanced prices, in which workers should share. With a new sense of urgency, he called for reports to be sent in not later than 30 June 1938 on the action to be taken.[61]

This was the state of play when on 6 September 1937 Ernest Bevin made his presidential speech to the TUC's Norwich Congress.

The TUC's Colonial Advisory Committee

Ernest Bevin's Intervention

Most of these developments passed over the heads of the TUC's International Committee and there was no specific reference to the colonies in the General Council's report to Congress, but Bevin perceived the significance of the outbreak in Trinidad.

Bevin's reputation in Britain at that time rested principally on his success as 'the dockers' KC' in an arbitration under the Industrial Courts Act in 1920 and as the architect of the TGWU, an amalgamation of twenty-two unions which gave him a dominant position on the TUC's General Council. But from his first journey abroad in 1915 as the TUC's fraternal delegate to the AFL he had begun to see British trade unionism in a wider context. In April 1919, at the first postwar conference which reconstituted the ITF, he moved the resolution for a re-established international federation which would include unions in India and the Far East; at the TUC's Congress in the following September, after Wadia's speech, he made the first of his interventions on India; later he made his mark at the ILO at Conferences and in the Joint Maritime Commission.[62] Initially he showed little interest in the colonies, and perhaps it was the 1929 ILO Conference which first opened his eyes to the worst abuses there, for he attended a preparatory meeting with Woolf and Buxton to discuss the Conference documents on forced labour. 'Bevin amazed me,' wrote Woolf. 'He knew nothing about what is now called colonialism or the facts about forced labour in colonies ... He picked our brains clause by clause and continually asked what line we advised him to take over every detail ... he was quick to see every point explained to him.'[63] Bevin did not sit in the Conference committee on forced labour, but the seed had been sown, and was subsequently nurtured in the Colonial Development Advisory Committee[64] set up under the Labour government's Colonial Development Act. When that was over, he did what he could to help Ballinger's work in South Africa.[65]

Bevin was also better informed than most general councillors. Though he left school at the age of 11 and hardly ever looked at a book, he read his documents thoroughly,[66] and constantly harped on the need to collect, and use, accurate information. From his own staff John Cliff went to the Whitley Commission in India, and Arthur Creech Jones, who served ten years as a national officer of the TGWU, enjoyed a close personal relationship with Bevin. After his election to Parliament in 1935 Creech Jones was assiduous in tabling Questions and contributing to colonial debates, and certainly fed Bevin with information on colonial issues.[67]

At the 1937 Congress[68] Bevin chose to stress British responsibility for conditions in the colonies:

> There are 66m. people, mainly coloured, ruled from the Colonial Office ... Most of them are voteless. A great responsibility rests upon us. The disturbances which have taken place in the West Indies are not without cause. A public survey of labour standards and conditions is absolutely imperative. I am certain that the citizens of this country do not want to be a party to the exploitation of dependent coloured peoples. This Congress could do a great work by initiating an investigation into colonial labour conditions and publishing the results, so that the public could be informed.

None of the Congress delegates picked up these remarks in the ensuing debates, but they were noted outside. The secretary of the International African Service Bureau, Wallace Johnson, wrote to Citrine expressing appreciation of Bevin's speech, which the Bureau intended to distribute to the local press throughout the colonies, and enclosed a memorandum which the Bureau had submitted to the Commission of Inquiry into the June disturbances in Trinidad. He wrote also to Bevin, who suggested to Citrine that his proposal for an investigation should be put to the General Council.[69] Citrine acted with

characteristic speed and thoroughness, and argued that extra staff
would be needed. By the end of November a new Colonial Advisory
Committee had been assembled,[70] and when it met for the first time on
22 December 1937 W. B. Kemmis, appointed as the TUC's first
colonial specialist, was there as secretary.

Preparing TUC Policy

As the office was preparing a programme of work for the new Colonial
Advisory Committee and sought expert advice as Bevin had suggested,
three new influences came into play.

The first was the International African Service Bureau, whose role
resembled that of the WWLI – but the organization was different in
character. The Indian associations with which the British Labour
movement were familiar were in close contact with the various
groupings in the Indian national movement, of which they were in a
sense a part, while the WWLI was initially the accredited agent of the
AITUC. No individual colony had such powerful political or trade
union bodies to direct or back the efforts of the few students, workers,
professional or business men who might be in Britain. They had to
function on a comparatively small scale and tended to group together
on a racial, rather than a national, basis. Such early bodies as the
African Progress Union had members from the West Indies and West
Africa, as did the West African and West Indians' Christian Union,
with the Trinidadian Audrey Jeffers as secretary, which gave support in
1920 to a delegation from what was then known as the South African
Native Congress.[71] Their British connections were with the churches,
the Anti-Slavery Society and with individual politicians rather than
with the Labour Party as such. John Richard Archer, chairman of the
African Progress Union, was Mayor of Battersea in 1913 and later
supported Saklatvala,[72] but he was not a national figure. The American
leader of Pan-Africanism, Dr W. E. Dubois, met the Webbs when
preparing for the Pan-African Congress held in London in 1921, and
the congress was addressed by Olivier and Dr Norman Leys; a further
congress held in 1923 heard Olivier, H. G. Wells and Harold Laski,
and received a message from Ramsay MacDonald.[73] In the 1930s,
Arthur Creech Jones and the Labour Member of Parliament Reginald
Sorensen worked with the West African Students' Union, the Negro
Welfare Association and Dr Harold Moody's League of Coloured
Peoples. The regularity with which the same few British names occur in
connection with colonial and Indian associations is in itself an
indication that these bodies touched only the fringe of British politics
and influenced British trade unionists, if at all, only at the bottom level
or indirectly. Yet it was from this specialist fringe that the forward-
looking policies for the colonies came in the Labour Party and, in the

case of the Forced Labour Convention, penetrated into the ILO and the TUC.

It was a new breed of professional, revolutionary politicians who came on to the scene after the Italian invasion of Abyssinia that made direct contact with the TUC. They also operated on the fringe, forming their closest links with the ILP, which was no longer affiliated to the Labour Party. When the TUC received the letter from the International African Service Bureau in 1937, most of the names carried at its head, except that of Kenyatta, were unfamiliar. An inquiry to the Labour Party elicited the reply that the party had no direct information about the Bureau but noted that its aims and some of its personnel coincided with those on a circular received in 1936 from the Pan-African Federation, when Gillies had inclined to the view that the Federation was a subsidiary of the LAI, with which Kenyatta was known to be connected.[74] Gillies may have known that when Kenyatta visited Russia in 1933, the Kikuyu Central Association had complained to Roden Buxton.[75]

The Communist link had been there, and in the trade union as well as the political field. The Bureau's secretary, Isaac Wallace Johnson, had in 1930 attended the LAI's First International Conference of Negro Workers in Hamburg, had written (under pseudonyms) for the *Negro Worker* published by the RILU's International Committee of Negro Workers, and had visited Moscow in 1932 in a group selected from the colonies.[76] By far the most travelled and experienced was the Trinidadian George Padmore, who had been a member of the American Communist Party, had attended the LAI's Frankfurt Congress in 1929 and organized its Conference of Negro Workers in 1930, and became head of the RILU's Negro Bureau.[77] Padmore resigned from the RILU after its International Committee of Negro Workers was disbanded, as part of a change in the Comintern line which in his view sacrificed support for the African and Asian liberation movements to the requirements of Russian foreign policy. In the Comintern view, Padmore was a petty bourgeois nationalist, pressing for the freedom of the colonies rather than the freedom of colonial workers, and he was formally expelled in January 1934.[78] But his Communist experience had certainly left its mark on Padmore's ideas, both on policy and on organization.

There is no indication that the TUC staff were aware of this controversy or of the significance of the Pan-African group in Britain. But Wallace Johnson's letter enclosed a statement of aims which coincided with TUC policy, and the evidence submitted to the Forster Commission on Trinidad was a competent memorandum which suggested that the International African Service Bureau was a serious organization. The Bureau's treasurer, T. R. Makonnen, visited the office in October. He was a practical organizer with an interest in the co-operative movement, who had worked and studied agriculture in America and in Denmark before settling in 1937 in Manchester,[79] where he had connections with the co-operative societies and with colonial workers in Liverpool. He was not a communist. In the TUC he left the impression that the Bureau had some representative status, with specialist knowledge and contacts which could be helpful to the colonial unions. He was given TUC publications and union rules, and subsequently the TUC, in replying to approaches from two unions in Trinidad and one in Jamaica, suggested that they should correspond also with the Bureau.[80]

This practice was short-lived. The Bureau's rules should have raised some doubts in the TUC, if only because active membership was open only to Africans and people of African descent. They also provided for affiliation by political, trade union, co-operative and cultural bodies throughout the world, and though it was stated that the Bureau did not aim to usurp their functions, it did hope to centralize and co-ordinate their activities and bring them into fraternal relations with one another and with sympathetic organizations in Britain and elsewhere. This opened up the possibility of a non-trade-union body in Britain claiming to represent and co-ordinate the work of trade unions in the colonies. If this outcome was foreseen in the TUC office, it was not recorded. Another defect was that the Bureau's leaders were primarily politicians. Only the Sierra Leonean, Wallace Johnson, who had briefly organized an African Workers' Union in Nigeria in 1931, returned to his own country in 1938 and helped to build the trade union movement.[81] Nevertheless the Bureau had provided the final impetus to Bevin and did arouse interest in the TUC at the critical moment.

The second new influence was that of Orde Browne. Having deferred the appointment of a Labour Adviser in the Colonial Office, Ormsby-Gore invited him to advise on the establishment of a labour department in Northern Rhodesia. Before his departure, Drummond Shiels took him to see Citrine. It was a fruitful meeting,[82] at which Citrine was introduced to the key administrative questions – Drummond Shiels's proposal for a Labour Adviser and Orde Browne's insistence that administrative officers were not competent to be responsible for labour supervision, which required specially trained inspectors and labour departments. Citrine was obviously feeling his way to a more positive approach. He observed that the colonies needed people with personal experience of industrial life: some scheme might be considered, he suggested, whereby trade union officials might go out to work not only as labour inspectors, but also in helping to establish trade unions. This appears to be the birth of the idea that later Orde

Browne and Citrine were to float in their reports on the West Indies, that trade unionists should actually work in labour departments. It was not in Orde Browne's mind in October 1937. Unlike the other former colonial servants who advised the Labour Party and the TUC, he was a radical Tory,[83] and in a memorandum that he prepared after this interview he expressed the view that the great bulk of labourers were primitive and uneducated men, the easy prey of any dishonest schemer, and therefore unable to build trade unions, not only in Africa but also in the West Indies and Mauritius.[84] He did admit, however, that some start must be made in the direction of trade unionism, as Ormsby-Gore had done in his despatch.

As an immediate consequence the TUC International Committee decided that there must be continuous pressure on the Colonial Office to see that labour departments were set up in the colonies and, if possible, to appoint labour specialists in the Office.[85] Citrine also wrote to Pugh to say that he had useful expert information that he would like to discuss with him before the Forster Commission's report was completed.[86] When the report came out in January 1938 it contained a recommendation that Trinidad should have a labour department headed by a person with wide experience in dealing with industrial questions and that it should help in the establishment of trade unions.

At this point Arthur Creech Jones entered the TUC's consultations. He had no colonial experience, but his interest in colonial issues can be traced to at least 1914, when he addressed the London Egyptian Debating Society on 'Socialism and Nationalism'.[87] He was already at that time secretary of the Camberwell Trades and Labour Council, and was the only one of the Labour Party's colonial advisers with a substantial trade union record. He acted immediately when Ormsby-Gore, in answer to a Question on 3 November, revealed that he had sent out a despatch on labour supervision. Creech Jones secured a copy (which was still confidential, but placed in the House of Commons Library). Gratified to find that it dealt with the issues which he and his colleagues had raised in the Estimates debate in June, he sent it to Bevin, who passed it on to Citrine. The TUC also received a memorandum which Creech Jones prepared for the Labour Party's Imperial Advisory Committee, and Buxton sent an exhaustive note on sources of information on colonial labour conditions.[88] In his memorandum Creech Jones included his suggestion previously made to Ormsby-Gore for the appointment of a labour advisory committee in the Colonial Office. Thus all the threads were now in Citrine's hands.

In preparing for the work of the new TUC Colonial Advisory Committee, Citrine also approached Ormsby-Gore, and the Colonial Office provided a memorandum[89] which described the position at that time. The Forced Labour Convention was in effect in all British territories, the Conventions on Night Work for Women and Minimum Wage for Employment at Sea were 'extensively' in force, and the 1936 Convention on Recruitment was about to be ratified. Two-thirds of the colonies had laws empowering governors to fix minimum wage rates and to set up advisory boards, and most had factory legislation. The provision for workmen's compensation was still unsatisfactory, but a model Ordinance had been circulated to the African colonies and changes were being prepared in Trinidad, Jamaica, Palestine, Malaya and Mauritius. The possibility of re-forming the labour inspectorates of Tanganyika and Uganda, and similar moves in some West Indian dependencies, were under consideration. All this was still protective. Nothing was said about conciliation or arbitration. On trade unions, the memorandum merely stated that many colonies had simple legislation sanctioning trade union organization. Clearly, there would be much for the TUC's new committee to do.

Its field of work as laid down by the General Council was the whole colonial empire: this left India and South Africa to the International Committee. It was to investigate labour conditions with the object of seeing how far the TUC could contribute towards raising the standard of life. The office document prepared for the inaugural meeting[90] referred to continued action in the ILO and embodied all the proposals put forward by the Labour Party experts, but recognized that the effects of administrative action could be only gradually felt. The document placed first the need to remedy immediate grievances such as underpayment, excessive hours, the truck system and repressive administration, and on trade unions set out the committee's work as 'to consider the best means of extending trade unionism among native workers, having regard to local conditions and difficulties, and with this object to formulate a simplified model system of trade union organization applicable to the colonies generally'. This ambitious programme went far beyond Bevin's initial proposal and beyond those of the Labour Party and the Colonial Office: it bears the stamp of Citrine, who shared with Albert Thomas the capacity to kick a ball placed before him into a goal beyond the one originally envisaged.

The First Fruits

The new Committee was chaired by H. H. Elvin, now chairman of the General Council, and the other General Council members were George Hicks, Ebby Edwards[91] and Arthur Shaw.[92] The outside members included Buxton and Polak from the old joint TUC/Labour Party committee, McGregor Ross from the former Advisory Committee on Forced Labour, Creech Jones, Drummond Shiels and J. F. N. Green from the Labour Party's Imperial Advisory Committee, and Professor W. M. Macmillan, whose *Warning From the West Indies* had been published in 1936. It advised the International Committee on ILO matters relevant to the colonies, and was the main committee for contact with colonial trade unions.

Already by the second meeting on 16 February 1938 appeals for help had come in from budding organizations in Trinidad, Jamaica, Sierra Leone and Kenya. By the end of May, model rules were in print. In accordance with previous practice, requests for colonial unions to affiliate to the TUC were refused: instead, unions were invited to associate themselves with the committee by sending in information, and a questionnaire on their organization was sent to them with the model rules.[93]

In January 1938 the report of the Forster Commission was published. Not only did it castigate the employers, but it revealed the extraordinary incompetence of the Trinidad administration. Despite all the despatches, hardly anything had been actually done: an Industrial Court Ordinance had been promulgated in 1920, but no Court was ever established; the Workmen's Compensation Ordinance 1926 still did not cover agricultural workers, contrary to the ILO Convention ratified by Great Britain; no effective action had been taken under the enabling Minimum Wage Ordinance 1936; no reply had been sent to MacDonald's 1935 despatch, and no action had been taken to set up a labour department, until after the 1937 disturbances, when the Deputy Colonial Secretary was temporarily appointed Secretary for Labour.[94] The impetus in the Colonial Office was now sustained. Lindon went to Trinidad, and by the end of the year all the West Indian colonies except Jamaica had labour officers of some sort at work.[95] In February Ormsby-Gore appointed Orde Browne Labour Adviser in the Colonial Office, and breaking with the Passfield tradition, urged him to keep in touch with Labour Members of Parliament and with Citrine.[96] In May Malcolm MacDonald returned for a further two-year stint at the Colonial Office. He arrived two weeks after further disturbances had broken out in Jamaica.

Meanwhile, the TUC's Colonial Advisory Committee had been preparing its bid for real influence in the Colonial Office. A deputation put its views to MacDonald on 23 June 1938,[97] and asked for a full-scale labour section in the Colonial Office and for the establishment of an advisory committee which would include representatives of the TUC. MacDonald replied that he could not take an immediate decision as he was exploring ways and means to increase expenditure on social services generally. Nor did he agree to a suggestion from Creech Jones that the TUC should have the opportunity to examine the drafts of colonial ordinances submitted to him for endorsement. But he acknowledged the TUC's interest by arranging for the Colonial Advisory Committee to have a full discussion with Orde,Browne and promised any assistance that his Office could give towards the development of trade unions. This development he hoped would be steady, but he thought it would be slow, commenting that his officials realized that their difficulties would be increased if the wrong sort of unions – that were wild and governed by bad judgement – were formed.[98] In fact, his officials, with J. G. Hibbert in charge of a labour section in the general department, did respond helpfully to requests for information and made extensive use of the TUC's model rules.[99]

The officials in the ILO's Native Labour Section also provided information,[100] and the deputation to MacDonald pressed for action to abolish penal sanctions for the enforcement of labour contracts. At the Blackpool Congress in September Hicks gave examples of low wages in the Gold Coast and of convictions for breach of contract – 1778 in Kenya alone in 1935 – and Shaw pointed out that the move against penal sanctions at Geneva had met with strenuous opposition from the employers and from many governments.

They were speaking in support of a General Council resolution deploring the continued existence of labour conditions which were incompatible with contemporary social and industrial standards, and calling for reforms including the application of relevant ILO conventions to all colonies, the introduction of collective bargaining, and a wide extension of the franchise. The General Council was pleased with the start made by its new committee, and the resolution instructed it to maintain the closest possible connection with colonial trade unions and to assist them.[101] Unlike the work of the Far Eastern Committee and on India, this was a case in which the General Council itself set out, without any pressure from below, to open up a new and extending field of activity.

Once they had done so, the Labour Party's Imperial Advisory Committee fell into second place as a source of colonial labour policy. This was recognized in 1939 when that committee abandoned an intention to recommend changes in the Colonial Office on the grounds that the subject was now being sufficiently covered by the Parliamentary Labour Party and the TUC.[102] The outside advisers on the TUC's own committee also gradually lost their importance. As the TUC build up its contacts with the colonial unions, it dealt direct with them, and its knowledge of developments on the ground soon surpassed the more general expertise of the advisers. Their contribution was, however, always acknowledged with gratitude and respect. The exceptions were McGregor Ross, who went again to the ILO in 1939 and was appointed a member of the Conference committee dealing with the convention on contracts,[103] and Creech Jones, who ultimately became Secretary of State.

The International African Service Bureau also ceased to influence the TUC. It was known that the Bureau had advised unions in Trinidad to write direct to them since correspondence sent to the TUC would be sent on to the Bureau for reply,[104] and in August 1938 a request from Makonnen to be allowed to represent colonial unions at Congress was refused.[105] At the same time the TUC rejected a suggestion that it should co-operate with the Negro Welfare Association in holding public meetings to raise a fund to support the West Indian unions.[106] Like the WWLI, the British-based organizations had overplayed their hand.

The TUC's contacts did not build up gradually, but came with a rush. From the point of view of the TUC and the colonial unions, MacDonald's most important decision was to appoint Citrine as a member of the West India Royal Commission. Its terms of reference, to investigate 'social and economic conditions ... and matters connected therewith',[107] were wide enough to cover anything that he might want to say or do. A new era opened up for the trade union movement when Citrine landed in Jamaica on 1 November 1938.

The Colonial Office and Trade Unionism

The Royal Commission visited all the West Indian colonies and arrived home on 7 April 1939. It took further evidence in London till June and completed its report in February 1940. Parallel with the Commission, from September 1938 to April 1939, Orde Browne was sent to carry out an official investigation. His report was published in July 1939. Thus for over a year following the TUC's deputation to MacDonald in June 1938, no new official material was published, though the public proceedings of the Royal Commission were reported in the British press.

The Social Services Department

Meanwhile the Colonial Office was moving. On 1 April 1939 a Social Services Department was formally established with G. M. Clauson, previously assistant secretary in the Economic Department, as secretary. MacDonald clearly envisaged co-operation with the TUC – he had sent prior information that it was to be set up, and in May Clauson explained its functions to Kemmis. This was not, as the TUC's Colonial Advisory Committee had feared, a mere internal re-organization. Though it would also deal with health, social problems and nutrition, it would cover all aspects of labour and approximately met the TUC's proposal for a specialist labour department. The request for an advisory committee was not conceded. Clauson explained that he personally hoped that a committee including TUC and employers' representatives would be established, but the selection of members might present difficulties and although the Secretary of State was in favour, some of the permanent staff would regard it as an unwelcome departure from tradition. However, the Colonial Office had realized that the colonial service could not staff the labour departments in the territories without help. Clauson told Kemmis that initial training in the Ministry of Labour was being considered, followed by attachment to one of the existing labour departments under an experienced officer such as Lindon in Trinidad. The first training course was held in London in October 1939.[108]

Clauson also sent a list of new labour departments set up in the previous year. It included British Guiana, the Gold Coast, Nyasaland and Tanganyika. A new department was being formed in Jamaica, where F. A. Norman, a Ministry of Labour assistant secretary with conciliation experience was appointed in May. Northern Rhodesia, following Orde Browne's mission, was preparing to set up a department. The TUC's Colonial Advisory Committee noted the absence of Fiji and Uganda from the list, and later deplored the fact that no spokesman from the TUC had been invited to take part in the labour officers' course in October.[109]

The appointment of Lindon and Norman was evidence that the Colonial Office was prepared to take an interest in the settlement of trade disputes. As the Forster Commission had pointed out, the Trinidad Government, having failed to use its own Industrial Court Ordinance, had no machinery through which grievances could be articulated. A Trade Disputes (Arbitration and Inquiry) Ordinance was enacted in 1938 and the newly founded Oilfields Workers' Trade Union (OWTU) used it in January 1939 to secure the first arbitration award in the West Indies. But arbitration was the end of the road after negotiation and conciliation had failed, and it presupposed the existence of a trade union able to present a case, or to secure competent outside advisers as the OWTU had done. Recognizing the difficulties of organization, the Forster Commission had expressed the view that workpeople would welcome assistance in getting unions established on proper lines and that when they were established, unions would appreciate the opportunity of having discussions with the Labour Department when contemplating negotiations with the employers.[110] In his report Orde Browne showed that this was borne out in practice.[111] He was able also to refer to the first comprehensive agreement on wages and working conditions negotiated in the West Indies, by the Trinidad Seamen and Waterfront Workers' Trade Union (SWWTU) and the Shipping Association in December 1938.

But was the Colonial Office ready to pursue such a promising line of advance? Clauson was not encouraging in his interview with Kemmis. While the Forster Commission had thought in terms of helping to redress grievances, Clauson said that the Office realized that the existence of recognized bargaining unions would be a safeguard against irresponsible and unfruitful labour agitation, but not in Africa. There, bearing in mind the disastrous effect of detribalization in South Africa, one of the chief aims of policy was the preservation of the tribal system. Even in West Africa, he thought, the up-country worker was likely to be better protected through the tribal structure, using the authority of the native headman for the solution of labour problems, than by a trade union movement led by the ambitious urban creole, who was generally a lazy and undeserving individual.

The West Indies, then, had to set the pace for trade unionism. There Orde Browne was changing his tone,[112] and in the Office a new voice began to be heard when T. I. K. Lloyd,[113] who had been secretary to the Royal Commission, returned in 1939. When Citrine's plans had been endorsed by the September Congress, Lloyd suggested that the attention of West Indian governors should be drawn to the Congress report. This was done, but not before Shuckburgh had altered the covering letter. He had thought that the first draft 'might overdo the note of cordiality. I am old-fashioned enough still to feel that the spread of trade unionism in the Colonies is an unavoidable embarrassment rather than a positive blessing. However, I know that our official policy is one of sympathy and cooperation and if it is thought fit to assume that Colonial Governors share our feelings, so be it'.[114]

Shuckburgh did not retire till 1942. It was scarcely surprising that when Citrine returned from the West Indies the TUC's remaining aim was still to be attained. Commenting on the General Council's report to Congress, Lloyd noted that a labour advisory committee remained a prime objective which Citrine might ensure was included in the forthcoming recommendations from the Royal Commission.[115]

The Royal Commission's Recommendations

Like Purcell and Hallsworth in India, Citrine was profoundly shocked by his first sight of a British dependency. His diary records mounting distress as he went round the islands and British Guiana. He noted in Jamaica, in the midst of a rural slum, that the only passable dwellings belonged to people who had returned from working in Panama or elsewhere with a knowledge of different surroundings, and in Trinidad that the American Trinidad Lake Company was more progressive than the British employers. Yet he went to meetings that ended with 'God Save the King', and commented on the modesty of the workers' demands. He observed the striving towards respectability, and was moved by the action of a woman in Antigua who hurriedly pulled a clean white dress over one of her children as he approached her miserable shack. In Barbados he found cane-cutters who worked all

day without a meal and had only a poor one on their return home. 'I
will bet that I shall do something for them before I finish with this
Commission,' he wrote. In the Guiana sugar estates he prophesied
violence, and on the day before it actually came on the Leonora
plantation, he commented bitterly, 'I believe that there are eight strikes
proceeding here at the moment, and for my part there can be eight
more'.[116] By the end, he was sickened by the subservience of the
local governments to employer and planter interests.[117]

Citrine was too experienced to prejudice future co-operation with the
new department in the Colonial Office or with the Labour Adviser,
whose path in the West Indies had several times coincided with his.
When he left Trinidad for home Citrine felt satisfied that Orde Browne
would support practically all the recommendations he intended to
make.[118] In drafting the labour section of the Commission's report, he
drew in his own senior staff, including George Woodcock,[119] who had
succeeded Milne-Bailey as head of the research department, and Kemmis
was required to ensure that no constructive suggestion from Orde
Browne's report was omitted. In the end, the failure of the West Indian
governments was so systematically exposed in all sections of the report
that the Cabinet, fearing the possible effect in neutral countries, especially
the USA, decided to withhold publication till the end of the war.
The recommendations were published immediately and, at Citrine's
insistence,[120] in full. The report itself was published in July 1945 together
with a statement of the action taken on the recommendations.[121]

By the time the recommendations were published, the West Indian
governments had been hastening to remedy the administrative and
legislative defects exposed by Orde Browne's investigation and by the
Commission's proceedings. This exposure was Citrine's first achievement. It began in Jamaica, where he quickly realized that labour legislation
was almost nonexistent. The public realized it too as local and British
press reports of the questioning of witnesses revealed that no action had
been taken on a despatch from Cunliffe-Lister in 1932 advocating simple
legislation on minimum wages, that there was no law requiring guards to
be fitted on machines in factories, and that the newly enacted ordinance
on workmen's compensation excluded domestic servants, clerks, shop
assistants, transport drivers, and agricultural workers apart from those
operating power-driven plants. Jamaica had had trade union legislation
since 1919: Citrine forced an admission from the Colonial Secretary that
protection from actions for damages in strikes had been deliberately
omitted from the 1919 Ordinance at the insistence of the Jamaican
government. As the Commission proceeded and he became increasingly
suspicious of both officials and employers, he deliberately prepared his
questions with the intention of extracting public commitments from
officials to alterations in the laws and from employers that they were in

principle willing to recognize trade unions.[122]

He also examined legislation that was in preparation. In Jamaica he had long discussions with the Attorney-General and the new Governor, Sir Arthur Richards, on the changes required in the 1919 Ordinance, which had been based on the Imperial Act of 1871. Their draft already included provisions for immunity and picketing which brought it into line with the British Act of 1906, but it also included the restrictions of the 1927 Trade Disputes Act. Citrine advised the omission of the 1927 provisions on political funds (contracting in) and on civil servants (prohibition against joining unions having members outside the government service or having political objects or connections), but thought he could not oppose the local government's right to make general strikes and political strikes illegal, as in Britain.[123] He was acutely aware of the position of the British unions in this respect, since at the 1938 Congress he had spelt it out to the General Council for the benefit of those who wanted to coerce the British Government into supplying arms to the Spanish Republicans. He had put to them the argument that parliamentary institutions were being derided by the Fascists with the taunt that democracy was played out, and it was not for the trade union movement to strike a blow at its institutions by trying to change by force the views of a democratically elected Parliament.[124] This argument took on a different colour when applied to an unrepresentative colonial legislature, but when he gave his advice in Jamaica Citrine already knew that the Governor was in favour of universal suffrage (which was established in 1944). Before he left Jamaica on 6 December 1938, he was satisfied that the amending legislation would be more favourable than the 1927 Act.[125] Two days later, the Bill was introduced. The Commission regarded its principles as generally satisfactory and recommended that the Jamaican legislation, now enacted, should be adopted elsewhere.

Barbados, with no experience of trade union legislation, had a Bill under discussion. Pointing out its defects to the governor, Citrine received the remarkable reply that the omission of immunities and of provisions for picketing had not been intentional.[126] The law subsequently enacted in December 1939 did prohibit prosecutions against unions for tortious acts and for damages in trade disputes, but did not include provisions for peaceful picketing, which had been deleted by the Legislative Council. This was a wholly nominated body, but the Governor had no reserve powers of his own. Faced with defeat on picketing, he chose to lose the clause rather than nominate a new Council. In the Legislative Assembly, wholly elected but on property and income qualifications which excluded the mass of the population from the franchise, Grantley Adams, leader of the Progressive League, protested,[127] but had the choice of losing the clause or the whole Bill. Barbados remained without protection for peaceful picketing until 1950.[128]

This issue of picketing had particularly impressed Citrine, especially in British Guiana, where workers' houses were often set back from the public roads on private plantations, often preventing access for trade union organization of any kind, as Purcell and Hallsworth had observed in Assam. The Commission recommended that in strikes pickets in reasonable numbers should be allowed access to workers at their homes and at factory gates. The Model Ordinance circulated to the colonies in July 1941 by the Secretary of State, Lord Moyne, who had been chairman of the Commission, followed this recommendation.

Like Pugh, Citrine did not object to compulsory registration, which he regarded as a protection for union members. There is evidence in correspondence with Kenya that the TUC did not consider compulsion to be an issue of principle, provided the practice was not arbitrary. While Citrine was in Jamaica, Kemmis replied to Makhan Singh, secretary of the Labour Trade Union of East Africa, using a note prepared by Woodcock. Singh had complained that the Kenya Trade Unions Ordinance 1937 allowed a union's registration to be cancelled at one month's notice and that all powers lay with the Registrar and the Governor-in-Council. Kemmis sent summaries of legislation with the comment that the bulk of union members in Britain were in voluntarily registered unions, and added 'The Registrar has no absolute power over the trade unions; his task is merely to accept or reject registration, and he deals with complaints from members regarding administration, especially in regard to the Political Fund'.[129] The 1941 Model Ordinance was silent on political funds but did include compulsory registration. Most colonial trade union leaders did not object to it and did not press for abolition when their own ministers came to power after the war. Even at an early stage, when they had had some experience of the legislation, they were in general not opposed to compulsory registration. By 1943 the Labour Party found it 'desirable' – on the grounds that the workers were inexperienced – provided that it was not used to interfere with unions' independence, that there was a legal obligation on Government to publish reasons for refusing or withdrawing registration, and that registration was refused to unions which directly or indirectly maintained a colour bar.[130]

Otherwise the Model Ordinance followed the British model, as the unions had constantly demanded in their evidence to the Royal Commission. At long last the Colonial Office had faced up to the defects in the Passfield Despatch. The early legislation in Jamaica, Trinidad and British Guiana[131] which had been found unsatisfactory actually met the proposals suggested in that despatch, and there had been ample time since 1930 for the Colonial Office to tell the colonies that these did not go far enough and to explain exactly what was needed. But now the whole climate in which trade union legislation was discussed had been transformed. In the labour sections of the Commission's report Citrine took his stand on 'the inherent right of free men to refuse wages and conditions of employment which they deem to be inadequate' and to exercize individually or in concert their right to refuse, without which the condition of the working man was 'tantamount to servitude'. Workers in the West Indies, Nigeria, Kenya and elsewhere had claimed this right. It was incompatible with the Colonial Office conception of unions as an unavoidable embarrassment or as organizations which might serve the beneficial purposes of Government on Government's terms.

But whatever the law, the principal obstacle to trade union achievement was unemployment, undercutting all standards to the extent that bargaining was almost impossible and wages and conditions were in effect determined by employers alone. The Commission caught glimpses of desperate cases, as in Barbados, where Morgan Jones[132] discovered that a porter licensed at the docks would be paid by the job and that his working days might add up to about three weeks a year. A lighterman might work five days in the crop season, but from August to April might not make a trip. One man[133] replied to his questions:

> *R. Clarke*: ... I have not made one from October until January ... I
> made one in January ... My boat is 5s. 3½d. a trip.
> *Morgan Jones*: How do you live?
> *R. Clarke*: I got my mother, Sir, and sisters who help me ...

The report acknowledged that the main social and economic defects of the West Indies had been investigated many times, and persisted because neither the colonial governments nor the Colonial Office commanded the resources to effect improvements. The Commission therefore recommended that the imperial exchequer should finance a sustained programme of development over at least 20 years, through a fund administered regionally by a Comptroller with his own expert staff. For the main industry – sugar – changes in the imperial sugar preferences were proposed to secure an increased price. To ensure that all the benefit did not go to the employers, Citrine suggested[134] a levy on each ton produced, to finance welfare schemes administered, on the model of the British Miners' Welfare Fund, through committees representing employers' organizations and trade unions working under the labour departments. This proposal was not adopted during the war,[135] but afterwards it was implemented with considerable effect in some of the territories, notably British Guiana.

In view of the Labour Party's sensitivity to any increase in British food prices, it is noteworthy that Woodcock, commenting on the welfare levy, argued that British consumers ought to pay more for sugar.[136] Nor was there any dissent from the Commission's proposal for a cement factory in Jamaica, which was accompanied by the bald statement, '... we do not think that the interests of the maintenance of the British export trade, or employment in Great Britain, should be allowed to stand in the way.'[137]

Coupled with this broader view of economic interest, and the improvement in West Indian conditions that was anticipated, the unions might be expected to grow. Until they did so, the Commission suggested a more positive role for the local governments in industrial relations, including an element of pressure on the employers. It was recommended that until trade unions were strong enough to negotiate there should be statutory wages boards, and that receipt of the assistance proposed for the sugar producers should be conditional on the full execution of these boards' decisions. Differences arising outside their scope should be handled by the labour departments or by arbitration, and the local governments should lead the move towards collective bargaining by forming Whitley Councils for civil servants and teachers.

This meant more responsibility for the labour departments. The Commission recommended that while the rest of their staffs should be locally recruited, the Labour Commissioners themselves should come from Great Britain. Here, with an echo of his first conversation with Orde Browne in 1937, Citrine suggested that some might be recruited from trade unions and employers' organizations and from those actually engaged in commerce and industry generally. The Commission endorsed Orde Browne's view that the labour departments should be assisted by advisory committees composed of workers' and employers' representatives and, as expected, Citrine argued that they should be backed by a competent and alert labour department in the Colonial Office, with an Advisory Committee for the Secretary of State.

The Colonial Development and Welfare Act 1940

When the Commission learnt in February 1940 that its report was not to be published, it was assured that its recommendations for a welfare and development fund had been adopted.[138] In July Sir Frank Stockdale was appointed Comptroller with responsibility to work out long-term programmes, to consider schemes suggested by local governments, and to advise the Secretary of State on applications for financial assistance. His brief covered land settlement and social services generally as well as the development of labour departments. From 1941–4 F. A. Norman acted as his adviser in labour matters, followed by Lindon.[139]

The conditions the Commission had investigated were not confined to the West Indies, and the remedies they proposed, although traditionally unwelcome to the Treasury, were not entirely new or devised by only one party. The proposals for the Colonial Development Act 1929 had been prepared by the outgoing

Conservatives and were taken over by the second Labour Government, and during MacDonald's first short term at the Colonial Office in 1935 he had realized that a new long-term development policy was required. As Secretary of State for the Dominions he was particularly shocked by the condition of the High Commission Territories in South Africa, which prompted him to begin preparation of such a policy when he returned to the Colonial Office in 1938. The West Indian disturbances, coinciding with unfavourable comparisons with other empires called up by Germany's demands for the return of its former colonies, gave him a weapon to use against the Treasury which was sharpened after the outbreak of war by Britain's need for American support. When the Cabinet sanctioned his appointment of the Royal Commission, it was in the expectation that its recommendations were bound to involve increased expenditure. MacDonald used the following months to work out the principles of a general policy which were established, but not finalized, until the recommendations were known. With the Commission's report in hand, MacDonald passed round the Cabinet table samples of the more horrifying passages, and pointed out that the criticisms made against British administration in the West Indies were applicable elsewhere.[140] The result was his *Statement of Policy on Colonial Development and Welfare*,[141] published on the same day as the Commission's recommendations. It was followed by the Colonial Development and Welfare Act 1940, which received the Royal Assent on 17 July, by which time MacDonald had become Minister of Health and Lord Lloyd was Secretary of State for the Colonies.

The primary purpose of the 1929 Act was to support economic projects which would utilize British manufacturing capacity and extend the market for British goods. They were useful to the colonies, but the Act's chief importance lay in the precedents established: that grants other than the regular grants-in-aid which propped up the poorest territories might be made, that an advisory committee with outside representation should assist in the allocation of the fund, and that colonial governments receiving allocations should report on conditions of labour on the assisted works, on which child labour was prohibited.[142]

The 1940 Act provided £5 million (as against £1 million) annually for ten years, to be expended on welfare and research as well as on economic projects, with the choice determined by colonial needs rather than by the possible effect on employment in Britain. With the fall of France and the arrival of German armies across the Channel expenditure of this order could not be sustained during the war, but it did start in the West Indies. In 1945 the fund was increased and the period extended to 1956.

This Act provided much more protection for the labour employed on the assisted works: no child under 14 might be employed, the conditions of labour must be fair, and before making any allocation for works the Secretary of State must satisfy himself that the general law of the colony provided 'reasonable facilities' for the establishment and activities of trade unions.[143] The 'trade union' clause was one of the first signs of a further shift in Colonial Office policy after Churchill became Prime Minister on 13 May 1940, Labour ministers joined the War Cabinet, and the former miner, George Hall, became parliamentary under-secretary of state.[144] The clause stemmed from an amendment moved by Creech Jones and David Adams at the committee stage of the Bill which Hall altered, on his own initiative, to the positive and general statement that was finally included in the Act.[145]

Subsequent controversy hung on the meaning of the words 'reasonable facilities'. They were loosely interpreted by Lord Lloyd, originally in a speech on the Bill, and after its enactment, in a reply he sent in August 1940 to a specific inquiry from the High Commission territories, stating that provided that the Secretary of State was satisfied that there was nothing in the law to prevent trade unions from forming and functioning, schemes might be started.[146] An internal office dispute began in January 1941 concerning irrigation works in Cyprus, when the head of the geographical department suggested that the simple legislation advocated by Lord Passfield would meet the requirement. But Hibbert[147] was now experienced in handling trade union legislation, and he was on strong ground after February when Lord Moyne, who had been through the whole argument in the West Indies, replaced Lloyd. Hibbert contended that the proviso had been included in the Act specifically to enable the Colonial Office to bring pressure to bear on local governments that were proving backward – as in Cyprus – in enacting satisfactory legislation, and the legal adviser, Sir Henry Grattan Bushe, doubted whether the House of Commons would agree that the nineteenth-century law of Great Britain provided 'reasonable facilities' for trade union activities, even in a colony.[148] The dispute was resolved by Moyne's circular despatch of July 1941 which enclosed the Model Ordinance.[149]

Moyne told the colonies that while the crucial words could to some extent be construed in relation to the social and economic conditions in a particular territory, there must be an irreducible minimum obtaining in all territories applying for grants. This minimum required, in addition to the provisions recommended in the Passfield Despatch, provisions for the rights of union members to combine and bring pressure on the employers, including the right to strike, immunity from civil actions for damages in trade disputes, and the protection of trade union funds from civil proceedings in tort. Only Jamaica, Nigeria, the Gold Coast and Sierra Leone met these requirements. All other colonies, including those in which some schemes had already been sanctioned, must review their legislation. In addition, it was desirable that provisions legalizing peaceful picketing should be enacted.

As a result, the High Commission Territories, which needed the grants, had trade union legislation for years before there were any trade unions. Only the Bahamas, which like Barbados had an old 'representative' constitution but lacked a Progressive League, declined to apply for grants under the Act. After the inevitable strike and riots which occurred in June 1942, it was revealed that the most up-to-date labour legislation that the colony possessed was the Combination of Workmen Act 1859.[150] The legislature passed a restrictive Trade Union Act in 1943 and clung to it for over a decade. The combined efforts of the Bahamas Federation of Labour, the TUC and the Colonial Office were required before a substantial improvement was secured in 1958.[151]

The Bahamas had been outside the scope of the West India Royal Commission. In general, though the Commission's report had in economic matters served mainly to support MacDonald's efforts, in this matter of trade union legislation it had proved decisive.

Trade Unionists in Labour Departments

While this reorientation of official policy was taking place, the outbreak of war had brought about a major change in the relations between the Government and the TUC in Britain. The mobilization of the population required more than the old ad hoc consultations, and in October 1939 a National Joint Council was set up under the Minister of Labour and National Service as the formal standing machinery for consultation with the TUC and the British Employers' Confederation. Its discussions covered major subjects such as the avoidance of disputes, but also day-to-day problems such as rationing for workers whose jobs required exceptional physical effort, air-raid precautions in factories, and a host of detailed questions which required almost continuous contact between officials. This did not directly concern the Colonial Office, but all round it in Whitehall the climate had already changed when George Hall decided that there was room for co-operation with the TUC, and invited representatives to meet him.

At this meeting on 4 July 1940[152] Hall wished to make progress on two suggestions from Orde Browne arising from his tour of the West Indies and a subsequent visit to West Africa. To help remedy inexperience amongst West Indian trade union officials, Orde Browne had proposed the provision of training in Britain, especially in the technicalities of negotiation, comparable to facilities already available for professional studies. The General Council had already decided to provide two scholarships, and candidates had been selected when Ruskin College closed down for the duration of the war. Hall saw a possible substitute in informal 'summer schools' in the West Indies. Orde Browne had also encountered organizational problems in trade unions, such as the form of organization required and the appropriate fields of recruitment for different classes of workers, and the restriction of membership and office-holding to persons actually engaged in the work concerned. He thought advice was needed, but would be more acceptable to local trade unionists if it came from the TUC rather than from himself or any other government official.[153] Hall suggested that the TUC might co-operate with the Office in producing a handbook of guidance, but he clearly intended that the source of guidance would be Government.

Hall stated that he intended to introduce some officers with a strong trade union background into labour departments and hoped the TUC might recommend some young trade unionists for this work. There was an initial misunderstanding, subsequently settled between Citrine and Hall, over who should choose them. Evidently, the TUC had expected to do so, but the telegram informing governors of the proposal laid particular emphasis on the importance attached by Hall and his officials to their appointment by the Colonial Office. It said plainly that in many colonies the trade unions were ill-organized and under irresponsible and misguided leadership, and the appointment of carefully selected, experienced and level-headed trade unionists from Britain might well assist and encourage the development of collective bargaining in preference to strikes. The appointments were seen as a very tentative experiment to be tried out in one or two colonies.[154]

There was an echo of Montagu in this, with the possible implication that the TUC could be used, but the decision was clearly right. The TUC was constantly advocating a positive role for the labour departments, whose officials could not work under a divided responsibility, and whatever measure of agreement might be reached between the Colonial Office and the TUC, they were different organizations with different functions and aims. Nor could the TUC ever have commanded the resources to establish officers under its own direction on the scale that was eventually achieved. The initial replies from governors reflected a generally favourable response, and when the candidates presented themselves at the Colonial Office the officials were surprised at their quality, which to Hibbert was 'a revelation'. By 1945 colonial governments were asking for more.[155]

By November 1941 the first appointments had been made: J. Stirling (Iron and Steel Trades) and I. G. Jones (South Wales Miners' Federation) as labour officers in Trinidad and the Gold Coast. They continued with: H. E. Chudleigh (AEU) as Inspector of Labour, Palestine; W. M. Bissell (Electrical Trades Union) as Deputy Commissioner of Labour, British Guiana; Edgar Parry (General and Municipal Workers) as Labour Officer, Sierra Leone; and P. H. Cook (NUR) as Labour and Welfare Officer, Nigerian Railways. They were soon reported to be doing admirable and useful work.[156] Though their position within the colonial administration sometimes raised difficulties for them, these pioneers proved that if competent men were prepared to go out from the British movement, they could give substantial help to the colonial unions.

Yet the TUC itself, having asked for a representative advisory committee in 1938, was held at arm's length for nearly four years.

The Colonial Labour Advisory Committee

Lord Moyne and Hall were transferred to other posts in February 1942. All the major decisions in labour policy had been taken by the time they left the Colonial Office, and the later war years were occupied in implementing them.

Following the recommendations on the West Indies, Moyne began a general move at the end of 1941 to bring unofficial advice to bear on policy. By 1943, labour advisory boards with representatives of workers and employers had been established in seven of the West Indian colonies, in the Bahamas and Bermuda, in seven African territories, and in Fiji and the Falkland Islands.[157] At the same time he decided to set up a Colonial Labour Advisory Committee at the Colonial Office and invited the TUC to submit nominations.[158] Hallsworth and Andrew Dalgleish were appointed. Dalgleish was national secretary of the Metal, Engineering and Chemical Group of the TGWU, and had served on a commission of inquiry into disturbances in Northern Rhodesia in 1940. He became a member of the TUC's Colonial Advisory Committee in November 1941. In the Colonial Office the old Colonial Labour Committee initiated by Drummond Shiels was disbanded and the new committee held its first meeting on 15 May 1942.

By that time the labour departments were in action, the character of colonial trade union legislation had been determined, and the key policy decisions had been taken. Moreover, the important directives were confidential, including Moyne's despatch defining 'reasonable facilities' for the purpose of the Colonial Development and Welfare Act, and the Model Ordinance did not appear in the TUC's files (as a Colonial Labour Advisory Committee document) until 1950. It was not even mentioned in the official summary *Labour Supervision in the Colonial Empire 1937-1943* which was published in 1943. Writing in

that year, Creech Jones observed that the Colonial Office had
produced reports for the Estimates debates in 1938 and 1939 but not
thereafter, that the annual reports of the individual territories had
ceased, that the report of the West India Royal Commission had not
been published, and the report of the Commission of Inquiry into the
Northern Rhodesia strikes could scarcely be obtained in London: the
Colonial Office was 'almost a silent office'.[159]

This was not entirely due to war conditions. The formation of the
Colonial Labour Advisory Committee resulted in more information
becoming available to its members, but its documents and minutes
were also confidential, which meant that the TUC generally had no
opportunity to brief its members beforehand, and reports to its own
Colonial Advisory Committee had to be given confidentially, if at all.
In reply to protests from Dalgleish, Harold Macmillan, who had
succeeded George Hall, agreed that he might keep the TUC informed
about the activities of the Committee, and in response to Citrine,
minutes and memoranda were subsequently sent direct to the TUC,[160]
but the practice was not sustained and this question – vital to the TUC
if its policies were to be based on complete information – remained an
issue between the two offices until long after the war had ended. The
problem was inherent in the practice of government committees. Even
colonial governments were not allowed to see the minutes of Colonial
Office advisory committees.[161] Similarly, although the TUC's Colonial
Advisory Committee stressed the importance of the right to introduce
subjects for discussion,[162] the formal position was that the Committee
would consider matters referred to it by the minister, who would decide
whether or not to accept their advice or convey it to the colonial
government concerned.

It was evident that the Colonial Office did not accord a high status to
the Colonial Labour Advisory Committee; nor, in consequence, did
the TUC. TUC nominees were not regarded as representatives, and
before appointments were made there was the customary preliminary
skirmish about how many names should be submitted[163] – the minister
had to be seen to choose. So the committee never became a channel for
TUC representations, which continued to be made direct. A revealing
incident occurred in 1943 when Hallsworth warned Citrine that the
committee was about to consider the possibility that the Jamaica
Maritime Union would affiliate to the National Maritime Union of
America, with the intention of securing access to American ports for its
members. For the government, this raised the question of the Jamaican
union's status under the law, but it had a wider colonial significance
and Citrine was anxious that the Colonial Office should not respond by
promoting legislation which could prevent colonial unions affiliating
to their appropriate international trade secretariats or, in the case of

national centres, to the IFTU. The subject was hastily removed from the agenda of the Colonial Labour Advisory Committee and the TUC's advice – that the Jamaican union should affiliate either to a British union or to the ITF, was conveyed independently to the Secretary of State.[164]

What, then, did the Colonial Labour Advisory Committee do? It received official documents such as reports from labour departments, on the conferences for labour officers held in Trinidad and in West Africa in 1942, and generally on the progress of the administrative reforms in which the TUC was interested. Information on unions registering was also given and there were discussions on the educational facilities that might be provided for them. The background against which the unions were trying to organize was gradually being filled in.

Their problems also began to emerge: access to plantations in the context of law and order in Ceylon, multiplicity of unions in Cyprus and Ceylon, the difficulty of collecting union dues in West Africa and whether they might be deducted from wages by employers. Dalgleish thought that this particular solution was unacceptable, and it was suggested that it might also be contrary to the Truck Acts. Everywhere there was the problem of leadership, often political, often from outside the membership. Hallsworth had encountered it in India and was adamant that good 'outsiders' who helped unions should not be excluded by restrictive requirements for registration designed to meet a problem which, in his view, would right itself in time. In such discussions the officials, TUC spokesmen and employers habitually argued from the standpoint of British practice – indeed, there was no other guide. Once the African unions moved into the picture, however, the cultural background of the workers brought its relevance into question. One example came from Jones in the Gold Coast where, he said, the workers did not understand trade unionism. On the one hand they expected it to bring a new world tomorrow morning, and on the other they suspected that unions would be part of a system of government control, since the government had enacted trade union legislation and appointed a trade unionist to assist in their formation. Such fundamental problems frequently arose in the Committee,[165] and their consideration must have been helpful to all concerned – especially for Dalgleish, who later undertook other important missions for the Colonial Office and for the TUC.

From an organizational point of view, perhaps the chief importance of the Colonial Labour Advisory Committee was that its existence gave the final stamp of authority to the policies of using TUC advice and positively encouraging the growth of unions. Labour departments used the TUC's model rules as a guide[166] and the attitude of both the Colonial Office officials and the local governments towards unions changed. In the West Indies Norman, whose brief as Labour Adviser to the Comptroller for Development and Welfare extended his influence beyond Jamaica, told workers explicitly that it was the duty of every worker to join a union and regularly pay dues and take a share in meetings.[167] This was a far cry from the hostility and neglect which had provoked the disturbances which caused the TUC to act in 1937. Whatever changes might have taken place in the Colonial Office, however, the TUC could not give effective help on the ground unless it could develop a network of relationships with the colonial unions themselves.

7   The TUC and the Colonial Trade Unions

If the administrative reforms provided some of the institutional structures through which the first object of the TUC's Colonial Advisory Committee – the redress of immediate grievances – might be pursued, they rested on the hope that colonial workers and their unions would be willing to use the services and advice of the labour departments. Lindon's experience in Trinidad provided an early indication that they would.

The second object – to find the best means of extending trade unionism – depended on the expectation that the unions would wish the TUC to co-operate with them. The TUC never went out to press advice or assistance on people who had not asked for it. They were already asking. In the first few months of the committee's work the problems that arose were so varied that it must quickly have become apparent that the TUC's ignorance of conditions on the ground would have to be remedied on a scale that would have taxed the resources of even the largest trade union organization. MacDonald's invitation to Citrine to serve on the Royal Commission was providential. His work in the West Indies provided the TUC with its initial and decisive experience.

As he crossed the Atlantic studying the preliminary papers provided for the Commission, Citrine had the Congress resolution of 1938 to back him, but felt that he knew little of the West Indies. In some quarters the appointment of the Commission had met with a negative response. The International African Service Bureau demanded that 'a native West Indian of African descent', preferably a representative of the labour organizations, should be appointed. The inclusion of Citrine and Morgan Jones, they believed, was not enough to inspire confidence, and the reaction of the West Indians would be the same as the Indian response to the Simon Commission.[1] There was also a report that the Trinidad Labour Party and the BGLU had decided to boycott the Commission unless the terms of reference were extended to include constitutional changes.[2] If the unions had boycotted the Commission Citrine would have found it very difficult to help them.

On arrival in Jamaica, Citrine noted a friendly expectancy amongst the crowd, but no cheering or anything of the sort.[3] The departure was very different. Thousands of singing workers assembled during the night on Kingston racecourse and moved off in procession at 3 a.m. for the long walk to the airport to bid Citrine goodbye.[4] As he went round the small islands there was a succession of public meetings, and in Barbados over 10,000 people assembled to hear Citrine deliver what the secretary of the Progressive League described as 'the most memorable address of my time, if not of this generation'.[5] There the Commission's proceedings had to be relayed by loudspeaker to the crowds massed outside, and Grantley Adams warned that while the people had no confidence in their own government, 'they look upon the Commission as a Saviour, and they are pathetically hoping that the Commission will do something for them. We have had to tell them that you are only here to investigate and to find out the facts'.[6]

Prelude to the Royal Commission

The facts included the movement towards trade unionism that was taking place before the Royal Commission arrived, and the approaches that had already been made to the TUC.

British Guiana

The TUC's earliest link had been with British Guiana, where the BGLU was suffering a temporary decline in 1938. Orde Browne found the unions definitely established and extending organization, though on a small scale. There were five unions in addition to the BGLU: the British Guiana Workers' League registered in 1931, the Man-Power Citizens' Association (MPCA) registered in November 1937, and the Seamen's Union, Transport Workers' and Post Office Workers' Unions registered in 1938.[7]

The Seamen's Union, which showed a clear desire to establish itself on industrial lines, had originally been affiliated to the Workers' League. With rules obtained from Critchlow, it was founded with twelve members on 10 October 1937, and came to the notice of the TUC through an approach to the Labour Party. The TUC put the new union in touch with the British National Union of Seamen and the ITF, and by 1 June 1938 it had seventy-two members.[8] The MPCA was a complete contrast. It organized some of the most depressed workers in the colony – the field workers on the sugar estates. They had been involved in strikes and disturbances in 1935, but did not then establish a permanent organization, and they had difficulty in throwing up their own leaders. The MPCA was strongly influenced by the East Indian Association: its secretary, Harri Barron, was a former secretary of the Association, and its president, C. R. Jacob, a Member of Legislative Council, was also president of the Association. Jacob had links with

H. S. L. Polak and Creech Jones, and the union asked for affiliation to the TUC in July 1938. This was refused,[9] but the weight of the MPCA's organizing potential would alone have commanded the continuing interest of the TUC.

Trinidad

In Trinidad fissures had developed within the trade union movement. The TUC's inclination was always to deal with one national centre, but as early as 1928 there was an indication that the TWMA's authority was not absolute, when the TUC refused an application for affiliation from the Trinidad Labouring Classes and Cocoa Planters Association. The same group, whose status was uncertain, then tried to form a Trinidad and Tobago Trade Union Centre, and after a triangular correspondence between the TUC, Cipriani and the IFTU its application to join the IFTU also failed.[10] The TUC received requests for rules from building and woodworkers after the enactment of the Trade Unions Ordinance in 1932 and from the Public Works Workers' Union after the 1937 riots. Both were advised to consult the TWMA/Trinidad Labour Party to avoid overlapping,[11] and when Citrine advised registration of the Clerks' Union in 1938, he informed the TLP. Though the TLP rejected his advice, the union was formed and registered.[12] Pugh visited the Public Works Workers' Union and the Federated Workers' Union. These and the SWWTU were registered by the end of 1937.[13]

The threat to Cipriani's influence in Port of Spain was matched in the rural areas by the formation of the British Empire Workers' and Citizens' Home Rule Party by Uriah Butler, after his expulsion from the TLP following his intervention in a strike on the Apex oilfield in 1935. The Forster Commission recorded that at the time of the 1937 riots Butler's party had about 100 paying members and 900 others,[14] but Butler's capacity as a mob orator made the actual membership almost irrelevant. There was no doubt that his activities and speeches in 1937 were incendiary, and his previous correspondence with government officials was shot through with bizarre political claims, such as that he was an anti-Catholic Protestant like Lord Carson, and that George V was not legitimately crowned. However, some of his demands – for 'lawful, not bastard' trade union laws, for improvements in workmen's compensation, and for 'the dole' for the unemployed – were justified and had met with no effective response from the administration.[15] Butler escaped arrest at the meeting at which a policeman was murdered and did not give himself up until December 1937, when he was sentenced to two years' hard labour for sedition. He was therefore out of action in the months before the Royal Commission arrived, but Cipriani had lost some popular support by dissociating himself publicly from the outbreaks, without further inquiry, immediately on landing when he returned to Trinidad.

The disturbances had stemmed initially from a strike on the oilfields in which the local TLP leaders were involved. This group – John Rojas, McDonald Moses and E. R. Blades – had been warned by the Governor, Sir Murchison Fletcher, that the employers would never agree to negotiate with a political party, and accordingly approached the barrister Cola Rienzi (Krishna D. Narayan) to draw up a constitution for a union.[16] The OWTU was registered in September 1937, and the All-Trinidad Sugar Estates and Factories Workers' Trade Union (ATSEFWTU) in November. Rienzi was president of both and applied on their behalf for affiliation to the TUC.[17] This was refused, but the association persisted. These two unions had the largest organizing potential on the island, and if trade unionism was to mean anything in Trinidad they had to succeed. Like the other new unions, they gave evidence before the Forster Commission, and Pugh noted that Rienzi had made a definite statement against the use of violence.[18]

The OWTU had the more stable organizing base and its leaders, even without Rienzi's great ability, were capable of building on it and of representing their members. They did not hesitate to use the strike weapon when necessary, but warned against violence and interference with machinery,[19] and were prepared to take the risk of going to arbitration in November 1938. The tribunal, appointed under the new Trade Disputes (Arbitration and Inquiry) Ordinance 1938, included John Jagger[20] and a British barrister, Dudley Collard, as workers' nominees. They were not satisfied with the award, but it did give an element of back pay, an increase in the hourly rate, time-and-a-half for all overtime and public holidays, and a week's holiday with pay after a year's service. More important, perhaps, was that it proved the leaders. The employers brought the best lawyer they could find to represent their case, but Jagger recorded that the union spokesmen were well able to stand up to him: the part-time secretary, E. R. Blades, who worked as a motor mechanic at $4\frac{1}{2}$d an hour, was thoroughly master of his job; the vice-president, McDonald Moses, made a remarkable criticism of the reports of the Cost of Living and Minimum Wages Committees set up by the government and presented a detailed schedule of living costs drawn up by the union; the assistant general secretary, Ralph Mentor, had prepared a memorandum on back pay under heads 'as a parson prepares his sermon', and delivered it with the fervour of a local preacher. Jagger also commented on the inclusion of a succession of rank and file witnesses whose evidence revealed an inconceivable depth of misery and poverty.

Thoroughly roused by what they saw and heard at the inquiry, Jagger and Collard spent all their spare time in investigations, union meetings and visits – including one to Butler in gaol. They helped the Public Works Union to prepare its case for its first meeting with the Public Works Department as employer, and helped nurses, civil service clerks and shop assistants to prepare their evidence for the Royal Commission.[21]

Also preparing for the Commission was the British Guiana and West Indies Labour Congress (BGWILC) originally set up in 1926. They had held a conference in Georgetown in June 1938 and in September Rienzi as secretary cabled the TUC Congress expressing the hope that the TUC would give help in organizing and building unions.[22] A further conference to prepare a memorandum for the Commission was held in Port of Spain in November. The need for unity was now being recognized, for Cipriani was in the chair. Though the Congress effectively represented only British Guiana and Trinidad, this meeting was marked by the first attendance of Barbados.

Barbados

The Barbadian representative was Grantley Adams.[23] He had earlier been in England to press the case for social and political reform and had met Labour Party spokesmen, including Creech Jones, but there is no record of any contact with the TUC until December 1938, when the Royal Commission was already in the Leeward Islands. A letter from W. H. Seale, Secretary of the Barbados Progressive League, asked for publications and stated the League's principal objects: to secure political expression for the law-abiding inhabitants of Barbados and 'to provide sane leadership for the workers in the various branches of industry and commerce, so as to enable them to conduct themselves in their respective organizations in such a manner as to avoid all possibility of future action which may be subversive to law and order'. Seale wrote that the leaders had been holding meetings to expound the doctrines of socialism and trade unionism, had already organized dockers, and were now concentrating on artisans, clerks and porters. As soon as finance and circumstances permitted, the Executive Committee intended to affiliate to the TUC.[24]

The League's objects, and the form of organization it adopted, bear an uncanny resemblance to those of the first organization in Barbados to appear in the records preserved by the TUC – the Barbados Labour League which prepared rules in 1909. Its objects included labour representation in the legislature, the provision of welfare benefits, the regulation of conditions of labour and the avoidance of strikes by the adjustment of disputes between capital and labour. It was to consist of wage earners, excluding liquor sellers, businessmen and landed proprietors from holding office, and it was to be divided into branches subject to central direction. The League asked to be seen as 'a patriotic effort to marshal and control the discontented, sadly underpaid worker; to keep the sinking ones from utter despair; to restrain the turbulent from overbearing demands; to present to the workers a possible escape from the debasing influence of an enforced poverty, and to enable them to see the opportunity by which they can take their place in the community as MEN'.[25] Apparently, it came to nothing, but the attempt was consistent with the later efforts of men of the middle class to achieve democratic representation and to channel the expression of workers' discontent into constructive trade unionism. When Roberts visited Barbados in 1926 he met representatives of the Democratic League founded by Charles Duncan O'Neal, who had been much influenced by the Fabian Society. O'Neal was also in touch with Cipriani and founded a Workingmen's Association[26] which included some craftsmen and at least one notable working-class leader, the former waterfront worker, L. Sebro.[27]

But Roberts had found no recognized unions. The most common form of organization was in friendly societies, which had 54,000 members in 1937.[28] In 1938, when preparing for Orde Browne's visit, the Barbados government stated that there were no trade unions and no trade union leaders who could fairly be regarded as representative.[29] Yet the groups that appeared to give evidence before the Royal Commission showed that attempts to form unions were being made. Some followed the riots of 1937 after a campaign of public meetings by Clement Payne, who arrived in March from Trinidad where, he claimed, he had been associated with Butler. But a bakers' union had been formed with over 100 members before the riots,[30] a strike of foundrymen was in progress before the disturbances, and another amongst lightermen and stevedores followed Payne's deportation in July.[31]

There was evidently a slight movement towards permanent combination, but the riots were an expression of general discontent. The Deane Commission that inquired into them recorded a consensus of opinion that the majority of employed workers took no part, but also that the disturbances spread to the countryside where Payne had no influence. The Commission reached the appalling conclusion that the cause was 'hunger, or the fear of hunger', and its report painted a terrible picture of overpopulation, unemployment and brutal labour relations. It proposed an immediate increase in the wages of agricultural and other unskilled manual workers and the appointment of a labour officer as initial liaison between employers and workers.[32]

This report was presented just after Ormsby-Gore's despatch was circulated. Before the Royal Commission arrived in January 1939, a Recruitment of Workers Act to implement the ILO Convention of 1936, a Labour (Minimum Wage) Act and a Labour Officer Act had been carried against opposition in the legislature, but a Workmen's Compensation Bill was still before the House of Assembly and the Trade Union Bill was bogged down in Select Committee. By that time it was clear that the move towards trade unionism had started, and that the new Progressive League intended to give a political lead.

The Smaller Islands

As elsewhere, the early labour leaders in the islands of the Leeward and Windward groups were middle class men who concentrated on securing seats in the legislatures and pressing for social legislation. Since they were not hampered by an archaic constitution like Barbados, these colonies did follow some at least of the despatches sent out by successive Secretaries of State. They had trade union laws, enacted in the Leeward Islands in 1931 and in the Windwards in 1933, and by the end of 1938 both groups had labour officers, had enacted workmen's compensation legislation and had abolished penal sanctions. The Windward Islands also had a minimum wage law and provisions governing the employment of women, young persons and children.[33] Much of the legislation was inadequate and some only recently activated. The defects of the trade union laws were recognized, at least in St Vincent, where the leaders of a Workingmen's Association founded in 1934 were in touch with Cipriani, who also advised Albert Marryshow in Grenada.[34]

In the light of the law and the depressed condition of the workers, trade union organization presented an almost impossible task, and the TUC had little contact with those who were attempting it. In 1930 Marryshow attended the Third Commonwealth Labour Conference under the wing of the TWMA, and in 1934 James McIntyre, secretary of the Grenada Workers' Association, visited the TUC office, and rules and recruiting material were sent to Owen C. Mathurin in St Lucia,[35] but there was no follow-up on either side. There were disturbances in St Kitts and St Vincent in 1935, but no trade unionist was sent out to inquire into them and thus, as in Barbados, there was no parallel to the crucial influence of Sir Arthur Pugh in Trinidad.

Orde Browne found no registered trade unions anywhere, but expressed the opinion that the Antigua Workingmen's Association and the Employers' and Employees' Association in St Vincent (registered as friendly societies), and in Grenada the Grenada Workers' Union and the Workingmen's Co-operative Association (registered as a limited company), had the capacity to become registered trade unions.[36] When the Royal Commission arrived, various other organizations appeared to give evidence – teachers' associations in several islands, civil service clerks in Dominica, the Workers' League in St Kitts – and little groups like a 'Labour

Deputation' in Dominica and the 'Artisans of Georgetown' in St Vincent.[37] There may have been no registered unions, but workers had learnt the first lesson, to express their views collectively.

Jamaica

A thousand miles from Trinidad, Jamaica was remote from the main centre of activity, but it was not remote from trade unionism. There were numerous attempts to form unions before and after the First World War, and the 1919 Trade Union Ordinance, unsatisfactory though it was, had been enacted in response to local demand. There was also provision for conciliation in trade disputes.[38] But permanent organization was not established, and much of the protest activity at the end of the war was amongst the unemployed, as was initially the case in the major disturbances which began on 3 May 1938.

As elsewhere, organization did not start with the riots, though it proceeded apace afterwards. In 1936 A. G. S. Coombs, a former policeman, began to organize sugar and banana workers in the Jamaica Workers' and Tradesmen Union. In February 1937, before the upheavals began elsewhere, Branch no. 3 of the Workers' and Tradesmen Union, Linstead, were the first to write to the TUC. Carefully handwritten, but with many spelling mistakes, their letter left no doubt that it came from working men. It asked for a rule book so that rules could be drawn up and submitted to the Attorney General for registration, which was voluntary under the 1919 Act. Rules were sent and nothing more was heard until May 1938, when Lord Olivier passed to the TUC a similar request from C. S. Maxwell, writing from Kingston as secretary of the Jamaica Workers' and Tradesmen Union, and the new model rules were sent. In June the reply from Maxwell, a carpenter, now carried a new letter head of the 'Jamaica Tradesmen Union' with the name, as president, of P. A. Aiken, an electrician who had led a strike on the government railway in 1919. Maxwell made it plain that his members were not connected with the disturbances that had broken out in Jamaica in May, but that they were unwilling – since most of them had spent years abroad – 'to live lives that are not suited to pigs'. In July a Builders' and Allied Trades Union was registered with Maxwell as secretary.[39]

In the same field was the Jamaica Artisans' Federated Union, with a membership of carpenters, masons, painters, plumbers and electricians. The secretary, R. E. L. Tummings, approached a British Member of Parliament for information in 1937, and was in contact with the TUC in 1938. This union also applied for registration, and both unions submitted evidence to the Royal Commission. Also forming in 1937 was the Jamaica Authoritative Trade Union, which approached the TUC in October. It intended to organize workers of all grades and occupations, to help small cultivators and to train women in domestic economy. It became the Jamaica Industrial Trade and Domestic Workers' Union, but had not secured registration by the time the Royal Commission arrived, nor did it submit evidence.[40]

It is apparent even from this fragmentary correspondence that Jamaican workers were trying to establish stable organization within the provisions of the 1919 Act, but without co-ordination by the Jamaica Workers' and Tradesmen Union or any other body, and without demarcation of fields of interest. The riots of 1938 brought in the politicians, who tried to provide direction.

The first clash with the police occurred in a sugar strike in January. In May a strike at the Frome Estate of the West Indies Sugar Company (Tate and Lyle) developed into a battle with four deaths and 89 arrests. The immediate dispute was settled with the help of Alexander Bustamante,[41] a businessman and moneylender who had begun to build up a reputation in 1937 with speeches on the platform of the Workers' and Tradesmen Union. In mass meetings after the Frome strike he became the focus and interpreter of discontent amongst the unemployed and some employed workers, who went on strike in municipal services and on the docks. On 24 May, after two days of disturbances, a state of emergency was declared and Bustamante was arrested for alleged sedition and incitement to riot. In the British Cabinet MacDonald warned his colleagues that there was likely to be a demand for a Royal Commission, but that there was little point in sending one unless some remedy for the economic situation could be found.[42] In Jamaica, the governor appointed a Conciliation Board.

Continued uproar in Kingston and the spread of strikes outside followed Bustamante's arrest. This left a vacuum which his cousin, the barrister Norman Manley[43] attempted to fill by mediation in the dock dispute and by representations on behalf of Bustamante. He was released on 28 May and went immediately to the Conciliation Board, where a settlement was reached.

Bustamante demonstrated by his interventions in actual disputes that he was essentially a mediator. In June he announced plans to establish five unions, for waterfront workers, transport, factory and municipal workers, and a general union for agricultural workers. He set up a co-ordinating headquarters under his own direction which recorded £44 collected in dues as its first cash book entry on 24 June 1938.[44] This became the nucleus of the Bustamante Industrial Trade Union (BITU) into which some of the existing unions were absorbed, and of which Bustamante was Life President. Bustamante was not in correspondence with the TUC either then or later. He co-operated with Citrine during the Royal Commission's visit, but he did not make the visit to Britain for which Citrine hoped.[45] It was not the habit of the

BITU to look outside Jamaica,[46] and in 1945 when Manley went to a meeting of Caribbean labour leaders in Barbados, Bustamante did not attend.[47]

Manley was aware of the wider links of the labour movement and more concerned with political action. He set up a committee to help existing unions and to form new ones, with Ken Hill, who was on the literary staff of the *Daily Gleaner*, as secretary. Hill approached the TUC for advice and publications and was sent the model rules and other material. He described the National Reform Association of Jamaica, of which he was also secretary, as a middle-class organization of socialist views and wrote of moves to form a Labour Party.[48] The People's National Party (PNP) was launched in September at a meeting addressed by Sir Stafford Cripps. Bustamante was on the platform, but political unity was not sustained and in 1943 he launched a separate Labour Party.

At the beginning there appeared to be a co-ordinated effort to build the unions. Hill wrote with approval of Bustamante's initial success in organizing the five unions[49] and led two transport unions which he had himself organized into the BITU, of which he became vice-president. Coombs remained apart, but his colleague in the Workers' and Tradesmen Union, H. C. Buchanan, left to become secretary of the BITU, though this did not last.[50]

Orde Browne recorded that at the beginning of 1939 there were six registered unions: the Workers' and Tradesmen Union led by Coombs, the Builders' and Allied Trades Union led by Maxwell, the Jamaica United Clerks' Association founded in 1937 with the barrister E. E. A. Campbell as president and the accountant Florizel Glasspole[51] as secretary, the Hotel Employees' Association, and two unions of the Jamaica Federation of Labour organized in 1918 by Bain Alves but inoperative by 1938. The BITU was registered in January 1939, and on 31 March 1939 showed a paying membership of 6,500 with assets of £3,235.[52] When the new trade union legislation was enacted, the existing registered unions were automatically registered under it.

This was the movement which was the first in the West Indies to meet the Royal Commission.

Citrine in the West Indies

There is substance in the view that Citrine's behaviour in the West Indies was more important than his recommendations.[53] He met the union leaders for discussions, but also went about with them amongst the public on exploratory visits outside the programme of the Commission. In Kingston and Spanish Town, with Bustamante, he was quickly surrounded by large singing crowds. Elsewhere, the visits were less noisy but conveyed a similar hope. This association of Citrine and the union leaders in the popular mind was good for both sides, and Citrine liked his colleagues personally and sensed the magnitude of their task, while they quickly realized that the Commission was more than a mere face-saving device for the colonial governments.

With Morgan Jones, Citrine insisted that as far as possible evidence should be taken in public. There was no attempt at elevated impartiality in his questioning of witnesses. He went out of his way to enable Bustamante to deny any seditious intention, and he made the most of Manley as a witness because of his high reputation as a lawyer.[54] He led government and employer representatives to express a belief in responsible trade unionism and social improvement, and was quick to pin them down on specific points, as in the case of the oral evidence given by the Trinidad Sugar Manufacturers[55] on the extension of workmen's compensation to agricultural workers:

> *E. A. Robinson:* ... the cocoa industry could not insure ... there are some 8,000 small proprietors who only employ labour ... perhaps a month or so a year ... They are poor labouring men. It would mean ... that over a little cut ... which would be all right in a week or two, some tout of a lawyer would start an action, and it would end in the small cocoa proprietor losing his property ... The same applies to cane farmers ...
>
> *Citrine:* ... what happens now if a man employed by these small or large people happens to injure himself? Does he get any payment whatever?
>
> *E. A. Robinson:* By the big people ... on an estate, we would always do something to help him.
>
> *Citrine:* There is no reason, then, if you always help them, why that should not be converted into a right ... Do you agree that, as far as the large estates are concerned, it would be equitable to include agricultural labour?
>
> *E. A. Robinson:* If the machinery can be evolved.
>
> *G. B. Westwood:* You will find ... that the number of accidents will ... increase as soon as you get workmen's compensation.
>
> *Citrine:* You think people go chopping off their fingers in order to get compensation?
>
> *G. B. Westwood:* More or less – not so seriously as that.
>
> *Citrine:* I do not think I should make suggestions like that if I were you ... It may be that workers who now neglect advancing a claim ... might advance that claim?
>
> *G. B. Westwood:* Yes.

He was walking the edge of a volcano. In Barbados, when he pointed

out to the government Agricultural Officer that figures on agricultural
wages that had been requested in July 1938 had been handed to the
commissioners as they entered for the hearing six months later, the
chairman's remonstrance and police calls for order could not quell the
cheers inside and outside the hall, and Citrine himself momentarily
feared a disturbance. In British Guiana, the Sugar Producers'
Association formally protested to Lord Moyne at his line of
questioning.[56] When the union representatives gave evidence in
Georgetown, there was unbearable tension, with the mutter of sugar
strikers who had been unable to get into the hall forming a 'menacing
background to the strained atmosphere within', and when the Elected
Members of the Legislative Council gave evidence the Chairman of the
Sugar Producers' Association, Frederick Seaford, was booed as he
entered.[57] That same day, there was a shooting on the Leonora Estate.
Attempts were made to associate Citrine with the violence, and it was
suggested that when the Commission moved on to Trinidad evidence
should be taken in private, but he overcame that proposal.[58]

Some of the representations made by the unions and the politicians
associated with them centred on political demands for representative
and responsible government, sometimes combined with federation for
the West Indies. At the same time, they managed to convey the
atmosphere of decay and frustration that overhung these tiny colonies.
Asked by Citrine and Morgan Jones whether they agreed with the
Deane Commission's conclusion that the cause of the 1937
disturbances was economic, and whether the conditions at that time
still existed, Grantley Adams replied[59] that they were possibly worse and
that all the inflammatory material was still there:

> *Citrine:* You have said here that 'the local Government is in the hands
> of a few wealthy families who ... display in many ways the mentality
> suitable to life before Emancipation ...' That is a very strong
> indictment, are you sure it is not exaggerated language?
> *H. Grantley Adams:* We wish we could say it was. What we feel is that
> they are indifferent. That they have, so to speak, run to seed. There
> was a time when the wealthy classes of Barbados were as keen and
> enlightened as the wealthy classes in England. Whether it is the sugar
> depression ... or for whatever reason, our experience in this colony
> is the wealthy classes care less and less for the people.

Against this background the union representatives put forward
general proposals, but also had to relate them to particular conditions.

The Union Evidence

The resolutions adopted at the Port of Spain conference of the

BGWILC in November 1938 provided the basis for memoranda from the southern organizations. They called for workmen's compensation for agricultural and domestic workers, a minimum wage system with union representation from each trade and industry on wages advisory boards, a 44-hour week without reduction of pay, ordinances on the lines of the United States Labour Relations Act to penalize unfair labour practices, trade union and factory legislation on the United Kingdom model, and the appointment of labour officers everywhere. The conference recommended legislation for old age pensions, national health and unemployment insurance, and national or municipal ownership of public utilities. There was a comprehensive attack on the plantation system in proposals for the redistribution of land and a ceiling on individual or company holdings, government ownership of all sugar factories, a single government agency in each colony to buy and export sugar, co-operative marketing of other agricultural products such as cocoa and rice, and facilities for agricultural workers to acquire plots to supplement their wages. The conference recommended an increased preference for sugar to be granted by the Imperial Government on condition that ten per cent went to employers and 90 per cent to cane farmers and to field and factory workers in increased wages.

Many of these proposals emerged in the Commission's report and could be found in the reports of previous commissions of inquiry, in the policies of the British Labour movement or in ILO conventions, or indeed in the Colonial Office, but no one had brought them to fruition. They demonstrated that the labour leaders were forward-looking, fully conversant with current ideas, and able to translate them, in general terms, into demands appropriate to the circumstances of their territories.

In presenting evidence applicable to the circumstances of particular groups of workers, perhaps the most successful body was the Committee of Industrial Organizations (CIO) in Trinidad, to which the oil, sugar and transport unions, and the Trinidad Citizens' League, were affiliated. Their evidence was printed as a pamphlet signed by Rienzi, Ralph Mentor, Blades, Rojas and Moses as officers, and by five others.[60] Like the BGLU evidence, this memorandum followed the November resolutions, but it specified the Sainte Madeleine Sugar Company as the first to be nationalized, because it had the best organized factory, and asked for the nationalization of the oil industry or a tax on petroleum exports to produce revenue for social services. It argued that ten of the seventeen producing companies accounted for nearly 90 per cent of total production and quoted the profits of these ten, all in the Oilfields Employers' Association. Figures on food and clothing requirements were submitted, and a demand was made for a response from Government to repeated requests for district labour offices to collect statistics on unemployment.

The CIO also submitted an account of negotiations between the Sugar Manufacturers' Association and the ATSEFWTU which had begun in January 1938 and had not reached a conclusion by the time the Commission arrived a year later. This account was important, because in countering the union's wage claim with a plea of inability to pay at current sugar prices, the employers had also challenged the representative standing of the Union. In oral evidence they charged the union with having called a strike without notice during negotiations.[61] The union evidence stated that an unofficial stoppage had occurred owing to delay in negotiations, and that in view of the possibility of disturbances the executive had recognized it in order to retain control of the situation. It showed that the union had brought in the Industrial Adviser, and that the employers had appeared unwilling to go to arbitration.

This union statement cast considerable light on the difficulties facing unions that were trying, in an atmosphere of strikes and riots, to establish themselves and to secure registration from the government and recognition from employers. In Trinidad in 1937 the Petroleum Association objected to dealing with the OWTU in the period between its initial formation and its registration.[62] In British Guiana, while the Royal Commission was actually taking evidence, MPCA officials were refused access to the Leonora Estate, and both Jacob and the Labour Officer had given prior warning that there would be trouble on the very day that the riot and the shooting took place. In this case, Citrine learned privately that the employers were withholding recognition from the union because they regarded Jacob as a political agitator, and he told them in exasperation that three people were lying dead that night as a result of their attitude. A week later, in Trinidad, he heard of fifteen strikes and martial law in British Guiana, but also that the sugar producers had agreed to deal with the union.[63]

Citrine was favourably impressed by the labour leaders' performance before the Commission, noting particularly that of Coombs and Manley in Jamaica, Adams and the Progressive League in Barbados, the combined unions in British Guiana (especially A. A. Thorne of the Workers' League), the CIO in Trinidad, and the St Kitts Workers' League (especially their principal witness, the Legislative Council member, T. Manchester).[64] The continuance of this success in representation required success in organization.

Advice to Unions

Citrine went out equipped with rule books and union publications in readiness for discussions with existing and potential union leaders.

Known as he was in Britain for introducing administrative order into the TUC, he paid attention to the basic essentials. Examining the books of the OWTU, he discovered that the auditor appointed by the government under the Trade Unions Ordinance had charged the union £40 for a six months' audit, and accordingly recommended in the Commission's report that audit should be done free by Labour Department officials.[65] At Bustamante's headquarters he found the accounts system satisfactory, but he also went over the rules prepared for registration with the union solicitor, and expressed his disapproval on the grounds that they put too much power into the hands of permanent officials and gave Bustamante the position of life president without election. In Barbados he gave rules and advice to the Progressive League, and information on a book-keeping system was sent direct from the TUC.[66] In St Vincent he advised the Workingmen's Association to postpone an application for registration as a union until it was known whether the law would be changed, and unlike Orde Browne, he ruled out the Employers' and Employees' Association as an attempt by the employers to counteract genuine trade unionism. In St Lucia he advised on the formation of a trade union, and in Antigua met officials of the friendly societies, being rewarded while in Trinidad with the news that the Antigua Trade and Labour Union had been established and already had 800 members and £80 in the bank.[67]

Recording his preliminary views on organization as he left the Leewards,[68] Citrine ruled out Dominica and Montserrat as having too few employed workers to sustain unions, and concluded that elsewhere there could not be more than one union in an island, with appropriate provision within it for the representation of sectional interests. Even then, they would be numerically weak when facing employers and governments and, at the best, parochial in outlook. The constant requests for affiliation to the TUC showed that the unions themselves feared this. Citrine found that some of them had already printed 'Affiliated to the British TUC' on their headed paper, but in a subsequent document he commented that affiliation would require alteration to the TUC's Standing Orders and would not be worthwhile for the unions. They would have to pay some affiliation fees, even if these were specially reduced, and it would be impossible for them to send delegates to Congress.[69] Nor could the TUC have given adequate service in return: in Guadeloupe, where a federation of unions paid contributions to the French CGT, Citrine was told that no one from the CGT had ever visited them,[70] and one of his objections in 1943 to the Jamaica Maritime Union's proposal to affiliate to the National Maritime Union of America was that affiliation would subordinate the Jamaican union.

An alternative was co-ordination within the West Indies. Before leaving Britain Citrine had formed the view that there would have to be some federal structure there, and by the end of his journey he hoped that this would include a central labour department, with uniform legislation and a travelling arbitration court that would be seen to be impartial in local disputes. The trade union counterpart would be a West Indian federation of trade unions with central financial provision and a good deal of autonomy for the local unions.[71] This thinking was in line with that of the British Guiana and West Indies Labour Congress, which submitted with its evidence to the Commission a draft Bill for a federal West Indian constitution in which friendly societies, trade unions and conciliation and arbitration in industrial disputes were federal subjects.[72] The Congress held a further trade union meeting in British Guiana in 1944, but it never performed the organizational function for which Citrine had hoped. The meeting in Barbados in 1945 saw its replacement by the Caribbean Labour Congress, which brought in Jamaica, but the new body included political party as well as trade union representatives, and the political influence was always dominant.

The TUC was the only trade union organization that could effectively represent the unions' interest where this was most needed at the time – in the Colonial Office – and it was the only one that was consistently and unanimously being asked to help. In 1939 Citrine thought that some form of association with the TUC might assist unions in gaining recognition from employers and government departments, and in recruiting, for such association might establish them as *bona fide* organizations in the eyes of the public. The TUC would have to approve their rules, and a union in association would have to be able to show that it had held its membership for a definite period, even if only for six or twelve months, for he had found that some registered unions existed only on paper, with a nominal membership of fifty or 100 and no published accounts. Within each colony he envisaged the formation of a trade union council with nominal affiliation fees and minimal administrative expenses, and rules based on a simplified form of the TUC's constitution. The TUC's recognition of a union would be conditional on its affiliation to the local council and on the council's approval of recognition. The BGWILC could be developed into a federation linking the councils together. This was in the future: initially, he envisaged the appointment of correspondents who would keep the TUC informed of union problems and activities, while the TUC would circulate a regular bulletin on activities throughout the West Indies.[73]

These ideas were developing as he met the unions, and throughout the tour he preached unity and directed his advice not only to the formation and practice of unions, but also to building a structured movement which could deal with inter-union rivalries, evolve common policies, and present them to governments, employers, and – in due course – to the international trade union organizations.

In this effort he had his greatest success in Barbados. The *Memorandum of the Barbados Progressive League to the Royal Commission 1939* stated that it was divided into three branches, political, social and economic. Its activities so far were mainly confined to the economic branch, which 'occupies a position similar to that of the British Trades Union Congress in relation to such Unions as are in the process of formation'. This was a misapprehension, since the TUC did not organize unions while the League was actively organizing on trade union lines within its own structure and was referred to as the 'Parent Body of Unions'.[74] In the vacuum that existed until the revised trade union legislation came into force in August 1940, trade unions had no legal status, and if the League's aim was to provide sane leadership to help workers' organizations to follow a constitutional path, it made sense to try to bring the associations that were forming under its own umbrella. Citrine found on arrival that the League had mapped out a skeleton organization for about eighteen unions – far too many, he thought, for the potential membership. He advised the formation of one union with separate sections.[75]

The leaders were very willing to take advice. In the expectant atmosphere to which the Commission had contributed, they were unable to produce quick results, while frustration burst out immediately in strikes which the League had not authorized and which it publicly condemned. The League also had its own teething problems,[76] but in April 1939 Edwy Talma, who followed Seale as secretary of the League, reported that it already had seventeen field secretaries and was preparing to form one union.[77]

The Barbados Workers' Union (BWU) was registered in October 1941. Six divisions organized by the League provided members for the first executive committee, and the BWU officially recognized that Citrine's advice on its structure had been decisive.[78] Though it had been fathered by the League, the union contained members who had been trying to organize before the League was started, and though it began with Adams as president and the League's secretary, Hugh Springer,[79] as secretary, both these men were genuinely interested in labour problems as such, and not merely in the union as a springboard to political power. The union successfully achieved the transition from political to trade union leadership. Springer, who was an outstanding administrator, had prepared for it when he resigned in 1947 to become Registrar of the University College of the West Indies. Adams resigned the presidency in 1954 when he became Premier of Barbados. Their successors, Frank Walcott as general secretary and McDonald Blunt, president of the Steamers' Warehouse Porters' Division, became long-service officers, and with the competence and the continuity that they provided, both the leadership and the structure of the Union stood the test of time.

It began modestly, with only two divisions paid-up and functioning. The long-promised Labour Officer, Guy Perrin, who had been deputy labour commissioner in Ceylon, had arrived in 1940. He chaired the Union's first negotiations, with the foundry employers. Pay increases were secured, with a minimum fixed for each grade, and the regulation of apprenticeship. By the end of the first year improvements in pay and conditions had also been secured in a biscuit factory and in one of the sugar factories, agreement had been reached on the preparation of a register of ships' carpenters and joiners, and the ships carpenters' division had gone to arbitration under the Trade Disputes Act 1939, securing a substantial wage increase. The Union had already shown that it was prepared and able to use every available means to advance its members' interests. By its fourth conference it had 5,587 members in twenty-two active divisions,[80] and it became one of the most competent unions in the colonial empire.

Obstacles

Elsewhere, formidable obstacles to unity were already embedded in some of the trade union movements. In Trinidad, Cipriani still regarded the new unions as rivals to the TLP and Butler's influence was only temporarily submerged by his imprisonment. In Jamaica, Bustamante's affectation of a Latin American flamboyance did not appeal to those leaders who leaned towards British respectability, nor did his political outlook – in many ways conservative – marry well with that of the Manley group who had connections with the left of the British Labour Party. It has been suggested that Manley (like Nehru) saw social regeneration, which included the development of trade unions, and the movement for self-government as two sides of the same coin, while Bustamante took the working class as the starting point for political action and dismissed self-government, at that time, as 'brown men government'. When he launched the Jamaica Labour Party in 1943 and led it to victory in the first elections by universal suffrage in 1944, the party was seen as the 'son' of the BITU.[81]

Citrine was disturbed to find that the initial attempt to form a co-ordinating council for the unions had already collapsed, but he was assured by Manley that Bustamante, who had at first agreed to co-operate, was utterly unselfish in regard to trade union organization and had the overwhelming support of the workers.[82] He saw that support for himself, and although such phenomena as the song 'We will follow

Bustamante till we die' and the formation of a uniformed bodyguard could have had little appeal for a European socialist acquainted with the rise of Mussolini, Citrine respected Bustamante and his achievement. Hoping that personal and political differences could be contained within a trade union movement concentrating primarily on its industrial functions, he called a meeting of all the unions with headquarters in Kingston and, with Bustamante present, secured provisional agreement for the establishment of a trade union council with Glasspole as correspondent to keep in touch with the TUC. After a similar meeting in Montego Bay he brought Bustamante and Coombs together, suggesting that the animosity between them might be overcome if the Workers' and Tradesmen Union, with Coombs, went into the BITU.[83]

After Citrine's departure these hopes were not fulfilled. Coombs was willing to divide the island into spheres of organization by the two unions, provided that each agreed not to attack the other and to discipline any of its officers that did so, and that both worked under the supervision of the projected Trade Union Council. Still no Council had been formed, however, when the rivalry between the two unions caused a strike and further disturbances in February 1939. In the ensuing state of emergency Manley, with Bustamante's approval, gave an undertaking to the Governor that one would be set up.[84]

The aims of the Trade Union Advisory Council (TUAC) that emerged were to advise on the organization, development and practical work of all affiliated trade unions, to promote their interests and secure united action on questions likely to affect them, and to develop union education programmes and international contacts.[85] Its chairman, N. N. Nethersole, was a leading light in the PNP but at that time had no trade union status except as a co-opted member of the council. The secretary, Richard Hart, was in the PNP but was also one of a 'small group of Marxist-Leninists which had begun to take shape in 1937'.[86] Moreover, as one of Manley's original co-ordinating committee, he had had the temerity to present Bustamante with a draft union constitution based on election by members. He was soon replaced by Glasspole.[87]

Shortly afterwards Citrine refused to take sides when he heard that Hill and other officers had resigned from the BITU in protest against the dictatorial conduct of the union. He advised against the formation of any other unions unless that step was specifically approved by the TUAC, but his letter crossed a report from Hill that four new unions, off-shoots of the BITU, were being organized, and that Bustamante had resigned from the TUAC, which had been reconstituted as the Trades Union Council. Bustamante's withdrawal had followed a formal complaint to the TUAC from Coombs that his union was being attacked, while it was suggested that Bustamante considered that the

BITU's membership justified greater representation on the TUAC Board, and that he anticipated interference with the BITU's rules after a TUAC decision that all member unions should have a uniform democratic constitution.[88] Citrine could only express regret and the hope that the reconstitution of the TUAC might contribute to the restoration of unity.[89] The rift proved to be permanent. Glasspole, as secretary of the new Trades Union Council, remained in touch with the TUC.

In British Guiana Citrine began his unity mission by advising union representatives to give their evidence to the Commission together, and was impressed by the way they did so. He held a public meeting and discussed union problems privately with the leaders, urging them to set up a committee, which they agreed to do,[90] but no trade union council was formed until 1941, and then unsuccessfully.[91]

In Trinidad Rienzi arranged a meeting with representatives of all the unions – the first time they had all met in the same room. Citrine sat with them later when they decided to form a provisional council with Rienzi as chairman and Rupert Gittens of the Public Works and Public Services Workers' Union as secretary. They agreed to draft the rules together and to plan the structure of the movement to avoid the formation of too many unions, with a committee to deal with possible overlapping. The revised Trade Unions Ordinance had not yet been enacted, and there was some anxiety that when it was the TLP would register some of its sections and that these would be in competition with unions already registered. The Trades Union Council was formed on 21 March 1939, and Citrine used his friendly relationship with Cipriani to bring its representatives, Gittens and Quintin O'Connor of the Shop Assistants' and Clerks' Union, to discussions with Cipriani and Vivian Henry as representatives of the TLP. He advised co-operation in planning the movement on the basis that the unions would affiliate to the TLP. He thought that this might antagonize the employers, but could see no other way. At the public meeting arranged for him he was unimpressed by the 'political tirades' of Cipriani and Rienzi, but at least they were together on the same platform. On his last day in Trinidad he explained to them in detail the relationship between the Labour Party and the unions in Britain and between the TUC and the National Council of Labour. He left with the impression that they would arrange a meeting of their executives to plan the movement with a jurisdiction committee whose decisions the parties would agree in advance to accept, and with affiliation to the TLP of all unions formed in accordance with the plan.[92]

In the light of subsequent history, it may be considered that this was the best piece of advice ever given to the Trinidad unions. But it presupposed that Cipriani would be able to command the support of the new generation of trade union leaders, or that the unions themselves would develop a revived party out of their industrial experience. Instead there was strong opposition to Cipriani until his death in 1945, and no coherent party emerged from the trade unions. Nor did Citrine's plan take Butler into account. Released from prison on 6 May 1939, he was given a public welcome by the OWTU and taken on as an organizer, but in August he was accused of flouting executive decisions and was expelled from the union with the support of branches.[93] Interned under Defence Regulations in February 1940, he re-emerged in 1945 to attempt to build his political and trade union organization in opposition to the OWTU and the existing unions.[94] Despite these and other tensions, the Trades Union Council survived.

The political undercurrents in the West Indies were extremely complicated, and apparently intensified rather than diminished by the small size of the movements involved. After meeting the executive of the little Negro Welfare Cultural and Social Association in Trinidad, Jagger commented that they were ready-made for martyrdom and locked into an isolationist creed which set them aside from the rest: 'There is only one bottle of the pure white milk of Socialism, and the NWCSA has got possession of that ... It is very unfortunate that a Labour movement which is so small should find it necessary to reproduce all the divisions which exist in either America or Great Britain, together with a few peculiar to themselves'.[95]

Some of the outside influences were constructive. America contributed the inspiration of the Wagner Act and the Committee for Industrial Organization[96] whose name was adopted in Trinidad, and the 'Harlem West Indians' were influential in the formation and organization of the PNP in Jamaica and of the Barbados Progressive League.[97] There was also, especially after the invasion of Abyssinia, the influence of Garveyism – negative in so far as it focused attention on aspirations which could not be fulfilled. In Barbados Ulric Grant, imprisoned for his part in the 1937 disturbances, was alleged to have urged his listeners to remember that Africa was their mother-country, that Ethiopia was stretching out her hands, and that 'princes shall come out of Egypt'.[98] Such utterances, addressed as they were to workers who were actually suffering, must have left their mark. So did the Indian National Congress non-co-operation movements amongst the political leaders of the sugar workers in Trinidad and British Guiana.

All the trade union leaders were nationalists, and well-acquainted with the political controversies in the British Labour movement, which was going through the 'Popular Front' agitation prior to Citrine's visit. There was the communist group in Jamaica, and in Trinidad a small group met regularly and studied Left Book Club and Communist publications.[99] Citrine was apparently unaware of the existence of the communist group in Jamaica – or at least, of its significance in the trade unions – and he did not believe that anyone in Trinidad was acting on Comintern or RILU directives, but he was aware of Rienzi's early association with Saklatvala and was amused to observe, in the OWTU's office, large portraits of Lenin and Stalin displayed alongside the TUC's own organizing posters.[100]

Yet the men who had put them up were prepared to co-operate with the government's Industrial Adviser and had just concluded a successful arbitration.[101] Time showed that they were first and foremost trade union organizers – Purcells rather than Pollitts – and there was nothing anywhere in the West Indies comparable to the Minority Movement in Britain or to the Indian Communist Party with its British Communist Party advisers active in the trade union movement. This was not for want of trying. In 1932 the government of Trinidad prohibited the import of any past or future issue of the *Negro Worker* and all other publications of the RILU's International Trade Union Committee of Negro Workers in Hamburg,[102] but Albert Gomes, who became president of the Federated Workers' Union but had previously edited a literary journal, *The Beacon*, recorded that prohibited publications were brought to him by seamen.[103] Seamen carried the message from Hamburg even into Barbados, urging workers to link up with revolutionary colleagues in Panama and Honduras and to expose 'the deception of Cipriani in Trinidad', with such extraordinary warnings as that the MacDonald government was preparing for a war against the Soviet Union in which millions of colonial peoples in Africa and the West Indies would be forced to lay down their lives.[104] This was in 1933 and the message changed after the Russian government's change of policy. But if they had little or no immediate impact, such communications, when they escaped the police, were unsettling, and West Indian workers were accustomed to working overseas, where the propaganda was overt. Whatever its content as policies changed, it was never conducive to the patient plodding required to build up trade unions.

It was not surprising that the union leaders in the three major territories could not achieve the unity on which the ultimate success of Citrine's plans depended. But everywhere the unions made sufficient progress, and followed enough of the TUC's advice, to make his effort worthwhile. All the contemporary witnesses and all the historians pay tribute to his role, perhaps best summed up by Knowles, 'in giving them confidence and courage to go ahead with what had, at first, appeared to be a hopeless task'.[105]

Assistance to Colonial Unions

In his final proposals after his return Citrine attached first importance to the existing and potential trade union councils. He recognized that they would reflect the uncertainty and instability of trade union membership, but he hoped that the TUC might exercize a unifying influence by treating them as the representative organizations in their colonies and channelling information and inquiries through their secretaries. He sent his first circular in May 1939 to Glasspole, Gittens, Seale, Thorne and Jacob in British Guiana, and in the small islands to Manchester, Samuel Henry (Antigua), R. E. A. Nichols (Mayor of Roseau, Dominica), E. Maresse Donovan (Grenada Trades Union), John H. Pilgrim (St Lucia) and James L. Cato of the St Vincent Workingmen's Cooperative Association. Subsequently, Seale was replaced by C. E. Talma in Barbados, Henry by B. A. Richards of the Antigua Trades and Labour Union, and the British Guiana correspondence was sent through Thorne.[106] In the office he arranged for a regular supply of information and publications to his correspondents and the staff prepared to adapt TUC study courses – including notes on keeping accounts – for the West Indies.

Citrine intended to formalize the link by establishing a West India Sub-Committee of the TUC's Colonial Advisory Committee, with which the recognized trade union councils would be associated. He had already decided that West Indian leaders should be invited to study in Britain, and he also proposed the appointment of a TUC representative who would work on the spot for 12 to 18 months, helping to complete the organization of the trade union councils, and to advise the unions and help them to establish collective bargaining. His choice was Victor Feather, then working in the TUC's Organization Department, and subsequently general secretary of the TUC.

The General Council endorsed all his proposals on 1 September 1939.[107] Two days later, Britain was at war. Circular letters went out to the correspondents, with publications and study courses, until October 1942, but the plan for a bulletin incorporating information received from them had to be abandoned. On nomination from their organizations, Glasspole in Jamaica and Blades in Trinidad – the latter subsequently replaced by Gittens – were ready to take up scholarships to Ruskin College in 1940, but had to postpone their arrival until 1945. Victor Feather remained at home. The special West India Sub-Committee of the Colonial Advisory Committee was not set up, and the Advisory Committee itself met only ten times during the war. With the TUC staff depleted by the call-up to the armed forces, with travel and postal services disrupted and even paper in short supply, Citrine was driven to the conclusion, in 1942, that the TUC could not carry out its plans for the colonial unions.[108]

Yet they did bear fruit, notably in the requests that came from the West Indies for help. Whereas before 1938, except for the TWMA, such organizations as existed faced their difficulties alone and the TUC had scarcely any contact with the Colonial Office, there was now a watchdog in Transport House. There were no local ministers in the West Indies and no government with the status of the Government of India. The Colonial Office could not plead lack of power to intervene, as Montagu and Birkenhead had done, nor did it try to do so. The steady representation of colonial grievances became part of the routine work of the TUC staff. Hitherto they had been general; now they were specific industrial problems. Ultimately, this handling of particular cases over a period of 25 years did more than anything else to build up the TUC's knowledge of colonial trade unionism.

Industrial Problems

Some of these problems raised general issues. Hallsworth's comments on 'outsiders' in the Colonial Labour Advisory Committee were made in a discussion on trade union legislation in Mauritius which confined membership to persons regularly and normally engaged in the industry which the association represented.[109] In 1942 the Jamaican Government Employees' Union, which was registered and in regular communication with the Railway Department, had this recognition withdrawn under a wartime Order on the grounds that its constitution allowed nonemployees to hold office. The union president and vice-president, Richard Hart and Nethersole, both lawyers, quickly realized that postal and public works department employees, who like the railway workers were not civil servants, could have a similar restriction applied to them. In the dispute which followed, the union was unable to go to arbitration since the railway was an essential service, and in October the police raided the union office and recognition was also withdrawn in respect of post and telegraph workers. When asking the Secretary of State for an inquiry Citrine stated that the TUC could not regard the appointment of nonemployees as officers as ground for refusing recognition to a union. The Order was withdrawn in November and negotiations followed immediately, with a joint request to the TUC from the union and the management for information on the terms and conditions of employment of railway workers in Britain.[110] This was provided by the NUR.

A long-running wartime problem arose from the Anglo-American agreement of March 1941 under which the USA constructed air and naval bases in the Caribbean. Thorne was the first to complain that the agreement that the American authorities would pay workers at the rates prevailing in each colony meant in British Guiana that the planting interests were actually preventing workers getting a decent wage from the Americans. He argued that no such heavy work had ever been done in the colony and no workers had been required to use machinery of the type the Americans introduced. Thorne asked for a board with representatives of employers and unions under a government chairman to fix wages.[111] A long correspondence between the TUC and the Colonial Office ensued, covering also complaints received from Jamaica and from Trinidad, where it was alleged in addition that the American forces were sidestepping union negotiations. The British Guiana government denied that the local comparison was with rates paid in sugar, Trinidad claimed that the construction work involved did not materially differ from that required for the airport and the deep-water harbour in Port of Spain, and Jamaica stated that its comparison was with wages paid for unskilled labour on the railway and public works and in industrial and commercial undertakings in Kingston. It was evident that the root of the matter lay with the low rates prevailing generally rather than with the United States authorities, and in this respect the correspondence was inconclusive. Consultations between the British and American governments did, however, produce a statement which the Colonial Office circulated to all the governors involved, that the US Navy and War Departments had no objection to their local representatives 'participating in conferences' with trade union representatives, provided it was understood that the US government would not be bound to their outcome or committed to recognizing any union as sole bargaining agency for local labour.[112]

There remained the underlying problem of the effect of wartime restrictions on customary union activities. These were accepted in Britain, but in Palestine the Histadrut complained that the Palestine Trade Disputes Order 1941 introduced a form of compulsory arbitration without the safeguards contained in the United Kingdom regulations. TUC representations secured no improvement on some concessions already granted by the Palestine government, and the TUC concluded that the legislation might be considered justifiable during hostilities.[113]

Other cases took the TUC on to less familiar ground. Dalgleish was appointed a member of the Commission of Inquiry into disturbances on the Northern Rhodesian Copperbelt in April 1940, and on his return discussed its recommendations with the TUC's International Committee.[114] A strike of African workers had followed a successful strike for higher wages by European miners, and resulted in seventeen Africans killed and seventy wounded after the military had been called in to repulse an attack on the compound office at Nkana. The Commission's report and a statement issued by the Northern Rhodesian government after discussing its recommendations with the mining companies[115] dealt with current problems, but also raised three

issues of long-term significance. The government accepted a recommendation that adequate married quarters should be available on the
mining compounds and the companies agreed to provide them, but the
government pointed out that it was not committed to a policy of
establishing a permanent industrialized African population on the
Copperbelt. It also had reservations about the Commission's proposal
that the mine managements should consider with the government and
with representatives of the [European] Northern Rhodesia Mineworkers' Union to what positions, not then open to them, the African
workers should be encouraged to advance. This raised problems of job
content, equal pay, colour bar and closed shop which could not be
tackled in wartime when the over-riding need was to secure copper
supplies, but it had to be dealt with after the war. It could not be settled
without proper representation of the African workers. In 1940 this was
provided by 'Elders' elected on a tribal basis in each compound. This
system had been introduced at Luanshya in 1931 and had spread to
other mines, but not to Nkana, where at the time of the riot the African
workers had no representative body of any kind. Though in most cases
the Elders were connected with chiefly families, they were themselves
employed in the industry, but they dealt with many domestic and
welfare problems as well as those arising at work, and election by tribe
did not provide for representation of different categories of workers. In
earlier disturbances in 1935 and in 1940 at Mufulira, where the
workers elected their own committee to run the strike, the Elders had
been swept aside. The Commission considered that this system was the
best available at the time and might be the seedbed of African trade
unionism. The government was prepared to explore this and other
possibilities through its labour department, and did in fact do so.[116]

The TUC's International Committee clearly felt they lacked the
knowledge to judge the Report, and sought the views of the South
African Trades and Labour Council, which suggested that a European
trade unionist with an intimate knowledge of African psychology
should be appointed to act as guide to the African workers. This was
impossible at the time. The TUC could only look to the Colonial
Office to see that the Commission's recommendations were carried
out, especially by the establishment of a fully fledged labour
department. For the TUC, the two most important questions were
those of the advancement of Africans in the industry and the
development of a trade union which would represent the African
workers. They were both tackled after the war, but it was not until
1953 that the four-year-old Northern Rhodesia African Mine Workers'
Trade Union secured the abolition of the tribal representatives.

This question of the natural channel of expression for African
workers was particularly acute where, as in Northern Rhodesia, large

numbers of workers drawn from many areas were employed away from the authority of their chiefs. It was one of the problems associated with the recruitment of migrant contract workers on which the ILO, the Labour Party and the TUC had already taken action. The Labour Party's colonial experts tended to see them in the context of the economic and political dominance of European settler interests, but beneath these were other labour problems inherent in African social structures, changing, but still dominant, especially in West Africa. The TUC had scarcely begun to think of these. An early example came in a request for help from Sierra Leone.

It was sent in 1942 by the secretary of the Freetown Maritime Workers' Union, P. D. Savage, writing from the Kroo Court House, Freetown. This union, already registered, was trying itself to replace the headmen who recruited stevedores on cargo vessels trading between West African ports by securing recognition for the union as the proper authority for the supply of labour. The union complained that workers had to pay gang headmen to obtain jobs and were subject to extortion while in employment. Correspondence with the Colonial Office revealed that this was not a simple issue. Most of the labourers were Kroos from the century-old Kroo settlement in Freetown who owed a customary payment to the Kroo tribal headman for such social purposes as relief of the poor and the education of their children. This was paid through the gang headmen – a system which frequently gave rise to disputes and afforded a loophole in the existing law that wages must be paid direct to the workmen without deductions. The TUC asked for an inquiry and suggested that if existing protective legislation could not be enforced, one solution might be found in a government employment exchange operated in agreement with the employers and the union.[117] This was only one aspect of what became a long-standing problem along the West African coast, where in time unions of seamen and dockworkers elsewhere demanded their share of work in their own ports and their members also faced difficulties in securing jobs. For many years the labour departments, unions in Sierra Leone, the Gold Coast and Nigeria, and the British National Union of Seamen, were concerned with these.

In handling requests for assistance in such cases, the TUC began to come to grips with industrial conditions and union problems in the colonies. There were other difficulties that were exacerbated in wartime but which were also part and parcel of the general state of political and civil liberties in territories under colonial rule.

Civil Liberty

Restrictions on civil liberty were primarily a matter for the Labour Party and were frequently raised in Parliamentary Questions. The

Labour Party's Imperial Advisory Committee began an examination of
sedition laws – into which the Colonial Office was trying to introduce a
measure of uniformity – in 1934, but the TUC was primarily
concerned with individual cases, initially that of Wallace Johnson in
the Gold Coast.[118] As the Meerut trial had shown, sedition laws could
have a side effect on trade union organization, and in the West Indies
Citrine became aware that the conduct of particular cases was not
always above criticism. Manley told him that when Bustamante was
first arrested in 1938 it took the police five hours to decide that they
could charge him with sedition, relying on a speech made two months
earlier. In St Vincent, the Labour Commissioner pointed out G. A.
McIntosh as the best workers' leader. In the minor riots of 1935 this
same man had been held for 19 days before being brought to trial on a
charge of 'waging war against the King', which was dismissed without
his having to give any evidence. In Barbados, Citrine was angered by the
record of proceedings against Ulric Grant and Isaac Lovell, sentenced
to ten and five years' imprisonment for sedition after the 1937 riots.
Despite the Governor's anxiety, he insisted on seeing them in gaol and
refused the prison governor's request to be present.[119]

Lovell was a carpenter and lay preacher who had concerned himself
with the positive aspects of Garveyism as president of a branch of the
Universal Negro Improvement Association. He gave telling evidence in
his petition to the Royal Commission, badly phrased and ill-spelt
though it was, explaining how jobs had been lost by amalgamation of
sugar estates and by the use of motor transport in place of small horse
and donkey carts. Citrine considered him to be a gentle man who could
not consciously have committed the crime of sedition. Grant, on the
other hand, was not an attractive figure. He had been deported from the
United States after two convictions for petty larceny and two for
burglary, and there he had been in touch with the Communist Party
leader, William Zak Foster. However, his petition to the Royal
Commission contained sensible proposals for reform such as a higher
price for sugar and reconstruction of the Legislative Council, he
asserted his loyalty to the Crown, and claimed to have been condemned
by a prejudiced jury. Though he had undoubtedly said some wild
things in his speeches to riotous crowds, it is hard to find any words in
either the indictment or the evidence at his trial which merited the
sentence.[120] Citrine questioned him closely, resolved to take up both
cases, and left with the impression that both men would soon be
released.[121] Lovell was pardoned in August 1939, but in 1941 Citrine
heard that Grant was still in gaol, and wrote to Lord Moyne to demand
an inquiry. On 20 December 1941, Grant was released.[122]

In the wartime crop of detentions under defence regulations an early
casualty was Bustamante, detained in September 1940 after a meeting

which called for a dock strike. A petition to Lord Moyne, sent by the BITU to the TUC in 1941, said that whereas the Jamaican Government claimed that Bustamante had not been arrested for calling the strike, but for seditious utterances, it had not stated what the allegedly seditious words were, and in any case sedition should be tried in an ordinary court. There had been no violence during the strike, even after his arrest, and from detention Bustamante had sent advice to the dockers to return to work and seek arbitration. The Governor, Sir Arthur Richards, took a very strong line – rejecting a petition for release in November 1940, refusing to see a union deputation in February 1941, and forbidding Bustamante to discuss union matters with the few visitors he was allowed to receive. When Citrine protested, Richards replied that the union had had ample time to make alternative arrangements for its administration, and the arrest was not due to only one utterance. The TUC representations did not secure any other explanation but an assurance was given that the case would be kept under review[123], and Bustamante was released in February 1942.

This intervention might have resulted in a renewal of the TUC's early relationship with the BITU but for a dispute within the union. The Jamaica Trades Union Council had asked for immediate intervention to avert a sugar strike over a wage increase demanded by the BITU. The Colonial Office and the Jamaican Government adopted the TUC's suggestion that a joint advisory board should be set up to investigate and report, and agreement was reached on terms acceptable to both sides.[124] This provided the wage increase demanded and, as the first agreement negotiated in sugar, was regarded as a milestone, but there were objections within the BITU to the hours of work it sanctioned, and it was negotiated by a caretaker administration of the union that was substantially assisted by the PNP. Proposals by the 'outsiders' for changes in the union's constitution precipitated a crisis in the executive which was resolved only by Bustamante's resumption of control after his release.[125] The TUC's attempt to assist the initiation of negotiations in the sugar dispute forestalled the anticipated use of wartime powers against the strike; the settlement, together with the representations made on behalf of Bustamante, must have helped towards his release. The TUC was in no way concerned with the internal battle in the union.

It was concerned with the side effects of the public services controversy in 1942. While the railway dispute was still unsettled, and after the police raid on the union offices, the 'Four Hs' – Richard Hart, V. Henry, Ken and Frank Hill, all union officers – were detained for 'being concerned in acts prejudicial to public safety or defence or in preparation or instigation of such acts'. The Secretary of State's denial that the detentions were concerned only with the railway dispute left a political slur on the detainees which was deeply resented. They regarded themselves as anti-Fascists *par excellence*, enthusiastically supporting the war effort, and Henry had served in Egypt and France during the First World War. These detentions were quickly terminated, on 18 March 1943.[126]

The denial that detentions were being used as weapons against unions in disputes, unaccompanied by any explanation of what the detainees had actually done to deserve imprisonment, was typical of detention cases. Government action, even if it might possibly have been justified in wartime, always appeared to be arbitrary. While the Jamaican dispute was in progress, two officers of the NRMU were detained in October 1942 and deported – one of them, the general secretary, F. S. Maybank, to Britain. The Northern Rhodesian government claimed that it had no intention of interfering with the normal activities of the union, but the pair had been leaders of a subversive agitation, planning to achieve their ends through the threat of disrupting the copper-mining industry. This had been designated as essential to the prosecution of the war, and in consequence strikes were prohibited. A sustained correspondence and two TUC deputations to the Secretary of State revealed no more than that the British government had been consulted throughout and had considered the evidence before the decision to deport had been taken. After discussions with Maybank, the General Council did not believe that he had intended subversion, and if he had, it was strange that he was allowed to visit the British coalfields as the guest of the Mineworkers' Federation. But the TUC had no means of disproving the charge, and Maybank was allowed to return only after the end of the war with Germany.[127]

The TUC was pursuing such cases despite Citrine's admission at the end of 1942 that it could not continue to give the colonial unions the organizational help that he had planned – that is to say, handling specific issues had become part of the normal work of the TUC office. By now Kemmis had had five years' experience of colonial work, and when Bolton retired in December Ernest Bell began a twelve-year stint as head of the International Department. 1942 had been a disastrous year. It began with the Japanese advance through Malaya and Singapore to take Rangoon in March. In India, now threatened with invasion, the Cripps Mission had failed to achieve a political settlement, and on 8 August the All-India Congress Committee initiated a mass campaign of civil disobedience with a call to Britain to quit India. With the immediate arrest of the Congress Working Committee, the entire British Asian empire except Ceylon was then either under enemy occupation or in a state of turmoil. Elsewhere there were some grounds for optimism. The Colonial Labour Advisory Committee had started work and there was frequent consultation between officials, the first trade unionists were in place in colonial labour departments, and the colonial unions were active and growing. There were also changes in the international scene that were destined to affect them.

Let us face the future

The League of Nations had disappeared, but with the Commonwealth and colonies, the United States and the Soviet Union fighting as allies, there was a hope not only that the war might be won, but that wartime co-operation might lead to new international institutions in which the Soviet Union would play a full part – even that at long last the trade union internationals might come together. The truncated ILO was operating from Canada. The IFTU had been housed with the TUC since 1940, when five of its affiliates were destroyed in the Nazi advance through Europe and three more were cut off from contact. However, some of the European leaders had escaped and were forming groups in Britain, and by September 1942 the London office was in touch with workers in occupied countries.[128] As the German army moved into Russia, the Comintern also lost contact with its European affiliates, but the military alliance enabled Citrine to go to Russia, and in 1941 an Anglo–Soviet Trade Union Council was established. The TUC again became the prime mover towards international trade union unity after the war.

The ILO

When the first war-time International Labour Conference met in New York in October 1941 the Colonial Office submitted a statement[129] on the changes made since 1937 in labour administration, trade union legislation and the application of ILO Conventions to the colonies. Labour policy was now being seen in a broader context. The Atlantic Charter proclaimed that 'freedom from want' was a war aim of the Allies, and a war for liberty was widely seen to be incompatible with the continuance of empires uncontrolled by their constituent peoples or by any international authority. The ILO's London representative, Wilfred Benson, was co-opted to the TUC's Colonial Advisory Committee in 1941, and with the approach of the crucial wartime International Labour Conference held in Philadelphia in 1944, pointed out to his colleagues that the ILO would need to shoulder a broader responsibility and to reconsider the position of colonial peoples. It was in this context that the inclusion of a colonial spokesman in the British workers' delegation was proposed.[130]

At Philadelphia E. E. Esua served on the Conference committee which considered a Recommendation on Minimum Standards of Social Policy in Dependent Territories.[131] It covered such subjects as housing and nutrition, and called for policies directed towards a general improvement in living standards through programmes of co-ordinated development with greater regional and international co-operation. The Conference also adopted a statement on the aims and purposes of the ILO which came to be known as the Philadelphia Charter. This specifically included the colonies in affirming that the progressive application of the principles of the new United Nations Charter was a matter of concern to the whole civilized world.[132]

The second issue concerning the ILO was its future status amongst the projected specialized agencies of the United Nations. Speaking as Minister of Labour in the Governing Body, Bevin stressed its value as the only international agency set up after the First World War in which workers and employers had a place, and the only one which had continued to function effectively. He insisted that it must not be made subordinate to the Economic and Social Council of the United Nations,[133] and in the event the ILO became a specialized agency of the United Nations in its own right. Its revised constitution required the metropolitan powers to report on conditions relevant to Conventions which they had not applied to their colonial dependencies as well as to those which they had ratified and applied. These changes did not take effect until 1946, but they were being prepared before the war ended.

The IFTU

At the outbreak of war, the IFTU still represented, overwhelmingly, the workers of the metropolitan countries, America and the Dominions. In the drive to extend organization after its London Congress in 1936, the AFL joined, but the ARCCTU responded to an IFTU delegation in 1937 by attaching unacceptable conditions to affiliation. At the Zurich Congress in July 1939 British and Norwegian resolutions urging a further approach to the Russians were defeated. In August the argument was ended by the Nazi–Soviet Pact. New affiliates came in from New Zealand, Egypt, South-West Africa, Mozambique, and from the French colonies through the CGT; but in 1939 Australia had still not affiliated, and negotiations with Trinidad had not been concluded.[134] In 1941 the Jewish Confederation of Labour in the Palestine mandate was still the only affiliate, outside India, in the British dependencies.

Now the IFTU's first task was to rebuild its shattered organization in Europe. In July 1942, with its surviving affiliates, and with the international trade secretariats and the refugee organizations which had established themselves in Britain, the IFTU was able to set up an Emergency International Trade Union Council, but it was not able to hold a full meeting of its General Council – the first since its Zurich Congress – until January 1945.

The Emergency International Trade Union Council decided at its inaugural meeting to consider the reconstruction of the international trade union movement, and in 1944 adopted proposals for a world-wide trade union federation. This implied the inclusion of former affiliates of the RILU and of the colonial unions. The Council also published a substantial report on the social and economic demands of workers in the postwar world which included a proposal for international supervision of the administration of colonial territories 'in order to ensure that the colonial peoples will be governed for their own benefit only and in view of their rapid evolution into independent and self-governing countries'.[135]

The prime obstacle to the formation of a world-wide trade union federation was removed in May 1943, when the Presidium of the Comintern called for its dissolution as 'the directing centre of the international working-class movement'. In fact, the Comintern had not called a congress since 1935, and in the Stalin purges most of its Russian and foreign leaders had disappeared. Its formal demise came in June 1943 in a statement that the Communist parties of 30 countries had approved the Presidium's proposal and that the organization was now dissolved. The RILU went with it. The main object was said to be to facilitate the development of unified national movements against Hitlerism by removing the 'calumny' that communist parties acted on outside orders. The Presidium's statement argued that it was becoming evident even before the war that central direction could not solve the varied problems of the labour movements of different countries, and that the war itself had drawn a division of function within the working class. Whereas in occupied countries its task was to sabotage the Hitlerite war effort, in the Allied countries the working class must support the military efforts of their governments, uniting the 'freedom-loving' peoples without distinction of party or religion.[136] If the Comintern Presidium itself had recognized the existence of historic and contemporary differences between the working-class movements of different countries, was it now possible for trade unions of different tendencies to co-operate in rebuilding the international structure after the war?

The World Federation of Trade Unions

The first requirement was a meeting of trade union representatives from the Allied countries. The TUC refused to allow the Anglo–Russian Trade Union Council to be used to initiate a new international,[137] but considered it unlikely that the Russians would accept an invitation from the IFTU. In some countries that would have to be included the IFTU had no affiliates, others were in neutral countries, and some underground. Outside occupied Europe the chief affiliates were the AFL and the TUC. The AFL regarded the Soviet trade unions as 'worker groups' which were in reality official branches of government and of the ruling Communist Party, operating without freedom of speech or assembly, and actively supporting worker blacklists, deportations and forced labour.[138] It would never regard an organization which included such 'groups' as a bona fide trade union body.

So the TUC made the first move. In September 1943 the Southport Congress empowered the General Council to call a world conference as soon as war conditions permitted, to consider problems of policy and organization affecting the interests of working people, and 'thereby to promote the widest possible unity, in aim and action, of the International Trade Union Movement'.[139] After the customary jurisdictional difficulties, a world conference met in London in February 1945.

All told, 164 delegates and 40 observers attended from 63 trade union organizations. They included representatives from Cyprus, British Guiana, Jamaica, Nigeria, Sierra Leone, the Gambia, the Gold Coast, Northern Rhodesia, the General Confederation of Jewish Labour and three Arab societies in Palestine, and from India and the Dominions. The AFL refused to attend, but the CIO was represented. The Conference had been postponed from the original date in June 1944 because this turned out to be the month of the Allied landings in Europe. As their countries were liberated the Belgian, Dutch and Luxembourg national centres re-emerged and rejoined the IFTU, and IFTU and TUC delegations travelled to France and Italy. The IFTU was able to call its General Council meeting in January 1945 and to participate in the World Conference. Since all movement and transport were still under wartime control, none of the incoming delegates could have attended without the permission and support of their governments. The colonial delegates, making their début on the world stage, did so with the blessing and help of the Colonial Office and of colonial governments.

The London Conference recorded its conviction that a world federation should be set up uniting trade union bodies 'on a basis of equality, regardless of race, creed, or political faith'. To implement its decisions an Administrative Committee was set up with Louis Saillant, one of the CGT resistance leaders, and a communist, as secretary. This committee worked from the CGT office in Paris and by May 1945 had drafted a provisional constitution for submission to national centres. This was put before the TUC Congress in September. In October a recalled conference met in Paris and turned itself into the first constituent congress of the World Federation of Trade Unions (WFTU).

The London Conference also called for world co-operation after victory to secure the development of undeveloped countries, stressed the need to end economic exploitation of colonies, and committed the participants to work in all countries, including colonies, for protective labour legislation and trade union rights. The purposes of the proposed world federation included assistance to workers in socially and industrially less-developed countries in setting up their trade unions, and the provisions for regional representation on the Executive Committee included a seat for Africa. The manifesto pledged the organization to work for the full exercise of the democratic rights and liberties of all peoples.[140]

The difficulties that arose in drafting and securing the adoption of the WFTU's constitution need not be dealt with here. They included some that had arisen in the IFTU, such as the degree of autonomy of affiliates and the position of the international trade secretariats. On a mundane level, the question of the absorption of the IFTU staff into the new body was a test of intention. At the Paris congress the TUC delegation tried to be accommodating. Though they had hoped for the appointment of Schevenels as general secretary, they bowed to the choice of Saillant.

The main difficulty was, as it had always been, political. Citrine had many reservations about the decisions on the structure of the organization, but hoped that they might fall into place if the spirit of the wartime alliance could be carried over into the peace. On one point he was adamant. In words reminiscent of Gompers in 1919, he told the Paris Congress:

> Our job here is to build a trade union international, an International to carry on practical day-to-day trade union work, to guide the activities of our different trade union centres and to secure practical results for the individual members of our unions ... I heard one speaker say yesterday that his organization was going to join the International because his country wanted their national independence and he wished to establish socialism. However laudable these desires may be, the World Federation of Trade Unions is not the medium whereby that is to be done. If once we get into the maze of politics, as surely as I am standing at this rostrum, the International will perish. It will split, because the different conceptions of political aspiration, desire, method and policy are so wide that they would divide us.[141]

He was immediately attacked in the Communist press with the customary venom, and returned to London with doubts about the new organization that many of the older trade union bodies shared.[142] Nevertheless, the IFTU dissolved itself in December, leaving the field to the WFTU. If the fears of the doubters should be confirmed, neither the Comintern nor the RILU was now needed to influence the colonial unions – the WFTU, with continuous access to them that the colonial governments had always tried to deny to Moscow and to Hamburg, was an open channel.

The Fifth Pan-African Congress 1945

The General Council went into the WFTU with its eyes open, for the TUC never forgot the Minority Movement. But it appears that no attention was given to the potential influence of the fringe groups in Britain. This was negligible in the West Indies, where the unions quickly established their status and threw up outstanding leaders of their own. It was not negligible in Africa, particularly West Africa.

The World Trade Union Conference provided new openings for the British organizations. In 1944 they formed a Pan-African Federation to develop their own policies on colonial affairs independently of the ideas of the British Communist Party and of the Labour Party. The Labour Party had issued a policy statement in 1943[143] which aimed at self-government for the colonies in the shortest possible time, but implied, as did the idea of international supervision, a preparatory period of trusteeship and training. Still associated with the Pan-African Congress of Dr Dubois, the British federation prepared the Fifth Pan-African Congress held in Manchester in 1945, timed specifically to enable the delegates to the Paris founding Congress of the WFTU to attend. The colonial delegates to the World Trade Union Conference in London were contacted while in Britain, and invitations to Manchester were sent to their organizations. Those who went to Paris were considered to represent their countries in political as well as trade union matters. Union delegates from the West Indies, Sierra Leone, the Gold Coast and Nigeria attended.

Most of the demands voiced at the Manchester Congress would have commanded support in any British Labour gathering, but there ran through the speeches and publications of the group in Britain before, during and after the Congress a settled distrust of nearly all British political leaders and of the entire apparatus of colonial government, including the recent improvements in labour administration. Padmore, for example, believed that in many colonies trade union legislation had been passed as a means of helping the war effort, and the Congress complained that the workers of West Africa had not been allowed to form independent trade unions without official interference. The legitimate rights of trade unions were understood and supported, but it was assumed that they would be politically led as part of a nationalist movement. One of the political secretaries of the Congress was Kwame Nkrumah, recently arrived from America and making his first appearance in Britain, and in Manchester the programme of non-co-operative 'positive action' which brought him to power in the Gold Coast was shaped. Finally, the Congress was still conceived on a racial basis, the aim being to promote the well-being and unity of African peoples and peoples of African descent,[144] whether in Africa, the West Indies, the United States or Britain.

It was, of course, undesirable as well as impossible to shield the colonial movements from political influences that did not share and might be hostile to the particular view of trade unionism held by the TUC, but if alternatives were to be put forward it would have been preferable for them to come from trade unionists. Except for Wallace Johnson, only Padmore had trade union experience, and that was in the USA and in the bureaucracy of the RILU, not in Africa. In 1945, the Nigerian unions demonstrated that they were capable of mass action, but with such a small proportion of the population in paid employment, the unions as organizations were still on the fringe of West African societies and needed time to develop on their own lines in their own circumstances. It is arguable that the TUC's empirical, practical approach was more likely to be useful to them than the destructive methods of communism or the permanent oppositionism of the Pan-African group. All three were derived from metropolitan experience and ideologies, but the TUC's views had at least been formed in actual trade union organization and allowed for different interests and attitudes amongst trade union members.

The TUC Congress of 1945

Such considerations were not in the minds of the delegates to the TUC's Congress in September. They met in confident mood. The wartime industrial effort had brought many new workers into the trade unions, and the TUC's affiliated membership now topped 6½ million. In June the Charter of the United Nations had been signed in San Francisco, and with the surrender of Japan in August the war was over. In July a Labour government had taken office, with 392 Members in the Commons as against 198 Conservatives. The outgoing chairman of the General Council, George Isaacs of the print workers, was Minister of Labour, Bevin was at the Foreign Office, George Hall and Creech Jones at the Colonial Office. Representatives came from the liberated trade union movements of Germany, Czechoslovakia and Austria. The Indian Federation of Labour and the AITUC had representatives amongst the visitors, as did the Ceylon Indian Workers' Federation. Jouhaux emerged from a Nazi gaol to address Congress as fraternal delegate from the CGT.

Congress adopted the General Council's recommendation to endorse the proposed constitution for the new world federation with reservations in regard to the international trade secretariats and the IFTU staff. If any delegates thought that the next conference in Paris would be plain sailing, they had no excuse, for Citrine gave a full explanation of the difficulties experienced in drafting the constitution and in calling the London Conference. There was also a startling speech by George Meany, then secretary of the AFL, making his first appearance as fraternal delegate. In his view the London Conference should never have been called, the officials of the IFTU had no right to prepare for the demise of their own organization, and it was impossible to co-operate with the controlled 'worker groups' that passed for trade unions in Soviet Russia. It was a characteristically vigorous speech, but not what the Congress wanted to hear. While Meany was interrupted, an enthusiastic welcome was given to the Soviet fraternal delegate, who dwelt on the wartime alliance and promised co-operation to strengthen the unity of the working class. Immediately after Congress, delegates would go to Paris for the first International Labour Conference of the peace and for the founding session of the world federation. 'We have never had such a chance to rebuild,' declared Ebby Edwards[145] from the presidential chair, and Congress believed that the chance should be seized.[146] The new world would take time to build, but its arrival in due course was confidently anticipated.

It would be idle to imagine that the delegates were thinking of the colonies in this new world. Even the Labour election manifesto had devoted only one sentence to the Commonwealth and Empire: 'the Labour Party will seek to promote mutual understanding and cordial cooperation between the Dominions of the British Commonwealth, the advancement of India to responsible self-government, and the planned progress of our Colonial Dependencies'.[147] The General Council's report recorded the work done by the Colonial Advisory Committee: preparation for the ILO's second discussion on Minimum Social Standards in Dependent Territories, and consideration of specific questions such as the appointment of trade unionists to the colonial service, labour conditions in Cyprus, a Trade Unions Ordinance in Gibraltar, the Maybank case, and the organization of seamen in West Africa. There was also a substantial report on South Africa from a member of the General Council who had recently visited the unions there. The Congress did not discuss these sections of the report. Attention was focused instead on the world conference, on the establishment of the United Nations Organization, and on a resolution demanding full recognition of India's claim to independence.[148]

The prime interest of the delegates, however, was in domestic matters. There were men in the Forces awaiting demobilization and return to their jobs, there was rationing of food and clothing, there was a shortage of raw materials while houses, factories and schools had to be rebuilt, run-down transport had to be restored and industry needed to be re-equipped. In many colonies the war had left similar legacies, and in those that had been occupied by the Japanese there had been appalling suffering, but it was not to be expected that trade union delegates, attending Congress to represent their members, would or could realize that a virtually bankrupt country was now required and pledged to develop viable self-governing states out of the wreckage. Nor, at this stage, could they see clearly how their unions could play a part in the process. This was still pre-eminently the concern of Citrine and the General Council.

For their part, Citrine and his colleagues had to hope that co-operation in the projected new international would have some success, and it was assumed that the colonial unions would benefit from participating in the attempt. With their embryonic organizations, they could not be expected to play a significant part in the forthcoming Paris conference or in the new federation, but they would gain experience of the wider world. As to building up their unions, the TUC was already pledged to help them. 'Let us face the future' the Labour manifesto had said in the general election. The General Council were willing to do so. Their colonial policy had been established, the initial plans for its implementation had been devised: they now had to be carried out.

Epilogue

The part to be played by the TUC in the colonies after the Second World War differed profoundly from its role at the end of the first. In the intervening period its task had been to participate in building new institutions and relationships, at home, in the inter-governmental structure of the ILO, in the international trade union movement, and in the dependencies.

Since it had set its hand to internal reorganization in 1916 the TUC had become a properly staffed and effective national centre. Instead of the haphazard collection of subjects that formerly made up a Congress agenda, instead of TUC representatives going to international conferences with briefs prepared in the back rooms of the Labour Party, Citrine had made sure that the office made proper preparations and made its own investigations. Given the resources in staff and money that were available in 1919, the Parliamentary Committee's contributions to the establishment of the ILO and the IFTU had been remarkable, but at the same time the TUC could do little more than applaud Wadia when he came from India. Even when the Committee took up the question of the Indian trade union legislation, the magnitude of the effort that would be required to give effective help to the new Indian trade union movement was not appreciated. The contrast between the handling of the St Kitts case in 1917 and Citrine's meticulous work on the West India Royal Commission was a measure of the organizational changes which enabled the TUC to follow up that work with practical assistance to the unions. The contrast between the status of the Parliamentary Committee and that of the General Council in 1945 – acknowledged domestically and internationally as the representative body of British trade unionism, regularly sending the British worker's representative and his advisers to the ILO, consulted by the government on a whole range of wartime issues and in continuous contact with the Colonial Office – was a measure of the change in the competence of the TUC itself.

This change was matched in the Colonial Office. Whatever success it might have had in administering backward dependencies before the first World War, whatever elementary protective measures might have been initiated in labour policy in the 1920s, the upheavals of the 1930s had cast a blinding light on its deficiencies. It would have been very easy in the circumstances for the Labour Party and the TUC to content themselves with negative attacks on imperialism. Instead, they applied their minds to the problems of administration. These were, after all, the problems that immediately concerned colonial governments and colonial workers. At the end of the war, constitutional changes were already in train, but in every territory except Ceylon the prime mover for some years would still be the administration, and the engine behind it still at Westminster. In the labour field, the British government's obligations to the ILO had resulted in significant changes in the functions of the Colonial Office and of colonial governments, but until the colonial unions were strong enough to influence both, the TUC's new-found liaison with the Colonial Office offered a convenient and effective channel of representation.

There was another channel that the TUC had not yet used in the colonies. Even before facing their governments, the colonial unions had to face employers. In the inter-war period the British employers had also been building up their organizations, but had not yet fully adapted them to deal with colonial problems. Their representatives sat down with those of the TUC in the ILO and in the Colonial Labour Advisory Committee, but the concept of a tripartite approach to the development and application of labour policy overseas was still in its infancy. In the colonies, except for Citrine's personal efforts while in the West Indies, the TUC had not yet approached employers direct in particular disputes, as it had done in India in the case of the Golmuri Tin Plate strike in 1929.

By the end of the war the TUC's first colleague in its approach to international, Indian and colonial problems had fallen into the background. The Labour Party had made an immense contribution to the development of institutions and policies, with the effect that the TUC was brought forward in its own right in the fields in which the Labour Party had been a pioneer. Henceforward the Party's role was primarily in Parliament, while the Parliamentary Committee's practice of raising issues through Parliamentary Questions fell into disuse in the TUC. One of the most promising joint efforts, the joint Commonwealth Labour Conferences, also fell into disuse, ultimately to be replaced by conferences of worker delegates from the Commonwealth meeting together at the annual International Labour Conferences in Geneva. The fact is that the trade union function is continuous, whereas the political parties form relationships and alliances according to their opinions and aspirations. It was no accident that the World Trade Union Conference fathered the WFTU while no corresponding expansion of the Labour and Socialist International took place.

However, the WFTU did not survive intact. Before and during the First World War both the Labour Party and the Second International had harboured many different and conflicting elements. In the following years the core of the Labour Party's beliefs had become more sharply defined, and with the formation of the Comintern a similar definition took place in Moscow and was imposed on its affiliates. Just as the Labour Party shed the Communist Party and the truncated ILP, so the Comintern and the 'bolshevized' British Communist Party shed their anarchists and the 'unreliable' left. The TUC, while drawing aside from organizational identification with the Labour Party and continuing to represent workers of all political persuasions, nevertheless in combating the NMM excluded the operation of the Communist Party as a distinct directing group within the trade union movement. It saw some of the continental movements divided by confessional and ideological differences, and was convinced by its own experience and that of the AITUC that such divisions were destructive of trade unionism. This conviction inspired its fruitless attempts to reach some accommodation with the Russians in the 1920s and 1930s and the wartime hope that the alliance against Nazi Germany might favour a renewed effort to establish a world international in which conflicting ideologies might be subordinated to a common trade union interest. The Soviet Union and the USA had abandoned their isolationist attitudes and joined the United Nations. If all were represented in the ILO there was scope for co-operation at Geneva, and if the normal rules and conventions of international organization were observed in the WFTU, the days of Comintern and RILU intervention in domestic affairs could pass into memory.

This did not mean that the TUC had no concept of trade unionism, though it was seldom made explicit and Lozovsky had found it indefinable. In all its actions the TUC demonstrated its rejection of revolutionary methods and displayed certain characteristics: it depended on the representation of workers by unions controlled by their members, which required freedom of expression and of association; its methods were persuasion, negotiation, and, where possible, voluntary agreement, which required recognition by employers; it was primarily industrial, but demanded and used political means of expression. The underlying concept was essentially political, derived from a liberal philosophy which recognized individual rights in a pluralist society: asserting that a worker had a right to a say in the determination of his wages and conditions of employment, that this right could be made effective by combinations, which in turn had their rights to freedom of action within the law and the opportunity to make their own distinctive contribution to that law and to the institutions reflecting and regulating social life. Although in its work for the dependencies the TUC was addressing itself to a series of practical problems as they arose, in sum, it was trying to project a whole ethos into the colonial scene.

The question naturally arises whether this ethos was relevant to the interests of the overseas trade unions in the conditions in which they had to work. The distinctive feature of their situation was the outside control of their countries. Though at varying stages along the line of development, none of them enjoyed full parliamentary democracy, and to the extent that their political institutions were in this respect defective, they could not enjoy all the means of association, expression and representation that were open to British workers. But British workers had not always enjoyed them, and had begun to organize even before they had the franchise. So did the workers of India and the colonies, raising in consequence the same problems for the state as had arisen in Britain. Left to themselves, the overseas unions might have found different solutions, but in practice they asked for British trade union rights, just as they asked for votes, parliaments and responsible governments. The remarkable outcome, that they gained the trade union rights first, was due not only to their own efforts but also to those of the British Labour movement.

Their principal gain, in this preliminary period of the TUC's effort to assist them, lay in the changes in laws and institutions – the legislation which recognized the status of trade unions, the provision for conciliation and arbitration and the immunities which protected trade union organization in the event of disputes, and the establishment of effective labour departments whose functions extended beyond protective supervision of labour conditions to the positive duty to help and consult trade unions. Such changes, spelt out in detail in the reports of the Whitley Commission in India and of the West India Royal Commission, presupposed the existence – actual or potential – of unions functioning on British lines. In India, the assumption that British trade unionism provided a basic model was challenged by the contrary view expressed by the Communist Party. The fact that this did not prevail, even after independence, and that Communist-led unions have continued to operate in a democratic pluralist state, suggests that the British model, considered in its historical setting, was not inappropriate. A second challenge came from the political use of industrial action in the nationalist struggle. The TUC had not achieved any meeting of minds with the National Congress leaders, and might well encounter non-co-operative nationalist forces elsewhere. Citrine's plans for the West Indies show that he hoped to do there what he would have liked to do in India – provide a continuing source of information and support to the unions. He was able to start this work in the West Indies because there was no effective Communist movement and because the nationalist politicians did not use the weapon of civil disobedience.

The West Indies were almost a special case. The dominant cultural influences were British and American; there were· some religious

revival and protest movements, but none comparable to the Bengal
agitation of the first decade of the century, or to Mahatma Gandhi's call
for regeneration through satyagraha. The colonial governments were
incompetent and reactionary, but they do not appear to have
presented that face of overweening arrogance and power that made the
Government of India a standing insult to the nationalist leaders. The
West Indian politicians were wedded to the parliamentary system in
which they had already begun to share, their main support was amongst
employed workers rather than peasants, and – by contrast with the
Whitley Commission, which was partially boycotted – their response
to the Royal Commission acted as a catalyst to both the political and
trade union movements. Partly because of Citrine's conduct, the
unions turned almost unanimously to the TUC, so that the changes in
Colonial Office labour policy, the establishment of permanent trade
unions, and the TUC's recognition of its own responsibility, went hand
in hand. The West Indian trade union leaders shared to an exceptional
degree the British Labour view of politics and of trade unionism. They
had some counterparts in Africa, but there the social system did not
appear to present a favourable environment for political democracy or
trade unionism – so far, nobody knew what opportunity might yield.
As for the East, the Chinese experience left no grounds for confidence
and Malaya was a closed book. As the war ended, the TUC had many
hopes and plans, but so far they were based on very limited
acquaintance with the colonial scene.

It would also have to direct attention to the purely practical
problems of how to give assistance to the unions. The TUC had had
some successes in representations to the India Office and the Colonial
Office; the Purcell/Hallsworth mission to India and Pugh's and
Citrine's visits to the West Indies had resulted in analyses of the
situations in which the unions were working, and consequent advice to
the unions; and a start had been made with supplying information and
preparing educational assistance, though both had been curtailed by
the war. On the other hand, Citrine's original proposals to send
representatives to work on the spot for a substantial period in India and
the West Indies had been frustrated. This was likely to have been the
most promising venture, but also the most expensive and the most
difficult to carry out. The success of all these methods would in the last
resort hinge on the capacity of the unions to make full use of any
assistance that was given.

Underlying every problem was that of organization, in the colonies
and in Britain. This had been clearly demonstrated by the TUC's own
failure in the early 1930s. Setting aside its preoccupation with India
and with the IFTU and the disasters befalling the TUC's trade union
friends in Europe, it still seems tragic that the period of greatest

suffering in the West Indies coincided with the political defeat of the Labour Party in Britain and the fall in trade union membership and resources which accompanied the economic slump. In the absence of pressure from the West Indies, there was little reason why the TUC should have diverted its attention from the hardships of its own membership when the first disturbances occurred, but the muddle over the trade union legislation in Trinidad – though largely attributable to the secrecy surrounding the Passfield despatch – was a serious lapse. The TWMA did ask for help, and it was in position to influence the other islands. The Commonwealth Labour Conferences, which had brought the West Indians to London and could have been useful in the 1930s, were allowed to lapse. These failures in organization were remedied after 1937, but they also indicate a certain failure in vision.

This study is a record of the decisions and activities of an organization. Within it, there were different interests and different attitudes, but there were no significant pressures from the membership to propel the leaders into the colonial field. Whatever was done was done at the initiative of a few men at the top. Why did they do it? Why did Citrine, in the middle of the war, exert himself to get Grant out of gaol? Why did Bevin, as Minister of Labour speaking to a conference of the Scottish TUC in December 1940, when the country had just by a hair's breadth escaped invasion, devote part of his address on trade unionists and the war to India? He intended, he told them, to stop the use of the word 'lascar' in any document, and British workmen and everybody else must stop referring to Indians as 'coolies', just as he, in negotiating union agreements, had refused to allow his members to be called 'labourers'.[1] It is a serious error to overlook the element of plain indignation at injustice and the strength, in the trade union movement, of a genuine spirit of fraternity which encompassed not only the great issues of the day but the small details that adversely affected workers' lives. The charge made by the Comintern that the British trade union leaders, allies of the bourgeoisie, were trying to control the Indian and colonial trade unions in the interests of British imperialism is, in the opinion of this writer, ridiculous, and proved to be so by the record and by our knowledge of the characters of the men concerned.

Unlike the Comintern leaders, they did not proceed from a theoretical analysis of imperialism. There had been such analyses in the British Labour movement, but the views of the trade union leaders on this general question were shaped in a Labour Party which accepted as read that empires were responsible for international rivalries and wars and for the economic exploitation and political repression of subject peoples. But it was a parliamentary party, with opportunities to seek mitigation of these evils even when in opposition, and to begin to remedy them when in government. The key figure behind the scenes in the Labour Party, Buxton, had no doubt that the 'old sterile stage of mere criticism and the repudiation of all responsibility' was past. 'It had the advantage,' he wrote, 'of saving us the whole trouble of thinking ... Its professors were made to feel virtuous and heroic; but they did no good whatever to the subject peoples.' He therefore embarked on 20 years of organizing Members of Parliament to put pressure on ministers, dealing at one end of the scale with the great issues of the paramountcy of African interests in East Africa and the need to ensure that the Protectorates in South Africa were not transferred to the Union, and at the other with minor matters, such as the inspection of camps used by migrant workers, which affected the sections of the population with which the TUC was concerned. 'These millions are dumb,' he told the House of Commons, 'and if anyone speaks for them, it must be we.'[2]

At the time (December 1929), African workers and farmers were, in Westminster terms, dumb, and their countries had none of the structures required to sustain independent states. Ten years later, Citrine, half-way round his tour of the impoverished West Indian islands, with their half-developed legislatures and largely official governments, wrote 'I have seen and heard of so many injustices in these islands that I can scarcely contain myself ... If we can do no better for these poor, simple and patient folk than we are doing at present, I for one do not wish to retain them in the British Empire. Let them have self-government entirely *or go to some other country which may try to do better for them*'[3] He saw it as his task to propose reforms which could be carried out for the benefit of these West Indian workers and to gain the General Council's support for a TUC programme to help them build their own organizations. In Buxton and Citrine we see what Gomes called 'colonial paternalism at its best'. Their attitudes were paternal in the sense that those of the 'outsiders' in the Indian trade union movement or the politicians of the Barbados Democratic League were paternal, and colonial in the sense that they were prepared to use the apparatus of imperial rule. However, no one in the Labour Party was impressed by the pomp and ceremony of that apparatus – Woolf in particular had a strong distaste for it – and Labour Party and TUC policy, if paternal, acknowledged the fact that children grow up.

Before 1945 no colony was equipped with the parliamentary institutions and the developed social services and trade unions required for the kind of independent state that the Labour Party and the TUC envisaged for the future. India already had parliaments, Indian Ministers and civil servants at the highest levels, armed forces that had proved their outstanding competence during the war, and trade unions that were fully capable of looking after themselves. In the

1945 election the Labour Party pledged itself to promote 'the advancement of India to responsible self-government' – unqualified – that is to say, independence. By comparison, Ceylon was just behind, and the West Indian colonies were already set on the same road; the African and Pacific colonies had scarcely started. But what was the end of the road, previously travelled by Canada, Australia, New Zealand and South Africa? Certainly not the severance of all existing relationships, but their preservation in the Commonwealth, still, at that time, symbolically held together by allegiance to the Crown. Two years later, when India became independent, the Labour government recognized the right of Burma, which was not prepared to continue that allegiance, to independence outside the Commonwealth. Subsequently, the circle was squared when India became a republic but was not asked to leave, and was followed in due course by many of the other dependencies.

The TUC did not make separate pronouncements on these political issues. Citrine was concerned to see colonial workers organized and represented in the WFTU. Like Gompers in 1919,[4] he saw the international federation as a forum in which labour problems of an international character could be identified and tackled, not as a political platform. Independence would bring the right to representation in the ILO: meanwhile, the TUC had shown itself willing to provide colonial representation at Geneva through its own delegation. The TUC was already accustomed to co-operating with the trade unions in the existing Dominions and in India, and the concept of the Commonwealth, with its freedom of movement for British subjects and its common effort in both wars, was deeply embedded in the mind of the British public. The question was not whether the links should be maintained, but whether the colonies, as and when they became self-governing, would wish to remain in the family, and if so, how they could be accommodated.

It was obvious that the interests of British workers could be affected if the colonies became independent states with the power to control their own economies and build their own industries, but this was not yet a pressing problem. Citrine had encountered it in the price of sugar and the manufacture of cement in the West Indies, and had put the interests of West Indian workers first; but the TUC represented British workers, and it would be a strange Commonwealth in which theirs were the only interests that should be disregarded. There was a potential source of conflict here, but in 1945 the TUC leaders do not appear to have been looking beyond the Colonial Development and Welfare Acts, which might benefit both colonial and British workers. Certainly they had no proposals to maintain the economic interests of Great Britain within a closed Commonwealth system, which past experience had always demonstrated would not in any case have been acceptable to the older Dominions or to India.

Bevin had recognized the interaction of British and Asian economic interests as early as 1919,[5] and his views widened with experience. After his intervention at Congress in 1937, he played no direct part in the development of the TUC's colonial policy. First, he was ill, and partly as a recuperative measure he went by sea to attend a conference on the Commonwealth in Australia in 1938, calling in at Bombay on the return journey. In May 1940 he became Minister of Labour and in October was taken into the War Cabinet. In 1945 he was appointed Foreign Secretary in Attlee's government. Thus his experience was more extensive than Citrine's, though he never had the opportunity given to Citrine to visit and study any colonial territory in depth. Citrine was a man of ideas, working them out in terms of organization. Bevin saw visions, on a world scale. They were not always consistent, and he can be seen over the years searching for the appropriate framework in which to translate them into reality.

He disliked empires, and as Minister of Labour in 1941 urged upon the Secretary of State for India his view that the time to establish Dominion status for India had come, 'to remove from all doubt the question of Indian freedom at the end of the war'.[6] But the links would remain. Referring primarily to the Dominions after his return from Australia, he wrote, 'Empires, as we have known them, must become a thing of the past,' but the Commonwealth was of great value to the world, capable of replacing the old conception of imperialism – with its tribute to a mother-country – by a balanced economy. How much better it would be for the world if Europe were a Commonwealth with a unified economy; certainly the collective body of British sovereign states should not be allowed to drift into disruption, but must hold together, possibly with an Assembly which could explain its purposes to the world. These would include the maintenance of democracy, the promotion of the human rights of labour, and a demonstration that it did not intend to follow a narrow exclusive policy in defence or trade. The Assembly could work out principles and suggestions which could help in the search for solutions to internal problems, such as the Irish boundary and the future of India, and 'a common contribution could be made towards the development of the Colonial Empire both in relation to defence, trade, and the recognition of equality'.[7]

Here, already visible in February 1939, is the seed which blossomed in 1950 into the Colombo Plan. Ill, and advised that he should not travel,[8] Bevin insisted on attending a meeting of Commonwealth ministers in Ceylon, which produced the Colombo Plan for South-East Asia. This was a marked improvement on the concepts underlying the Colonial Development and Welfare Acts: it covered independent

India, Pakistan and Ceylon as well as the remaining British dependencies in South-East Asia, it brought in the old Dominions, and it envisaged an interchange between the recipients as well as the donors, through a Commonwealth Technical Assistance Committee with headquarters in Colombo.

The emphasis was on technical assistance, which included the sharing of expertise on labour administration, industrial relations and trade union education, in which the TUC in the postwar years was called upon to play a part. Citrine had started this idea in the Colonial Office, and it was given a characteristic expansion in Bevin's plan to bring Indian industrial workers for training in Britain during the war. Not only did they improve their skills, but they were taken to visit union branches as an integral part of their work. As Minister of Labour, Bevin pushed this scheme through the War Cabinet against the opposition of the India Office and the Viceroy,[9] and in 1945 he was able to tell the Labour Party Conference that just under 1,000 trainees had been through the course. He welcomed the industrialization of India, which would help to get rid of poverty and the moneylender, but other workers also had to be taken into account: no one was so poor as the peasant; no one had lower purchasing power. It was no use to talk about finding markets unless they were in a position to have a proper exchange of commodities. If British industrial workers were to maintain a decent standard of life, they must be just to the peasant.[10]

A much more coherent view of colonial needs was beginning to emerge. The West India Royal Commission had come to the conclusion that social and economic problems could not be entirely separated from those of constitutional advance, if only because the demand for a larger voice in the management of their affairs represented a growing political consciousness amongst the people which made it doubtful whether any schemes of social reform would be completely successful unless they were accompanied by the largest possible measure of constitutional development.[11] The truth of this had been demonstrated by the Indian nationalist response to the Whitley Commission. Conversely, the adoption of a policy of colonial development recognized that self-government in poverty-stricken, neglected territories would be a cruel deception of the people. This must be taken into account, as Bevin pointed out, when economic planning was considered in Great Britain itself. And the new Labour government intended to plan the economy.

However, the shape of the colonial empire would change. India had never been part of it, but Ceylon had, and was now close to independence. Constitutional development in the West Indies was really a matter for local negotiation. West Indians already held most of the posts in the civil service, a new university was planned, the

Development and Welfare Organization was in place and was a potential forerunner of federation, and – by contrast with the Mediterranean and the Middle East – there were no major defence issues involved. Even if there had been, the war had demonstrated that *in extremis* the protection of the Caribbean was largely a matter for North America. In future, the colonial empire would be largely an African empire. The West Indies were going through a period of conscious nation-building. Would, or could, they be followed by the African territories?

In 1943 the Labour Party Conference adopted a policy statement, *The Colonies: The Labour Party's Post-War Policy for the African and Pacific Colonies*, which revised previous publications by the Advisory Committee on Imperial Questions and was much influenced by Creech Jones.[12] Here were colonies where indigenous institutions were largely tribal, and discussions on constitutional development were not about universal suffrage and responsible ministers, but about direct and indirect rule, the position of chiefs in local government, the entry of Africans into the civil service, and the paramountcy of African interests in areas of European settlement. Self-government would not come 'for a considerable time'. Much of the statement was devoted to land policy, co-operatives and education, but the expansion of industry was envisaged, notably in the processing of local raw materials. There were also mining and transport to be taken into consideraation. In general, industry should be gradually developed under control, 'the object being to combine such development with deliberate prevention of those evils which accompanied it everywhere in Europe'. In this context, labour policy would become increasingly important. The 'protective' phase had not yet passed, but the new phase was also covered in some detail. In sum, the statement envisaged a slow process of nation-building from the grass roots, with political institutions developing in parallel with social and economic change.

In 1945, then, the TUC had to look forward to a period of much greater difficulty in the colonies. In the 'paternal' period, the essential legislative measures to protect the powerless worker and to legitimize trade union organization had been worked out. They still had to be applied in detail, but this was largely the responsibility of government machinery. The problems of trade union organization would require greater understanding and knowledge than the TUC yet possessed, despite all that had been learnt in India and the West Indies. What would African workers expect from their trade unions? Would they give their loyalties to them, not sporadically, but continuously for the periods required to build organization? Would they allow politicians to lead or to manipulate their unions? How would they regard the government trade union advisers, or emissaries from the TUC? What part would be played by the Indian workers in East Africa? By the 'European' workers in the Rhodesias? The questions were legion, and would not be answered by general statements from Transport House.

The answers, as always, would have to be found in organization, in the colonies, and in the TUC itself. The work in the West Indies would continue and a new sphere of activity would open up in Malaya; new issues would arise in the ILO; old issues would re-surface in the trade union internationals, and their part in colonial advancement would have to be determined. The personnel would change: Albert Thomas and Buxton were dead, Bevin and Creech Jones in government, Citrine went to the Coal Board in 1946. They left behind a sound foundation on which a new generation of trade union leaders, in Britain, in the internationals, and in the colonies, could build.

Notes

Chapter 1

1 Albert Gomes, *Through a Maze of Colour* (Trinidad: Key Caribbean Publications, 1974), p. 42.
2 Sir Vincent Tewson: 1925–31 Secretary, TUC Organization Department; 1931–46 Assistant General Secretary; 1946–60 General Secretary.
3 Ben Tillett: 1887 founder, Tea Workers' and General Labourers' Union; 1889 Secretary, Sea Operatives' and General Labourers' Union (later Dock, Wharf, Riverside and General Workers' Union, known as Dockers' Union); 1923–30 Secretary, Political and International Department, TGWU; 1892–4 member of TUC Parliamentary Committee, 1921–31 member of TUC General Council, 1929 President of TUC Congress.
4 Ernest Bevin: 1913 assistant national organizer, 1920 Assistant General Secretary, Dockers' Union; 1922–46 General Secretary, Transport and General Workers' Union; 1925–40 member of TUC General Council, 1937 President of Congress; May 1940 Minister of Labour, 1945–51 Secretary of State for Foreign Affairs.
5 Walter Citrine: 1914 first full-time District Secretary, 1920 Assistant General Secretary, Electrical Trades Union; January 1924 Assistant General Secretary, 1926–46 General Secretary, TUC.
6 Lord Citrine, *Men and Work* (London: Hutchinson, 1964), p. 32.
7 Alan Bullock, *The Life and Times of Ernest Bevin*, Vol. II: *Minister of Labour* (London: Heinemann, 1967), p. 206.
8 Citrine Papers: *Diary*, 26–7 December 1938.
9 *Labour International Handbook* (London: Labour Research Department, 1921), p. 202.

Chapter 2

1 Charles Bowerman: 1892–1906 General Secretary, London Society of Compositors; 1897–1923 Member of Parliamentary Committee, 1911–23 Secretary, TUC; 1906 MP for Deptford.
2 W. J. Bolton: 1903 clerical assistant, TUC; 1921–42 secretary, TUC International Department.
3 *Congress Report*, 1916, *passim*.
4 Harry Gosling: 1895–1921 General Secretary, Amalgamated Society of Watermen, Lightermen and Bargemen; 1921 President, Transport and General Workers' Union; 1908–23 Member of Parliamentary Committee and General Council, 1916 President of Congress; 1923 MP for Whitechapel, 1924 Minister of Transport.
5 *Congress Report*, 1917, *passim*.

6   ibid.; Parliamentary Committee *Minutes*, 23 March, 18 April, 1917; Record of Deputation, TUC File 712.5.

7   *Labour International Handbook* (1921), pp. 181–182.

8   B. C. Roberts, *The Trades Union Congress 1868–1921* (London: Allen & Unwin, 1958), p. 89.

9   *International Trades Union Review*, no.1 (London: Trades Union Congress, August 1918).

10 Max Beer, 'Some Reminiscences of the London International Congress', *Trade Union Unity*, Vol. I, no.7 (October 1925).

11 *Congress Report*, 1895, 1896, *passim*.

12 *Congress Report*, 1904, *passim*.

13 John Price, *The International Labour Movement* (London: Oxford University Press, 1945), pp. 16–17.

14 Walter Schevenels, *Forty Five Years: International Federation of Trade Unions 1901–1945*. (Brussels: IFTU Board of Trustees, 1956).

15 Tom Mann: 1896 co-founder, Ship, Dock and River Workers' International (precursor of ITF); 1919–21 Secretary, Amalgamated Engineering Union; 1921 member of Executive, Red International of Labour Unions.

16 *Labour International Handbook* (1921), p. 198 (Emphasis added).

17 Patrick Renshaw, *The Wobblies: The Story of Syndicalism in the United States* (London: Eyre & Spottiswoode, 1967), p. 168.

18 *International Trades Union Review*, no.1 (August 1918).

19 Henry Broadhurst: 1874–1879, 1893–94 member of Parliamentary Committee; 1875–84, 1886–89 secretary of Parliamentary Committee.

20 G. D. H. Cole and Raymond Postgate, *The Common People, 1746–1938* (London: Methuen, 1938), pp. 394–5.

21 Winston S. Churchill, *My Early Life* (London: Collins, 1959), pp. 228–9.

22 *Congress Report*, 1904.

23 Herbert Tracey, ed., *The Book of the Labour Party*, Vol. I (London: Caxton, 1925), pp. 121–2.

24 Roberts, *The TUC*, pp. 191, 229–30.

25 Arthur Henderson: 1892 organizing district delegate, Friendly Society of Ironfounders; 1904 elected to Parliament with support of Ironfounders; 1911–34 Secretary, Labour Party; 1915 President, Board of Education; December 1916–11 August 1917 member of War Cabinet without portfolio; 1924 Home Secretary; 1929–31 Foreign Secretary.

26 Tracey, *The Book of the Labour Party*, Vol. I, p. 119.

27 2 March by the Russian calendar. Russia adopted the western calendar on 1 February 1918.

28 Jane Degras, ed., *The Communist International 1919–43. Documents*, Vol. I. (London: Frank Cass, 1971), p. 1.

29 David Marquand, *Ramsay MacDonald* (London: Jonathan Cape, 1977), pp. 200, 209.

30 Will Thorne: 1889 General Secretary, National Union of Gas Workers and General Labourers. 1924 General Secretary, National Union of

General and Municipal Workers; 1894–1933 member of Parliamentary Committee and General Council, 1912 President of Congress; 1906 Member of Parliament for West Ham.

31 Parliamentary Committee *Minutes*, 30 May 1917; *Congress Report*, 1917.

32 Parliamentary Committee *Minutes*, 6 June 1917; *Congress Report*, 1917.

33 Tracey, *The Book of the Labour Party*, Vol. I, pp. 198–9.

34 Parliamentary Committee *Minutes*, 19 July 1917.

35 Parliamentary Committee *Minutes*, 25 July 1917, with correspondence Bowerman/Henderson 25 July, J. Middleton/Bowerman 26 July, 1917.

36 David Lloyd George, *War Memoirs*, Vol. II (London: Odhams Press, 1938), p. 1132.

37 Tracey, *The Book of the Labour Party*, Vol. I, p. 199; Parliamentary Committee *Minutes*, 7 August 1917; *Congress Report*, 1917.

38 Robert Smillie: member of Parliamentary Committee and General Council 1917, 1920–26; 1923 Member of Parliament.

39 J. Havelock Wilson: 1896 Co-founder, Ship, Dock and River Workers' International and active in forming ITF; 1889–97, 1918 member of Parliamentary Committee; 1892 Member of Parliament.

40 *Congress Report*, 1917.

41 Parliamentary Committee *Minutes*, 19 July, 27 August, 4 September, 6 September, 1917.

42 Fred Bramley: 1912 organizing secretary, Furnishing Trades Association; 1916–17 member of Parliamentary Committee; February 1918 assistant, June 1919 assistant secretary, September 1923–October 1925 General Secretary, TUC.

43 Sidney Webb: 1881–91 clerk (Class I), Colonial Office; 1915 member Labour Party Executive representing Fabian Society; 1922 Member of Parliament; January–November 1924 President of Board of Trade; June 1929–August 1931 (as Lord Passfield) Secretary of State for the Colonies.

44 David Lloyd George, *War Memoirs*, Vol. II, pp. 1492, 1510–17; Tracey, *The Book of the Labour Party*, Vol. I, p. 206.

45 Tracey, *The Book of the Labour Party*, Vol. I, pp. 207–8; *Congress Report*, 1918, *passim*.

46 Arthur Henderson, *Memorandum on the International Peace Congress*. Undated, apparently prepared for a meeting of the TUC/Labour International Joint Committee held on 17 December 1918. The minutes of this meeting have not been preserved in the TUC, but it is recorded that they were endorsed by the Parliamentary Committee on 18 December.

47 James T. Shotwell, ed., *The Origins of the International Labour Organization*, *Vol. I* (New York: Columbia University Press, 1934), pp. 60–61, 64, 66.

48 Margaret Cole, *Makers of the Labour Movement* (London: Longman, 1948), p. 253.

49 Roberts, *TUC*, pp. 298, 262–65.

50 W. A. Appleton, *Trade Unions, Their Past, Present and Future* (London: Philip Allen, 1925), p. 121.

51 In this context, the term almost certainly means the Dominions.

52 *International Trades Union Review*, no.1 (August 1918).

53 Tom Shaw: 1892 official of Colne Workers' Association, later first Secretary of Northern Counties Textile Trades Federation; 1911–38 Secretary, International Textile Association; 1918 Member of Parliament for Preston; 1924 Minister of Labour; 1929–31 Minister of War.

54 *Congress Report*, 1918, *passim*.

55 Parliamentary Committee *Minutes*, 8 October 1918.

56 Shotwell, *The Origins of the International Labour Organization*, Vol. I, p. xx.

57 Parliamentary Committee *Minutes*, 17 May, 6 September, 1 December, 1918.

58 Parliamentary Committee *Minutes*, 8 January, 20 January, 1919; *International Trades Union Review*, no. 3. (July 1919).

59 Degras, *The Communist International. Documents*, Vol. I, pp. 1–5.

60 David Lloyd George, *War Memoirs*, Vol. II, p. 1904.

61 G. D. H. Cole, *Socialist Thought*, Vol. IV, Pt I. (London: Macmillan, 1958), p. 294.

62 *International Trades Union Review* (January 1921).

63 Parliamentary Committee *Minutes*, 11 June 1919; *Congress Report*, 1919.

64 *International Trades Union Review* (July 1919).

65 Walter Schevenels, *Forty Five Years*, p. 79.

66 Parliamentary Committee *Minutes*, 8, 20, 21, January, 12 March, 10 April, 11 June, 1919.

67 *Congress Report*, 1919.

68 Walter Schevenels, *Forty Five Years*, pp. 118–121.

69 Price, *International Labour Movement*, p. 55.

70 *Congress Report*, 1919, 1920.

71 Rt Hon. G. N. Barnes, MP: 1906–7 member of Parliamentary Committee, December 1916 Minister of Pensions; August 1917 Minister of Labour, succeeding Henderson as member of War Cabinet.

72 J. H. Thomas, MP: 1916 General Secretary, National Union of Railwaymen; 1917–23, 1924–28 member of Parliamentary Committee and General Council, 1920 President of Congress; 1909 Member of Parliament; 1924, August–November 1931, November 1935–May 1936, Secretary of State for the Colonies, 1930 Secretary of State for Dominion Affairs.

73 J. Stuart-Bunning: 1916–20 member of Parliamentary Committee, 1919 President of Congress.

74 Robert Shirkie: 1918–1919 member of Parliamentary Committee.

75 The following details are drawn from Shotwell, *International Labour Organization*, pp. 119–125, which gives a fuller account than the delegates' reports submitted to the Parliamentary Committee and to the 1919 Congress.

76 Parliamentary Committee *Minutes*, 3 February 1919; *Congress Report*, 1919.

77 Shotwell, *International Labour Organization*, pp. 186–8, 212, 217–8, 267, 270–71, 288, 290–3.

78   Margaret Bondfield: 1898 assistant secretary, Shop Assistants' Union, 1914 organizing secretary, National Federation of Women Workers, 1921 chief woman officer, National Union of General Workers; 1917–24, 1925–29 member of Parliamentary Committee and General Council, 1923–January 1924 Chairman of General Council; 1923 Member of Parliament for Northampton; January 1924 Parliamentary Secretary, Ministry of Labour, 1929–31 Minister of Labour.

79   Parliamentary Committee *Minutes*, 14 August, 11, 12, 25 September 1919, 15 June 1921; *Congress Report*, 1920.

80   Shotwell, *International Labour Organization*, pp. 171–5, 444.

81   N. M. Joshi: 1920 assistant secretary, 1925 joint general secretary, 1927 General Secretary, All-India Trade Union Congress; 1919, 1921, 1922, 1925, 1934–37, 1945, 1947, Indian Workers' Delegate to International Labour Conference; 1922–34 deputy member, 1934–44, 1946–48 member, ILO Governing Body.

82   V. B. Karnik, *N. M. Joshi, Servant of India.* (Bombay: United Asia Publications, 1972), pp. 20–22, 28–31, 33; *International Trades Union Review*, no. 8, July 1921.

83   Parliamentary Committee *Minutes*, 8, 9 October 1919.

84   S. A. Dange, *AITUC: Fifty Years, Documents*, Vol. I. (New Delhi: All-India Trade Union Congress, 1973), pp. xxxv, lxviii, xxxvi, 3.

85   *Congress Report*, 1920, pp. 137–8, 140; *International Trades Union Review*, no. 10, January 1922, p. 11.

86   *Congress Report*, 1919, *passim*.

87   Parliamentary Committee *Minutes*, 14 August 1919.

88   B. P. Wadia, *Aims of the Labour Movement in India.* Articles reprinted from *Shama'a*, October 1920. Published by Miss M. Chattopadhyay, Madras, pp. 3–5.

89   Interview with G. Shelvapathy Chetty, 15 January 1973.

90   B. Shiva Rao, *The Industrial Worker in India* (London: Allen & Unwin, 1939). pp. 13–14, 19.

Chapter 3

1   *Congress Report*, 1920. *Standing Orders.*

2   General Council *Minutes*, 5, 21 September, 4 October, 1920.

3   ibid., 28 February 1923; *Congress Report*, 1923.

4   Lord Citrine, *Men and Work*, pp. 79, 97.

5   General Council *Minutes*, 27 February 1924.

6   John Bromley: 1921–35 member of General Council; 1932 President of Congress.

7   Parliamentary Committee *Minutes*, 20 July 1921.

8   *Labour Party Conference Report* October 1924; *Congress Report*, 1923.

9   The Minutes of the International Joint Committee filed by the TUC are incomplete, but those that remain, and reference to the Minutes of the Parliamentary Committee and of the Joint Executives make it clear that its meetings ran continuously from 17 October 1917 to the Joint International Committee established under the Co-ordination Scheme.

10 International Joint Committee *Minutes*, 17 November 1921.

11 General Council *Minutes*, 5 October 1921. This committee was subsequently known in the TUC as the International Committee.

12 General Council *Minutes*, 4 January 1922; Joint Executives *Minutes* 4 January 1922.

13 *Memoranda on International Labour Legislation: The Economic Structure of the League of Nations*. With an Introduction by Sidney Webb and the text of the Berne *Labour Charter* (London: Labour Party, undated).

14 *Congress Report*, 1923.

15 Eglantyne Buxton, informal note, 1972. MSS *Brit. Emp. s405. Buxton 5/3.1*, and *passim*. Oxford University Colonial Records Project (OUCRP).

16 Harold Snell: 1922–31 Member of Parliament; 1926 member of British Guiana Constitutional Committee; 1931 Parliamentary Under-secretary of State for India.

17 Joint International Department Advisory Committee on International Questions *Minutes*, Imperial Questions Sub-Committee, *Minutes*. *passim*.

18 Shapurji Saklatvala: employed at London office of Tata Iron and Steel Company till 1926; 1905 came to England; 1910–20 member of ILP, 1921 member of CPGB; founder member of Workers' Welfare League of India; 1922–23, 1924–29 Member of Parliament. Saklatvala became ineligible for appointment by the Labour Party to TUC/Labour Party joint committees after the 1924 Labour Party Conference's decision to exclude Communists from membership was implemented. His last attendance at the Imperial Advisory Joint Sub-Commitee was on 16 July 1925.

19 Leonard Woolf, *The Journey not the Arrival Matters*. (London: Hogarth Press, 1969), p. 159.

20 General Council *Minutes*, 27 June 1923; International Committee *Minutes*, 11 July 1923; *Congress Report*, 1923.

21 General Council *Minutes*, 26 September, 31 October, 1923; Joint Executives *Minutes*, 27 September 1923.

22 Finance Committee *Minutes*, 5 November 1923, 21 January 1924, 14 April, 23 June, 1924.

23 Functions Committee *Minutes*, 19 November 1924 – 21 January 1926; *Report from the Chairman and Secretaries of the Labour Party Executive and the TUC General Council to the Functions Committee* 21 January 1926; General Council *Minutes*, 24 September 1924, 27 January 1926.

24 Letter from Lord Citrine to author, 28 August 1978.

25 A. A. Purcell: 1898 General Secretary, Amalgamated Society of French Polishers, 1910 Chief Organizer, National Amagamated Furnishing Trades Association (NAFTA); 1929 full-time secretary, Manchester and Salford Trades Council; 1919–27 member of Parliamentary Committee and General Council, 1924 President of Congress; 1924–27 President, IFTU; 1923–29 Member of Parliament.

26 International Committee *Minutes*, 17 July 1924; *Congress Report*, 1924, p. 319.

27 International Committee *Minutes*, 12 March 1925.

28 H. W. Lee: 1885–1911 secretary, Social Democratic Federation; 1913–24 editor, SDF journal *Justice*.

29 Gillies/Citrine, undated note; note dated 15 January 1926.

30 Finance Committee *Minutes*, 4 May 1925.

31 Interview with Sir Vincent Tewson 7 October 1980.

32 The Joint Advisory Committee *Minutes* 16 April 1924 to 13 January 1926 show that Woolf made 15 attendances, Tillett four and R. Williams one. The *Minutes* of the Labour Party's Imperial Advisory Committee 30 October 1929 to 13 March 1940 show that on one occasion, 13 July 1938, a member of the TUC staff, H. B. Kemmis, attended. There was no trade union representation on this Labour Party committee.

33 Margaret Cole, ed., *The Webbs and Their Work* (London: Frederick Muller, 1949), p. 175.

34 J. H. Thomas, *My Story* (London: Hutchinson, 1937), p. 78.

35 Leonard Woolf, *Downhill all the Way* (London: Hogarth Press, 1967), p. 223; *The Empire in Africa: Labour's Policy* (London: Labour Party, undated).

36 *Congress Report*, 1925, pp. 553–4.

37 C. Delisle Burns, 'The British Commonwealth of Nations', *The Book of the Labour Party*, Vol. III, p. 82. Delisle Burns was on the staff of the TUC/Labour Party Joint Research and Information Department.

38 Joint International Committee *Minutes*, 27 March, 13 June, 1923; General Council *Minutes*, 20 January 1922, 12 December 1923; Joint Executives *Minutes*, 26 July 1923; TUC/Labour Party circular 29 August 1924; *Congress Report*, 1924, pp. 263–4.

39 E. L. Poulton: 1908–29 General Secretary, National Union of Boot and Shoe Operatives; 1917–29 member of Parliamentary Committee and General Council, 1921 President of Congress; 1921–30 member of ILO Governing Body.

40 Joint Executives *Minutes*, 4 December 1924.

41 Pencilled notes by Citrine, 18 November 1929.

42 *Report of the First British Commonwealth Labour Conference, London, 27 July–1 August 1925*. (London: TUC and Labour Party, 1925).

43 George Lansbury: 1910–12, 1922–40 Member of Parliament; 1929–31 Minister of Works; 1931–35 leader of the Labour Party; 1913 director and editor of the *Daily Herald*.

44 Joint Advisory Committee on Imperial Questions *Minutes*, 2 December 1925, 13 January 1926.

45 *Report of First British Commonwealth Labour Conference*, p. 82.

46 C. V. Alert, *The Life and Work of Nathaniel Critchlow* [Hubert Nathaniel]. (Georgetown, 1949). *passim*.

47 Joint Executives *Minutes*, 26 November 1925.

48 Alfred Richards, *Trinidad Discovery Day Celebrations Souvenir, 1927*; Alderman Alfred Richards, *Mayoral Candidature 1936*. MSS Brit.Emp.s332, ACJ 25/5, 2. OUCRP.

49 Ron Ramdin, *From Chattel Slave to Wage Earner* (London: Martin Brian & O'Keefe, 1982), p. 114.

50   *Trinidad in Parliament – The Political, Social and Industrial Situation. Being a Report presented to the Executive Committee of the Trinidad Workingmen's Association (Incorporated), affiliated to the Labour Party of England, by their Delegate Mr W. Howard-Bishop Jnr, Official Organiser of the Association, of his mission in Great Britain during the month of August 1921.* (London: National Labour Press, 1921).

51   Richard Hart, 'Aspects of Early Caribbean Workers' Struggles', *Caribbean Societies*, Vol. I. Collected Seminar Papers no. 29 (London: University of London Institute of Commonwealth Studies, 1982), pp. 36, 39.

52   *Report by the Rt. Hon. F. O. Roberts MP on His Visit to the West Indies, 1926, with First West Indian Labour Conference, 11–14 January inclusive, 1926, Minutes,* prepared by the secretary to the Conference, C. C. Holmes; *Congress Report,* 1926.

53   *International Trades Union Review,* June 1920.

54   Parliamentary Committee *Minutes,* 10 May 1920.

55   *Congress Report,* 1920; International Joint Committee *Minutes* 10 November 1920.

56   Parliamentary Committee *Minutes,* 9 October 1919; *Minutes* of Meeting, 27 November 1919, of British Delegation to the International Congress at Geneva, 1920.

57   *International Trades Union Review,* January 1921.

58   *Congress Report,* 1923: 'Constitution of the Labour and Socialist International'.

59   Ronald Hingley, *Joseph Stalin: Man and Legend* (London: Hutchinson, 1974), pp. 136–7.

60   'Interim Report to the Trades Union Congress and the Labour Party', *International Trades Union Review,* June 1920.

61   *International Trades Union Review,* January 1921.

62   *Labour Magazine,* (London: TUC and Labour Party), no. 1, May 1922, p. 36.

63   Jane Degras, ed., *The Communist International 1919–1943. Documents,* Vol. I. (London: Frank Cass, 1971), p. 341.

64   *Labour Magazine,* no. 3, July 1922, pp. 122–3, 132.

65   Walter Kolarz, *Russia and Her Colonies* (London: George Philip, 1952), p. 226.

66   Marquand, *Ramsay MacDonald,* p. 261; James Ramsay MacDonald, *Wanderings and Excursions* (London: Jonathan Cape, 1932), pp. 143–52.

67   Hingley, *Stalin,* p. 131.

68   *Labour Magazine,* May 1922.

69   Joint International Committee *Minutes,* 29 May 1922.

70   Degras, *Communist International,* p. 351.

71   Memorandum, *The International Labour and Socialist Congress, Hamburg, May 1923* (Printed, undated).

72   I. Deutscher, *Stalin: A Political Biography* (London: Oxford University Press, 1949), pp. 184–5.

73   Walter Kolarz, *Russia and Her Colonies* pp. 13, 263–7, 271, 276, 278.

74　'Theses on the Agrarian Question Adopted by the Second Comintern Congress 4 August 1920'; Degras, *Communist International*, pp. 155–161; C. H. Ellis, *The Transcaspian Episode 1918–1919* (London: Hutchinson, 1963), *passim*; Peter Hopkirk, *Setting the East Ablaze* (London: John Murray, 1984), *passim*.

75　Hendrik Sneevliet: 1914 founded first Marxist organization in Asia, the Social Democratic Association of the Indies, which became the Communist Party of Indonesia (PKI) in 1920. Expelled by the Dutch in 1918, under his party name of Maring served as Comintern representative in the Netherlands and China. Subsequently left the Communist Party and led the Dutch Revolutionary Socialist Party. 1942 shot by the Germans in Amsterdam.

76　Edgar Snow, *Red Star over China* (London: Victor Gollancz, 1968), p. 336. (Emphasis added).

77　Helmut Gruber, *Soviet Russia Masters the Comintern* (New York: Anchor Books, 1974), pp. 297, 257, 341.

78　V. I. Lenin, *British Labour and British Imperialism* (London: Lawrence and Wishart, 1969). (Text based on 3rd Russian edition of Lenin's *Collected Works* and authorized by the Marx–Engels–Lenin Institute, Moscow), pp. 236–42, 264.

79　Nikolai Lenin, *'Left Wing' Communism: An Infantile Disorder* (London: Communist Party), p. 68. (Undated: apparently contemporary and used in this version in TUC office).

80　V. I. Lenin, *British Imperialism*, p. 219.

81　Degras, *Communist International*, Vol. I, pp. 165, 168–72, 258–63, 267–9.

82　*Labour Party Conference Reports*, June 1921, October 1924, October 1925.

83　'Theses on the Tactics in the Trade Union Movement', Fifth Comintern World Congress 1924, Gruber, *Comintern*, p. 146.

84　*Labour International Handbook*, p. 201.

85　J. T. Murphy, *The 'Reds' in Congress: Preliminary Report of the First World Congress of the Red International of Trade and Industrial Unions* (London: British Bureau of the Red International of Trade and Industrial Unions, 1921), pp. 21, 28, 12–17; A. S. Losovsky, *The World's Trade Union Movement* (London: National Minority Movement, 1925), p. 207.

86　*Report of the Executive Bureau to the Third Congress of the RILU 1924*, Chapter XII. (Typed copy.)

87　Losovsky, *World's Trade Union Movement*, p. 141.

88　ibid., p. 92.

89　'Programme of Action', Murphy, *Reds in Congress*, p. 26.

90　Losovsky, *World's Trade Union Movement*, pp. 202–10.

91　*Executive Bureau Report*, Chapters XII, XIV.

92　Francis Meynell, *My Lives* (London: The Bodley Head, 1971). pp. 120–123.

93　Labour Research Department: Originally an offshoot of the Fabian Society with G. D. H. Cole as honorary secretary, providing information for trade unions and co-operative societies. In 1919 it set up an international section under Rajani Palme Dutt, who became a foundation member of the Communist Party in 1920. The LRD then fell increasingly under communist influence and some of its staff left, but some unions continued to use its information services.

94 Dame Margaret Cole, *The Life of G. D. H. Cole* (London: Macmillan, 1971), p. 125; *Congress Report* 1929, p. 173.

95 Marquand, *MacDonald*, p. 382.

96 Daniel F. Calhoun, *The United Front: The TUC and the Russians, 1923-1928*. (Cambridge: Cambridge University Press, 1976), pp. 44, 28, 239.

97 Roderick Martin, *Communism and the British Trade Unions*. (London: Oxford University Press, 1969). pp. 1, 44.

98 General Council *Minutes*, 22 March 1927; Walter M. Citrine, *Democracy or Disruption* (London: TUC, 1928), pp. 16-21.

99 Report of Meeting of London Members of Parliamentary Committee and Delegates from Russian Trade Unions, 12 April 1920. *International Trades Union Review*, no. 5, June 1920, pp. 26-7.

100 *British Labour Delegation to Russia 1920: Report*. (London: TUC and Labour Party, 1920). pp. 63-71, 119-21.

101 *Congress Report* 1920, p. 260.

102 Robert Williams: 1920 Delegate to Congress for National Amalgamated Labourers' Union; secretary, National Transport Workers' Federation; delegate to ITF and IFTU; April 1921 expelled from British Communist Party; 1926-7 chairman, Labour Party Executive.

103 Murphy, *Reds in Congress*, p. 7; E. H. Carr, *The Bolshevik Revolution 1917-1923*, Vol. III, Part V. (London: Penguin Books, 1966), p. 209; Losovsky, *World's Trade Union Movement*, pp. 128-9.

104 *International Trades Union Review*, no. 6, September 1920, p. 24.

105 J. T. Murphy: shop stewards' leader, AEU, member of Provisional Committee of International Council of Trade and Industrial Unions, and of committees of RILU and of its British Bureau; founder member of British Communist Party, expelled 1932.

106 Harry Pollitt, *Serving My Time* (London: Lawrence & Wishart, 1940), pp. 127-8.

107 *International Trades Union Review*, June, July, October, 1921, January 1922.

108 *Report of International Trade Union Congress, Rome, 20-26 April 1922*. (Amsterdam: IFTU, 1923), p. 44.

109 *Congress Report*, 1924, p. 249.

110 Degras, *Communist International*, Vol. I, p. 204.

111 *International Trades Union Review*, June 1920.

112 Schevenels, *Forty Five Years*, pp. 138-144.

113 General Council *Minutes*, 23 May 1923 - 27 February 1924, *passim*; *Congress Reports* 1921, 1922, Accounts.

114 International Committee *Minutes*, 10 December 1923; W. Citrine, *The Trades Union Congress at Work: Headquarters Organization* (London: TUC, 1931).

115 J. H. Thomas, *My Story* (London: Hutchinson, 1937), p. 88.

116   General Council *Minutes*, 23 January 1924; Bramley/Council of People's Commissars, TUC File 947.

117   *Russia and International Unity: Report to Affiliated Societies.* (London: TUC, March 1925).

118   General Council *Minutes*, 5 September 1924.

119   *Congress Report* 1924, pp. 393–4.

120   George Young: former diplomat, examiner in Ottoman Law, London University, 1920 accompanied Labour Delegation to Russia; A. R. McDonell: 1907–16 British Consul in Baku, 1916–19 served in British forces in Persia and the Caucasus.

121   Calhoun, *The United Front*, pp. 102–105, 107.

122   Citrine, *Men and Work*, pp. 96–97.

123   *Russia: Official Report of the British Trade Union Delegation to Russia, November–December 1924* (London: TUC, February 1925).

124   Friedrich Adler, cited in *Trade Union Unity* (London: May 1925). Vol. I, no. 2, pp. 24–25.

125   Hingley, *Stalin.* pp. 143–149; Victor Serge, *Memoirs of a Revolutionary 1901–1941*, ed. Peter Sedgwick. (London: Oxford University Press, 1963), p. 177.

126   Bertrand Russell, *The Theory and Practice of Bolshevism* (London: Allen & Unwin, 1962), pp. 9, 22. (First published 1920.)

127   Citrine, *Men and Work*, p. 97.

128   Sir Walter Citrine, *I Search for Truth in Russia.* (London: Routledge, 1938), p. 307.

129   *Labour Magazine* (London: TUC and Labour Party, May 1925, March 1926).

130   *Russia and International Unity*; General Council *Minutes*, 1 December 1925, Joint Meeting with IFTU Delegation; *Congress Report*, 1926, p. 243.

131   *Summarized History of the Anglo-Russian Joint Advisory Committee.* General Council Document, 28 February 1936. TUC File 947/220.

132   *Congress Reports*, 1926, 1927.

133   Helmut Gruber, *Comintern.* p. 122.

134   Resolution on Russian Trading Relations, *Congress Report*, 1925.

135   Citrine, *Democracy or Disruption*, p. 5.

136   Joseph Berger, *Shipwreck of a Generation* (London: Harvill Press, 1971). pp. 103–104.

Chapter 4

1   Presidential Address. *Congress Report*, 1924.

2   M. K. Gandhi, *The Story of My Experiments with Truth: An Autobiography* (London: Phoenix Press, 1949), pp. 266, 380–85, 390–91.

3   Arthur Swinson, *Six Minutes to Sunset* (London: Peter Davies, 1964), *passim.* E. Thompson and G. T. Garratt, *Rise and Fulfilment of British Rule in India* (London: Macmillan, 1935), pp. 608–11.

4   Gandhi, *Autobiography*, p. 416; C. F. Andrews, *Mahatma Gandhi's Ideas.* (London: Allen & Unwin, 1929), pp. 284–289; Jawaharlal

Nehru, *Jawaharlal Nehru: An Autobiography* (London: John Lane, The Bodley Head, 1938), pp. 69–73, 76–7, 79–81.

5   Joint International Committee *Minutes*, 15 February 1922; National Joint Council *Minutes*, 21 February 1922.

6   Arthur H. Nethercot, *The Last Four Lives of Annie Besant* (London: Rupert Hart-Davis, 1963), pp. 296, 302–4.

7   Durga Das, *India from Curzon to Nehru and After* (London: Collins, 1969), p. 77.

8   Fenner Brockway, *Inside the Left* (London: Allen & Unwin, 1942), p. 119. *Towards Tomorrow*. (London: Hart-Davis, MacGibbon, 1977), p. 59.

9   Josiah Wedgwood: 1906–19 Member of Parliament (Liberal); 1919–42 Member of Parliament (Labour).

10   The Second Earl of Birkenhead, *Halifax* (London: Hamish Hamilton, 1965), p. 273.

11   Cmd. 2768; 22 Geo. V, ch. 4.

12   Gandhi, *Autobiography*, p. 346.

13   S. Saklatvala MP and M. K. Gandhi, *Is India Different? The Class Struggle In India: Correspondence on the Indian Labour Movement and Modern Conditions* (London: Communist Party of Great Britain, 1927), p. 26.

14   Nehru, *Autobiography*, p. 192.

15   Joint International Committee *Minutes*, 16 July 1924; Joint Executives *Minutes*, 26 June 1924; *Congress Report*, 1924, pp. 262–3.

16   Joint International Department, Advisory Committee on Imperial Questions *Minutes*, 11 March 1925.

17   Advisory Committee on Imperial Questions *Minutes*, 29 April 1925; Joint International Committee *Minutes*, 21 May 1925; Joint Executives *Minutes*, 28 May 1925.

18   The Second Earl of Birkenhead, *The Life of F. E. Smith, First Earl of Birkenhead* (London: Eyre & Spottiswoode, 1965), pp. 507–8.

19   Nethercot, *Annie Besant*, pp. 351–2, 357–9.

20   *Labour Party Conference Report 1925*, pp. 236–7.

21   *AITUC: Fifty Years*, p. 57.

22   Karnik, *Joshi*, p. 120.

23   V. V. Giri: President, Bengal-Nagpur Railway Union and one of the founders of the All-India Railwaymen's Federation: 1946–7 Minister of Labour, Madras; 1952–4 Union Minister of Labour; 1957 governor, Uttar Pradesh; 1967–9 Vice-President of India, 1969–74 President of India.

24   Karnik, *Joshi*, pp. 75–6.

25   Mukunda Lall Sircar, secretary, Bengal Trade Union Federation (Bengal Provincial Committee, AITUC), *Memorandum* circulated by him to Members of the Indian legislatures and to Members of Parliament, August 1926, and to the TUC by the WWLI London, October 1926.

26   Joint International Committee *Minutes*, 4 December 1924.

27   The Second Earl of Birkenhead, *F. E. Smith*, p. 512.

28   The Second Earl of Birkenhead, *Halifax*, pp. 237, 240.

29   Nethercot, *Annie Besant*, p. 378.

30 *Congress Report*, 1926, p. 410.
31 Nehru, *Autobiography*, p. 156.
32 *Labour Party Conference Report* 1927, p. 255.
33 Nehru, *Autobiography*, pp. 157, 176.
34 Michael Brecher, *Nehru: A Political Biography* (London: Oxford University Press, 1959), p. 129.
35 *Report on Labour Conditions in India by A. A. Purcell* MP *and J. Hallsworth (British Trades Union Congress Delegation to India), November 1927 to March 1928.* (London: TUC General Council, 1928), p. 3.
36 International Committee *Minutes*, 20 October 1927; General Council *Minutes*, 26 October 1927; *Congress Report*, 1927, p. 351.
37 Lord Morley: Secretary of State for India 1905-10.
38 *International Trades Union Review*, October 1921.
39 *Congress Reports*: 1922, pp. 457-8; 1923, p. 411; 1924, pp. 445-7.
40 Arthur Pugh: 1890 branch secretary, 1906 national assistant secretary, British Steel Smelters' Association; 1917 General Secretary, British Iron and Steel and Kindred Trades Association; 1920-35 member of Parliamentary Committee and General Council, 1926 President of Congress.
41 Far Eastern Labour Conditions Committee *Minutes*, 25 June 1925 – 13 August 1926; Functions Committee *Minutes*, 22 October 1925; *Congress Reports*: 1925, p. 317; 1926, pp. 219-22.
42 Sweated Goods Committee Interim Report, *Sweated Imports and International Labour Standards.* (London: Labour Party, 1925).
43 *Congress Report*, 1925, pp. 487-8, 553-4, 490.
44 *Congress Reports*: 1926, pp. 226, 416-8; 1927, p. 219.
45 B. C. Roberts, *Labour in the Tropical Territories of the Commonwealth.* (London: G. Bell and Sons, 1964), p. 22; *Labour Magazine*, Vol. I, no. 2, June 1922, p. 92.
46 *Congress Report*, 1926, pp. 225, 224; *The Chinese Disturbances*, unsigned note, undated, but after 11 September 1925. TUC File 950.
47 *IFTU Press Report no. 46*, 20 November 1924; *Labour Magazine*, January 1925, May 1925.
48 Interview H. W. Lee, Dame Adelaide Anderson, Pierre Henry (ILO) 15 December 1926; Letter Henry/Lee 14 January 1927. TUC File 925.I.
49 Henry McAleavy, *The Modern History of China* (London: Weidenfeld & Nicolson, 1967), p. 238; Gruber, *Comintern*, p. 324; *Congress Report*, 1925, p. 315. Accounts differ in detail: e.g., the TUC Report refers to the first man killed as a workman, McAleavy as a Communist Party member leading the strike.
50 Gregory Haines, *Gunboats on the Great River, A History of the Royal Navy on the Yangtse* (London: Macdonald & Jane's, 1976), p. 68.
51 *Congress Report*, 1925, p. 489.
52 ibid, pp. 315-7; *Congress Report*, 1926, p. 251.
53 *Congress Report*, 1927, pp. 221-2.
54 Haines, *Gunboats*, p. 78.
55 General Council *Minutes*, 12, 24, June 1925; *Congress Reports*: 1925, pp. 314-6, 1927, p. 347; *The Chinese Disturbances*.

56   *The Chinese Disturbances.*
57   *Congress Report*, 1926, p. 225.
58   Sz-Toh-Li, 'The Fourth All-China Trade Union Congress', *The Pan-Pacific Worker*. Pan-Pacific Trade Union Secretariat, Hankow, Vol. I, no. 2, 15 July 1927, p. 6; Gruber, *Comintern*, pp. 324–6.
59   Roberts, *Tropical Territories*, p. 23; Gruber, *Comintern*, pp. 418–9.
60   Nora Waln, *The House of Exile.* (Harmondsworth: Penguin Books, 1944), p. 152. The author, who was in Canton during the 1925 strike, records that an old man who sold her two melons was tried, wrapped in thin wire, and laid out in the sun to die of slow strangulation.
61   McAleavy, *Modern History*, pp. 246, 247, 249; Gruber, *Comintern*, pp. 436, 441; Snow, *Red Star*, p. 75.
62   Finance and General Purposes Committee *Minutes*, 22 March 1927.
63   Haines, *Gunboats*, pp. 89–94; *Congress Report*, 1927, p. 223.
64   TUC Document R.274 22. 31 August 1927.
65   *Congress Report*, 1925, pp. 487–9; Calhoun, *The United Front*, pp. 176, 314; *China's Fight is Labour's Fight: An Appeal to the Trades Union Congress* (London: Chinese Information Bureau, 1925).
66   Finance and General Purposes Committee *Minutes*, 17 January 1927; International Committee *Minutes*, 18 January 1927; General Council *Minutes*, 23 February 1927; Citrine, *Disruption*, p. 18; *Statement by Labour Party National Executive* 4 January 1927.
67   Calhoun, *The United Front*, pp. 314, 339.
68   *Congress Report*, 1927, pp. 221, 384–5.
69   Gruber, *Comintern*, pp. 369–70, 373.
70   Snow, *Red Star*, pp. 452, 158, 423.
71   Dan N. Jacobs, *Stalin's Man in China* (Cambridge, Mass. and London: Harvard University Press, 1981), pp. 101–9, 116, 149–50; RILU, *Report of Executive Bureau*; Sz-Toh-Li *Fourth All-China TUC*, p. 6.
72   TUC *International Trades Union Review*, no. 6, September 1920.
73   Anthony Short, *The Communist Insurrection in Malaya 1948–60* (London: Frederick Muller, 1975), p. 20; Roberts, *Tropical Territories*, pp. 24–25.
74   Losovsky, *World's Trade Union Movement*, pp. 208–9; *Draft Propaganda Thesis on Pan-Pacific Labour Conference*, Canton, 1927. TUC File 909.3.
75   Joint International Committee *Minutes*, 19 January 1926; International Committee *Minutes*, 11 April 1927; H. W. Lee, *Pan-Pacific Labour Conference*, Document I.C.8 (1926–27), 24 March 1927; unsigned, undated note by Lee; cable, Holloway, secretary Melbourne Trades Hall/Citrine 12 April 1927. TUC File 909.3.
76   V. B. Karnik, *M. N. Roy, A Political Biography* (Bombay: Nav Jagriti Samaj, 1978), p. 241.
77   TUC File 909.3; Mei-Li, 'History of the Pan-Pacific Trade Union Secretariat and its Tasks'. *Eastern and Colonial Bulletin*. RILU, Vol. II, nos 2–3, February–March 1929, p. 20; *Pan-Pacific Worker*. Vol. I, no. 2, 15 July 1927.
78   *Trud*, Moscow, 23 June, 1 July, 1927; *Daily News*, London, 1 April 1927; *Pan-Pacific Worker*, Vol. I, no. 7, 1 October 1927, p. 4.

79   E. J. Phelan, *Yes and Albert Thomas* (London: Cresset Press, 1949), p. 201.
80   *Eastern and Colonial Bulletin*, Vol. I, nos 24–25, 15 November 1928, p. 2; Vol. II, nos 2–3, February–March 1929, p. 20; no. 10, October 1929, Appendix.
81   Anthony Short, *Communist Insurrection*, p. 20. F. W. Deakin and G. R. Storry, *The Case of Richard Sorge* (London: Chatto & Windus, 1966), pp. 85–88, 92.
82   R. Bridgeman/Citrine 28 November 1931; office notes Lee/Citrine, Citrine/Lee 30 November 1931. TUC File 951.
83   At that time the Secretary of the SATUC was the Communist, W. H. Andrews, whose trade union record went back to his participation, as a member of the Amalgamated Society of Engineers, in the Transvaal miners' strike of 1897; 1931 expelled from the Communist Party. The African union ICU was also invited and split on the issue. Several Communist officials were expelled from the Union, including the General Secretary, J. La Guma, who subsequently attended the Brussels Congress.
84   Finance and General Purposes Committee *Minutes*, 31 January 1927; Citrine/Gibarti 2 February 1927. TUC File 778.24.
85   *Labour Party Conference Report* 1930, p. 33.
86   Nehru, *Autobiography*, pp. 161–2.
87   W. Gillies/Citrine 28 August 1929, TUC File 778.24; Fenner Brockway, *Inside the Left* (London: Allen & Unwin, 1942), p. 167.
88   Jacques Ventadour, *Report on the Congress 10–15 February 1927, Bulletin de la Ligue Contre l'Oppression Coloniale at l'Imperialisme*, Special Number (Neuilly sur Seine, undated). File *League Against Imperialism*, Institute of Social Studies, Amsterdam.
89   Lee/Citrine 5 February 1927. TUC File 778.24.
90   *Bulletin d'Information* no. 1, 15 March 1928. International Secretariat, LAI, Berlin. Institute of Social Studies, Amsterdam.
91   *Congress Report*, 1929, p. 173.
92   Dr F. Adler, 'The True and False United Front', *Labour Magazine*, Vol. III, no. 8, December 1924, p. 350. Joint International Committee *Minutes* 16 June, 4 December, 1924, 21 January, 21 May, 1925.
93   Bramley/General Council 23.3.1925. TUC File 910.3.
94   *Labour Party Conference Report* 1930, pp. 30, 33. (Comintern resolution cited from *International Press Correspondence* 13 May 1926.)
95   Bridgeman/Milne-Bailey 2 February 1930; Bridgeman/Lee 23 January 1930 and *Rules*, LAI (British Section). TUC File 778.24.
96   *Labour Party Conference Report*, 1930, p. 34. (Resolution of LAI 18–20 August 1928 cited from *International Press Correspondence* 31 August 1928).
97   Brockway, *Inside the Left*, p. 168.
98   Citrine/secretary, Birmingham Trades Council 22 April 1929. TUC File 778.24 (citing Resolution of the LSI Executive, Zurich, 11–12 September 1927). (Emphasis added.)
99   Brecher, *Nehru*, p. 113.

100 *Labour Party Conference Report*, 1928, pp. 335–8.
101 D. Chaman Lall MLA, C. F. Andrews, R. R. Bakhale, P. C. Bose, Mahabub-ul Huq, Devaki Prasad Sinha.
102 *Second British Commonwealth Labour Conference 2–6 July 1928: Report* (London: TUC and Labour Party, 1928).
103 The Conference was originally scheduled to meet in 1927. On 29 July 1926 the Joint Executives referred the composite draft to a subcommittee of MacDonald, Lansbury, Henderson and Thomas, and some alterations were made by MacDonald and Lansbury. In February 1928 the TUC Finance and General Purposes Committee referred the revised 1926 draft to a subcommittee of Ben Turner, E. L. Poulton, Gillies and Bolton, which met on 29 February 1928 and made further minor changes.
104 P. S. Gupta, *Imperialism and the British Labour Movement* (London: Macmillan, 1975). p. 81; J. F. N. Green: 1896 joined Colonial Office staff, 1920–33 assistant secretary.
105 *Congress Report*, 1928, p. 390.
106 The Second Earl of Birkenhead, *Halifax*, p. 274.
107 Brecher, *Nehru*, p. 141.
108 Nehru, *Autobiography*, Appendix A, p. 601.
109 The Second Earl of Birkenhead, *Halifax*, p. 222.
110 'Manifesto of the ECCI 26 March 1929', *Pravda*, Moscow, 27 March 1929.
111 Karnik, M. N. Roy, pp. 147, 139, 153, 158, 199.
112 *Communist Activities in India* (London: HMSO, 1924), Cmd. 2309.
113 Interview R. Bridgeman/W. J. Bolton, H. W. Lee, 8 April 1929. TUC File 954/710 F.1.
114 *India: Deputation to Mr Wedgwood Benn 9 July 1929*, Document I.C.10/1 1928–9, 24 July 1929; *India: Meerut Prisoners: History of Case*, TUC File 954 F1; *Congress Report*, 1931, p. 373.
115 *The Times*, 1 December 1929; *Labour Party Conference Report*, 1929, pp. 271, 190–92.
116 Nehru, *Autobiography*, p. 215, Appendix B, p. 603.
117 Gruber, *Comintern*, p. 125.
118 ibid., p. 222.
119 Karnik, M. N. Roy, pp. 127, 145, 160; Hopkirk, *Setting The East Ablaze*, p. 212.
120 H. H. Elvin (National Union of Clerks): 1925–39 member of General Council; 1938 President of Congress.
121 *Congress Report*, 1929, p. 405; Bridgeman/Milne-Bailey, 2 February 1930 Milne-Bailey/Bridgeman, 19 February 1930. TUC File 778.24.
122 'Second Anti-Imperialist World Congress', *Information and Press Service no. 4* (Frankfurt: LAI) p. 2.
123 *Labour Party Conference Report*, 1930, p. 34.
124 *Memorandum of Interview* Citrine/Sir Malcolm Seton, deputy under-secretary, India Office, 12 October 1931. TUC File 954/920.
125 Citrine/Secretary, Birmingham Trades Council.
126 Walter M. Citrine, *Democracy or Disruption: An Examination of*

Communist Influences in the Trade Unions. Labour Magazine, Vol. VI, nos 8, 9, 10, December 1927–February 1928. Subsequently collated as a pamphlet under the same title. (London: TUC, 1928).

127   *Congress Reports*: 1928, pp. 356–61; 1929, pp. 168–82, 344–8, 403–5.

128   *Labour Party Conference Report* 1930, p. 29; G. R. Shepherd (Labour Party)/Milne-Bailey 4 March 1930. TUC File 778.24.

129   TUC Circulars: no. 120, 5 June 1934, nos 16 and 17, 26 October 1934.

130   Citrine/Heads of Departments, 7 February 1934. Staff were instructed to adopt a similar attitude if Bridgeman called personally. TUC File 778.24. It was already office practice, confirmed by the General Council on 27 April 1927, to send only formal acknowledgements to correspondence from the Communist Party and the NMM.

131   Brecher, *Nehru*, p. 115.

132   Nehru, *Autobiography*, p. 165.

133   Degras, *Communist International*, Vol. II, pp. 531, 541–547.

134   ibid., p. 558.

135   *The Times*, London, 3 August, 4 December, 1929; 16 January 1930; Nigel West, *MI5: British Security Operations 1909–1945* (London: Bodley Head, 1981), pp. 63–71.

136   Degras, *Communist International*, pp. 557, 559, 563; Karnik, M. N. *Roy*, pp. 222, 227, 230, 234–7, 243–5, 249.

137   Lee/Joshi 15 July 1925; Lee/Joshi 29 January 1926, Joshi/Lee 25 January 1926; Lee/Joshi 18 May 1927 (handwritten, marked 'Personal and Private'). *N. M. Joshi Papers*, Nehru Memorial Museum, New Delhi. Files no. 16 part I, no. 17 part I, no. 18.

138   Karnik, *Joshi*, pp. 147–8.

139   First Annual Report (1 January–31 December 1926) (Bombay: Bombay Textile Labour Union, 1927).

140   Sukomal Sen, *Working Class of India: History of Emergence and Movement 1830–1970.* (Calcutta: K. P. Bagchi, 1977), pp. 293–4.

141   *Report of the Royal Commission on Labour in India* (Whitley Report) (London: HMSO, June 1931), Cmd. 3883, pp. 339, 344, 215.

142   *Industrial Review, Vol. III, no. 5.* TUC, June 1929, p. 14; Karnik, *Joshi*, pp. 63–4.

143   Sukomal Sen, *Working Class*, pp. 264–5; Whitley Report, p. 319.

144   *Congress Report*, 1926, p. 226.

145   Dange ed., *AITUC*, pp. xxiii, xxxvii, lxix-lxxii, lxxvi, 40.

146   Nehru, *Autobiography*, pp. 187, 197–98.

147   Brecher, *Nehru*, p. 141.

148   B. Shiva Rao, *The Industrial Worker in India.* (London: Allen & Unwin, 1939), p. 155.

149   *Congress Report*, 1930, p. 190.

150   Shiva Rao, *Industrial Worker*, p. 152.

151   Sukomal Sen, *Working Class*, pp. 280, 287–8.

152   Dange, ed., *AITUC*, pp. lxxviii, 6, 170; Karnik, *Joshi*, pp. 59, 149.

153   Lee/Joshi (personal) 7 January 1926; Citrine/Joshi (private and confidential) 11 March 1926; Joshi/Lee (personal) 9 April 1926. *N. M. Joshi Papers*, File no. 17, part II.

154 Sukomal Sen, *Working Class*, p. 304.
155 According to the Purcell-Hallsworth Report, p. 14, this union's affiliated membership was 3,000 in December 1927.
156 *TUC Report*, 1930, pp. 190–91; Karnik, *Joshi*, p. 85.
157 Conrad Noel (Chairman, British Section, LAI), citing letter from F. J. Ginwala (newly elected treasurer, AITUC), in *Bombay Chronicle* 10 December 1929/Herbert Tracey, TUC, 27 January 1930, with Lee's note on letter. TUC File 778.24; Document I.C./10/5/1928–9, 27 August 1929.
158 Sukomal Sen, *Working Class*, pp. 301, 316 note 26.
159 Harold Crouch, *Trade Unions and Politics in India* (Bombay: Manaktalas, 1966), p. 66; Sukomal Sen, *Working Class*, pp. 309–10.
160 *Congress Report*, 1930, p. 191; Karnik, *Joshi*, pp. 88–9.
161 Dange, ed., *AITUC*, p. 51; A. S. and J. S. Mathur, *The Trade Union Movement in India* (Allahabad: Chaitanya Publishing House, 1957), p. 258.
162 *Congress Report*, 1930, p. 317; *Deputation to Mr Wedgwood Benn, 9 July 1929*.
163 *Congress Reports*: 1930, p. 189; 1931. p. 373.
164 *Parliamentary Debates*, 9 February 1933.
165 National Joint Council Sub-Committee on Meerut Prisoners *Minutes*, 15 March 1933, Appendix; National Joint Council Circular, *Meerut, Release the Prisoners!*, April 1933; TUC File 954 F1; *Manchester Guardian* 16 November 1933; *Daily Herald* 19 December 1934.
166 Karnik, M. N. Roy, pp. 315–17, 321, 352; General Council *Minutes*, 9 September 1931; TUC File 954/710 F.1.
167 Karnik, *Joshi*, pp. 89–92; M. N. Roy, p. 485; International Committee *Minutes*, 20 June 1944; *Congress Report*, 1944.
168 *Third British Commonwealth Labour Conference 21–25 July 1930: Report*. (London: TUC and Labour Party, 1930).
169 R. R. Bakhale/TUC. TUC File 957.30.
170 At the First Round Table Conference 12 November 1930 – 19 January 1931 Joshi represented Labour and Shiva Rao the Home Rule League. V. V. Giri was appointed additional Labour representative for the second session 7 September – 1 December 1931. Joshi attended the third session 17 November–24 December 1932. Shiva Rao served on the Lothian Committee which investigated the franchise. Joshi, Shiva Rao and Aftab Ali gave evidence on behalf of the NTUF to the Joint Select Committee of Parliament which considered the British government's White Paper before the enactment of the Government of India Act 1935.
171 Joe Hallsworth: 1902 full-time official Amalgamated Union of Co-operative Employees, 1921 General-Secretary National Union of Distributive and Allied Workers; 1926–46 member of TUC General Council, 1939 President of Congress; 1927–8 member of TUC delegation to India; 1927–37 member of British workers' delegation to ILO Conferences, 1938–47 British Workers' Delegate.
172 Jawaharlal Nehru, *Presidential Address*. Indian National Congress, 49th

Session, Lucknow, April 1936, p. 16.
173   British Commonwealth Labour Conference 1930, TWMA *Memorandum*, 27 May 1930, TUC File 937.29; C. L. R. James, *The Life of Captain Cipriani* (Nelson, Lancs., 1932). pp. 104–7.
174   *Commonwealth Labour Conference, Industrial Relations.* Document G.C.8/1/1927–28. TUC File 937.28.
175   International Committee *Minutes*, 25 August 1925, 23 November 1926; General Council *Minutes*, 24 November 1926; *Report of Fourth Ordinary Congress of the IFTU, Paris, 1–6 August 1927.* (Amsterdam, IFTU), p. 37.
176   James, *Cipriani*, p. 104.
177   Ras Makonnen, *Pan-Africanism From Within.* (London and Nairobi: Oxford University Press, 1973), p. 160.

Chapter 5

1   Parliamentary Committee *Minutes*, 18 April 1917.
2   *Congress Report*, 1921, p. 101; *Report of Deputations to Ministers, 1922.* (London: TUC, 1922), pp. 27–8.
3   3 December 1925, TUC File 954, International Committee *Minutes*, 3 November 1927; General Council *Minutes*, 13 August, 3 September, 24 November, 1926, International Committee *Minutes*, 17 March 1927, General Council *Minutes*, 23 May 1928, International Committee *Minutes*, 29 June 1928; 9 July 1929, TUC File 954/710 F1.1., International Committee *Minutes*, 10 March 1931.
4   3 December 1925.
5   Parliamentary Committee *Minutes*, 16 February 1921; *Congress Report*, 1921, pp. 99–106.
6   Montagu referred to ad hoc conciliation and inquiry in Madras and Bombay, but the deputation remained unaware that three months earlier the Viceroy had expressed the view that legislation on the lines of the English Industrial Courts Act 1919 would be premature – see Sukomal Sen, *Working Class*, pp. 133, 158.
7   *Congress Report*, 1921, p. 84.
8   International Committee *Minutes*, 3 November 1927.
9   A. B. Swales (AEU): 1919–34 member of Parliamentary Committee and General Council; 1925 President of Congress.
10   *Congress Report*, 1922, p. 102. The confidential memoranda were not filed by the TUC, but their contents were reported to Congress.
11   George Hicks (Amalgamated Union of Building Trade Workers): 1921–40 member of General Council; 1927 President of Congress.
12   General Council *Minutes*, 2 November 1921, 4 January 1922; *Legislation in India: Registration and Protection of Trade Unions and Workmen's Compensation*, Report by Ben Tillett and G. Hicks.
13   *Report of Deputations to Ministers, 1922*, pp. 23–9.
14   *Legislative Assembly Debates. 8 February 1926, Vol. VII no. 11, Official Report.* (Delhi: Government of India Press, 1926). Speeches by N. M. Joshi, Lala Lajpat Rai, Dewan Chaman Lall, pp. 923, 913, 921.

15 Interview with G. Shelvapathy Chetti. Madras, 15 January 1973.
16 General Council *Minutes*, 14 March, 27 March, 25 June, 1924; Joint Advisory Committee on Imperial Questions *Minutes*, 2 July, 16 July, 1924; *Congress Reports*, 1924 p. 263, 1925 p. 319.
17 Whitley Report, p. 319.
18 *Legislative Assembly Debates*, 8 February 1926. Speech by W. S. J. Willson (Associated Chambers of Commerce: Nominated Non-official), p. 910.
19 *Congress Report*, 1925, p. 317; General Council *Minutes*, 28 October 1925; H. W. Lee, *The Textile Crisis in Bombay*, 12 November 1925, and *Further Note, The System of Managing Agencies*, 17 November 1925, TUC File 954 Industrial Disputes: Bombay Textile Strike, Documents; Deputation to Lord Birkenhead 3 December 1925, TUC File 954 Bombay Textile Strike.
20 Second Earl of Birkenhead, *Life of F. E. Smith*, pp. 138–41, 484–5, 527.
21 Stanley Jackson, *The Sassoons*. (London: Heinemann, 1968), p. 210.
22 *Congress Report*, 1927, p. 221.
23 Finance and General Purposes Committee *Minutes*, 17 March 1927; *Congress Report*, 1927, pp. 217–18; International Committee *Minutes*, 3 November 1927; Document I.C.2/4 1927–28, TUC File 954 C3.
24 General Council *Minutes*, 25 April 1928.
25 *Deputation to Mr Wedgwood Benn 9 July 1929*. Document I.C.10/1/1928–9.
26 Whitley Report, pp. 347–8.
27 Shiva Rao, *Industrial Worker*, pp. 195, 206.
28 V. V. Giri, *Labour Problems in Indian Industry*. (Bombay: Asia Publishing House 1972), p. 84.
29 Shiva Rao, *Industrial Worker*, p. 182.
30 ibid., pp. 188–9.
31 ibid., p. 194.
32 *Congress Report*, 1929, p. 368.
33 A. S. and J. S. Mathur, *Trade Union Movement in India* (Allahabad: Chaitanya Publishing House, 1957), p. 178
34 Citrine/Passfield 12 September 1929, TUC File 954.9; International Committee *Minutes*, 20 August 1929, 11 April 1930; Document I.C.14/4 1929–30; Note on telephone conversation and interview Lee, Firth/Leggett 15 May 1930; Document I.C.16/10 1929–30, 3 June 1930; *Congress Report*, 1931, p. 237.
35 Confidential Despatch 17 September 1930. C.O.854 173 70218/30, General.
36 General Council *Minutes*, 28 October 1925; TUC Circular No. 5/1925–26 30 October 1925; *Congress Report*, 1926, p. 226.
37 Bombay Textile Labour Union, *First Annual Report*, p. 1.
38 General Council *Minutes*, 26 June, 24 July, 31 August, 1929; Document I.C.7/7 1929–30 TUC File 954 C7.
39 G. Ramanujam, *From the Babul Tree – Story of Indian Labour* (New Delhi: Indian National Trade Union Congress, 1967), p. 33.
40 A. S. and J. S. Mathur, *Trade Union Movement*, p. 25.

41 *Eastern and Colonial Bulletin*. RILU, November 1929, p. 8, October 1929, pp. 11–12.

42 International Committee *Minutes*, 10 December 1929 and documents; 10 April 1930, Document I.C.14/5 1929–30.

43 Finance and General Purposes Committee *Minutes*, 4 February, 25 February, 1929; General Council *Minutes*, 27 February 1929.

44 Finance and General Purposes Committee *Minutes*, 9 January, 6 February, 23 April, 7 May, 1928, 22 April 1929.

45 General Council *Minutes*, 23 May 1928, Finance and General Purposes Committee *Minutes*, 25 June 1928.

46 International Committee *Minutes*, 3 November 1927, 29 June 1928; Document I.C.2/1 1927–28, TUC File 954.

47 Parliamentary Committee *Minutes*, 20 July 1921; *Labour Monthly*, Vol. 1, no. 5, 15 November 1921, (London: Labour Publishing Co.), p. 448; *Labour International Handbook*; Sukomal Sen, *Working Class*, p. 166; P. S. Gupta, *Imperialism and the British Labour Movement*. (London: Macmillan, 1975), p. 45.

48 WWLI, *Objects*, undated.

49 Parliamentary Committee *Minutes*, 21 April, 21 July, 17 August, 31 August, 4 September 1920.

50 Gupta, *Imperialism and the British Labour Movement*, p. 49; Joint International Committee, Imperial Questions Sub-Committee *Minutes*, 16 April, 11 June, 2 July, 16 July 1924; *Congress Report*, pp. 262–3.

51 *Labour Monthly*, Vol. 2, no. 3, 15 March 1922, p. 232.

52 Parliamentary Committee *Minutes*, 9 August, 29 August 1921; General Council *Minutes*, 2 November 1921; Joint International Committee *Minutes*, 20 March 1924.

53 Dange, ed. *AITUC*, p. 181.

54 Imperial Questions Sub-Committee *Minutes*, 11 June 1924.

55 General Council *Minutes*, 6 September, 8 September 1926.

56 Dange, ed. *AITUC*, p. 171.

57 WWLI, *Seventh Annual Report*, London, 1925.

58 General Council *Minutes*, 27 March 1924.

59 H. S. L. Polak/Joshi 1 July 1926; Joshi/Polak 16 July 1926. *Joshi Papers*, File no. 17, part I.

60 Joshi/Lee 29 April 1927; Lee/Joshi 18 May 1927. ibid., File no. 18.

61 International Committee *Minutes*, 3 November 1927.

62 ibid., 3 April 1928.

63 Documents I.C.6/7/1928-9, I.C.9/8/1928-9. TUC File 954, Documents.

64 *Eastern and Colonial Bulletin* Vol. II, No. 2–3. RILU. February–March 1929, p. 4; *Industrial Review*, Vol. III, no. 4. TUC. April 1929, p. 13; Document I.C.9/8/1928–29. 6 June 1929. TUC File 954 A.1.

65 L.B., 'Coming (Xth) Session of the All-India Trade Union Congress'. *Eastern and Colonial Bulletin* Vol. II, no. 11. RILU, November 1929, p. 10; L. Burns, 'Split in Indian Trade Union Movement and Tasks of the Left Wing'. ibid., Vol. III, no. 1–2. January–February 1930.

66 L. Burns, 'India and the British Reformists'. ibid., Vol. I, no. 5.

1 November 1927, p. 1; 'Coming Congress of Indian Trade Unions'. ibid., Vol. I, no. 6. 15 November 1927, p. 6.

67 Purcell and Hallsworth, *Report*.

68 General Council *Minutes*, 13 August, 3 September, 1926; *Congress Report* 1927, p. 219.

69 M. K. Gandhi, *The Story of My Experiments with Truth* (London: Phoenix Press, 1949), p. 356.

70 Whitley Report, pp. 320, 328, 336.

71 Interview with Mahesh Desai, General Secretary, Hind Mazdoor Sabha, Bombay, 2 January 1973.

72 V. K. Krishna Menon, ed. *Condition of India, Being the Report of the Delegation sent to India by the India League in 1932*. (London: Essential Books, 1933), pp. 438–9, 442–3.

73 Saklatvala and Gandhi, *Is India Different?* p. 25.

74 International Committee *Minutes*, 11 May 1928; Document I.C.7/4/1927–28, TUC File 954/230; *Congress Report*, 1928, pp. 258–9.

75 General Council *Minutes*, 26 October 1927; Document I.C.8/1/1927–28. TUC File 954/230.

76 *Interview with Sir Atul Chatterjee, High Commissioner for India, June 8th 1928, at Geneva.* Document I.C.8/2/1927–28, ibid.

77 General Council *Minutes*, 23 May, 25 July, 1928; *Congress Report*, 1928, pp. 471–3.

78 Interview Sir Walter Citrine/N. M. Joshi, December 1936. TUC File 954/230; Typewritten note, 7 October 1937, ibid.; Finance and General Purposes Committee *Minutes*, 22 November 1937, with memorandum, *Organization of Indian Workers*; *India: Labour Advisers*, History of Case. TUC File 954/230.

79 Document I.C.6/7/1928–29. TUC File 954 Documents.

80 Interview with B. Shiva Rao, New Delhi, 22 January 1973.

81 Whitley Report, p. i; John Cliff: former tram conductor and member of executive committee, Amalgamated Association of Tramway and Vehicle Workers; 1919 Joint Secretary, National Joint Council for the Tramways Industry; 1922 National Secretary of Passenger Workers' Group, 1924 Assistant General Secretary, Transport and General Workers' Union; 1935 full-time member, 1947–55 Deputy Chairman, London Transport Executive.

82 Whitley Report. Appendix I, pp. 494–528.

83 ibid., pp. 332, 348, 465–70.

84 ibid., pp. 331, 328–30.

85 V. K. R. Menon, 'The Influence of International Labour Conventions on Indian Labour Legislation', *International Labour Review* (Geneva: International Labour Organization, June 1956), p. 557.

86 N. M. Joshi, Fraternal Delegate's speech, *Congress Report*, 1931, p. 391; Interview with B. Shiva Rao, New Delhi, 22 January 1973; Interview with V. V. Giri, New Delhi, 24 January 1973.

87 *Congress Reports*: 1930 p. 317, 1931 pp. 235–236, 1933 pp. 182, 183, 312, 1935 p. 178.

88 Whitley Report, pp. 472–4; Document I.C.3/7 1934–35; note by

Jamnadas Mehta 20 February 1935. TUC File 954 General.

89 *Congress Report*, 1931, p. 392; Whitley Report, pp. 462–4; Government of India Act 1935 (26 Geo. 5. Ch. 2), Schedules I and V.

90 *Returns Showing the Results of Elections in India in 1937*, Cmd. 559. (London: HMSO November 1937).

91 *Congress Report*, 1935, p. 178.

92 E. A. Landy, *The Effectiveness of International Supervision* (London: Stevens, Oceana, 1966), pp. 173–4.

93 Shotwell, *Origins of the ILO*, pp. 316–8.

94 E. J. Phelan, *Yes and Albert Thomas* (London: Cresset Press, 1949).

95 ILO, *The International Labour Organization: The First Decade* (London: Allen & Unwin, 1931), pp. 333–6.

96 International Labour Conference, Tenth Session, 1927, *Proceedings*, p. 333; ILO Governing Body, 42nd Session, October 1928, *Minutes*, p. 589; International Labour Conference, 12th Session, 1929, *Proceedings*, Vol. I p. 1056; 15th Session, 1931, p. 583; 16th Session, 1932, p. 594; ILO Governing Body, 60th Session, October 1932, *Minutes*, p. 559.

97 *Note on ILO Committee of Experts on Native Labour, 27 October – 2 November 1932*, enclosed with Circular Despatch, 28 April 1934. C.O.854.174. 90094/3/32. Secret and Confidential Despatches.

98 International Committee *Minutes*, 13 April 1926; 3 April 1928; Document I.C.6/2/1927–28, TUC File 926.1; IFTU Circulars September 1928, 3 October 1928, TUC File 932.1.

99 'A Pillar of the ILO, A Tribute to the late Harold Grimshaw'. *Industrial Review* Vol. III, no. 8. TUC. August 1929, p. 15.

100 Citrine/Grimshaw, 12 November 1928; Record of Interview 21 December 1928. TUC File 932.1.

101 General Council *Minutes*, 24 April 1929; International Committee *Minutes*, 11 April 1930; *Congress Report*, 1938, p. 202.

102 *ILO Conference 1930, Forced Labour: Report to the TUC International Committee by J. Bromley.* TUC File 932.1; International Labour Conference, 14th Session, 1930, *Proceedings. Debate on Report of Committee on Forced Labour*, p. 291.

103 International Committee *Minutes*, 20 November 1934, 22 January 1935; *Congress Report*, 1935, p. 169; Ballinger/Citrine 21 June 1935. TUC File 932.2.

104 *Congress Reports*: 1946, p. 142; 1954, p. 216; 1955, p. 210.

105 *Congress Reports*: 1954, pp. 215–6; 1955, p. 210.

106 Landy, *International Supervision*, pp. 17–20; IFTU Circulars 23 March, 21 April, 24 May, 1928; 18 February 1929. TUC File 925.41 I.

107 Circular Despatches, C.O.854 80: 2 April 1931, X/J 7196; 8 April 1931, 80014/3/31; 10 April 1931, 80014/5/31 General; 11 April 1931, 80014/4/31 General.

108 Secret and Confidential Circulars. 10 April 1930. C.O.854.173.

109 Note by R. V. Vernon, 14 June 1937. C.O.888. 1 CLC 30.

110 13 August 1930. C.O.854.173. Secret and Confidential Circulars.

111 E. Mahaim, chairman of the Governing Body. *Special Meeting of the Governing Body of the International Labour Office, Geneva, 30 June 1932.*

112 ILO Governing Body, *Minutes of 30th Session, January 1926*. First supplementary report of Director, p. 85; Discussion on report, p. 52; A. H. Findlay (Patternmakers' Union): 1921–40 member of General Council, 1936 president of Congress.

113 ILO Governing Body: *Minutes of 32nd Session, 25 May – 4 June 1926*. Director's report, Annex A, *Memorandum on the Study of Questions Relating to Native Labour*, p. 299. *Supplementary Note Submitted to Governing Body, 4 June 1926*, p. 302. Discussions, pp. 279, 302; *Minutes of 33rd Session, 14–16 October 1926*. Director's Report, Appendix IV, p. 437. Appendix VIII, p. 452; *Minutes of 34th Session, 28–30 January 1927*. Director's Report, Appendix II, p. 73.

114 ILO Governing Body, *Minutes of 37th Session, 11–14 October 1927*. Director's report, pp. 440, 467 and seqq.; *Minutes of 43rd Session, 11–12 March 1929*. Appendix XII, *Record of Meeting of Committee of Experts on Native Labour 4–8 December 1928*. pp. 116 and seqq.

115 IFTU, 3 October 1928, 6 November·1928. TUC File 932.1 *Forced Labour*.

116 International Committee Minutes, 17 January 1929; *Congress Report*, 1929, p. 220.

117 TUC File 932.2 Documents.

118 *League of Nations Union Conference on Forced Labour 6–7 March 1929*; International Committee Minutes, 20 February 1929; W. McGregor Ross, *Comment on Definition of Forced Labour*. LNU Document SG 3012, 14 November 1929. TUC File 932.1.

119 *Congress Report*, 1929, p. 221; Forced Labour: ILO Questionnaire, TUC File 932.3.

120 Convention no. 29 concerning Forced or Compulsory Labour, 1930. *Conventions and Recommendations Adopted by the International Labour Conference 1919–1966* (Geneva: International Labour Office, 1966), pp. 155–165.

121 International Labour Conference, 14th Session, 10–28 June 1930. *Appendix V to Report of Proceedings, Report of Committee on Forced Labour*, pp. 671–684; *Workers' Group Minority Report*, p. 725; *Congress Report*, 1930, p. 172.

122 International Labour Conference, 12th Session, 30 May–21 June 1929, *Minutes. Debate on Report of Committee on Forced Labour*, pp. 394, 410, 416; Sidney Webb/Citrine 10 June 1929; A. S. Firth/Poulton 13 June 1929, Citrine/Poulton 15 June 1929. TUC File 932.1.

123 *Congress Report*, 1939, pp. 232–234.

124 International Committee Minutes, 14 May 1930.

125 Comment by Arthur Pugh. ILO Governing Body, 32nd Session, 25 May–4 June 1926, *Minutes*. Discussion on Director's Report, Annex A, *Study of Questions Relating to Native Labour*, p. 279.

Chapter 6

1 G. D. Tarrant, *The British Colonial Office and the Labour Question in the Dependencies in the Inter-War Years*. (Ph.D. Thesis, University of Manitoba, 1977), p. 354.

2 Landy, *International Supervision*, p. 233.
3 *Colonial Labour Committee 1931-1941*. C.O. 88.1. CLC (1).
4 *Despatch* 8 September 1930, enclosing Memoranda, Papers and Stenographic Notes of Meetings 23 June – 15 July 1930. C.O.854. 173. 71539/30.
5 Tarrant, *Colonial Office and Labour Question*, p. 135.
6 General Council *Minutes*, 24 July 1929.
7 Lord Citrine, *Men and Work*, pp. 267-71.
8 General Council *Minutes*, 24 September, 17 December, 1930.
9 Tarrant, *Colonial Office and Labour Question*, p. 329.
10 Margaret Cole, ed., *The Webbs and Their Work*. (London: Frederick Muller, 1949), p. 207.
11 ibid., pp. 213, 216, 217.
12 Tarrant, *Colonial Office and Labour Question*, pp. 329-30.
13 Secret and Confidential Circulars. C.O.844. 173. 70218/30.
14 Gupta, *Imperialism and British Labour Movement*, pp. 142-4.
15 Cole, ed. *The Webbs and Their Work*, p. 255. (Emphasis added.)
16 Note of telephone conversation with F. W. Leggett, 15 May 1930, on Ceylon. TUC File 954.9.
17 Gupta, *Imperialism and British Labour Movement*, p. 194.
18 Circular Despatch 12 July 1941. Enclosure, *An Ordinance to Regulate Trade Unions and Trade Disputes*. CLAC (50)28. Appendix 2. TUC File 932.5 II.
19 For full account see Roberts, *Labour in Tropical Territories*, pp. 281-94.
20 (2) The purposes of any trade union shall not, by reason merely that they are in restraint of trade, be deemed to be unlawful, so as to render any member of such trade union liable to criminal prosecution for conspiracy or otherwise.
(3) The purposes of any trade union shall not, by reason merely that they are in restraint of trade, be deemed to be unlawful so as to render void or voidable any agreement or trust'.
21 Tarrant, *Colonial Office and Labour Question*, p. 332.
22 T. M. Yesufu, *An Introduction to Industrial Relations in Nigeria*. (London: Oxford University Press, 1962), p. 29.
23 In a letter to the author dated 13 September 1974 Lord Citrine, then aged 87, stated that he had no recollection of Passfield consulting the TUC, but if he had done so Citrine would have reported to the TUC's Colonial Advisory Committee. [This would appear to rule out even an informal discussion. The TUC had no Colonial Advisory Committee until 1937, but in 1930 Citrine would have reported to the International Committee.] Lord Citrine also wrote, 'On the merits of registration of colonial unions, I would have supported this, but with safeguards against arbitrary actions of the Governors'.
24 Cipriani/Citrine 30 May 1932; Citrine/Cipriani cable and letter 20 June 1932; Citrine/V. E. Henry 9 February 1933; V. E. Henry/Citrine 2 March 1933; V. E. Henry/Citrine 16 February 1934; Citrine/V. E. Henry 29 March 1934. TUC File 972.9.
25 *Trinidad and Tobago Disturbances 1937, Report of Commission* (London:

HMSO, 1938), Cmd. 5641, p. 48.

26 Cipriani/Middleton 5 July 1937. TUC File 972.9.

27 Cipriani/Sutherland, 13 October 1937. TUC File 972.9/200.

28 Citrine/Rowland Sawyer, Secretary, Negro Welfare Association, 3 November 1937. TUC File 972.981 G1.

29 Pugh/Citrine 7 December 1937, with copy of and Pugh's comments on letter Cipriani/Gillies 19 November 1937. TUC File 972.9/200.

30 Quintin O'Connor/Citrine 23 May 1938; Citrine/O'Connor 3 June 1938. TUC File 972.9/200.

31 *Forster Report*, p. 87.

32 Colonial Advisory Committee *Minutes*, 16 February 1938, with document C.A.C. 2/3, TUC File 972.9.

33 Labour Party Imperial Advisory Committee *Minutes*, 16 February, 2, 16, 30 March 1938; Memorandum no. 191 by J. F. N. Green 2 March 1938; Memorandum no. 191A as passed for transmission to the Party Executive 30 March 1938; Fabian Colonial Bureau, *Trade Unionism in the Colonies*. Labour Committee document, 12 August 1941.

34 Minute by J. E. W. Flood 3 October 1936. *Appointment of a Labour Officer at the Colonial Office*. C.O.866/29. 1166. 1936.

35 Tarrant, *Colonial Office and Labour Question*, p. 73.

36 C.O. 888.1 CLC 25, 26, 27, 28, 29; P.S.Gupta, *Imperialism and British Labour Movement*, p. 248.

37 *The Colonial Office and Native Labour Problems*. TUC Colonial Advisory Committee Document C.A.C. 1/5 17 December 1937.

38 D. J. Morgan, *The Origins of British Aid Policy 1924–1945, The Official History of Colonial Development, Vol. I* (London: Macmillan, 1980), pp. xix, xxiii, 46–7.

39 Citrine/Green 17 December 1934, TUC File 932.2; International Committee *Minutes*, 17 February 1935 and document I.C. 3/4, 1934–5 17 January 1935.

40 *Congress Report*, 1933, p. 183; Correspondence with Jamnadas Mehta and Citrine/Sir Samuel Hoare, Secretary of State for India, 1934–5; document I.C.3/7 1934–5, 18 February 1935, TUC File 926.1.

41 General Council *Minutes*, 31 August 1931; IFTU Executive *Minutes*, Berlin 9–10 June 1932, TUC File 950 J.3.

42 IFTU Congress, London 8–11 July 1936, *Triennial Report 1933–5* (Paris: IFTU, 1937); *Congress Report*, 1937, pp. 182–83.

43 Sir Walter Citrine, *I Search for Truth in Russia* (London: Routledge, 1938), pp. 81, 132.

44 Telegram de Brouckère, Adler, LSI, Citrine, Schevenels, IFTU/President of the People's Commissariat, Moscow 21 August 1936. TUC File 947 F.

45 *Congress Report*, 1938, Accounts.

46 *West India Royal Commission Report* (London, 1945), Cmd. 6607, p. 196.

47 *The Colonies*. (London: Labour Party, 1933). Policy Report no. 6, p. 12.

48 See discussions on Northern Rhodesia, Nyasaland, the Gold Coast and the West Indies in *Minutes*, 10, 19, June, 11 November, 1936, 10

February 1937; *Interim Report of the Sub-Committee on the West Indies*, Document LP/Imp.A.C./1/188.

49 *Report of the East Africa Commission* (London: 1925), Cmd. 2387, p. 43.

50 C.O.854.97. 1766/35 General. 9 November 1935.

51 Correspondence Orde Browne/Weaver (ILO) June 1933–March 1935, MSS Afr.s1117 Orde Browne, Box3 OB 3/4 35, 37; J. J. Paskin (Colonial Office)/Orde Browne 6 December 1933, OB 3/4 14; MSS Brit. Emp. s 405 Box 6, Buxton 6/7 3–4, 2, 5, 110; MSS Afr.s1117 Orde Browne, Orde Browne/William Lunn MP 14 February 1934, Box 4, OB 4/2 49, 53, 96; 17, 25, 41, 45, 54, 62, 66, 67, 98, 103, 133, 177. OUCRP.

52 Drummond Shiels/Ormsby-Gore 24 September 1936; Minute by Sir John Shuckburgh 13 October 1936; *Final Note* by J. G. Hibbert 25 September 1937. *Appointment of a Labour Officer at the Colonial Office*, C.O./866/29 1166.

53 Wogu Ananaba, *The Trade Union Movement in Nigeria.* (London: Hurst, 1969), p. 18.

54 Sir William Geary: a British lawyer resident in Lagos, whose *Nigeria under British Rule* (1927) was an early classic.

55 Tarrant, *Colonial Office and Labour Question*, p. 336.

56 Richard Sandbrook and Robin Cohen, ed., *The Development of an African Working Class.* (London: Longman, 1976), pp. 32–4.

57 Tarrant, *Colonial Office and Labour Question*, p. 336.

58 A. Creech Jones/Ormsby-Gore 22 July 1937, Lord Dufferin/Creech Jones 28 July 1937, Creech Jones/Ormsby-Gore 3 August 1937, Dufferin/Creech Jones 7 August 1937. MSS Brit. Emp. s332, Box 14, File 1, A.C.J. OUCRP.

59 L.P.Imp.A.C. *Minutes*, 14 July 1937.

60 Note by R. V. Vernon 14 June 1937. *Supervision of Labour Conditions*, C.O.888.1. CLC 30. 1766/2/35 General.

61 Circular Despatch 24 August 1937. *The Colonial Empire in 1937/38.* Cmd. 5760, 1938. Appendix.

62 'In Memoriam Ernest Bevin', *ITF Journal* (London: International Transport Workers' Federation, November-December 1951), pp. 54, 58.

63 Leonard Woolf, *Beginning Again* (London: Hogarth Press, 1964), p. 220.

64 Alan Bullock, *The Life and Times of Ernest Bevin, Vol. 1. Trade Union Leader.* (London: Heinemann, 1960), pp. 474, 542.

65 General Council *Minutes* 28 November 1931.

66 Alan Bullock, *Ernest Bevin, Foreign Secretary, 1945–51* (London: Heinemann, 1983), p. 99.

67 Bevin/Citrine 28 September 1937, enclosing documents received from Creech Jones; Creech Jones/Bevin 23 November 1937. TUC Files 932, 932.3.

68 *Congress Report*, 1937, pp. 74–75.

69 I. Wallace Johnson/Citrine 8 September 1937; Bevin/Citrine 16 September 1937. TUC File 932.

70 General Council *Minutes*, 22 September 1937; International Committee *Minutes*, 26 October, 23 November, 21 December, 1937.

71 See *Some of the Legal Disabilities Suffered by the Native Population of the Union of South Africa and Imperial Responsibility* (London: St Clements Press 1920). MSS Brit. Emp. s 405, Box 5, Buxton 5/1 2. OUCRP.

72 Information given to author by Jeffrey P. Green, 29 November 1981.

73 George Padmore, *Pan-Africanism or Communism?* (London: Dennis Dobson, 1956), pp. 129–30, 139–40.

74 Internal office note 17 September 1937. TUC File 932.

75 Harry Thuku/C. Roden Buxton 10 March 1933. MSS Brit. Emp. s 405, Box 6, Buxton 6/5 45. OUCRP.

76 James R. Hooker, *Black Revolutionary* (London: Pall Mall Press, 1967), pp. 17, 51, 18. James S. Coleman, *Nigeria: Background to Nationalism.* (Berkeley and Los Angeles: University of California, 1958), p. 208.

77 Hooker, *Black Revolutionary*, pp. 8–15.

78 Padmore, *Pan-Africanism*, p. 330; Hooker, *Black Revolutionary*, pp. 31, 33, 34.

79 Ras Makonnen, *Pan-Africanism From Within* (London and Nairobi: Oxford University Press, 1973), p. ix.

80 Bolton/Makonnen 26 October 1937. TUC File 972.

81 James S. Coleman, *Nigeria*, p. 208; James R. Hooker, *Black Revolutionary*, p. 50.

82 *Memorandum of Interview* 12 October 1937. TUC File 932.

83 Ormsby-Gore/Orde Browne 8 April 1938. MSS Afr.s1117 Orde Browne, Box 2, OB2/5 83. OUCRP.

84 *Labour Organization in the Colonies.* Sent by Orde Browne to Drummond Shiels 16.10.37 and by Shiels to Citrine 18.10.37. TUC File 932.

85 International Committee *Minutes* 26 October 1937.

86 Citrine/Pugh 9 November 1937. TUC File 972.9/200.

87 2 May 1914. Published in *African Times and Orient Review*, ed. Duse Mohamed, London, 16 June 1914. MSS Brit. Emp. s332. Box 9, ACJ 9/1 1. OUCRP.

88 Creech Jones/Bevin 23 November 1937, TUC File 932.3; *Labour Problems at the Colonial Office* by A. Creech Jones, L.P.Imp.A.C. Document no.189, November 1937, TUC File 936; *Labour Conditions in British Dependencies: Sources of Information* by C. Roden Buxton, 3 December 1937, TUC File 932.3.

89 *The Colonial Office and Native Labour Problems.* Colonial Advisory Committee Document 1/5 17 December 1937. TUC File 932.

90 *Memorandum for Inaugural Meeting 22 December 1937.* Colonial Advisory Committee Document 1/1. TUC File 939.9 I.

91 Ebby Edwards (Miners' Federation): 1931–46 member of General Council, 1944 president of Congress.

92 Arthur Shaw (Textile Workers): 1929–38 member of General Council. Died February 1939. Replaced by G. H. Bagnall (Dyers, Bleachers and Textile Workers): 1939–47 member of General Council.

93 Colonial Advisory Committee *Minutes*, 16 February, 30 March, 22 June, 1938; *Congress Report*, 1938, pp. 205–6.

94 *Forster Report*, pp. 47–51.

95 *Labour Conditions in the West Indies: Report by Major G. St J. Orde Browne.* (London: July 1939), Cmd. 6070, pp. 142, 49.

96 MSS Afr.s1117 Orde Browne. Box 2, O.B. 2/5 71, 75, 83. OUCRP.

97 *Deputation to Malcolm MacDonald 23 June 1938*, TUC File 712.5. MacDonald/Citrine 3 August 1938, *Special Colonial Advisory Committee Meeting with Orde Browne*, TUC File 932; Colonial Advisory Committee *Minutes*, 5 August 1938.

99 J. G. Hibbert/Kemmis 15 August 1938; Kemmis/N. A. Bavan, Ministry of Labour 26 May 1938; Hibbert/Kemmis 30 September 1939. TUC File 932.5 I.

100 *Congress Report*, 1938, p. 207.

101 ibid., pp. 433–5.

102 L.P.Imp.A.C. *Minutes*, 26 July 1939, with note.

103 *Congress Report*, 1939, pp. 232–34.

104 Cipriani/Gillies 19 November 1937. TUC File 932.9/200.

105 *Interview* Kemmis, Makonnen 24 August 1938. TUC File 972.

106 *Interview* Kemmis, Peter Blackman 19 August 1938. TUC File 932; TUC/Blackman 24 August 1938. TUC File 972.

107 Colonial Advisory Committee *Minutes*, 22 June 1938; *West India Royal Commission Report* (London: June 1945), Cmd. 6607, p. xi.

108 G. L. M. Clauson/Vincent Tewson 5 March 1939; Colonial Advisory Committee *Minutes*, 26 April 1939; *Interview* Clauson, Kemmis 9 May 1939. TUC File 931 I; *Labour Supervision in the Colonial Empire 1937–1943*. Colonial no. 185, 1943. p.2.

109 Clauson/Kemmis 9 June 1939 TUC File 932.3; Colonial Advisory Committee *Minutes*, 14 June, 9 November, 1939.

110 *Forster Report*, p. 88.

111 *Orde Browne Report, West Indies*, pp. 121–2.

112 ibid., p. 44.

113 T. I. K. Lloyd: 1921 assistant principal, Colonial Office; 1929 principal; 1938–9 secretary, West India Royal Commission; 1939 assistant secretary; 1947 permanent under-secretary of state.

114 22 December 1939. C.O.859.11.1790.

115 *Congress Report*, 1939, p. 234; Note by T. I. K. Lloyd, 8 November 1939, C.O.859.11.1790.

116 *Citrine Papers: Diary.* Jamaica 2 December 1938; Trinidad 6 March 1939; Antigua 30 December 1938; Barbados 19 January 1939; British Guiana 13, 15 February 1939.

117 Interview with Lord Citrine, 20 March 1975.

118 *Citrine Papers: Diary.* Trinidad 7 March 1939.

119 George Woodcock (Weavers' Association): 1936 secretary, TUC Research Department, 1947 assistant general secretary, 1960–69 General Secretary; 1954 member, British Guiana Constitutional Commission; *Citrine Papers: West India Royal Commission* Drawers I. V, VI.

120 Morgan, *British Aid Policy*, pp. 76–7.

121 *Recommendations of the West India Royal Commission*, February 1940, Cmd. 6174; *West India Royal Commission Report*, July 1945, Cmd. 6607;

West India Royal Commission 1938–39, Statement of Action Taken on the Recommendations, July 1945, Cmd. 6656.

122   Interviews with Lord Citrine. 25, 27, 31 September 1976.

123   *Trade Disputes and Trade Unions Act 1927*: '1 (I) (a) ... any strike is illegal if it – (i) has any object other than or in addition to the furtherance of a trade dispute within the trade or industry in which the strikers are engaged; and (ii) is a strike designed or calculated to coerce the Government either directly or by inflicting hardship upon the community ... and it is further declared that it is illegal to commence, or continue, or to apply any sums in furtherance or support of, any such illegal strike or lockout ... (4) The provisions of the Trade Disputes Act 1906 shall not ... apply to any act done in contemplation or furtherance of a strike or lockout which is by this Act illegal, and any such act shall not be deemed for the purposes of any enactment to be done in contemplation or furtherance of a trade dispute.'

124   Lord Citrine, *Men and Work*, p. 360.

125   *Citrine Papers: Diary*. 21, 25, November, 5 December 1938.

126   ibid., 23 January 1939.

127   Francis Mark, *The History of the Barbados Workers' Union* (Barbados Workers' Union, 1969), pp. 67–8.

128   *Trade Union (Amendment) Act 1949*. Barbados, 9 February 1950.

129   Makhan Singh/Citrine 8 July 1938; internal office note Woodcock/Kemmis 17 November 1938; Kemmis/Singh 18 November 1938. TUC File 967 I.

130   *Report of Fabian Colonial Bureau Meeting with Colonial Delegates to the World Trade Union Conference 19 February 1945*. MSS Brit. Emp. s332, ACJ 14/4. 5. OUCRP; Labour Party, The Colonies: The Labour Party's Post-war Policy for the African and Pacific Colonies. (London: March 1943) p. 11.

131   The British Guiana ordinance of 1919 provided protection against actions for damages in strikes, but did not protect peaceful picketing.

132   Morgan Jones: 1921–39 Labour Member of Parliament; 1932–4 member of Joint Select Committee on Indian Constitutional Reform; 1938–9 member of West India Royal Commission, died immediately on return.

133   *Citrine Papers: West India Royal Commission*. Oral evidence 1.2.1939.

134   *West Indies Welfare Local Levy (Memorandum by Sir Walter Citrine)* 14 August 1939. Citrine Papers, West India Royal Commission, Drawer 1. III.

135   *Action on Recommendations*, p. 55.

136   *Citrine Papers: West India Royal Commission*, Drawer 1, V.

137   *Royal Commission Report*, p. 249.

138   Urgent Confidential Circular, with letter MacDonald/Moyne, 13 February 1940. *Citrine Papers: West India Royal Commission*, Drawer 1, IV (2).

139   *Action on Recommendations*, pp. 4–6.

140   D. J. Morgan, *British Aid Policy*, pp. 41, xiv–xvi, 76–7.

141   *Statement of Policy on Colonial Development and Welfare*. Cmd. 6175.

20 February 1940.

142 *First Interim Report of Colonial Development Advisory Committee, 1 August 1929 - 28 February 1930.* Cmd. 3540. Enclosed with Confidential Circular 24 April 1930. C.O. 854. 173.71261/1930 (5).

143 *Colonial Development and Welfare Act 1940.* 3 and 4 Geo. 6, Ch. 40. Section 1 (2) (a).

144 George Hall (South Wales Miners' Federation): 1922–46 Labour Member of Parliament for Aberdare; 1940–42 Parliamentary Under-Secretary of State for the Colonies; August 1945–October 1946 Secretary of State for the Colonies.

145 Tarrant, *Colonial Office and Labour Question,* pp. 339–41.

146 Morgan, *British Aid Policy,* p. 124.

147 J. G. Hibbert: 1930 joined Colonial Office; principal 1936; 1943 assistant secretary, Ministry of Fuel and Power; 1947 assistant secretary, Colonial Office.

148 Tarrant, *Colonial Office and Labour Question,* pp. 342–3.

149 Confidential Circular 12 July 1941. C.O. 859/49/41/122254/3.

150 The report of the Commission of Inquiry was made available only to Members of Parliament, but was summarized in *Empire* Vol. V, no.5, pp. 9–12 and Vol. VI no. 1, p. 2. Fabian Colonial Bureau, 1943.

151 *Congress Reports:* 1956, p. 224; 1957, p. 227; 1958, p. 239; 1959, p. 252.

152 Hall/Citrine 24 June 1940, TUC File 930 (1); *Discussion at Colonial Office, 4 July 1940,* TUC File 932.51; International Committee *Minutes 23 July 1940.*

153 *Orde Browne Report, West Indies,* p. 44; Orde Browne/Hibbert 9 May 1940 with *A Memorandum on Colonial Trade Unionism and the Trade Union Council,* Hibbert/Orde Browne 10, 13, May 1940, MSS Afr. s1117 2/4, 102, 115, 117, OUCRP.

154 Sir Cosmo Parkinson/C. G. Eastwood 11 January 1941, Hibbert/Stockdale 7 March 1941, C.O.859/59 1941 12278; Citrine/Hall 29 May 1941, TUC File 932.3.

155 Replies to Circular Telegram of 7 February 1941, Notes by Hibbert 1, 23, September 1941, C.O.859/59 1941 12278/A; Sir George Gater/Citrine 27 February 1945, TUC File 932.33.

156 *Labour Supervision in the Colonial Empire 1937–1943,* p. 8. Colonial Advisory Committee *Minutes,* 18 November 1941.

157 ibid., pp. 8–9.

158 C. J. Jeffries/Citrine 12 December 1941, TUC File 932.93; General Council *Minutes,* 17 December 1941.

159 MSS Brit. Emp. s 332 ACJ 11/4, 5. OUCRP.

160 Dalgleish/Citrine, Citrine/Dalgleish, 22 October 1942. TUC File 932.93.

161 Morgan, *British Aid Policy,* p. 195.

162 Colonial Advisory Committee *Minutes,* 29 April 1942; MSS Brit. Emp. s332 ACJ 11/4, 25. OUCRP.

163 Jeffries/Citrine 12 December 1941; K. W. Blaxter/Citrine 29 May 1945, Citrine/Blaxter 1 June 1945. TUC File 932.93.

164 Hallsworth/Citrine 4 November 1943 with CLAC document no. 40; Citrine/Hallsworth 15 November, 7 December, 1943; Secretary of State (Col. Oliver Stanley)/Citrine 10 January 1944; TUC FGPC *Minutes*, 20 December 1943, International Committee *Minutes*, 18 January 1944 with document I.C.3/6; Citrine/Stanley 21 January 1944. TUC File 932.5 I.

165 Colonial Labour Advisory Committee 1942–3: Papers and Minutes. C.O.888/2.

166 ibid., Gold Coast Railway Workers' Union; Hibbert/Kemmis 16 September 1942, Kemmis/Hibbert 28 September 1942, Barbados Workers' Union. TUC File 932.5.

167 Foreword to *BBC Broadcast to the West Indies* (Barbados: Comptroller for Development and Welfare, 1943).

Chapter 7

1 Letter to *Manchester Guardian* 5 August 1938.

2 *Daily Herald* 31 August 1938.

3 *Citrine Papers: Diary* 1 November 1938.

4 *Jamaica 1938: The Birth of the Bustamante Industrial Trade Union* (Kingston BITU, 1968). (Pages not numbered.)

5 C. E. Talma/Kemmis 15 April 1939. TUC File 972.27.

6 *West India Royal Commission Report*, p. xviii; Oral evidence, 24 January 1939.

7 *Orde Browne Report: West Indies*, pp. 177, 184, 183.

8 George S. Anthony/Labour Party 1 November 1937; Citrine/W. R. Spence (NUS) 25 November 1937; Anthony/Fimmen (ITF) 6 January 1938, Fimmen/Citrine 20 January 1938; Citrine/Anthony, 26 November 1937–10 June 1938, *passim*. TUC File 972.8.

9 Citrine/C. R. Jacob 31 May 1938, H. Barron/Citrine 6 July 1938, Citrine/Barron 25 July 1938. TUC File 972.8.

10 Helena Manuel/Citrine 1 July 1928, Citrine/Manuel 28 July 1928; Sassenbach (IFTU)/Citrine 23 August 1929, Citrine/Cipriani 6 March, 17 September 1930, internal office note 25 September 1930; TUC File 972.9. Citrine/Officers (Merchant Navy) Federation 26 March 1936, TUC File 972.9/200.

11 Charles Atkinson/Citrine 18 November 1933 – 29 May 1936; A. S. Mondezie/Citrine 16 September, Gaskynd A. Grainger/Citrine 22 November, 1937. TUC Files 972.9, 972.9/200.

12 G. Maurice Hann (British Shop Asistants' Union)/Citrine, with correspondence from TLP Clerks' Union 1 January 1938, Citrine/Hann 3 January 1938; Quintin O'Connor/Citrine 23 May–11 July 1938; C. James Harris (TLP Clerks Union), V. E. Henry (TLP)/Citrine 25 May–4 July 1938. TUC File 972.9/200.

13 Sylvestre L. Patrick/Citrine 11 October 1937, TUC File 972.9; *Orde Browne Report: West Indies*, p. 132.

14 *Forster Report*, p. 58.

15 W. Richard Jacobs, ed., *Butler Versus the King* (Port of Spain: Key

Caribbean Publications, 1976), pp. 224, 230, 206–9.

16 Interview with John Rojas, Arima, 7 February 1976.

17 *Orde Browne Report: West Indies*, p. 132; C. Rienzi/Citrine 31 March 1938, TUC File 972.9.

18 *Forster Report*, pp. 93, 24; Pugh/Citrine 7 December 1937, with comments on Cipriani/Gillies 19 November 1937. TUC File 972.9/200.

19 *Port of Spain Gazette* 8 April 1938.

20 John Jagger: 1915–20 Yorkshire divisional officer, Amalgamated Union of Cooperative Employees; 1920 General President, National Union of Distributive and Allied Workers; 1935 Member of Parliament.

21 John Jagger MP, *Trinidad and the Tribunal, November 1938–February 1939: A Descriptive Diary*. Duplicated typescript, 1939, *passim*.

22 G. S. Anthony/Citrine 10 June 1938, C. R. Jacob/Citrine 8 August 1938, TUC File 972.8; *Congress Report*, 1938, p. 435.

23 G. H. Grantley Adams (later Sir): 1936 Member of Colonial Parliament; 1938 vice-president, Barbados Progressive League; 1941 President, Barbados Workers' Union; 1949 Member of ILO Committee of Experts on the Application of Conventions; 1954 Premier, 1958 Prime Minister of Barbados; 1958–62 Prime Minister of West Indies Federation.

24 W. H. Seale/TUC 14 December 1938. TUC File 972.27.

25 *Rules of the Barbados Labour League, 7 January 1909* (Bridgetown: Times Printing Office, 1909).

26 *Short History of Trade Unionism in Barbados and 19th Annual Report* (Bridgetown: Barbados Workers' Union, 1960), p. 6.

27 Interview with Erskine R. Ward, Hastings, Barbados, 10 February 1976.

28 *Annual Report on the Social and Economic Progress of the People of Barbados 1937–38*. HMSO no. 1861, 1938.

29 *Replies to Questionnaire on Labour*, prepared in compliance with Secretary of State's despatch no. 151 of 26 July 1938. Serial no. 617, Citrine Papers: Royal Commission. Drawer 4A, 4.

30 *Report of Commission appointed to inquire into the disturbances which took place in Barbados on 27 July 1937 and subsequent days* (Deane Report) (Bridgetown: 2 November 1937), para. 44.

31 Mark, *Barbados Workers' Union*, p. 7.

32 *Deane Report, passim*.

33 *Orde Browne Report: West Indies*, pp. 101, 145, 150, 157, 49, 148, 156, 158.

34 William H. Knowles, *Trade Union Development and Industrial Relations in the British West Indies* (Berkeley and Los Angeles: University of California Press, 1959), pp. 113, 143.

35 Cipriani/Milne-Bailey 6 May 1934, Interview McIntyre/Bolton 28 May 1934; Owen G. Mathurin (*Voice of St Lucia*)/TUC 30 November 1934, TUC/Mathurin 20 December 1934. TUC File 972.9.

36 *Orde Browne Report: West Indies*, pp. 149, 104, 145, 157.

37 *Royal Commission Report*, pp. 461–6, 478.

38   Zin Henry, *Labour Relations and Industrial Conflict in Commonwealth Caribbean Countries*. (Trinidad: Columbus Publishers, 1972), p. 33.

39   I am indebted to Mr Richard Hart for drawing my attention to a police report dated 3 May 1938 filed in the Public Record Office (CO 137/827 File 68868/2) which states that Coombs was replaced as president of the JWTU by Aiken in February but was contesting Aiken's claim, which was also not recognized in some of the rural branches. The report suggested that by the end of March Aiken and Maxwell had decided to leave the JWTU and start a new union. There was no indication in the TUC correspondence that the union asking for rules in May was a breakaway.

40   L. E. Barnett (Linstead)/Citrine 19 February–8 March 1937; Citrine/Maxwell 26 May–24 June 1938, Maxwell/*Daily Gleaner*, Kingston, 20 December 1938; J. R. Leslie MP/Vincent Tewson 30 May 1938, Citrine/Tummings 31 May 1938; Samuel McLean, C. Floyd (Authoritative Trade Union/Citrine 4 October 1937–30 December 1938, Kemmis/Makonnen 18–20 January 1939; TUC File 972.1. *Orde Browne Report: West Indies*, p. 98. *Royal Commission Report*, pp. 459, 476.

41   Alexander Bustamante (later Sir): 1938 Life President, Bustamante Industrial Trade Union; 1943 President, Jamaica Labour Party; 1944 Member of House of Representatives; 1955 Chief Minister, 1962–7 Prime Minister of Jamaica.

42   Morgan, *British Aid Policy*, p. 27.

43   Norman Manley: 1938 Leader, People's National Party; 1949 Member of House of Representatives; 1955–62 Premier of Jamaica.

44   *Jamaica 1938*.

45   *Citrine Papers: Diary* 28 February 1939.

46   Interview with Miss Edith Nelson and senior officers, BITU, Kingston, 27 January 1976.

47   R. Nettleford, ed. *Manley and the New Jamaica, Selected Speeches and Writings 1938–1968*. (London: Longman Caribbean, 1971), p. xlvii.

48   Ken Hill/Citrine 11 June 1938, Citrine/Hill 13 July 1938. TUC File 972.1.

49   Hill/Citrine 4 August 1938, ibid.

50   Hart, *Caribbean Working Class*, p. 418.

51   Florizel Glasspole (later Sir): 1937 General Secretary, Jamaica United Clerks Association; 1939 Secretary, Trade Union Advisory Council; 1952 General Secretary, National Workers' Union; 1944–72 Member of House of Representatives; 1955 Minister of Labour; 1957, 1972, Minister of Education; 1972 Governor-General of Jamaica.

52   *Orde Browne Report: West Indies*, p. 98; *Jamaica 1938*.

53   Interview with Dr Zin Henry, Port of Spain, 4 February 1976.

54   Lord Citrine, *Men and Work*, pp. 332–3; *Citrine Papers: Diary* 14 November 1938.

55   Oral evidence 27 February 1939.

56   *Citrine Papers: Diary* 19 January, 14 February, 1939.

57   *Daily Chronicle*, Georgetown. 16 February, 20 February, 1939.

58   *Citrine Papers: Diary* 17–20 February 1939.

59 Oral evidence 24 January 1939.
60 *The Workers' Case for a Better Trinidad. Memorandum from the Committee for Industrial Organization to the Royal Commission.* (San Fernando: CIO, 1938).
61 *Memorandum Submitted by the Sugar Manufacturers of Trinidad on the Sugar Industry;* Oral Evidence, 27 February 1939.
62 *Memorandum Submitted by Petroleum Association of Trinidad.* Appendix D.
63 *Citrine Papers: Diary.* 16, 24, February 1939.
64 ibid., 2 December 1938; 24 January, 14 February, 9 March 1939; 22 December 1938.
65 ibid., 2 March 1939; *Royal Commission Report,* p. 199.
66 *Citrine Papers: Diary* 6 November, 1 December, 1938, 23 January 1939; W. Seale/TUC Accounts Department 10 February 1939, TUC File 972.27.
67 *Citrine Papers: Diary* 17 January, 16 January, 1939, 23 December 1938; R. St Clair Stevens (president), Berkely A. Richards (secretary), Antigua Trade and Labour Union/Citrine 18 March 1939. TUC File 972.21.
68 *Citrine Papers: Diary* 3 January, 9 January 1939.
69 Sir Walter Citrine, *Trade Unionism in the West Indies,* 3 May 1939 (draft of TUC Committee document). *Citrine Papers: Royal Commission,* Drawer 1, IV 3.
70 *Citrine Papers: Diary* 13 January 1939.
71 Interview with Lord Citrine 25 September 1976; *Citrine Papers: Diary* 12 January, 9 January, 1939.
72 *Citrine Papers: Royal Commission.* Drawer 6, G.
73 Sir Walter Citrine, *Trade Unionism in the West Indies.* TUC File 972.27.
74 *Memorandum;* C. E. Talma, 'What the Progressive League Represents'; *Barbados Observer* 20 May 1939.
75 *Citrine Papers: Diary* 25 January 1939.
76 Mark, *Barbados Workers' Union,* pp. 93–4.
77 C. E. Talma/TUC Accounts Department 15 April 1939. TUC File 972.27.
78 Hugh W. Springer/Citrine 11 October 1942. TUC File 972.27.
79 Hugh Springer (later Sir): 1941—7 General Secretary, BWU; 1940—7 Member of House of Assembly; 1947—63 Registrar, University of West Indies; 1970—80 Secretary-General, Association of Commonwealth Universities; 1984 Governor-General of Barbados.
80 *First Annual Report* to first Annual Delegate Conference, 28 March 1942, Barbados Workers' Union. TUC File 972.27; *Five Years of Trade Unionism, The Barbados Workers' Union Fifth Anniversary.* (Bridgetown: Advocate Company, 1946), p. 24.
81 Nettleford, *Manley,* pp. xliv, xlviii; *Jamaica 1938.*
82 *Citrine Papers: Diary* 22 November, 6 November, 1938.
83 ibid., 30 November, 5 December, 1938; *Daily Gleaner* 6 December 1938.
84 *Daily Gleaner* 15, 19, December 1938; Hart, *Caribbean Working*

Class, p. 418.

85 *Report on the Trades Union Congress of Jamaica to 30 June 1946*. Mimeo, Kingston, 1946. p. 2. Cited in Jeffrey Harrod, *Trade Union Foreign Policy: A Study of British and American Trade Union Activities in Jamaica*. (London: Macmillan, 1972), p. 177.

86 Hart, *Caribbean Working Class*, p. 417.

87 F. Glasspole/Kemmis 27 March 1939. TUC File 972.1.

88 *Daily Gleaner* 17, 26, 28, 29, April 1939.

89 Hill/Citrine 22 April 1939, Citrine/Hill 2 May 1939, Hill/Citrine 5 May 1939; Glasspole/Citrine 22 May 1939, Citrine/Glasspole 9 June 1939. TUC File 972.1.

90 *Citrine Papers: Diary* 7, 14, 17, February 1939.

91 Rawle Farley, 'A Note on the British Guiana Trade Union Congress', *The Caribbean Trade Unionist*. (Georgetown: *Daily Chronicle* 1958), pp. 69–74.

92 *Citrine Papers: Diary* 2, 17, 3, 22, 23, March 1939.

93 Cable, OWTU/TUC 10 August 1939. TUC File 972.

94 F. W. Dalley, *Trade Union Organization and Industrial Relations in Trinidad*. Colonial no. 215 (HMSO: 1947), pp. 7, 41–43.

95 John Jagger MP, *Trinidad and the Tribunal*, p. 28.

96 In November 1938 the unions in the American Committee, having been suspended by the AFL, converted it into a federation of unions, the Congress of Industrial Organizations.

97 Knowles, *Trade Union Development*, pp. 128–9.

98 *Rex v. Ulric Grant*, Court of Grand Sessions, Barbados. Enclosure in Despatch no. 81 of 14 March 1938.

99 Interview with McDonald Moses, Port of Spain, 2 February 1976.

100 Interview with Lord Citrine, 31 September 1976; *Citrine Papers: Diary* 2 March 1939; I am indebted to Richard Hart for the information that the communist group in Jamaica had connections with the Jamaica Progressive League founded in New York in 1936, but not with the Comintern or the RILU, and that after Pollitt's visit to Jamaica he made contact with Bed Bradley in the CPGB, but received little information or comment on the information he sent to Bradley.

101 The choice of Collard as one of the workers' nominees on the arbitration board suggests a left-wing, if not Communist Party, connection. The secretary of the CPGB, Harry Pollitt, on a convalescent cruise, travelled on the same boat as Jagger and Collard and landed briefly in Trinidad and in Jamaica, where he arrived on the day of Citrine's departure.

102 *Proclamation*, 14 April 1932. Trinidad and Tobago no. 24 of 1932.

103 Gomes, *Maze of Colour*, p. 19.

104 Inspector-General of Police/Colonial Secretary Barbados, 17 June 1933, with leaflet *Resist the War Plans of the McDonald Government* and *West Indian Organizer*, vol. I January 1933. Barbados Archives ACC no. 38 GH 3/6/4.

105 Knowles, *Trade Union Development*, p. 195.

106 Circular Letters Kemmis/Correspondents 6 March 1939, Citrine/Correspondents May 1939, TUC File 972/202; Corrected list, November

1940, TUC File 972.

107 Colonial Advisory Committee *Minutes*, 14 June 1939; General Council *Minutes*, 1 September 1939 and document G.C.26 *Trade Unionism in the West Indies* 29 August 1939.

108 *Assistance to West Indian Trade Unions: Memorandum by Sir Walter Citrine* 14 October 1942; General Council *Minutes*, 30 September 1942.

109 Colonial Labour Advisory Committee *Minutes*, 6 August 1943. C.O.888/2.

110 Nethersole, JTUC/Citrine 14 October–30 December 1942; Citrine/ Cranborne (Secretary of State) 14 October–3 November 1942; Citrine/NUR 31 December 1942. TUC File 972.1.

111 Thorne/Citrine 21 January, 21 March, 1941 (received in TUC on 4 March and 9 April, respectively). TUC File 972/111.

112 Citrine/Moyne 17 April 1941, Citrine/Cranborne 30 March 1942, TUC File 972/111; Colonial Advisory Committee *Minutes*, 18 November 1941 and document Col. Adv. Cttee. 1/1941–42, TUC File 930; General Council *Minutes*, 26 November 1941.

113 Document Col. Adv. Cttee. 1/1941–42, TUC File 930.

114 International Committee *Minutes*, 27 August 1940, 21 January – 22 July 1941; Document I.C.3/1 1940–41. TUC File 968.1.

115 *Report of the Commission Appointed to Inquire into the Disturbances in the Copperbelt, Northern Rhodesia, in April 1940* (Lusaka: Government Printer, 1941); *Statement by the Government of Northern Rhodesia on the Report of the Copperbelt Commission* (London: Colonial Office, February 1941).

116 A. L. Epstein, *Politics in an Urban African Community* (Manchester University Press, 1958), p. 62; and *passim* for full account of tribal elder system.

117 P. D. Savage/TUC 27 March 1942; Colonial Advisory Committee *Minutes*, 29 April 1942; Wilfred Benson (ILO London Office)/Kemmis 30 April 1942; Citrine/Cranborne 10 June 1942, Cranborne/Tewson 6 July 1942. TUC File 966.4.

118 *Sedition in Our Overseas Dependencies.* L.P.Imp.A.C. no. 141, June 1934, Labour Party; Colonial Advisory Committee *Minutes*, 15 March, 26 April, 9 November, 1939; Kemmis/Hibbert 30 March 1939, W. J. Bigg (Colonial Office)/Kemmis 19 April 1939. TUC File 930.

119 *Citrine Papers: Diary* 6 November 1938, 17, 21, 23, 25, January 1939.

120 *Citrine Papers: Royal Commission.* Serial no. 626; Serial no. 620, Petition of Ulric McDonald Grant, 2 October 1938, and Note, Drawer 4B; *Rex v. Ulric Grant.*

121 *Citrine Papers: Diary* 25 January 1939.

122 Citrine/Moyne 29 September 1941, Moyne/Citrine 2 October 1941, Private secretary to Secretary of State/Citrine 23 December 1941. TUC File 972.27.

123 H. M. Shirley, vice-president, on behalf of BITU Executive/Citrine 8 April 1941, with petition 17 February 1941; Citrine/Moyne 19 May 1941, Moyne/Citrine 30 May, 12 August, 1941; Citrine/Shirley 26 August 1941. TUC File 972.1.

124 Colonial Advisory Committee *Minutes*, 18 November 1941; Document Col.Adv.Cttee. 1/1941–42, TUC File 930.

125 Michael Manley, *A Voice at the Workplace* (London: Andre Deutsch, 1975), p. 37; Interview with Miss Edith Nelson, General Secretary, BITU, 27 January 1976; *Jamaica 1938.*

126 Ken Hill/Citrine 7 December 1942; Citrine/Stanley 3 February 1943, Stanley/Citrine 19 February 1943; Henry/Citrine 27 December 1942, 30 April 1943. TUC File 972.1.

127 *Congress Reports:* 1943 pp. 97, 297; 1944 p. 123; 1945 p. 145.

128 *Congress Reports:* 1941 p. 349; 1942 p. 261.

129 *Supervision of Conditions under which Labour is Employed in the Colonial Empire.* Colonial Office, October 1941. Stencilled.

130 Colonial Advisory Committee *Minutes*, 18 November 1941, 21 October 1943.

131 *Congress Reports:* 1944 pp. 113, 122; 1945 p. 144.

132 *Congress Report* 1944 pp. 114–15.

133 ILO Governing Body, 94th Session, London, 25 January 1945.

134 *Congress Report*, 1939 pp. 215–19; Schevenels, *Forty Five Years*, p. 193.

135 *Congress Reports:* 1943 p. 92, 1944 p. 104 and seqq.; International Committee *Minutes*, 20 June 1944; *Social and Economic Demands of the International Trade Union Movement for the Post-War World.* Emergency International Trade Union Council. (London: IFTU, April 1944).

136 *Resolution of the ECCI Presidium*, Moscow, 15 May 1943; *Statement of the ECCI Presidium on the Dissolution of the Communist International*, Moscow, 8 June 1943. Jane Degras, ed., *The Communist International, 1919–1943, Documents*, Vol. III (London: Oxford University Press, 1965 pp. 477–9, 480–81.

137 Document I.C.5/3, 20 April 1948.

138 *Congress Report*, 1945 p. 355.

139 *Congress Report*, 1943 p. 373.

140 *Congress Report*, 1945 pp. 100–116, 138, 140–41, 144.

141 *The TUC and the WFTU* (London: TUC 1948) p. 4.

142 Lord Citrine, *Two Careers* (London: Hutchinson, 1967), p. 231.

143 *The Colonies: The Labour Party's Post-War Policy for the African and Pacific Colonies.* (London: Labour Party, 1943).

144 George Padmore, *Pan-Africanism or Communism?* (London: Dennis Dobson, 1956), pp. 149–51, 154–6, 163–5.

145 Ebby Edwards: 1931 General Secretary, 1932 President, Miners' Federation of Great Britain; 1931–46 Member of TUC General Council, 1944 and 1945 President of Congress.

146 *Congress Report*, 1945 pp. 363–72, 21, 23, 5–6, 260, 406, 353–6, 291, 99, 115, 9.

147 *Let Us Face the Future, A Declaration of Labour Policy for the Consideration of the Nation.* (London: Labour Party, April 1945) p. 11.

148 *Congress Report*, 1945 pp. 144, 152–6, 421.

Chapter 8

1   Ernest Bevin, *Trade Unionists and the War*. Address given under the auspices of the Scottish TUC General Council. Edinburgh, 14 December 1940.
2   Buxton 5/3. 9; 5/3. 173–5. OUCRP.
3   Citrine Papers: *Diary* 27 December 1938. (Emphasis added.)
4   See Chapter 2, p. 24, above.
5   See Chapter 2, p. 36, above.
6   Alan Bullock, *Bevin*, Vol. II, p. 206.
7   *The Spectator* 3 February 1939.
8   Bullock, *Ernest Bevin, Foreign Secretary*, p. 746.
9   Bullock, *Bevin*, Vol. II. pp. 206–7.
10 *The Labour Party's Policy on International Affairs*. Speech by the Rt Hon. Ernest Bevin, MP, at the Labour Party Conference at Blackpool, 23 May 1945.
11 *West India Royal Commission Report*, p. 373.
12 *The Colonies*. For a fuller treatment, see David Goldsworthy, *Colonial Issues in British Politics 1945–1961* (London: Oxford University Press, 1971) pp. 120–21.

Sources and Select Bibliography

(Further details and references are given in the notes to Chapters.)

1 Unpublished Sources

TUC

Subject files.

Minutes of Parliamentary Committee and General Council, and of the following subordinate committees:

Finance, Functions, Finance and General Purposes, International, Far Eastern Labour Conditions, Forced Labour, Colonial Advisory.

Labour Party

Minutes of Advisory Committee on Imperial Affairs.

TUC/Labour Party joint committees.

Minutes of the following committees:

International Joint Committee, 1917.

During period of joint working:

Joint Executives, National Joint Council (with Parliamentary Labour Party), Joint International Committee, Advisory Committee on International Questions and Imperial Questions Sub-Committee.

1933 National Joint Council Sub-Committee on Meerut Prisoners.

Colonial Office Records

Classified in the Public Records Office as follows:

Circular despatches C.O.854, Colonial Labour Committee and Colonial Labour Advisory Committee C.O.888, internal Office notes C.O.859, C.O.866.

Collections of private papers

Lord Citrine: West India Royal Commission papers (TUC), Diary (Lord Citrine).

Oxford University Colonial Records Project, Rhodes House, Oxford: Major Orde Browne, Charles Roden Buxton, Arthur Creech Jones.

Nehru Memorial Library, New Delhi: N. M. Joshi Papers.

Institute of Social Studies, Amsterdam: File on League Against Imperialism, Schevenels Archive.

John Jagger, *Trinidad and the Tribunal, A Descriptive Diary*. Filed in Lord Citrine's West India Royal Commission papers.

2. Published Sources

Proceedings and Policy Statements

Trades Union Congress: Congress Reports.
  Russia and International Unity, 1925.
  Democracy or Disruption, 1928.
Labour Party: Annual Conference Reports.
  Memorandum on War Aims, 1918.
  Memoranda on International Labour Legislation (prepared for Berne Congress)
    with Berne Labour Charter.
  Labour and the New Social Order, 1918.
  The Empire in Africa: Labour's Policy undated. (Apparently 1920. According
    to Woolf, drafted by Roden Buxton.)
  Sweated Imports and International Labour Standards, 1925.
  The Colonial Empire, 1933.
  *The Colonies: The Labour Party's Post-War Policy for the African and Pacific
    Colonies*, 1943.
  Let Us Face the Future, 1945.
Labour Party and TUC:
  Labour and the Empire: Africa, 1926.
  Report of First British Commonwealth Labour Conference, 1925.
  Report of Second British Commonwealth Labour Conference, 1928
    (duplicated typescript).
  Report of Third British Commonwealth Labour Conference, 1930
    (duplicated typescript).

International Federation of Trade Unions:
  Emergency International Trade Union Council, *Social and Economic
    Demands of the International Trade Union Movement for the Post-War
    World*, 1944.

International Labour Organisation:
  Proceedings of International Labour Conferences.
  Minutes of Governing Body.
  *Conventions and Recommendations Adopted by the International Labour
    Conference 1919–1966*, 1966.

Barbados Labour League: *Rules*. Times Printing Office, Bridgetown, 1909 (in
  TUC Library).
Workers' Welfare League of India: *Objects*, undated.
Red International of Labour Unions:
  J. T. Murphy, *The 'Reds' in Congress, Preliminary Report of the First World
    Congress of the Red International of Trade and Industrial Unions*. British
    Bureau, London, 1921.
  Report of Executive Bureau to Third Congress of RILU 1924. (typed copy,
    TUC Library).
Committee for Industrial Organization, Trinidad:

The Workers' Case for a Better Trinidad, Memorandum to the Royal Commission.
(San Fernando: CIO, 1938).

Journals
TUC:
International Trades Union Review 1918–1922.
Industrial Review (begins January 1927).
Labour (begins September 1938).
TUC and Labour Party: Labour Magazine 1922–1927.
Labour Research Department: Trade Union Unity 1925–1926.
RILU, Moscow: Eastern and Colonial Bulletin 1927–1931.
Pan-Pacific Trade Union Secretariat, Hankow: Pan-Pacific Worker 1927 (TUC
File 909.3).

Government Reports

Report of the Royal Commission on Labour in India, 1931. Cmd. 3883.
Trinidad and Tobago Disturbances, 1937: Report of Commission, 1937. Cmd.
5641.
Report of Commission Appointed to Enquire into the Disturbances which Took Place
in Barbados on 27 July 1937 and Subsequent Days. Bridgetown, November
1937 (not numbered).
Annual Report on the Social and Economic Progress of the People of Barbados
1937–8. HMSO no. 1861, 1938.
Returns Showing the Results of Elections in India in 1937. Cmd. 559, November
1937.
The Colonial Empire in 1937–38. Cmd. 5760, 1938.
Labour Conditions in the West Indies, Report by Major G. St J. Orde Browne, OBE
Cmd. 6070, July 1939.
Recommendations of the West India Royal Commission. Cmd. 6174, 1940.
West India Royal Commission Report. Cmd. 6607, July 1945.
West India Royal Commission 1938–39, Statement of Action Taken on the
Recommendations. Cmd. 6656, July 1945.
Statement of Policy on Colonial Development and Welfare. Cmd. 6175, 1940.
Report of the Commission Appointed to Enquire into the Disturbances in the
Copperbelt, Northern Rhodesia, October 1935. Cmd. 5009.
Report of the Commission Appointed to Enquire into the Disturbances in the
Copperbelt, Northern Rhodesia, in April 1940. Government Printer, Lusaka,
1941 (not numbered).
Labour Supervision in the Colonial Empire 1937–1943. Colonial no. 185, 1943.

Other Reports
TUC:
Official Report of the British Trades Union Delegation to Russia in November and
December 1924, 1925.
Report on Labour Conditions in India by A. A. Purcell MP and J. Hallsworth
(British Trades Union Congress Delegation to India) November 1927 to
March 1928, 1928.
International Labour Conference 1930, Forced Labour: Report to the TUC

International Committee by J. Bromley (Not printed, TUC File 932.1).

TUC and Labour Party:
  British Labour Delegation to Russia 1920: Report, 1920.
  Report by the Rt Hon. F. O. Roberts, MP, on his Visit to the West Indies, 1926, to the Members of the Labour Party Executive and the TUC General Council. With Minutes of First West Indian Labour Conference 11–14 January 1926, and extract from 1925 Annual Report of the TWMA (Not printed, TUC File 972.9)

Textile Labour Union, Ahmedabad: *Annual Report 1925*.

Bombay Textile Labour Union: *First Annual Report 1926* (Bombay, 1927).

India League: *The Condition of India, Being the Report of the Delegation sent to India by the India League in 1932*, ed. V. K. Krishna Menon (London, 1933).

Trinidad Workingmen's Association: *Trinidad in Parliament, Report by W. Howard–Bishop Jnr.* (London: National Labour Press, 1921).

Barbados Workers' Union:
  First Annual Report to First Annual Delegate Conference, 28 March 1942. (Not printed, TUC File 972.27).
  Five Years Of Trade Unionism, The Barbados Workers' Union Fifth Anniversary. (Bridgetown: Advocate Company, 1946).
  Short History of Trade Unionism in Barbados and 19th Annual Report (Bridgetown, 1960).

Pamphlets

C. V. Alert, *The Life and Work of Hubert Nathaniel Critchlow* (Georgetown, 1949).

Rawle Farley, *The Caribbean Trade Unionist* (Georgetown: Daily Chronicle, 1958).

C. L. R. James, *The Life of Captain Cipriani* (Nelson, Lancs, 1932).

Nikolai Lenin, *'Left Wing' Communism, An Infantile Disorder.* (London: The Communist Party, undated).

A. A. Purcell MP, *Workers of the World Unite! The Speech which Startled the Paris Congress.* With Foreword by James Maxton MP (London: ILP Publications, 1927).

S. Saklatvala MP and M. K. Gandhi, *Is India Different? The Class Struggle in India, Correspondence on the Indian Labour Movement and Modern Conditions.* (London: Communist Party of Great Britain, 1927).

B. P. Wadia, *Aims of the Labour Movement in India.* Reprinted from *Shama'a*, October 1920 (Madras: M. Chattopadhyay, 1920).

Articles, Papers and Theses

Richard Hart, 'Aspects of Early Caribbean Workers' Struggles'. *Caribbean Societies*, Vol. 1. Collected Seminar Papers, no. 29. (University of London Institute of Commonwealth Studies, 1982).

'In Memoriam Ernest Bevin'. *ITF Journal*, November–December 1951 (London: International Transport Workers' Federation).

G. D. Tarrant, *The British Colonial Office and the Labour Question in the*

Dependencies in the Inter-War Years. Dissertation for PhD degree. University of Manitoba. Canadian Theses on Microfiche 30078, 1977. British Library.

3 Interviews

Great Britain 1975–1980
Lord Citrine, Harry Hurst, Sir Frederick Leggett, Sir Vincent Tewson.

Geneva 1975
ILO: H. Dunning, E. A. Landy, W. Sansom.

India 1975
J. Ajmera, Abid Ali MP, J. Appasamy, N. Babu, A. T. Bhosale, G. Shelvapathy Chetty, S. A. Dange, Mahesh Desai, L. D. Gandhi, President V. V. Giri, V. R. Hoshing MLA, V. Kabra, R. K. K. Khadilkar MP, B. W. Kulkarni, V. S. Mathur, V. K. Krishna Menon, H. D. Mukerjee MLA, M. D. Patwardhan, G. Ramanujam, R. G. Rane, B. Shiva Rao, Ram Lal Thakar, K. P. Tripathi, H. M. Trivedi MLA.

West Indies 1976
Barbados: E. Greaves MP, Dr K. Hunte, R. L. Morris, L. Trotman, F. L. Walcott MP, E. Ward.
Jamaica: L. Beckford, Sir Florizel Glasspole, L. Goodleigh, F. Hill, D. Nelson, Miss Edith Nelson, R. Nettleford, B. Purkiss, C. Stone.
Trinidad: D. Bedeau, B. Bougouneau, H. Dunmore, Senator V. H. Glean, C. Gonzales, I. S. Gonzales, J. Grannum, N. D. Grannum, Dr Zin Henry, Mrs E. Ien, J. James, S. John, H. Johnson, McDonald Moses, F. Mungroo, G. Munroe, J. Rojas, R. Singh, V. A. Stanford, J. T. Theodore.

4 Books

All-India Trade Union Congress, *AITUC: Fifty Years, Documents*, Vol. I, with an Introduction by S. A. Dange (New Delhi: AITUC, 1973).
Wogu Ananaba, *The Trade Union Movement in Nigeria* (London: Hurst, 1969).
W. Appleton, *Trade Unions, Their Past, Present and Future* (London: Philip Allen, 1925).
Joseph Berger, *Shipwreck of a Generation* (London: Harvill Press, 1971).
Earl of Birkenhead, *F. E., First Earl of Birkenhead* (London: Eyre and Spottiswoode, 1965).
Earl of Birkenhead, *Halifax: The Life of Lord Halifax* (London: Hamish Hamilton, 1965).
Michael Brecher, *Nehru: A Political Biography* (London: Oxford University Press, 1959).
F. Brockway, *Inside the Left* (London: Allen & Unwin, 1942).
Alan Bullock, *The Life and Times of Ernest Bevin*. Vol. I, *Trade Union Leader* (London: Heinemann, 1960). Vol. II, *Minister of Labour* (London: Heinemann, 1967).

Alan Bullock, *Ernest Bevin, Foreign Secretary, 1945-51* (London: Heinemann, 1983).

Bustamante Industrial Trade Union, *Jamaica 1938: The Birth of the Bustamante Industrial Trade Union* (Kingston: BITU, 1968).

D. Calhoun, *The United Front, The TUC and the Russians 1923-1928* (Cambridge: Cambridge University Press, 1976).

Citrine (Sir Walter), *I Search for Truth in Russia*, revised edn (London: Routledge, 1938).

Citrine (Lord), *Men and Work: An Autobiography*. Hutchinson, London, 1964.

Citrine (Lord), *Two Careers: A Second Volume of Autobiography* (London: Hutchinson, 1967).

Margaret Cole, ed. *The Webbs and Their Work* (London: Frederick Muller, 1949).

F. W. Deakin and G. R. Storry, *The Case of Richard Sorge* (London: Chatto and Windus, 1966).

Jane Degras, ed. *The Communist International, 1919-1943: Documents*. Vol. I, 1919-23, Vol. II, 1923-28 (London: Frank Cass, 1971); Vol. III, 1929-43 (London: Oxford University Press, 1965).

A. L. Epstein, *Politics in an Urban African Community* (Manchester: Manchester University Press, 1958).

Edo Fimmen, *The International Federation of Trade Unions: Development and Aims* (Amsterdam: International Federation of Trade Unions, 1922).

M. K. Gandhi, *The Story of My Experiments with Truth: An Autobiography* (London: Phoenix Press, 1949).

V. V. Giri, *Labour Problems and Indian Industry* (Bombay: Asia Publishing House, 1972).

David Goldsworthy, *Colonial Issues in British Politics 1945-61* (London: Oxford University Press, 1971).

Albert Gomes, *Through a Maze of Colour* (Port of Spain, Trinidad: Key Caribbean Publications, 1974).

Helmut Gruber, *Soviet Russia Masters the Comintern* (New York: Anchor Press/Doubleday, 1974).

Partha Sarathi Gupta, *Imperialism and the British Labour Movement* (London: Macmillan, 1975).

Zin Henry, *Labour Relations and Industrial Conflict in Commonwealth Caribbean Countries* (Trinidad: Columbus Publishers, 1972).

Ronald Hingley, *Joseph Stalin: Man and Legend* (London: Hutchinson, 1974).

J. R. Hooker, *Black Revolutionary* (London: Pall Mall Press, 1967).

International Labour Office, *The International Labour Organisation: The First Decade* (London: Allen & Unwin, 1931).

Dan N. Jacobs, *Borodin: Stalin's Man in China* (Cambridge, Harvard University Press, Mass. and London, England: 1981).

Richard Jacobs, ed. *Butler Versus the King* (Port of Spain, Trinidad: Key Caribbean Publications, 1976).

V. B. Karnik, *N. M. Joshi: Servant of India* (Bombay: United Asia Publications, 1972).

V. B. Karnik, *M. N. Roy: Political Biography* (Bombay: Nav Nagriti Samaj, 1978).

William H. Knowles, *Trade Union Development and Industrial Relations in the British West Indies* (Berkeley and Los Angeles: University of California Press, 1959).

E. A. Landy, *The Effectiveness of International Supervision: Thirty Years of ILO Experience* (London and New York: Stevens, Oceana, 1966).

V. I. Lenin, *British Labour and British Imperialism* (London: Lawrence and Wishart, 1969).

A. Losovsky, *The World's Trade Union Movement* (London: National Minority Movement, 1925).

Henry McAleavy, *The Modern History of China* (London: Weidenfeld & Nicolson, 1967).

James Ramsay MacDonald, *Wanderings and Excursions* (London: Jonathan Cape, 1932).

Ras Makonnen, *Pan-Africanism from Within* (London and Nairobi: Oxford University Press, 1973).

Michael Manley, *A Voice at the Workplace* (London: Andre Deutsch, 1975).

Francis Mark, *The History of the Barbados Workers' Union* (Bridgetown: Barbados Workers' Union, 1969).

David Marquand, *Ramsay MacDonald* (London: Jonathan Cape, 1977).

Roderick Martin, *Communism and the British Trade Unions: A Study of the National Minority Movement* (Oxford: Clarendon Press, 1969).

A. S. and J. S. Mathur, *Trade Union Movement in India* (Allahabad: Chaitanya Publishing House, 1957).

D. J. Morgan, *The Origins of British Aid Policy 1924–45, The Official History of Colonial Development*, Vol. I (London: Macmillan, 1980).

W. H. Morris-Jones, *The Government and Politics of India* (London: Hutchinson, 1971).

Jawaharlal Nehru, *An Autobiography* (London: The Bodley Head, 1938).

Arthur H. Nethercot, *The Last Four Lives of Annie Besant* (London: Rupert Hart-Davis, 1963).

Rex Nettleford, ed. *Manley and the New Jamaica: Selected Speeches and Writings 1938–1968* (London: Longman Caribbean, 1971).

George Padmore, *Pan-Africanism or Communism?* (London: Dennis Dobson, 1956).

E. J. Phelan, *Yes and Albert Thomas* (London: Cresset Press, 1949).

Harry Pollitt, *Serving My Time* (London: Lawrence & Wishart, 1940).

J. Price, *The International Labour Movement* (London: Oxford University Press, 1945).

C. Ramanujam, *From the Babul Tree: Story of Indian Labour* (New Delhi: Indian National Trade Union Congress, 1967).

Ron Ramdin, *From Chattel Slave to Wage Earner* (London: Martin Brian & O'Keefe, 1982).

B. Shiva Rao, *The Industrial Worker in India* (London: Allen & Unwin, 1939).

B. C. Roberts, *The Trades Union Congress 1868–1921* (London: Allen & Unwin, 1958).

B. C. Roberts, *Labour in the Tropical Territories of the Commonwealth* (London: Bell & Sons, 1964).

W. Schevenels, *Forty Five Years: 1901–1945* (Brussels: IFTU Board of Trustees, 1956).

Sukomal Sen, *Working Class of India: History of Emergence and Movement 1830–1970* (Calcutta: K. P. Bagchi, 1977).

Victor Serge, *Memoirs of a Revolutionary 1901–1941* (London: Oxford University Press, 1963).

James R. Shotwell, ed. *The Origins of the International Labour Organization* (New York: Columbia University Press, 1934).

Edgar Snow, *Red Star Over China*, revised edn (London: Victor Gollancz, 1968).

Herbert Tracey, ed. *The Book of the Labour Party*, 3 vols (London: Caxton Publishing House, 1925).

L. Woolf, *Beginning Again 1911–1918* (London: Hogarth Press, 1964).

L. Woolf, *Downhill all the Way 1919–1939* (London: Hogarth Press, 1967).

L. Woolf, *The Journey not the Arrival Matters 1919–1969* (London: Hogarth Press, 1969).

T. M. Yesufu, *An Introduction to Industrial Relations in Nigeria* (London: Oxford University Press, 1962).

Index

Prepared by Maureen Webley

Prepared by Maureen Webley
Names

sentatives 240
Northern Rhodesia Mineworkers'
Union 240
charges of subversive agitation 244
Nyasaland 188, 200

Palestine 45, 110, 129, 130, 178, 211
General Federation of Jewish Labour
167
Palestine Federation of Labour 132
wartime restrictions on union activities
239
Pan-Africanism 192, 193
Pan-African Federation 250
5th Pan-African Congress 1945 250–1
Pan-Pacific Trade Union Secretariat 103–6
affiliation to League Against Imperialism
107
penal sanctions
elimination aims 189, 198
in British Guiana 53
in India 156
ILO Convention 171, 174–5
People's National Party (Jamaica) 224
Petrograd Soviet 14, 16
and Stockholm Conference 16
delegation to London 17–18
Philadelphia Charter 246
picketing 140–1, 181, 203–4, 209
police
pressure on Indian trade union movement 127–8, 141–2
political funds 140, 204
political influences
and early TUC organization 12–14
and trade union aims 11, 79–81
and WFTU 249
on British trade union movement 2
on colonial trade union movement 230,
235, 250–1, 260–1
on Indian trade union movement 128–9
Postmen's Federation 30
Purcell-Hallsworth Report (India) 155–60
recommendations to TUC 158–9

railway industry
Indian disputes 145, 151
Indian trade union organization 156
Jamaican dispute 238, 243–4
Nigerian strikes 188
recruitment 185
ILO Convention 196
migrant labour 168

Red International of Labour Unions 70,
150
aims 66
and colonial aims 66
British Bureau 65, 66–7
dissolution 247
establishment 65
international propaganda committees 70
links with China 103–4
Negro Bureau 193
propaganda into India 153
propaganda into West Indies 236
relations with WWLI 153
relationship with Comintern 65, 66
registration of trade unions 179, 183
in Trinidad 182
procedures 142, 143, 162
see also compulsory registration
representation
at early international conferences 9, 10
at ILO 166–9
problems of 11, 175
and AITUC 151–5
in Indian Government 92–3, 162–4
representative internationalism 22
revolutionary trade unionism 104–5, 119,
236
TUC rejection 68, 105–6, 256
see also RILU
rights
of native workers 47
of workers 2, 174, 205, 256
trade union 21, 256
Royal Commission of Inquiry into Trade
Unions 6
Royal Commission on Labour in India *see*
Whitley Commission
Russia
delegations 16; 1920 57, 69; 1924 74–7
Revolution 14, 20
TUC/Labour Party views on 15–18,
57
self-determination policy 60–1
trade unions 15–16
see also Bolsheviks; Mensheviks; USSR

Sailors' and Firemen's Union 36
St Kitts 137, 221
TUC intervention 8, 254
St Lucia 221, 229
St Vincent 222, 242
Workingmen's Association 221, 229